Volker

Schlöndorff's

Cinema

Volker

Schlöndorff's

Cinema

ADAPTATION, POLITICS, AND THE "MOVIE-APPROPRIATE"

Hans-Bernhard Moeller and George Lellis

Southern Illinois University Press   Carbondale and Edwardsville

Library of Congress Cataloging-in-Publication Data

Moeller, Hans-Bernhard.
    Volker Schlöndorff's cinema : adaptation, politics, and the "movie-appropriate" / Hans-Bernhard Moeller and George Lellis.
        p. ; cm.
    Includes bibliographical references and index.
    1. Schlöndorff, Volker—Criticism and interpretation. I. Lellis,
George. II. Title.

PN1998.3.S353 M64 2002
791.43'0233'092—dc21

                                                            2002018804
    ISBN 0-8093-2451-2 (cloth : alk. paper)

Printed on recycled paper. ♻

Contents

Illustrations

Acknowledgments

We thank colleagues who read sections of our manuscript at various stages, including Robert Reimer, Hubert Heinen, Kathie Arens, Charles Ramirez Berg, Lois Gibson, Cristóbal Serrán-Pagán, Charles Affron, David Desser, and Klaus Phillips. We are grateful to the two anonymous readers who reviewed our manuscript on behalf of Southern Illinois University Press and provided helpful criticism to us.

Our gratitude is also directed to many institutions and archives for their support and the use of their facilities. The University of Texas at Austin awarded a crucial early research grant and provided the continued stimulus of students' involvement in film courses. Coker College provided faculty development funds, a sabbatical, and much encouragement, and particular mention is due Malcolm C. Doubles and Ronald L. Carter. We also cite Hessischer Rundfunk; the DAAD (German Academic Exchange Service), which provided an early research grant; the Niedersächsische Landeszentrale für Politische Bildung; the Goethe Institute; the Munich Filmmuseum; the Stiftung Deutsche Kinemathek, especially the ever-helpful staff of the Library Archive; the Hochschule für Fernsehen und Film in Munich; the Technische Universität Berlin; the Universität/Gesamthochschule Wuppertal; the Universität Marburg; the Filmausschnittsammlung der Volkshochschule Dortmund; the Kommunales Kino Dortmund; the Frankfurt/M. Opera; the Berlin Opera; Handicap International; Franz Seitz Filmproduktion; dpa (Deutsche Presse-Agentur); *Süddeutsche Zeitung; Der Spiegel;* and *Die Zeit.* We are indebted to the Academy of Motion Picture Arts and Sciences for both the release of the text of Schlöndorff's acceptance speech to us and permission to quote from it here. (Copyright © Academy of Motion Picture Arts and Sciences, 1980.)

Special people we should mention are Peter Hoffmann, Ute Gräfin von Baudissin, Helga Belach, Gero Gandert, Friedrich Knilli, Thomas Koebner, Norbert Kückelmann, Ulrich Kurowski, Wolfgang Längsfeld, Günter Giesenfeld, Hans Prescher, Enno Patalas, Horst Schäfer, Klaus Bertisch, Sylvia Sommella, Ernst Schreckenberg, Frau Bien, and Siegfried Zielinski. All helped us use the resources of their respective institutions to full advantage. Karl Heinz Stahl made available to us Petra Schubert-Scheinmann's *Magisterarbeit.*

We owe a debt to Bioskop Films and the Babelsberg Studios for the information and materials provided. Particular thanks go to Eberhard Junkersdorf, Henriette Letzner, Reinhard Hauff, and Peter Fleischmann.

We are indebted to several distributors and their representatives for assisting in making films available to us and acquiring stills. They include Gabriele Caroti of Kino International *(The Legend of Rita)*, Frau Bachman of Warner Home Video *(The Ogre)*, Gisela Schmeer of WDR Cologne *(Making of The Ogre)*, Linda Duchin of TeleCulture *(War and Peace)*, New Line Cinema ("Antigone" from *Germany in Autumn*), Atlas Film and AV, and Kinowelt Orion Classics. Hans-Peter Reichmann and Beate Dannhorn of the Deutsches Filmmuseum Frankfurt am Main; Olivia Just of the Deutsches Filminstitut-DIF, also in Frankfurt; Mary Corliss of the Museum of Modern Art Film Stills Archive; Sally Schoen Bergman; Beate Bauer; and Klaus Phillips supplied us with stills.

Grateful acknowledgments are due to colleagues who provided papers in their early forms or who otherwise shared their research and thoughts with us, especially David Head, Heidemarie Kesselmann, Marianne Barnett, Karla Leeper, and Robert Rowland. Friend and colleague Laurence A. Gretsky was always there to help find just the right word, and Jane Park offered invaluable stylistic suggestions while pruning overgrown sentences. We are also indebted to those who contributed information, energy, and high standards to numerous conferences in which we participated or which we organized. They helped focus our thoughts and transform our arguments, and without them we could not have written this study of Schlöndorff in its present form.

And we thank all those whose varied kind acts, both large and small, helped smooth the road for our research and writing. These include Mary Lathan Steele, John Thompson-Haas, Kim Chalmers, Greg Tillou, Peter Pantsari, Thom Roberts, Gisela Hundertmark, Michael Conner, Patrick Couture, Marlis Schroeder, and Heinz-Dieter Möller. Included here as well are those whose names may be forgotten or overlooked, if in some cases we even knew them. For any such oversights, we offer our apologies.

Finally, let us recognize our wives, Sheila Johnson and Susan Lellis, and our children, Nicole, Julie, and Martine, who have both explicitly and implicitly supported us with consideration and love through the whole process of writing this book.

Volker

Schlöndorff's

Cinema

1

Introduction:
The Historical Importance
of Schlöndorff

During the 1960s, cinema redefined itself. Baby boomers worldwide were entering their teens and young adulthood—the demographic ages at which moviegoing peaks. At the same time, the classicists of the Hollywood cinema, like John Ford, Howard Hawks, and Alfred Hitchcock, were moving into the twilight of their careers. They were leaving behind a Hollywood studio system battered by competition from television, antitrust legislation, and unpredictable audiences. This system would never—despite the new Hollywood's ongoing economic clout—regain its former glory. Technological change was making film production easier, cheaper, and less dependent on a large-scale industrial model: low-budget, personal movies could coexist with monumental blockbusters.

Film culture became Janus-faced. On the one hand, a body of film had emerged over the medium's sixty-year history that demanded to be reassessed, reclassified, and reappreciated by younger generations. On the other hand, youthful audiences demanded change: they had new ideas about what could be filmed and how it should be filmed. This demand for change emerged in West Germany in the 1960s with the Young German film movement. In 1966, two remarkable features by first-time West German filmmakers startled and provoked film festival audiences and art house patrons. Alexander Kluge's *Yesterday Girl (Abschied von gestern)* and Volker Schlöndorff's *Young Törless (Der junge Törless)* became the first serious harbingers of the New German Cinema that was to become a major force in international film during the 1970s. Stylistically, they were nearly polar opposites. Kluge's film was an avant-garde cinematic essay about a young woman adrift and confused in a modern, morally sterile West Germany obsessed with the "economic miracle." Schlöndorff's more classical film honored the legacy of the

1

great prewar German filmmakers as it looked back to the early 1900s, presenting an oppressive boarding school for boys as a breeding place for Nazi ideology. Both motion pictures exemplified the youthful energy, literary character,
political commitment, and pragmatic ambition of the West German new wave.
Schlöndorff and Kluge hinted at aspects of 1960s political radicalism and alternative culture that were to inform their following films.

Schlöndorff directed some ten features in the dozen years following *Young
Törless*. The success of *The Tin Drum (Die Blechtrommel)* in 1979 fully legitimized
the New German Cinema as an international commercial and popular force.
Schlöndorff succeeded, in part because he, Kluge, Edgar Reitz, Rainer Werner
Fassbinder, and others successfully fought for a state film subsidy system. For
nearly a decade, this system had given Schlöndorff the opportunity to direct
an astonishing array of politically sharp and formally innovative motion pictures. This period culminated with *The Tin Drum,* with which West Germany
garnered the Academy Award for best foreign film and shared the Cannes
Golden Palm. By this time, Schlöndorff had become a major cultural figure, not
only within the Federal Republic of Germany but also internationally.

As the liberal political climate of the 1960s evolved into the conservatism of
the 1980s, however, Schlöndorff found himself caught in the middle. During
the 1970s, he had to withstand repeated attacks from the right-wing establishment, as well as culturally based sniping from radicals on the left. Specifically,
in collaborating with Nobel prize–winning novelist Heinrich Böll on *The Lost
Honor of Katharina Blum (Die verlorene Ehre der Katharina Blum,* 1975), the director drew fire from the reactionary Springer Press. By the mid-1970s, terrorism
had become the domestic political issue that most stirred up the West German
citizenry, and conservatives saw this film as the work of sympathizers with the
Baader-Meinhof terrorist gang. Simultaneous with this political censure from
the right was continued criticism from the left. Cultural radicals perceived
Schlöndorff as stylistically traditional, approaching norms of middlebrow commercial cinema, especially in *The Tin Drum.*

The fall of the Helmut Schmidt government and the rise to power of Helmut
Kohl in 1982 marked the practical end of the New German Cinema.
Schlöndorff, like several of his colleagues, began to work abroad—first in
France, then in the United States. After the fall of communism and the 1990
reunification of Germany, Schlöndorff returned and for five years led the commercially risky and artistically ambitious attempt to transform the renowned
but outdated East German Babelsberg studio into a profit-making operation.
In the course of three decades, the outsider had become an establishment figure. In a 1995 survey of film historians, editors, journalists, and filmmakers,

three of Schlöndorff's features were listed among the top fifty German films of all time (Jacobson). Clearly, *Young Törless* (ranked thirty-eighth), *The Lost Honor of Katharina Blum* (forty-ninth), and *The Tin Drum* (thirty-fourth) have earned Schlöndorff his position in film history. In addition, the omnibus film *Germany in Autumn* (*Deutschland im Herbst*, 1978), to which Schlöndorff contributed the "Antigone" episode, ranked twenty-eighth. Only Fritz Lang and Wolfgang Staudte rated a comparable four or more mentions in the top fifty.

Despite this status, a number of serious discussions of the New German Cinema have either ignored Schlöndorff or marginalized him. For example, two important and otherwise praiseworthy monographs on postwar German film, Eric Santner's *Stranded Objects* and Richard W. McCormick's *Politics of the Self*, make absolutely no mention of Schlöndorff. Other studies, like Thomas Elsaesser's *New German Cinema* and Anton Kaes's *From Hitler to Heimat*, have dismissed Schlöndorff in a few sentences or paragraphs. This study of Schlöndorff intends to fill a gap in the English-language critical literature.

Schlöndorff is important for three main reasons. First, in those politically committed films that have earned him one of the broadest receptions among New German Cinema directors, the filmmaker achieved an exciting merger between rhetoric and poetics. Second, his work and his philosophy of filmmaking embody many intriguing contradictions about the commercial and artistic natures of film. Third, he has tended to pursue literary adaptation, which in itself puts him at the center of critical controversies about issues of fidelity and medium integrity. We argue that the contradictions within Schlöndorff's work and his creative treatments of literature are a source of its vitality.

Schlöndorff's most widely acclaimed films—*Young Törless, The Lost Honor of Katharina Blum,* and *The Tin Drum*—adapt works by major German-language writers and do what Schlöndorff has been justifiably praised for achieving. They take politically charged subject matter, present it with immediacy and conviction, and develop ideas through sophisticated use of image and sound. They work as rhetoric, as provocative discourse about issues of Nazism, terrorism, and militarism. As poetic expression, they are structurally elaborate and aesthetically precise. Schlöndorff's greatest works represent a convergence of rhetorical force with poetic grace.

On their rhetorical side, Schlöndorff's movies have been relevant to their times, having covered such topical issues as youthful rebellion, collective resistance to oppression, victimization of women, relations between the arts and society, German-Polish conflicts, the Lebanese civil war of the late 1970s and, finally, the post–World War II rehabilitation of the German cultural traditions driven out by the Third Reich. They are counterparts to works by filmmakers like Constantin Costa-Gavras and Oliver Stone.

At the same time, Schlöndorff's movies are not merely rhetorical artifacts whose interest will diminish as the issues they address become history. Although they have been entertaining enough to engage a mass audience, Schlöndorff's successful films go beyond mere topicality and diversion to hold up under close aesthetic scrutiny. Our study shows in particular Schlöndorff's careful positioning of the spectator to achieve, as needed, both identification with and distance from his protagonists. Patterns of the gaze articulate point of view in ways that go beyond Hollywood's standard use of eyeline match, whereby a shot of a person looking is followed by a point-of-view shot of what that person sees. In addition, we explore how Schlöndorff uses leitmotif techniques that produce meaning through connotation and implication. These significant recurring objects, images, and sounds serve to demarcate character and to integrate and unify narratives, as well as to establish subtle associations or subtexts. In some cases, Schlöndorff borrows point-of-view and leitmotif structures from the literary texts he adapts, but in others they are cinema-specific inventions.

This interest in merging political expression with formal expressiveness links Schlöndorff to his New German Cinema colleagues like Rainer Werner Fassbinder, Alexander Kluge, and Edgar Reitz. All share the antifascist perspective, a vision of a different kind of German film that would explore both the country's past and its present problems. He joined with them to create a formally challenging national cinema and succeeded better than any in bringing it to a wide audience.

Tensions and Contradictions

Schlöndorff has earned a reputation as a specialist in adapting often difficult literature to the screen. He has usually been faithful to his literary models in matters of plot sequencing, dialogue, and characterization. But mixed with this often scrupulous fidelity is what Schlöndorff calls his *kinogerecht*, or "movie-appropriate," criterion. By this, the director means a film product that is popular in two senses. It is right for the movie house in terms of the cinema both as a mass-audience social institution and as a specifically visual communication medium. Film must not, in other words, be measured in terms of the standards of any other art form but rather in terms of its developed cultural traditions and formal potentialities.

The *kinogerecht* film is the mass entertainment film, the opposite of the esoteric work of screen art. Although his movies have mainly been shown in art theaters in the United States, for most of his career Schlöndorff has positioned himself in Germany as a commercial filmmaker intent on reaching a wide audience. Schlöndorff's insisting on the *kinogerecht* quality comes from an extreme ambivalence about high culture. Yet he has pursued box office success without sacrificing intellectual ambition and without turning his back on positive aspects of traditional culture. He believes that film can express complex ideas and oppositional ideologies, and that a mass audience can comprehend them. The very positive box office figures for challenging works like *The Lost Honor of Katharina Blum* and *The Tin Drum* bear this out.

To reach a wide audience, Schlöndorff knows how to employ a relatively traditional film vocabulary that, on immediate observation, avoids calling attention to itself. He structures his narratives according to many of the conventional patterns of film genre: the Hollywood Western, the crime film, the women's film, and the German *Heimatfilm*. At the same time, he undermines genre structures by including subversive elements that analyze, deconstruct, and even parody traditional genre codes. Thus the films can play it both ways. They gratify the viewer, even while being stylistically complex, self-reflexive, and politically avant-garde. On the one hand, they embody the work of a rationalist intellectual; on the other, they express a popular inclination toward pleasure seeking, rebellion, and emotional release.

Adaptation Theory

Dealing with an adaptation specialist such as Schlöndorff requires defining our position vis-à-vis adaptation issues. Film theory has undergone considerable changes in this subdiscipline. Critical focus about adaptation theory has shifted from "fidelity ranking," which conceives of a movie as a "reflection" of a literary work of art, to consideration of adaptation as transformation. Most serious film critics would now argue that when filmmakers adapt literary works, they always interpret them. Comparative critics of the 1990s, like Millicent Marcus, James Griffith, and Brian McFarlane, offer highly qualified conceptualizations of the notion of fidelity, acknowledging the inevitable differences that will result from moving from one medium to another.

This current thinking avoids the Platonistic concept of adaptation as a process in which the film copy can only approach the literary ideal. The traditional "fidelity" position implies superiority of the medium of literature over that of cinema. Those critics who prize absolute fidelity in adaptation ascribe to the original work a transcendent value.

An opposing tradition comes from the theater of Bertolt Brecht. In writing his plays, Brecht would openly steal, modify, and update the plots, characters, and ideas of earlier writers. The implication for Brecht is that the original, and by extension literature in general, is anything but sacred and exists to be used and reshaped in whatever way suits the more contemporary artist. We discuss in subsequent chapters Brecht's influence on Schlöndorff, but it is important to see the film director as coming out of this tradition that puts the literary canon "up for grabs" by whoever wants to use it. Although it may shock traditionalists, such an approach does not necessarily indicate a disrespect for literature. Rather, it makes literature into discourse that grows and changes and thus continues to be useful and relevant in new social and aesthetic contexts. One can apply Jacques Derrida's description of translation to this approach to adaptation: It "augments and modifies the original, which, insofar as it is living on, never ceases to be transformed and to grow" (122).

At the extreme opposite of the fidelity position, there are equally wrongheaded critics who argue that a film adaptation must always stand completely independent of its original source. In point of fact, no film is produced in a cultural vacuum, and any film audience is composed of members with varying cultural and literary awareness. Those who create movies based on extremely popular novels and plays, for example, can reasonably expect their audiences to have some familiarity with the book or performance. Any preceding source, be it a comic strip for *Batman,* the television show for a *Star Trek* or *X-Files* movie, or the Bible for countless Hollywood spectacles, can be part of a film's context for reception. To deny this would be to fall into a different kind of Platonic idealism.

In the larger cultural view, all creation can be considered adaptation within the overarching system of intertextuality. Following this view, every artist bases his works on preexisting cultural models. The "reworking" may follow the model closely and completely, as in remakes or parodies, or it may involve only a partial lifting from the original of aspects such as genre, motif, scene, and quote. According to Roland Barthes, any text qualifies as a "tissue of quotations drawn from the innumerable centers of culture" (146). In this theoretical model of adaptation, the literary source becomes, in the words of Christopher Orr, who cites Barthes as above, merely "one of a series of pre-texts which share some of the same narrative conventions as the film adaptation" (72). Because the intertextuality between the film adaptation and the preestablished literary text is but one of several such shared elements, fidelity-biased critics run the critical risk of disregarding other intertextualities. They may well ignore these other "quotations" as the source of variations from the literary model in film adaptation. For instance, a critic who views Wim Wenders's *The Scarlet Letter* (*Der scharlachrote Buchstabe*, 1972) solely as an adaptation of Nathaniel Hawthorne misses its reference to the American Western and thus can only partially appreciate the film.

Many film adaptations can be seen in part as comments on the original literary sources. They can, in effect, function as works of literary criticism on film. For example, Schlöndorff's *Swann in Love (Un amour de Swann)* can be read as an "essay," albeit an unsystematic one, on both the mechanisms of class structure and the taboo against homosexuality in Proust's cycle of novels. In a similar way, the David Cronenberg 1990 adaptation of *Naked Lunch* is as much a discourse on the life, times, and cultural significance of William Burroughs, the author, as it is a filmic presentation of the novel itself. In short, film adaptations are not just reflections of the original; they are part of the discourse about the original.

How a novel converts to a motion picture becomes a function of qualities specific to each medium. Movies involve certain modes of perception and representation impossible to achieve on the printed page. For instance, effects of light and shadow routinely influence the significance of scenes in film. A visible prairie or expanse of desert is central to many Westerns. Movies are also uniquely capable of producing immediate physiological reactions, such as to the sight of blood or to the slime in *Ghostbusters* (1985) and *Men in Black* (1997). To realize fully their particular medium's potential, filmmakers need to maximize the effect of those signifiers that the medium is most equipped to handle. Filmmakers adapting literature to film must transform mental impressions into material ones. Writers start with signs that are by their nature abstractions through which readers can imagine a specific physical world. Filmmakers, by contrast, begin with the specific physical world from which viewers can abstract ideas. As Dudley Andrew reminds us in his *Concepts in Film Theory*, the "analysis of adaptation then must point to the achievement of equivalent narrative units in the absolutely different semiotic systems of film and language" (103).

Concern with the place and quality of literary adaptations is a central issue to postwar cinema criticism. François Truffaut's key essay "A Certain Tendency in French Cinema" attacked the French so-called tradition of quality and those literary adaptations within it that the director regarded as empty and soulless. In this essay, Truffaut set up a dichotomy between the auteur, that is, the filmmaker with a constant and consistent unity of theme and style, and the *metteur en scène* who more mechanically stages a preexisting text. A major implication of Truffaut's argument is that the art of film consists of much more than solely dialogue and performance. Truffaut did not categorically reject adaptation. He did

warn of the potential of both knee-jerk leftist moralizing and middle-class stuffi-
ness in adaptation, and thus initiated a tradition of adaptation skepticism.

The tradition has extended into commentary on the German film. Some film
scholars have rejected literary adaptation as "uncreative," bourgeois cinema,
detached from societal needs. Eric Rentschler, an American academic and critic
of German film, along with journalistic polemists in the West German press, censured the New German Cinema's adaptations as the *"Literaturverfilmungskrise,"*
or crisis of literary adaptation. He seized on 1976–77 as "a juncture where literature adaptations had a most detrimental effect on German film"
("Deutschland" 1979). Rentschler likewise saw the political turn to conservatism, a response to Baader-Meinhof anarchism, as stifling to the alternative
thinking and political protest expressed by the New German Cinema works
during the first half of the 1970s. The movement's subsequent output had
turned into a "retelling" cinema (Rentschler, "Deutschland" [1980] 15). The
West German state subsidy system and its film selection boards had effectively
paralyzed critical cinematic creativity and had instead encouraged tame and
domesticated adaptations of the classics. This antiadaption bias may, in part,
explain why Schlöndorff has been marginalized in much of the writing on the
New German Cinema.

Adaptation bashers have customarily accepted Truffaut's dichotomy
between the auteur and the *metteur en scène.* But Schlöndorff himself has said,
"I think that a cinéaste should efface himself behind the film he is making; I am
not an auteur, I am perhaps a stylist" ("Sur le tambour" 20). This vision of
Schlöndorff as a "profi," an "altruistic servant" of art and the specific subject
at hand, has been the premise of at least one book-length study (Wydra 7–8).
The director does consistently represent a sensibility willing to privilege other
authors' ideas and concepts. But we also argue that there is in Schlöndorff's
work an auteurlike consistency of theme and style regardless of the specific
movie's source. When Schlöndorff's films are successful, they are often so
because they find ways to transform literary ideas through fully cinematic
means into effective motion picture ideas. The question is not whether they are
better or worse than their literary antecedents but rather whether they successfully generate ideas in image and sound.

Periods in Schlöndorff's Work

We divide our discussion of Schlöndorff's oeuvre into five different periods,
considering them also in relation to the rest of the New German Cinema and
the historical and social contexts that produced them. We recognize that any

periods we propose are somewhat arbitrary and overlapping. They are devices for structuring discourse and orienting the reader, not ironclad categories. We indeed look for cross-period connections in subject matter and approach.

The first period comprises the director's first three features, *Young Törless, A Degree of Murder* (*Mord und Totschlag*, 1967), and *Michael Kohlhaas* (1969). In these three greatly different films, we see early articulations of themes and issues developed throughout the filmmaker's career. Paramount is the endeavor, not always successful, to revitalize German film production through youth-oriented subjects, formal vitality, and creative adaptation of literary classics.

In the second period, Schlöndorff relies heavily on German television and state subsidies to create largely low-budget, innovative works. This is a period marked by interest in social repression, political commitment, feminism, and particularly German subject matter. Accompanying these interests is a related preoccupation with the cinematic application of the dramatic theories and practice of Bertolt Brecht. This second period begins with the adaptation of Brecht's play *Baal* (1970) and extends to Schlöndorff's "Antigone" contribution to the 1978 omnibus film *Germany in Autumn.*

Period three, which includes *The Tin Drum, Circle of Deceit* (*Die Fälschung*, 1981), and *Swann in Love,* is marked by a movement into large-scale European coproductions and internationally prominent casts. These commercially ambitious movies reinforce Schlöndorff's international reputation. With this growing internationalism comes, in the latter two films, a turning away from specifically German subject matter with an increasing awareness of non-German audiences. This period also features more nationally focused documentaries and contributions to group projects.

The fourth period comprises *Death of a Salesman* (1985), *A Gathering of Old Men* (1987) and *The Handmaid's Tale* (1989). This is Schlöndorff's American period, defined by his own move across the Atlantic and the choice of the United States as setting for his films. In this period, Schlöndorff begins to work comfortably within the American production system, initially for television. Schlöndorff collaborates with American and British playwrights and explores issues of theatrical adaptation and the use of theaterlike forms.

The fifth period begins with *Voyager* (1990), a kind of multicontinental road movie that has one foot each in the New and Old Worlds respectively. The period continues into the present. It has Schlöndorff performing the role of a multinational film production facilitator, as well as the director of the big-budget European project of *The Ogre* and the low-budget, specifically German *The Legend of Rita* (*Die Stille nach dem Schuss*, 2000).

If there is a story to be told in Schlöndorff's work, it is one that historically parallels a branch of the middle-class left in the late twentieth century. We can follow the director from the anarchistic optimism in the late 1960s to a 1970s disillusionment and theorization, through a 1980s acceptance of the failure of traditional dogmatic communism, and to an attempt to create in the 1990s a brand of capitalism that is socially sensitive. Schlöndorff reflects the postmodern condition in his ability to commingle the social and cultural goals of the political left, the economic mechanisms of the capitalist marketplace, and the poetic and mythic dimensions of literature.

2

Schlöndorff and His Sources

In surveying Volker Schlöndorff's development as a filmmaker, one can note how he merges two major traditions—one French, one German. If his chronologically more immediate model is the French cinema of the late 1950s and early 1960s, the works' basic aesthetic heritage is the German cinema of the Weimar period and its extension in exile.

Influences: The French Cinema

If one were sketching out a transnational cinema history, one might easily describe the New German Cinema as an offshoot of the French New Wave. In 1962, in the city of Oberhausen, the Young German cinema proclaimed its goals in a public document known as the Oberhausen Manifesto. In some ways, this document presents the new German generation's positive reaction to the success that their French contemporaries—François Truffaut, Alain Resnais, Jean-Luc Godard, and Claude Chabrol—had in redefining their national cinema. The young Germans saw the French as a model for a cinema that would reject the confining subjects, styles, and economic structures of *Opas Kino*, to use the term of derision of that younger generation for "granddaddy's cinema." Both the young French filmmakers and their German counterparts wanted to propose something new and vigorous.

One would expect Schlöndorff's cinema to reinforce this general pattern. After all, the filmmaker lived in Paris from 1956 to 1964, precisely the years in which the New Wave renewed the French cinema. He received his *baccalauréat* from the Lycée Henri V. As part of his high school experience at a French boarding school, he became friends with his classmate Bertrand Tavernier, who himself was to develop into a major figure in the French cinema. Schlöndorff then pursued studies in economics and political science before being accepted into

France's major film school, then known as the Institute des Hautes Études Cinématographiques (IDHEC). In the early 1960s, he served as an assistant on movies by Louis Malle, Alain Resnais, and Jean-Pierre Melville. French director Jean-Daniel Pollet has mentioned how Schlöndorff accompanied him on the shoot of Pollet's highly experimental *Méditerranée* (1963), a film linked to the *nouveau roman* and the advanced literary work of Philippe Sollers (Pollet).

Schlöndorff is not the only figure of the New German Cinema to have been shaped in part by French film culture. A detailed general history of Franco-German cinematic relations since 1960 has yet to be written, but we can acknowledge certain connections at this point. Peter Fleischmann, for example, was also an IDHEC student, completing his studies in 1962. Wim Wenders, although unsuccessful in being admitted to IDHEC, like Schlöndorff discovered much of the German film tradition at the French Cinémathèque. Jean-Marie Straub, although Alsatian by birth, became a major figure in the New German Cinema after seeking asylum in Germany to avoid fighting in the Algerian war. And many German women filmmakers, including Ula Stöckl, Claudia von Alemann, Jutta Brückner, Margarethe von Trotta, and Ulrike Ottinger, have studied or worked in France.

It would be foolish to argue for overly direct influence of French filmmakers on Schlöndorff's work. He himself has suggested in interviews that such influences have been more in the area of technique than anything else ("An Interview" 28). At the same time, when one compares Schlöndorff's work with that of his French mentors and colleagues, one cannot help noticing affinities. Let us consider some of them under five overlapping categories: professionalism, pluralism, respect for genre, austerity, and political commitment.

1. Professionalism. Unlike those members of the French or German new waves who came to filmmaking from the starting point of criticism, Schlöndorff from the beginning approached his craft from a practical rather than journalistic or historical-critical orientation. His training came from his schooling at IDHEC, and, more important, from the apprenticeships that accompanied and followed it. Although his official biographies always list his acceptance into IDHEC, he never completed the school's curriculum and by his own admission studied there only one year (Bronnen and Brocher 82; Pflaum and Prinzler, *Film* 385). He appears to have abandoned formal film education as soon as his production assistant experiences led to regular work (Fleischmann). One suspects that he used the ethos of IDHEC attendance as leverage in getting his first projects under way.

Although IDHEC may or may not have had much direct effect on Schlöndorff, two of his mentors from the time, Louis Malle and Alain Resnais, had also attended the school and were major figures among the new filmmakers of the period. Although certain stylistic characteristics are associated with the French New Wave, such as the use of hand-held cameras, location shooting, direct sound, and jump cuts, these techniques were by no means adopted by all of the filmmakers involved. In contrast to the spontaneity, technical casualness, and penchant for improvisation shown by filmmakers like Truffaut, Godard, Chabrol, and Jacques Rivette, those New Wave figures who emerged from IDHEC tended toward a far more calculated approach to filmmaking. These more classically oriented filmmakers included Malle and Resnais as well as those far less known abroad, like Claude Sautet, Robert Enrico, or Alain Cavalier. If the one branch of the New Wave grows out of and extends the line begun by Italian Neorealism, IDHEC produced a parallel group of filmmakers whose work was characterized by craftsmanship, seriousness, and in the opinion of some, academicism (Martin, "France" 71; Les étudiants 56).

The most important French influence on Schlöndorff, however, was undoubtedly Jean-Pierre Melville, to whom Schlöndorff was introduced by his friend Bertrand Tavernier. Schlöndorff was, with Tavernier, an assistant director on *Léon Morin, Priest* (*Léon Morin, prêtre*, 1961) and *Le doulos* (1962), and he helped with the preparation of *The Magnet of Doom* (*L'aîné des ferchaux*, 1962) and "Three Rooms in Manhattan," the latter of which was never shot. Melville has said of Schlöndorff that on meeting him in 1960, "[a]lmost immediately I felt that I had met my spiritual son" (Nogueira 89). Schlöndorff, in turn, has written, "He was my first master, and the one from whom I learned the most" ("A Parisian-American in Paris" 45).

Melville is remembered by U.S. filmgoers for his appearance in Jean-Luc Godard's *Breathless*, in which Godard established him as a kind of spiritual father of the French New Wave. Like Godard, Melville knew, loved, and respected the American cinema, but his admiration led him in a far different direction, and he and Godard differed significantly in their tastes. Melville saw the Hollywood film as having reached its apogee in the 1930s, under a rigid studio system. Rather than celebrate Alfred Hitchcock or Howard Hawks, Melville reserved his greatest admiration, at least according to Schlöndorff, for William Wyler and Robert Wise ("A Parisian-American in Paris" 44). The *Cahiers du cinéma*–influenced critics of the 1950s and 1960s disdained Wyler and Wise as showing little personal vision in their work. Today as well, Wyler and Wise tend to be respected as Hollywood professionals but also considered rather cold, even somewhat mechanical craftsmen. A highly independent entrepreneur who had his own film studio, Melville was also his own producer and as a result maintained a high degree of individual control over his work.

2. Pluralism. This professionalist, craftsmanship-oriented approach to film-making would, at least in the case of someone like Malle, result in a versatility that allowed Malle to work in different tones, styles, and genres. Malle was thus able to move from steamy sex drama (*The Lovers/Les amants*, 1958), to anarchic comedy (*Zazie*, 1960), to star vehicles for Brigitte Bardot (*A Very Private Affair/Vie privée*, 1962; *Viva Maria!*, 1965), to documentary (*Vive la tour*, 1962), to morose literary adaptation (*The Fire Within/Le feu follet*, 1963). With *Zazie* in particular, which provided for Schlöndorff's first apprentice experience with Malle, the French filmmaker chose a reputedly "unfilmable" novel by Raymond Queneau, one filled with puns and word-specific flourishes. He brought it successfully to the screen in a way that would suggest the position, taken later by Schlöndorff, that a skillful mise-en-scène equivalent can be found to almost any literary effort. Like Malle, Schlöndorff has worked in both fiction and documentary and has experimented with a variety of genres, styles, literary collaborators, adaptation projects, production situations, and degrees of political commitment.

3. Respect for Genre. The qualities of professionalism and adaptability very much suit a commitment to working within a commercial production system, and Schlöndorff has shared with the French New Wave the appreciation for established filmmaking genres. This respect for genre may have arisen in part through his association with Tavernier, whose critical writings on the Hollywood cinema show an admiration for creative experimentation within commercial formulas and whose own films have reformulated the classical Western and police film. Even more important, Melville worked almost exclusively in the gangster film and has also commented that almost all of his films are "transposed Westerns" (Nogueira 100). It is no surprise, then, that we find patterns from the Western and the police thriller in a number of Schlöndorff's works. Indeed, Schlöndorff's cinematic homage to Melville, *Coup de Grâce* (*Der Fangschuss*, 1976) with its fortress-estate on the frontier of the Baltic wars, its assertive and headstrong woman who must make her way in a world of men, its (anti)hero who must choose between male bonding and heterosexual love, can be seen as an art film reworking of fundamental narrative configurations from the Western. As with many genre-oriented films of the French New Wave, in some cases Schlöndorff's references to classical formulas are to be taken seriously; in other cases they are ironic reversals of convention meant to impose a modernist self-referentiality on the work.

4. Austerity. Melville's work is stylistically sober and very simple. He has boasted that Robert Bresson, a filmmaker noted for his extremely ascetic, austere style, copied Melville's first film, *The Silence of the Sea* (*Le silence de la mer*,

1947), in realizing his far more famous *Diary of a Country Priest* (*Journal d'un curé de campagne*, 1950) (Nogueira 27). One cannot help finding a comparable austerity, not in every Schlöndorff film but in a significant number of them, for example, *Young Törless, The Sudden Wealth of the Poor People of Kombach* (*Der plötzliche Reichtum der armen Leute von Kombach*, 1970), *Coup de Grâce*. In each, a bleak black-and-white style of photography, simple sets and costumes, uncomplicated camera setups, a quiet acting style drained of declamation and excess affect, and spare music all combine to provide for a minimalist, dedramatized, rather cold style. It is a style Malle himself used in *The Fire Within*, on which Schlöndorff worked, and one brought to an extreme by Jean-Marie Straub in a work like *Unreconciled* (*Unversöhnt*, 1965). If one considers that both Malle and Straub had worked with Bresson on *A Man Escaped* (*Un condamné à mort s'est échappé*, 1956), this line of austerity—and it is a stylistic quality very much associated with early works from the New German Cinema—may come into Schlöndorff's work from more than one French source ("Straub/Huillet" F1). Although the style may grow in part out of constraints of low-budget production, it can also involve turning these constraints into virtues.

5. Political Commitment. Schlöndorff's stay in Paris coincided with the controversy and dissent surrounding the Algerian war, and he was involved to some extent in activism and protest. It may or may not be coincidental that among the extraordinarily few French works about the war that were produced in the early 1960s, almost all were by IDHEC-connected cinéastes: Malle's uncompleted *Alger 1961* (1961–62), Enrico's *La belle vie* (1962), Resnais's *Muriel* (1963), Jean Herman's *La quille* (1963), and Cavalier's *L'insoumis* (1964).

It is not surprising, then, that Schlöndorff's very first short, *Who Cares?* (*Wen kümmert's?*, 1960), dealt with youths troubled by political situations. The story revolves around a young Arab who is considering dropping out of the FLN, the Algerian Liberation Front, and a young German, a refugee from the German Democratic Republic. The two encourage each other to return to their homelands and to stand up for their convictions there. The short was banned in West Germany for political reasons (Patalas 63).

IDHEC had produced, in the words of Raymond Durgnat, "left-wing social moralists" who were in opposition to the "bourgeois anarchists" of the French New Wave (4). Perhaps the most striking alumnus of IDHEC from this period, and subsequently one of the most successful, was Greek expatriate Constantin Costa-Gavras. In work like *Z* (1969), *The Confession* (*L'aveau*, 1971), and *State of Siege* (*État de siège*, 1973), he established what was to become known as the leftist "political thriller." Like Schlöndorff, Costa-Gavras has been a filmmaker always ready to work within the established industry. He uses popular entertainment genre structures to support leftist political messages, a tactic that has caused him to be denigrated by both the right and the left. Surely Schlöndorff's *The Lost Honor of Katharina Blum* qualifies as a political thriller in much this same way, although we shall see how it has other agendas as well. One can only wonder about the extent to which Schlöndorff and Costa-Gavras, foreigners each, were similarly shaped by the cultural ambience of Paris in the late 1950s and early 1960s.

One must not underestimate the importance of French culture for Schlöndorff, as he himself has said he embraced it as something of a rebellion against the German culture of Nazism. Yet the probable influences described above suggest a pattern that is not entirely rebellious in character. IDHEC, Malle, Melville, and Tavernier all have their relatively conservative sides, have embraced tendencies toward a cinema of careful craftsmanship and traditional storytelling, and represent modes of cooperation with an existing economic and cultural system. This approach seems more moderate than the revolt and anarchic freedom often associated with the French New Wave and especially its post–May 1968 by-products. Other figures of the New German Cinema, such as Kluge, Fassbinder, Straub, and Wenders, seem to owe far more to the antiprofessionalist, antinarrative attitude of the Godardian wing of the French New Wave. Schlöndorff, for sure, flirts with these more subversive tendencies, especially in films like *A Degree of Murder* or *Baal,* not to mention his involvement with Brechtian theory. But he also has another foot firmly planted in a tradition of quality and French classicism; one could certainly argue that he has as much in common with this craft-oriented French tradition as with the New German Cinema.

How does one explain the apparent contradiction? Let us suggest that Schlöndorff's links to both the classic and the alternative French film traditions explain only one half of his aesthetic formation as a filmmaker. To examine the other half, we must consider his ties to the German film tradition that he formed, ironically enough, during his stay in France.

Roots in Classical German and Exile Film Traditions

Schlöndorff's first short, *Who Cares?*, was dedicated to Fritz Lang, a compliment which shows that from the very beginning Schlöndorff sought to link his work to older traditions of German filmmaking. One can find throughout the work of Schlöndorff references and similarities to both the classic works of the 1920s and early 1930s and to the exile legacy resulting from so many German filmmakers having fled to Hollywood with the rise of the Third Reich.

Schlöndorff is surely not the only filmmaker of the New German Cinema to acknowledge a debt to this past. Other examples abound. Werner Herzog's 1978 remake of Friedrich Wilhelm Murnau's *Nosferatu* (1922) pays homage to the expressionist tradition; Wim Wenders very specifically cites Fritz Lang's *Nibelungen* (1922–24) in the opening dialogue of *Kings of the Road* (*Im Laufe der Zeit*, 1975); and Rainer Werner Fassbinder has repeatedly invoked the spirit and techniques of Douglas Sirk (Detlef Sierck) as often as those of Brecht. But Schlöndorff's incorporation of the German filmmaking past has perhaps been the broadest and most eclectic in the New German Cinema.

Schlöndorff's knowledge of this specific film history began in his years in Paris, a fact as telling as any about the radical break in the German cultural tradition caused by the fascist regime of 1933–45. He met the exile Lotte H. Eisner, a major scholar and preserver of the German expressionist film and a curator at the French Cinémathèque, who took the young man under her wing. He obtained a job at the Cinémathèque as a translator of intertitles and subtitles for classic German films. He thus acquired an intimate familiarity with these works, not to mention free admission to Cinémathèque screenings, a perquisite he reportedly took daily advantage of ("Die Prinzessin" 169). The impact of these constant contacts can scarcely be overrated; note that the Schlöndorff of the mid-1970s maintains that the movies he has seen are his "real influence as a filmmaker" ("An Interview" 27). And the director of the mid-1980s reflects on the seminal significance of these film screenings: "The forgotten and humiliated came out of exile into the dark auditorium, where their honor was returned to them and they had us pledge the oath to uphold their heritage" ("Die Prinzessin" 169). The filmmaker describes his generation as one that wants to link up with the tradition of the 1920s ("Von den 'Alten'" 115).

Within this German film legacy, one finds at least four styles and approaches. They include the expressionist movement, the social pictorialism of Fritz Lang and G. W. Pabst, the analytical-critical realism of Bertolt Brecht, and the satiric-comic tradition of an Ernst Lubitsch or Billy Wilder. Schlöndorff's work contains allusions to and affinities with all four of these modes, and all extend to the humanist, antifascist exile tradition of the cinematic "Other Germany."

The first two categories frequently overlap. The expressionist movement in film produced studio-shot movies in which elaborate sets were often purposely distorted to parallel visually the anxious or disturbed interior states of their characters, for example, *The Cabinet of Dr. Caligari* (*Das Kabinett des Dr. Caligari*, 1919) and *Nosferatu*. As a movement in the silent film, it represented a pushing of the limits of signification derived from the construction of the image itself rather than from editing. What we have called a social pictorialism borrows the same basis in mise-en-scène for constructing visual meaning but involves more realistic environments and less emphasis on reflecting extremes of internalized emotion, as in Murnau's *The Last Laugh* (*Der letzte Mann*, 1924) and Lang's *M* (1931).

Schlöndorff recognized both of these traditions and responded initially to this call from the past when embarking on his first feature film, *Young Törless*.

> I was attracted to Fritz Lang's films, also the silent films of Murnau and Pabst. . . . I thought it was very important for me to relate to the tradition of German films. *Young Törless* (1965) is perhaps most influenced by this German filmmaking. When I worked on *Young Törless* I was thinking a lot of *M* (1931). ("An Interview" 27–28)

In his attempt to establish stylistic ties with the German film legacy, Schlöndorff not only availed himself of a story in "such a 'German' setting as a cadet academy . . . a linkage to German film traditions—Stroheim and Lang," ("Tribüne" 309); he even involved the cast by screening *M* for them. This classic orienting of the actors is especially evident in such *Törless* episodes as the interrogation of Basini in the boarding school attic. Film scholar Eric Rentschler associates this particular scene with Lang's child murderer facing the underworld jury in *M* (*German Film and Literature* 186).

Rentschler further observes the cinematic expressionist legacy imprinted on *Törless*'s passageways, vaults, and concealed attic room so characteristic of that classical German film architecture. Exterior space, here and even in landscapes, mirrors the inner condition of characters (184–85). One recognizes in Schlöndorff's debut feature a mode of filmmaking that is image-based rather than dialogue-oriented, a correlative to an entire line of French mise-en-scène criticism derived from a specific appreciation of expressionism and social pictorialism.

Other suggestive images and examples support the continuity of these German film traditions. One recalls the orderly procession of workers in Fritz Lang's *Metropolis* when one watches the geometric groupings of women perform bizarre rituals in *The Handmaid's Tale*. The gray war-torn trenches of Pabst's *Westfront 1918* reappear in *Coup de Grâce*. Schlöndorff extends the tradition of the street film in the reconstruction of a Danzig neighborhood in *The Tin Drum*.

An additional major piece of evidence is the director's work with Valeska Gert. Actress, mime, and avant-garde dancer, cabaret performer and writer, Gert (1892–1978) was a characteristic stage and screen personality during the

1. *Coup de Grâce.* Valeska Gert *(brightly lit in center),* an icon of Weimar culture, as Aunt Praskovia. Photo: Museum of Modern Art/Film Stills Archive.

Weimar Republic who had to survive in exile after the fascists assumed power. Pabst cast her in his *The Joyless Street (Die freudlose Gasse,* 1925) as the seamstress Greifer; in *Diary of a Lost Girl (Tagebuch einer Verlorenen,* 1929) as the governess;· and in *The Threepenny Opera (Die Dreigroschenoper,* 1930) as Mrs. Peachum. Several New German Cinema filmmakers drew on this living link to Pabst and Weimar cinematic culture, most prominently Schlöndorff, who not only assigned Gert an important role in *Coup de Grâce* (1976) but also based his documentary *Just for Fun, Just for Play—Kaleidoscope Valeska Gert (Nur zum Spaß, nur zum Spiel—Kaleidoskop Valeska Gert,* 1977) on her. (See illustration 1.)

In addition to appearing in Pabst's film of the *Threepenny Opera* by Bertolt Brecht, Gert also appeared in stage reviews and film inserts for a choral play (*Chorspiel*) by the playwright. She even physically shared the limelight with him as Canaille in his *Der Abnormitätenwirt (The Innkeeper of Perversities)* at the noted Munich Kammerspiele theater (Peter 65). She thus becomes a link to the third tradition, that of the ironic and detached political engagement of Brecht and the critical realism of the New Objectivity. Brecht himself incorporates another major link to Weimar culture for Schlöndorff. By the time the filmmaker met and cast Gert personally, he had himself realized his own television film based on Brecht's *Baal* (1969).

Brecht's comprehensive aesthetic approach to stage, screen, and general writing encompassed not only the rationalistic realism for which he is generally noted, particularly in German stagecraft and writing, but also facets of the Central European satiric-comic tradition. In terms of pure screen art, Ernst Lubitsch and Billy Wilder best embody this fourth tradition, even though their work in Berlin perhaps has received less than its appropriate recognition. Films that demonstrate Schlöndorff's working in this tradition, specifically the satirical vein, originated during the first half of the 1970s. They include *The Morals of Ruth Halbfass* (*Die Moral der Ruth Halbfass*, 1971), *A Free Woman* (*Strohfeuer*, 1972), and the television film *Overnight Stay in Tyrol* (*Übernachtung in Tirol*, 1973). The comic tradition comes even more overtly to the fore in *The Andechs Feeling* (*Das Andechser Gefühl*, 1974), a film produced by Schlöndorff. It is the story of a rebellious teacher spoofing the German-village film genre, starring Herbert Achternbusch, the writer-director. Schlöndorff planned to work further in this line in one of his unrealized projects from the 1980s, "The Most Powerful Man in the World," which was to have been a comedy about a summit conference, with Steve Martin playing the president of the United States ("German Film Production"). Schlöndorff's scriptwriter on the project was Walter Reisch, a Hollywood veteran who was part of the exile generation from the Hitler era. In Wilder's case, Schlöndorff has acknowledged his debt to the older filmmaker. A four-and-a-half-hour video and 16-mm documentary, *Billy, How Did You Do It?* (1992), gives a detailed portrait of Wilder a decade before his death in 2002. We will discuss this portrait later.

A significant overlap may suffice to highlight both Wilder's European past and the multifaceted connections between Schlöndorff and the earlier German tradition: Valeska Gert played a role in *People on Sunday* (*Menschen am Sonntag*, 1929), the collaborative film that teamed Wilder with Robert Siodmak and Edgar G. Ulmer, as well as others, prior to their flight—en masse—from the swastika. As we trace Schlöndorff's career through his international and American periods, we see an odd parallel to the émigré tradition. At their best, filmmakers like Lang or Wilder not only adapted to the Hollywood production system but brought to the American cinema a special insight into both positive and negative aspects of U.S. society. In developing a film like *A Gathering of Old Men* (1987), Schlöndorff had to be conscious of the way he was pursuing something similar to what Fritz Lang had accomplished in his first American film, *Fury* (1936). Both filmmakers examine the American system of justice with equal portions of admiration and calls for vigilance. In a similar way, both Billy Wilder's *The Apartment* (1961) and Schlöndorff's *Death of a Salesman* (1985) criticize the inhumanity of American capitalism with sharpness and understanding.

In his published writings, Schlöndorff has given tribute to some of the past figures from the German world of culture in general and film in particular. Others he acknowledged verbally in interviews and, above all, in his homage to the exile filmmakers in Hollywood during his acceptance speech on the occasion of West Germany receiving the 1979 Academy Award for best foreign film for *The Tin Drum*. For instance, Schlöndorff wrote an extensive review of Lotte H. Eisner's memoirs for the German magazine *Der Spiegel* and contributed a short text to a collection of testimonials in honor of Fritz Lang ("Die Prinzessin"). He also recognized in his Academy Award address "all those whose tradition we want to pick up and follow and who worked and lived here. . . . Fritz Lang, Billy Wilder, Lubitsch, Murnau, Pabst" (Acceptance speech).

Schlöndorff's energetic post–Berlin Wall, post–German unification efforts on behalf of Berlin-Babelsberg can be understood as another bow to the cinematic Weimar legacy. In the short film shown to all visitors at the beginning of popular studio tours, Schlöndorff takes on the role of screen guide through the facility of Babelsberg.

In the director's introduction (*Präsentationsfilm*, 1990), the history of the Babelsberg studio claims no small significance; Schlöndorff here extends the bow he has been taking toward the past German film culture for decades. Babelsberg traces its origins back to the grand epoch of silent German film when Deutsche Bioscop film production in 1911 erected its studio here. The company was named after the Bioscop double-image projector *(Doppelbildprojektor)* that German movie pioneer Max Skladanowsky had developed to initiate the popular history of the movies in Germany in 1895. In the Bioscop studios, "the ancestral cell of the later Ufa city" Babelsberg (Kreimeier 27), Paul Wegener inaugurated the classic German cinema with *The Student of Prague* (*Der Student von Prag*, 1913). Although management organization and ownership periodically shifted, the studio's operations expanded and it became the production site of such works as *The Cabinet of Dr. Caligari* (*Das Kabinett des Dr. Caligari*, 1919); Lang's *Dr. Mabuse, the Gambler* (*Dr. Mabuse, der Spieler*, 1922), *Nibelungen*, and *Metropolis* (1926); Murnau's *Faust* (1926); and Josef von Sternberg's *The Blue Angel* (*Der blaue Engel*, 1930), starring Marlene Dietrich. This tradition was suppressed by the Third Reich, during which the studio became a center of Nazi propaganda and escapist entertainment.

2. Schlöndorff and Billy Wilder in Berlin, reclaiming the Weimar and exile traditions.
Photo: Volker Schlöndorff.

The creators associated with this classical German Babelsberg cinema—
directors, producers, actors, and support staff, with few exceptions—would
seek asylum abroad after the Nazi assumption of power. Lang and Siodmak,
Wilder and producer Eric Pommer, Gert and Brecht: it is to this cinematic
"Other Germany" and to its pre-1933 legacy that Schlöndorff bowed by choosing the name "Bioskop" for his second production company in 1973, thus
directly referring back to the origins of Babelsberg. He was to come full circle
after a period of filmmaking in the United States and demonstrated in the 1990s
his continued sense of past German cinematic accomplishments within and
outside Germany by pursuing a vision for a renewed Babelsberg. (See illustration 2.) In assuming this responsibility, Schlöndorff tied together artistic and
professional traditions, opting for a synthesis and embedding a future German
cinema in the larger context that can "unite European audiences" ("Inside
Europe").

Part One

**THE EARLY SCHLÖNDORFF:
SUPPRESSION, POP, AND PROTEST**

3

Young Törless

In May 1966, for the first time in the postwar era, West Germany had a real contender at the Cannes film festival. After two decades of mostly marginal and irrelevant film production, Germany had produced a work that made the festival audience sit up and take notice: Volker Schlöndorff's *Young Törless (Der junge Törless)*. FIPRESCI (Fédération Internationale de la Presse Cinématographique) awarded the film its international critics' prize, and other awards soon followed. At home, *Young Törless* garnered three federal film prizes for the year's best direction, script, and screenplay. In Nantes, France, during the European Film Days, the jury presented it with the Max Ophüls-Prize. In the United States, *Variety* praised it as "a very impressive directorial debut" (Hans 19). The 1967 *International Film Guide* listed *Young Törless* as one of the top ten films of the preceding year and referred to Schlöndorff as "the foremost hope of the new German cinema" (Cowie, *1967* 5, 78).

The film set up a pattern followed by dozens of subsequent works from the New German Cinema. It took a renowned literary text, assertively enacted it to strong cinematic effect, and dispassionately reflected on themes relevant to postwar West German culture: innocence and guilt, conformity and rebellion, solipsism and engagement. The movie evoked from spectators and critics a broad variety of interpretations. Some have analyzed *Young Törless* as a study of adolescence. Others debated whether the film proposed a political model of Middle European militarism. The film is effective on both counts. A viewer can best approach its psychological aspects by comparing the *Törless* film with the genre of literary and filmic narratives about adolescents and boarding schools that had preceded it. Similarly, an awareness of the way in which Schlöndorff's literary contemporaries had reinterpreted Robert Musil's novel makes clearer the motion picture's metaphoric import for postwar Europe.

The director translated to the screen, in convincing and inventive fashion, a classic of German-language fiction. During the 1950s and 1960s, West German critics and readers rediscovered Robert Musil's 1906 novel, *Die Verwirrungen des*

Zöglings Törless, a work driven into intellectual exile when its author was forced to leave his country during the Third Reich. A highly subjective, modernist book that at first glance appears ill-suited for cinematic adaptation, the novel stands out as a work of experimental fiction. Its modernist self-consciousness questions the principles of nineteenth-century realism both through its psychological depth and its *Sprachskepsis,* a philosophical skepticism about the ability of language to articulate reality. The book relies on an omniscient, interpreting narrator to convey abstract ideas about its young protagonist.

Schlöndorff omitted certain aspects of the novel's intellectual quality when he undertook the adaptation. Contrary to John Sandford's accusations in *The New German Cinema,* however, Schlöndorff did not make these changes out of facile reductionism, nor did he unambiguously simplify the novel by externalizing its depiction of characters' internal states (37). Rather, our thesis is that the filmmaker's choices complement the specificity of his medium: he created cinematic equivalents of Törless's inner life and employed a network of leitmotifs to stimulate the viewer's reflections.

Both novel and film are set in a military academy in the eastern provinces of Austria. Törless's experiences are at the center of the story. Sent by his father, Privy Councillor Törless, to obtain a first-rate education at this elitist institution, the student becomes involved in sadistic peer-group experimentation. Reiting and Beineberg, the student's school friends, acquire complete control over a classmate when they gain knowledge of a break-in that he has committed. Törless witnesses the brutalities to which the pair subject the thief Basini in the boarding school's attic, a space which the two, with a near-masochistic collaboration by their victim, have turned into a torture chamber. As the excesses against Basini increase and threaten to end with a class lynching, the victim admits his crime to the school authorities and is expelled. Törless leaves the academy of his own accord.

In general, the film's individual boarding school students follow the characterizations of the novel. Basini (Marian Seidowsky) is the sensitive one. Because of his immaturity and inferiority complex, he is a show-off, an endangered, sometimes feminine adolescent who commits an act of theft. Reiting (Alfred Dietz), who like Beineberg (Bernd Tischer) is physically bigger and older than Basini, exemplifies the smart, brutal criminal. He is the rough, inhuman torturer who gives in to all impulses as long as he has complete control over the victim. Beineberg's contempt for humanity and his manipulative drives are more mystic and exotic than Reiting's, though both boys are merciless and power-hungry. The power of controlling Basini tempts Törless (Matthieu Carrière), but that thrill disappears quickly. Törless is more intellectual and searching than Beineberg but also more passive, a voyeuristic observer. Neither empathizing with Basini nor actively ending his pain, Törless loses himself in his own thoughts or in abstract, speculative questions, as when he tries to discover Basini's breaking point in the attic.

By any account, Musil's *Die Verwirrungen des Zöglings Törless* renders a portrait of adolescence and a school story similar to Hermann Hesse's *Beneath the Wheel (Unterm Rad)* and James Joyce's *Portrait of the Artist as a Young Man*. All three are semiautobiographical works (Corino). Characteristically, the genre's hero undergoes the crisis of initiation into the world of adults—a "passage" that mixes day and night, light and dark, ethics and moral corruption. Self-discovery, a fundamental part of adolescence and a basic feature of the literature and films about youth, characterizes *Törless*.

In addition, Musil's *Törless* sketches a psychosexual portrayal of youth prophetic of William Golding's *Lord of the Flies* (1954) and Günter Grass's *Cat and Mouse (Katz und Maus*, 1961), including the theme of adolescent sadism. Through violence and peer-group rejection, Musil's and Golding's characters exorcise a schoolmate's identity. Schlöndorff's adaptation captures the tensions of this process with a claustrophobic boarding-school setting and authoritarian ambience reminiscent of Leontine Sagan's classic film *Girls in Uniform (Mädchen in Uniform*, 1931). In this way, he synthesizes a literary tradition with the stylistic legacy of the pre-Nazi German cinema.

As a film, Schlöndorff's *Young Törless* is characterized by moody black-and-white photography, spare dialogue, and a somewhat languid, reflective pace. Schlöndorff follows certain conventions of the 1960s art film in this respect. But we shall see in our discussions of *Törless*'s mise-en-scène how the filmmaker's decisions in visualizing Musil's narrative involve careful use of composition and editing patterns to maintain the subjectivity of point of view and moral ambiguity of the literary source. We examine how the filmmaker visually articulates two major issues of adolescence found in Musil's novel: first, Törless's emerging sexuality, which involves his desire for women and changes in his perceptions of them; second, the issue of how an adolescent defines himself through peer relations, with individual values coming into conflict with group behavior. By merging the first, personal, more poetic side of maturation with the second, more political side, Schlöndorff achieves a complex discourse about German culture and politics in the mid-twentieth century. We also show how the director's leitmotif structure unifies this discourse through three different visual tropes: a metaphoric use of animals, a self-reflexive creation of voyeuristic viewing patterns, and graphic emphasis on confining circular forms. All of these elements work together to depict a proto-Nazi microcosm.

Adolescence and Sexuality

In keeping with the sexual side of the youth genre, young Törless must further his personal development by overcoming the stereotypical images of women that he holds. Along with initiation into the adult world, he must confront a distorted dichotomy in which women function only as one of two contrasting archetypes: the pure mother and the impure prostitute. His experiences with women force Törless to adjust to a complex world in which morality is not black and white. The character's growing sexual sophistication parallels a moral sophistry he begins to develop. In both the novel and film, three core scenes demonstrate this link: (1) the departure of Törless's parents from the school-town's train station; (2) the joint visit with classmate Beineberg to Bozena, the prostitute; and (3) Törless's own final departure from the school. It is revealing to examine these scenes in greater detail. In both media, the two departures take place at the outset and conclusion of the narrative—thereby framing an adolescent's coming of age.

During the initial departure at the small train station, Törless's affectionate embrace of his mother (Hanna Axmann–von Rezzori) establishes the boy's motherly image of the female. Schlöndorff reinforces this image with the gaze that passes between them in shot/reverse-shot through the train window—with the low angle up at the mother supporting her authority, the high angle down to Törless emphasizing his passivity. The novel's flashback to the protagonist's early isolated days in the military academy portrays in detail his yearning for his mother and his idealization of her at this station. In just a few shots, the filmmaker encapsulates several pages of text.

This Madonna-like image of women is tested during Törless's visit to Bozena (Barbara Steele). The novel uses the protagonist's reflections to establish the conflict raging inside him when he faces Bozena, the confrontation of two types of women that he wants so desperately to keep neatly separated: "How *can* it be like this—this woman, who is for me a maze of sexual lust, and my mother, who up to now moved through my life like a star, beyond the reach of all desire, in some cloudless distance, clear and without depths . . . " (Musil, *Young Törless* 39). In this scene, Törless's childlike need to idealize his mother clashes with disturbing realities. Both in the novel and in the film, Bozena teases Törless. Turning to Beineberg, the film's prostitute remarks: "Your friend acts as if he's never seen a woman before in his life. And his mother is a very pretty person. . . . She surely caught the eye of more than one when she was young." Bozena accurately senses the conflict she is stirring in the protagonist's mind. Later she turns directly to Törless and disturbs his reflections by asking: "You don't like

3. *Young Törless.* The title figure glancing at his mother at the end. Photo: Deutsches Filminstitut, Frankfurt.

me telling you about your mother? . . . You think your mother and I are not the same, huh?" Bozena goes even further by equating her visitors with their parents: "You are exactly like your parents, hypocritical, cowardly, and untruthful." At this early juncture, however, the boarding school student opposes these equations.

The cyclic end of both the novel and film versions of *Törless* illustrates the boy's maturation by indicating his changed relationship to his mother. In the last scene, as both are riding in a coach to the train station, he shoots a sidelong glance at his mother. "What is it?" she asks. "Nothing, Mamma. I was just thinking," Törless replies. Here the text and Schlöndorff's written scenario continue: "And, drawing a deep breath, he considered the faint whiff of scent that rose from his mother's corseted waist" (Musil, *Young Törless* 173; Schlöndorff, "Der junge" 56). (See illustration 3.)

Schlöndorff closely follows Musil's text in its chronology and details, as well as in its implication of Törless's emotional development. Because his reply "I was just thinking" comes right as the carriage passes the prostitute's quarters, it alludes (for the viewer) to Bozena's sobering reduction of his mother and aunt to their sexual roles. At this very moment, the director shows the character glancing down to his mother's lap. The final interaction between mother and son has attained a different, more equal status in comparison with the film's initial departure scene: the camera, which no longer looks up to the mother and down to the son, now stays at the same angle for both. We can conclude from this scene that Törless now perceives the woman as both a sexually active human and a mother. This ending is standard for a story of this genre: a youngster has come of age.

In both versions of *Young Törless*, we can recognize separate but related modes of expression and imagery common to this genre of novel and film about adolescence. The scene in Bozena's room provides a suitable example of medium specificity. In the novel, particularly in a modernist work as cerebral as *Törless*, Musil works constantly with the protagonist's reflections and memories, including those about both women. To avoid a voice-over narration to represent his hero's inner voice, Schlöndorff instead gives Bozena—a younger, more appealing woman than in the book—a child. Bozena's crying baby becomes a cinematic "match" to elaborate on certain analogous relations: the parallel between the prostitute and her infant, on the one hand, and Mrs. Privy Councillor Törless and the protagonist, on the other. The baby screams and Bozena points to it. "You think you are more than that there? You're wrong." Through visual association and dialogue, the filmmaker has created a cinematic equivalent.

Subjectivity, Group Behavior, and Fascism

Schlöndorff seems to have brought to his task of adaptation little respect for traditional views that place internal, hidden life in the domain of literary representation, while viewing the cinema as a medium that represents empirical and material reality. This attitude is most evident in the way Schlöndorff conveys Törless's inner conflicts about wanting to be part of the group but also wanting to follow his own conscience. Schlöndorff uses visual means to suggest Törless's strong internal states, even as the director develops detailed images of the adolescent's objective environment that help tell the story.

We find an example of this dual use of the image in the schoolboys' return from the rail station after the departure of Törless's parents. The cerebral character of Musil's novel challenges the filmmaker not only to reproduce the empirical reality in which the boys cross the fields and reenter the school town but also to recreate the inner cosmos of Törless, a second world no less significant and rich than the material world. The sign systems of both the novel and the film portray the students strolling into town and trying to flirt with the young peasant women in precocious, awkward macho ways. According to the novel, "Törless took no part in this display of overweening . . . manliness" (19). In both evocative imagery and explicit narration, however, the novel makes clear that the boy abstains only because of "his own peculiar kind of sensuality, which was more deeply hidden, more forceful, and of a darker hue than that of his friends and more slow and difficult in its manifestations"(20).

How can the filmmaker recreate visual evidence for Törless's surging inner state? The filmmaker relates him visually to objects that attract his desire. First, Schlöndorff repeatedly singles out Törless from the group of students: he almost always walks alone. Second, Schlöndorff guides the viewer's eye to Törless when the group enters the town by cutting to close-ups of the adolescent. By means of montage, he inserts a series of eyeline match shots into a traveling sequence. In each pair of shots, we first see Törless in close-up and then the various objects of his gaze—a woman in the interior of a narrow home, a woman on a patio, a slaughtered pig. The filmmaker uses classic editing technique to go beyond the pure reproduction of the external reality and lead the viewer to identify with Törless's internal states.

Schlöndorff's medium-specific transformation of the novel is even more successful during the film's five-minute cake-shop sequence that occurs the next evening. In the novel's lengthy scene, Törless and Beineberg enjoy the ambience of a café while sipping liqueur, talking, and yawning. Beineberg finishes an extended tale about his father's British service in India that bores Törless because he has heard it so many times. The adolescent's resentment of his schoolmate increases as Beineberg rolls himself a cigarette and reads a story from the daily paper. Törless breaks the tense spell by starting a routine dialogue about meals, school subjects, and the irrelevance of the boarding school as preparation for life.

Again through editing, the film version immediately introduces the viewer to Törless's internally articulated dislikes, urges, and moods that then permeate the entire scene. After a long shot that shows the students in the café, Schlöndorff cuts to a medium shot that places a waitress next to Törless, whose glass she is refilling. (See illustration 4.) The relation between Törless and the waitress is established visually when the camera follows Törless's glance as it glides over the woman's arm. In a montage of close-ups and medium close-ups, the camera begins to capture fragments of the waitress's body—her neck, mouth, hands. By reducing the woman to eroticized body parts, Schlöndorff conveys his character's subjective experience. While closely observing the woman, Törless (in close-up) licks his lips. The next shot presents the mouth of the waitress, who also licks her lips. This montage editing of close-ups and tongue gestures demonstrates Törless's sexual arousal, while the segmental representation of the waitress emphasizes the impersonal nature of Törless's feelings. Having once produced this sensual aura, the director transfers it through the same stylistic means to the relation between Törless and Beineberg. Again Schlöndorff cuts between close-ups of Törless's glance and the close-up fragments of the other's body (Beineberg's hand straightening a cigarette, his fingers, his eyes, his hand striking a match and moving to his mouth, his lips). Törless's glance meets Beineberg's and endures it. The long take of the glance conjures up exactly the degree of tension necessary to express Törless's hostility. From this montage, filmgoers can infer Törless's inner states and dynamics. By concentrating on central elements of this ten-page scene from the novel, Schlöndorff masterfully represents Törless's libido, including the student's simultaneous homoerotic attraction to and detesting of his classmate.

To the point-of-view shots just described that highlight the film's psychosexual subtext, Schlöndorff adds a more objective element, using deep-focus shots and comparative editing to generate a discourse on political power. When the filmmaker expands the cake-shop scene by adding a second strand of action, he makes the scene complex in a different way by replacing literary signs with visual ones. Schlöndorff deviates from the original narrative by placing Basini and Reiting, who discuss a case of theft, in a separate wing of the cake shop at the same time that Beineberg and Törless are talking. In both the novel and the film, the specific interaction between Basini and Reiting lays the groundwork for the blackmailing relationships that later develop inside the peer group quartet. In the novel, apart from a reference of Bozena's to Basini, this relationship begins after the visit with the prostitute. By then, Reiting has already caught the thief and is explaining to his comrades how he trapped Basini into confession and elicited his pledge to do whatever Reiting demands. Musil explicitly renders Reiting's report, including the remark that Basini "actually invited me to have a drink with him downtown. He ordered wine, cake, and cigarettes, and pressed it all on me" (*Young Törless* 52). Here then lies the source of the parallel structure whereby Reiting intimidates Basini in the cake shop.

The filmmaker clearly felt it was important to introduce Basini's character earlier and more thoroughly than Musil does in the novel. To do so, the filmmaker establishes a number of new scenes and moves others to positions earlier in the plot. Toward the end of the pupils' return from the railroad station, the trio of Törless, Reiting, and Basini enters an inn. Basini stands out right

4. *Young Törless*. Matthieu Carrière *(left)* as Törless. The adolescent's sensuality emerging in the cake shop. Photo: Franz Seitz Filmproduktion.

away when he orders drinks not only for his comrades but also for some strangers. In addition, he is the only one of the trio who is drawn into a game of chance, in which he promptly loses his wager. This episode is altogether newly created, as is the scene showing Basini vainly combing his hair and posing in the academy's washroom before retiring for the night. Another addition shows a gloved hand stealing from Beineberg's locker late at night, with the final shot of the sequence identifying the thief as Basini. Thus, the viewers have known Basini for some time before they, along with Törless and Beineberg, learn from Bozena about Basini's naïveté and boasting. In the comparable scene in the novel, this is the first indication of Basini altogether.

Like Basini, Reiting's character also receives greater attention in the film than in the novel. Before the spectator encounters him at the cake shop with Basini, Reiting is seen with the same school friend in a pub and in three scenes constructed for the film that are set in the study room, the classroom, and the bathroom. Reiting's aggressiveness is brought forth twice by the filmmaker, once as he tortures a fly while sitting at Törless's table and another time in the classroom as he takes a student's sport shoe and throws it at Basini. Neither incident appears in Musil's book.

Although the students in the film are individually characterized much as they are in the novel, the group they form nevertheless gains added weight on the screen, sometimes at the expense of the character of Törless. In the cakeshop scene, the spectator sees Törless as he relates to the three classmates in the film. If the relation of Beineberg and Reiting to Basini is one of complicity between torturers and victim, Törless also plays a role in this sadomasochistic trio, one that displays the curiosity of the voyeur rather than the compassion of a social activist. Motivated by youthful searching and questioning, Törless repeatedly takes part in the double life of the "good" boarding-school cadets who at night degrade and sadistically torment their comrade.

The central student quartet's double life in the *Törless* novel has, since the Third Reich, frequently evoked association with the historical Nazi state, and Schlöndorff deepened these associations. Diverse voices of literary life have recognized the resemblance, including exiled novelist Musil himself, who wrote in his diary: "Reiting, Beineberg: Today's dictators *in nucleo*" (*Tagebücher* 441). Publishers' blurbs in post–World War II editions and translations of the novel, like the Rowohlt German reissue of 1959, saw the novel prefiguring in visionary manner "the picture of a coming dictatorship and the rape of the individuals by the system" (2). Similarly, Third Reich exile Jean Améry turned Törless into a Hitler party member in an imaginative extension of the character's fictional life ("Gespräch"). Améry's Törless wrote for Goebbels' weekly, then died of a heart attack in precisely those days when Nazi cruelties became fully known. Likewise, Wilfried Berghahn, author of the popular Musil biography of 1963, commented that "the methodology of the concentration camps" could be perceived in the students' clandestine behavior (28–29). The director chose Berghahn as his literary advisor.

Before this backdrop, the *Törless* of the mid-1960s was not the same work of art as the *Törless* of 1906. Musil's narrator assures the reader: "Later, when he had got over his adolescent experiences, Törless became a young man whose mind was both subtle and sensitive"(137). Schlöndorff, by contrast, rejects Musil's optimistic conclusions and understands the book in the mirror of historical knowledge. Schlöndorff's *Young Törless* replaces the positive moral interpretation of events provided by Musil's narrator with far more ambiguous images.

Leitmotifs: Animals, Voyeurs, Circles

Instead of simplifying and debasing *Törless*'s complexity, as Sandford alleges, Schlöndorff amplifies many aspects of the prose narrative through a leitmotif structure that increases the multivalenced meaning of the story. Images and incidents relating to animals, voyeurism, and imprisoning circles surface repeatedly throughout the film to form a network of associations and references. Individually, these images may be quite simple, but together, they provide a visual discourse of a richness comparable to Musil's verbal one: what Sandford calls reductionism is rather an attempt to express ideas through pictures rather than words.

Animal metaphors abound in Schlöndorff's *Törless* and reflect the sadism of Beineberg and Reiting. The film's bullies force Basini to call himself a dog. The slaughtered pig—slit open and hanging at the village entrance—and the mouse dangling by its tail both foreshadow the lynching scene in the gym where Basini hangs like the other creatures, head downward. (See illustration 5.) (A key, hanging on a thread, used by Beineberg to hypnotize Basini, also forms a link in this leitmotif network.)

Similarly, Schlöndorff's compositions and editing present the Törless figure as wavering between voyeurism and a posture of resistance as he watches the trapped victims. Schlöndorff's leitmotif technique allows the spectator to contemplate the adolescent character "trying on" different ethical positions. When, in the newly developed scene in the study room, Törless watches Reiting catch a fly and torture it, he does no more than show disgust and criticism. When he observes Beineberg's half-mystic levitation experiment in the attic, he finally walks out without helping. When Törless takes a walk in front of the board-

5. *Young Törless*. Basini, the victim, hanging upside down in the gym. Photo: Museum of Modern Art/Film Stills Archive.

ing school, he meets a group of students. They see Reiting holding a mouse by the tail and letting it swing back and forth. In this case, Törless does not continue to watch the torment. He intervenes by grabbing the animal and kills it to stop its suffering. Like the film audience, Törless takes ambivalent pleasure in watching human cruelty unfold.

The film's Törless has the option to act responsibly, which becomes apparent in a part of the cake-shop scene. Musil describes the scene in the following way: "Beineberg had taken up a newspaper. . . . Now Beineberg glanced up from the newspaper. Then he read a paragraph aloud, laid the newspaper aside and yawned"(25–26). In the film, however, Schlöndorff lets Beineberg read a complete article about a waitress who kills her abusive live-in lover. Why did the filmmaker expand this scene? At first sight, it merely suggests an anticipation of the youthful aberrations and sadomasochism that follow in the narrative. At second sight, it becomes clear that the relationship between the waitress and the lover parallels not only that of Basini and Reiting/Beineberg and that of Basini and Törless but also that of Törless and Reiting/Beineberg. The interrelated motifs of bondage, sexual services, sadism, all tinged with pseudoreligious overtones, occur in all three cases. The newspaper reader's detached fascination with the violent incident parallels the same morbid interest that Törless, and by extension the audience, takes in his friends' sick behavior. At the same time, we have a case in which a dominated, oppressed victim could have refused the victim role. In other words, like the murderous waitress, Törless and Basini are put in positions from which they can rebel. Significantly, Törless chooses to watch— rather than act in this scene. The filmmaker shows Törless's ambivalence, not only through his "spiteful satisfaction . . . that with some extra faculty he had, he got more out of these happenings than his companions did" but also through his amoral observation.

This interposing of Törless between the stance of responsibility and voyeurism is central to Schlöndorff's film, and it is an option that the filmmaker also extends to the spectator. Eric Rentschler has further pursued the figure of Törless's voyeurism (*German Film and Literature* 186). Törless appears at the edge of frames, in the dark background—much as the filmgoer in the darkened movie house. "He, like we, is a cinema fetishist, a private person enchanted by the possibilities before him, captivated by the theater of shadows transpiring in front of him" (188). The metaphor of the voyeur, then, suggests that the film audience may itself incline to a similar socially irresponsible stance. We along with Schlöndorff know that historically the German intellectual tradition during the Third Reich—except for the "Other Germany" of the exiles—leaned toward the apolitical position. Implicitly, then—in his representation of Törless as voyeur—Schlöndorff develops a forceful critique of traditional German society, especially of the intellectuals who were most likely to comprise Musil's audience.

Although Schlöndorff's Törless, like Musil's, finds his way thanks to his own special sensitivity, the filmmaker expresses much more historical skepticism. The film conveys this attitude through the major metaphor of the circle. Enclosure is the primary spatial quality of much of the cinematic *Young Törless:* the castlelike boarding-school complex, its inner court, classrooms, dormitory, gymnasium, and finally, the attic. More specific, Schlöndorff has developed confining circles into a subnetwork of film images that are frequently integrated with the animal leitmotifs. As noted earlier, the torturer Beineberg strives to hypnotize his victim in the attic with the imprisoning orbits of the pendulum. As early as 1966, Ernst Wendt noted in the German magazine, *Film,* the correspondence between the circle that Reiting draws around his victim, the fly, and the remorseless circle that the boarding school students draw around their victim, Basini, at the end of the film (18). At first, Törless participates impulsively in the lynching scene, pushing Basini into the circle, then tries to break into the circle from the outside to intervene on behalf of the victim. However, he does not succeed in disrupting the sadistic merry-go-round of the youthful pre-Holocaust torturers. Schlöndorff combines threatening circular motifs with imagery of hypnotism and control in homage to similar elements in the films of Fritz Lang. Just two years earlier, Jean-Luc Godard, in his own homage to Lang, the science-fiction film *Alphaville,* had created similar associations between circles and evil (Roud 166).

Eventually, though, the film expresses through visual imagery that Törless will soon stand outside the circle. This message is sharpened in the film through nuance, leitmotif, and composition—particularly in the last scene. Wendt has also noted that the opening of the film includes two panning shots, each forming a quarter circle around the train station; at the end of the film, a similar pan forms a half circle (17). With the last scene of the film, therefore, the circle has grown to a full 360 degrees, as Alberto Cattini has observed (12). Does Schlöndorff mean then to close the vicious circle of brutality around Törless? The train station as a place of departure suggests the opposite to enclosing Törless in the circle, as does Schlöndorff's preceding scene in which Törless no longer faces his mother as the child of the film's beginning. In addition, on the psychological level, this mature Törless seems to have no further interest in complying with brutal boyish secret games.

In terms of political metaphor, however, Törless may not have escaped the surrounding circle of conformity. His waffling between responsibility and voyeurism, his occasionally narcissist self-absorption, and his association with the historical Nazi guilt stimulate viewer ambivalence toward the protagonist. The cinematic pull toward identification now alternates with the spectator's inclination to detach from Törless. As a historicocultural metaphor, Törless can be understood but not forgiven. This political power level is enriched by the audience's awareness of past Austro-German history, by meticulous mise-en-scène, and by a carefully structured leitmotif network. Rather than being a simple reduction of the book, Schlöndorff's film simultaneously updates Musil and richly superimposes a contemplation of Central European history over a study of adolescent development.

4

A Degree of Murder and "An Uneasy Moment"

When an interviewer asked Rainer Werner Fassbinder in 1974 whether any films by contemporary young German filmmakers particularly appealed to him, his response mentioned Schlöndorff's *A Degree of Murder* (*Mord und Totschlag*, 1967) (Wiegand, "Interview" 69). The affinity between the two directors was at its peak during the second half of the 1960s, when both were based in Munich and *A Degree of Murder* emerged. Nonetheless, why Fassbinder chose to privilege Schlöndorff's second feature film remains an intriguing question. Surely during the later sixties there were parallels between the two filmmakers' attitudes, creative stances, and objectives. In *A Degree of Murder*, Marie (Anita Pallenberg) recruits two strangers to help her dispose of the corpse of her lover, whom she accidentally shot in self-defense. Both Schlöndorff in *A Degree of Murder* and Fassbinder in *Gods of the Plague* (*Götter der Pest*, 1969) structure plots in which two men and a woman restlessly drive into the countryside.

Given his sense of rebellion, the young Fassbinder probably liked how *A Degree of Murder* broke with the past. Schlöndorff used the success of *Young Törless* as a springboard to introduce, with his second film, a new element of pop culture visual splashiness into the German film. *A Degree of Murder*, however, made before the institution of extensive state subsidies and television financing, also maintained certain production conventions from an earlier, more traditional generation. Schlöndorff changed producers, moving from Franz Seitz, Jr., an establishment fixture, to Rob Houwer, who was closely associated with the first generation of the New German Cinema. However, even with this younger-generation producer, financing in the traditional German system largely had to come from advances from the distributor. Schlöndorff and producer Houwer secured the considerable advance of five hundred thousand German marks from the German Constantin Verleih distributorship.

Counting on income through the sale of the worldwide screening rights apparently looked like a good risk. Shortly upon completion of the picture, Houwer did sell the non-German rights for *A Degree of Murder* to Universal for the sum of $185,000, which at the time equalled seven hundred thousand marks (Bronnen and Brocher 82). This transaction earned a small profit for the producer, although the film's box office take ultimately did not realize the domestic distributor's guarantee. On top of that, Universal failed altogether to release the picture to the international market (Bronnen and Brocher 82–83). The film did not receive a New York theatrical premiere until 1980, after the success of *The Tin Drum* (Buckley).

A New Wave Youth Film

A Degree of Murder used its comparatively high budget of more than a million marks to step into a new visual culture. It not only introduced color photography to the New German Cinema and the limited "wide screen" 1.66:1 standard; it brought the Young German cinema up to date with international pop art and new wave aesthetics. Plugging the novel ambience of his second film in an interview, the young director emphasized his dislike for black-and-white. "In the movies," he continued, "I'm not happy until color lifts off from the screen as the curtain opens, and even more so in 'Scope to boot" (Hopf, "Fragen"). The filmmaker began to turn away from the more elitist sensibility of *Young Törless* toward a sensibility characterized by spontaneity, sensuality, and consumption.

　　Most important, the film embodied a link to the French New Wave. One innovation of *nouvelle vague* film practice had been the movement of filmmakers out of the studio and onto the streets of Paris. In *A Degree of Murder*, Schlöndorff correspondingly focused on young people adrift in the city and moving out to the countryside, using "50% exterior shooting," by his own report ("Volker Schlöndorff bleibt"). Another forte of the contemporary French films, their mark of novelty, had been the mixture of genres and pervasive shifts in temperament—now comic, now serious. The Schlöndorff of *A Degree of Murder* worked similarly: "I was interested in the discontinuity. At first, there is a murder, then there's laughing again. The basic idea is the surprise assault against traditional biases. There no longer is a five-week mourning period" ("Entsetzliches").

　　A Degree of Murder, then, shares with such French *nouvelle vague* films as François Truffaut's *Shoot the Piano Player* (1959) and Jean-Luc Godard's *Band of Outsiders* (*Bande à part*, 1964) the undramatic narrative structure, mood changes, gags, and playful treatment of the fictional crime motif. In an interview,

Schlöndorff described his film as one "with no great dramatic conflicts" ("Volker Schlöndorff bleibt"). Elsewhere, he speaks of "a lyric film" ("Ist Michael Kohlhaas"). Like *Shoot the Piano Player,* Schlöndorff's film contains the strong element of popular culture, and like *Band of Outsiders,* it has a woman and two men involved in criminal activity presented in a light and careless manner.

The sixties' sensibility here is one that combines violence and frivolity, or crime and brutality associated with—to borrow the title of a contemporary review of *A Degree of Murder*—"neither guilt nor atonement" (Peters). The film-maker, who himself emphasized, "There's hardly a statement, much less a moral message" (Hopf, "Fragen"), employed two strategies to avoid moral issues. First, as Klaus Eder has pointed out, *A Degree of Murder* is a crime story acted out not by criminal types but by everyday youngsters ("Vom Umgang" 17). Second, not unlike the makers of *Thelma and Louise* (1990), Schlöndorff por-trays a heroine who is both guilty and innocent. In both films, the central female characters are subjected to unwelcome sexual approaches and react out of self-defense. At the same time, these heroines are guilty of taking the law into their own hands and failing to report the crime to the police. By creating heroines sympathetic to the audience, both films omit the edifying element, forgo the moral lesson, and deny the category of guilt (Nettelbeck).

Schlöndorff's point of departure was a crime story, and he has stated that he was aiming for the certain quality of "the American action movies of the thir-ties" (Hopf, "Fragen"). The director drew on a press report for the dramatic material of his second picture, following a tradition from the French cinema of basing films on sensational journalistic accounts, the *faites diverses.* In fact, the original idea from which *A Degree of Murder* emerged was the very news-paper article about a prostitute shooting her pimp that Beineberg reads to Törless in Schlöndorff's first film. Yet the filmmaker has completely transposed the news story by isolating it from its original milieu of prostitution and cor-ruption. The press materials for the film describe its characters as being like comic-strip figures, in effect abstractions from reality (Constantin-Film 4).

Hollywood Genre and Its Subversion

A Degree of Murder has been considered one of a group of films from the late 1960s, drawn from American action movies, sometimes referred to as "antithrillers." They abound in quotes from earlier movies, seem derived from the culture industry rather than life, and foreshadow in style and approach a more recent film like Quentin Tarantino's *Pulp Fiction* (1995). *A Degree of Murder,* with its mixture of familiar film patterns, genre minimotifs, quotes from sensational newspaper yarns or earlier popular films, and intentionally abstracted characters, has been seen "as the most amusing and masterly attempt in this direction" (Pflaum and Prinzler, *Cinema* 18). Thomas Elsaesser has argued in "Towards a Genre Cinema?" that *A Degree of Murder* and Klaus Lemke's *48 Hours to Acapulco (48 Stunden bis Acapulco)*, from the same year, 1967, are "both thrillers that harked back to those of Don Siegel and Sam Fuller in the 1950s" (*New German Cinema* 120). But one might counter that the "antithriller" designation is far more accurate: *A Degree of Murder* operates with *topoi* of the crime film but shows ambivalence about following the rules of the genre too closely.

Indeed, *A Degree of Murder* demonstrates a light and decidedly early postmodern synthesis that cites, repeats, and pastiches elements from earlier authors, works, and styles. The director is playing with a handful of genre elements. In addition to the thriller or antithriller, there are elements of the youth film (involving precomputerized slot and pinball machines, games of highway chicken, careless love, and amoralism). There are patterns of the *Heimatfilm*, or German regional nostalgia genre (as seen in the stop at the aunt's farm house or Fritz's causing mayhem with a farmer's horse).

There are also moments of black comedy—Hitchcock comes to mind first. Consider how the small-town setting of *The Trouble with Harry* (1956) clashes with a macabre plot about the burying and reburying of a corpse. Hitchcock's orderly provincial types seem as displaced with their morbid activity as the trio of youngsters in *A Degree of Murder*. (See illustration 6.) Or, comparably, we might recall Hitchcock's *Rope* (1948), which also involves the hiding of an inconvenient corpse. Schlöndorff may well be citing Hitchcock, who lights the concluding scene of *Rope* with a flashing red neon sign, when the younger filmmaker lights the struggle that ends in Marie's shooting Hans (Werner Enke) with a similarly blinking Pepsi sign. On a different level, the shot of Marie lacing the shoes that stick out of the carpet used to hide the corpse is a striking moment of black comedy.

There is, finally, the newly emerging genre of the road film seen in the latter half of *A Degree of Murder*. Open spaces contrast with metropolitan Munich; the city dwellers experience nature; Marie tastes the raindrops splashing through the open rear window on her face; the trio enjoys the thrill of speed, the beat of the music, and the liberating drives on the open road.

Citing different genres is thus part of the postmodern synthesis in *A Degree of Murder*—one that is salted with a good dose of humor. Contemporary music is another spice that complements the film's visual approach. Brian Jones of the Rolling Stones contributed a score that sets a lively, popular beat, is strong on

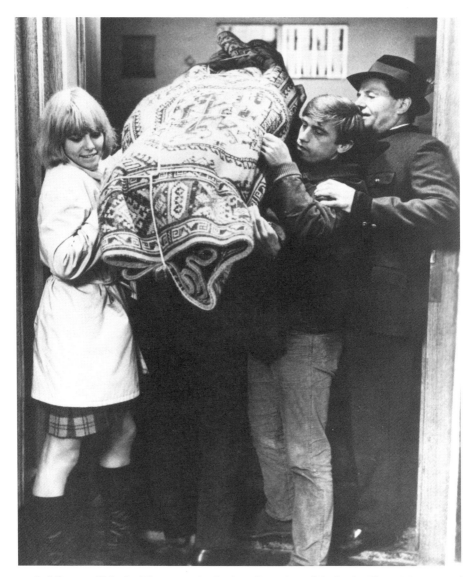

6. *A Degree of Murder.* The young hedonists disposing of the body. Photo: Museum of Modern Art/Film Stills Archive.

drums, and sparingly employs the reedy wail of the harmonica and flute. It is closely associated with the musical accompaniment of films such as Michelangelo Antonioni's 1966 *Blow-Up,* wherein rock music likewise blends with pop sensibility and murder and strong, colorful images.

Like *Blow-Up, A Degree of Murder* also draws the portrait of a generation that was as music-oriented as it was bent on increasing consumption. Schlöndorff, in an interview, referred to Marie and her two male helpers as "children of the age" (Hopf, "Fragen"). The trio embodies the generation immediately preceding the student protest movement. If there is rebellion in their life, it amounts to no more than a playful cultural stab at the establishment. This is the generation of the "now" sensibility, but one that is content to play table soccer, drive around in cars, and sleep with one another if the moment feels right. Marie may be reminiscing about her childhood from under a chair, playing with a stuffed animal one moment and seducing helper Günther (Hanspeter Hallwachs) the next. Schlöndorff depicts a generation that has few scruples. A case in point is the film's ending. It intercuts Marie waiting on tables at her usual café job with shots of earthmoving equipment uncovering and suspending the corpse of her former lover on a crane, midair.

Schlöndorff's approach thus employs characters who do not analyze their own situation, in a narrative that in turn discourages viewer analysis. *A Degree of Murder* may not have been prompted by Susan Sontag's "Against Interpretation," but it does in retrospect suggest an artistic answer to this manifesto. Together with Leslie Fiedler's influential writings, Sontag's essay declared "serious" art and scholarship as "out" in the 1960s. Art that privileged content, art designed to involve the intellect on several levels, art that challenged the audience toward interpretation was disqualified, if not considered reactionary. Sontag was calling for "direct" works of art, art to "recover our senses. We must learn to *see* more, to *hear* more, to *feel* more" (14). Schlöndorff likewise emphasized the nonanalytical attitude of both his trio of heroes and his film *A Degree of Murder* itself: "They accept, they don't analyze. They go with the flow" ("Volker Schlöndorff bleibt"). Clearly, Schlöndorff here forgoes the aesthetics of *Young Törless,* whose approach is characterized by carefully woven leitmotifs that construct a complex subtext. *A Degree of Murder* is unconcerned with deeper levels of meaning, analytical representation, and analytical reception.

Apparently Schlöndorff quite consciously opted for this aesthetic distance between his debut film and his second feature, although he continued to address a young audience. *A Degree of Murder* nevertheless signified a radical change to the culturally sophisticated segment of filmgoers familiar with *Young Törless.* In both films, adults are peripheral and young people stand prominently in the foreground. Yet critic Karl Korn correctly perceived that Schlöndorff's new film could also be understood as a challenge to the critics of *Young Törless.* In addition to producing a film that moved away from the horizon of expectations established by *Törless*, Schlöndorff provokingly for-mulated his intent: "No film for academics! A film for the elite of the 15- to 17-year-olds! A film for Barbarella!" (Hopf, "Fragen"). Indeed, *A Degree of Murder* is, in the words of a contemporary critic, "in every respect the youngest of all Young German cinema films" (Peters).

Critics did not generally reward Schlöndorff for his radical departure, and they often responded negatively to the film's apparent lack of values. It is true that *A Degree of Murder* was nominated as the official German entry to the 1967 Cannes film festival. And individual critics praised it as "another hit" (Hebecker), the "formally most masterful film of the new German wave" (Korn), and even as "the best film . . . which the Young Germans have produced so far" (WMH). For many critics, however, the film qualified as "the convinc-ing and to many perhaps questionable portrayal of a generation, a certain men-tality" (Peters). According to critic Marianne Dommermuth, the picture was restricted to viewers over eighteen, thus largely locking out Schlöndorff's tar-get audience. Similarly, the *Neue Zürcher Zeitung* reported that Swiss movie house operators at first opposed showing the film. "They confused im-moral with a-moral; and some critics have appropriately followed suit. They indig-nantly reject the film, because they react moralistically to the crucial point towards which Schlöndorff's brutal picture leads" (sb). Moral considerations, youth-excluding ratings, and Schlöndorff's massive deviation from the crit-ics' horizon of expectations after *Young Törless* seem to have prevented the film from succeeding at the box office. Still, the very qualities that undermined the public success of the film may have garnered it a place on the list prepared by Fassbinder in the early 1980s of what he considered the ten best productions of the New German Cinema (Baer 224).

"An Uneasy Moment"

After *A Degree of Murder,* Schlöndorff rejoined the coproducer of *Young Törless,* Franz Seitz, Jr., this time for a five-part omnibus film project entitled *Der Paukenspieler* (The Kettledrummer, 1967). Seitz, one of the most active post–World War II West German producers, assembled a team of contempo-raries that included such establishment directors as Rolf Thiele and the more ambitious and respected Bernhard Wicki. Schlöndorff was the only one to rep-resent the younger generation in this project. Themes of public violence and social pressures further link the short films.

Although Schlöndorff collaborated with Helmut Rimbach on both scripting and directing "An Uneasy Moment" ("Ein unheimlicher Moment"), this episode continues the filmmaker's mid-1960s focus on adolescents, "games," and violence. When Mrs. Weber returns from shopping, she finds her son Franz playing with his father's rifle. In an ensuing argument, the gun discharges. At the sound of the shot, the mother panics and flees from the apartment. Her agitation results in the neighbors' calling the police. In an attempt to peacefully resolve the incident, the police first hand the mother a megaphone to use in pacifying her son who remains in the apartment. But the strange instrument only further disorients the mother. Soon the situation escalates out of control. The law brings to bear all of its technical apparatus and, depersonalized behind the gas masks, the force finally invades the apartment. Inside, Franz has committed suicide with his father's gun. Structurally, Schlöndorff juxtaposes to the events a narrator's voice that tells the story while also delivering a laconic running commentary on it. Observations such as "Reporters solicit instant perspectives of the man on the street about what's happening" or "Hence a second front is opened [by the police]" underscore the inappropriate responses of the media and the police. Action and commentary clash and produce an irony that at times approaches the black humor of *A Degree of Murder.*

As a document of social protest, Schlöndorff's contribution is as interesting an experiment as any in the entire omnibus film. The filmmaker was to vary the same theme in the mid-1970s with *The Lost Honor of Katharina Blum.* However, "An Uneasy Moment" remained almost without public echo, as did the larger work itself: Schlöndorff's thirteen-minute episode was first released as a short in 1970 (Lewandowski 1) and a second time, as part of the entire eighty-seven-minute *Der Paukenspieler,* in a 1981 noncommercial premiere at the Frankfurt/M. Kommunales Kino ("Volker Schlöndorff" Lg. 23: F 3–4).

5

Michael Kohlhaas

Critics generally regard *Michael Kohlhaas* (*Michael Kohlhaas—Der Rebell*, 1969) to be one of Schlöndorff's failures, a film whose story leaves audiences cool, whose acting is inappropriate and unaffecting, one that fails as literary adaptation, as precise political analysis, and as popular entertainment. As literary adaptation, it brings the text of Heinrich von Kleist to the screen. In updating Kleist, Schlöndorff deliberately relates the rebellion of the character Kohlhaas to the social unrest of the late 1960s, rendering *Kohlhaas* a work that mirrors and comments on the student and worker revolts of the more modern period. As mass entertainment, *Kohlhaas* evokes two popular film genres—the archetypal Hollywood form of the Western and the distinctively German genre of the *Heimatfilm*. The result is a motion picture pulled by the three often contradictory forces of literature, politics, and film genre. These tensions make *Kohlhaas* both interesting and inconsistent.

Schlöndorff's decision to adapt Kleist's short novel, which was drawn from an authentic chronicle of sixteenth-century events, would seem to have held potential for a commercially successful film. Kleist's novella tells of an honest, hard-working, religiously devout horse trader, Michael Kohlhaas, who becomes a terrorist, a guerrilla warrior against an aristocrat. Junker Wenzel von Tronka has cheated him out of two fine black horses. Kohlhaas becomes a popular Robin Hood–like hero among oppressed peasants in the land, a rebel against abusive authority, a leader with grass roots appeal. Yet *Michael Kohlhaas* is also a story of failure, of corrupted revolution. Characters like Stern, a stable hand who turns into a wastrel; Katrina, a prostitute; and Nagel (Nagelschmidt in Kleist's original), an opportunistic robber, join up with Kohlhaas not out of a sense of justice or righteousness, but out of their own self-interest. Kohlhaas's revolution, doomed as it is to political failure, ends up losing its moral direction as well. This pessimistic outcome may well be one reason why the work had trouble finding a popular audience.

Michael Kohlhaas is a very different movie for a German audience than for a foreign one. For Germans, Kleist's novel is a familiar classic; for international audiences it is largely unfamiliar. Schlöndorff's choice of source material reveals a kind of ambivalence that has permeated much of Schlöndorff's work as a literary adaptor: the movie *Michael Kohlhaas* is both a tribute to and a revision of Kleist, an homage to a major cultural stream in German literature and a modification of that source for a contemporary audience. Schlöndorff clearly wanted to explore the topicality of this subject. On European prints of the film, the credits appear over newsreel footage of student demonstrations in four countries around the world. Given the film's time—the protest years of the Vietnam War era—producers clearly must have thought the subject would catch on with a young audience. The result is the first large international coproduction of the then Young German Cinema (the first wave of the New German Cinema). It surely hoped to capitalize on the success in the mid-1960s of the so-called "spaghetti Westerns" produced by Italy at the time.

An International Production

Schlöndorff reportedly began the project by writing the first script in German himself. This version of the screenplay is more faithful to Kleist than is the finished product (Schlöndorff). The producers then brought in Clement Biddle-Wood to work with Schlöndorff on an English version. The final screenplay was written in collaboration with Edward Bond, the British leftist playwright whose earlier plays, *The Pope's Wedding* (1962) and *Saved* (1965), had approached themes similar to those of *Kohlhaas* in their attempts to show violence arising from class oppression. One commentator has claimed, inaccurately, that the movie script was based not on Kleist's classic novella but rather on the sixteenth-century chronicle that had served the German writer as well (*Munziger-Archiv.* K: 13049). Although some of the scriptwriters' departures reflect a return to the original chronicle—the film's ending in particular—other parts of the movie retain elements of Kleist's reworking. The adaptation remains generally faithful to the narrative lines of Kleist's version. Overlaid on the structure, however, are various updatings and topical references, particularly to the student unrests that culminated—during the very shooting of the film in April through June of the same year—in the events of May 1968.

Schlöndorff gave the film, which was shot in English, an international cast. Kohlhaas was played by David Warner, the British actor who first achieved international recognition in Karel Reisz's film *Morgan—A Suitable Case for Treatment* (1966). The Danish actress Anna Karina, famous for her work in the

French cinema with her former husband Jean-Luc Godard, played Kohlhaas's wife Elisabeth. The remainder of the cast for the film, much of which was shot in the former Czechoslovakia, included German, British, and Czech performers. For his director of photography, Schlöndorff used Belgian cinematographer Willy Kurant, a former collaborator with Godard on *Masculin-féminin* (1966) and with Orson Welles on *Immortal Story* (1968). The general consensus about *Michael Kohlhaas*, however, has been that its collection of international talent proved as much a handicap as a help and that Schlöndorff was unsuccessful at bringing the disparate elements together in a coherent and satisfying way.

Kohlhaas shares with a number of movies from the mid- to late 1960s the then-fashionable concern with revolution and rebellion. The movie represented West Germany at the 1969 Cannes film festival, whose prizewinners, Lindsay Anderson's *If. . .*, Bo Widerberg's *Adalen '31*, Costa-Gavras's *Z*, Glauber Rocha's *Antonio das Mortes*, Vojtěch Jasný 's *Moravian Chronicle (Všichni dobří rodáci)*, Karel Reisz's *Isadora*, and Dennis Hopper's *Easy Rider*, all treated aspects of personal and collective revolt. In this respect, Schlöndorff's *Kohlhaas* grew out of his previous *A Degree of Murder*, which in its own manner embodied the same spirit of youthful confrontation with and assault on traditional values and authoritarian structures: both movies place their audiences in the position of identifying with heroes who break the law and defy social norms.

If Schlöndorff's *Kohlhaas* had much in common with the international cinema of its time, it also finds parallels with the other arts, in particular in the West German theater. For example, Peter Zadek's 1966 production of Schiller's *The Robbers (Die Räuber)* took, as *Kohlhaas* does, a literary classic with a Robin Hood–like theme and presented it as a text relevant to the youthful rebellion of the 1960s. Dieter Forte's *Martin Luther and Thomas Münzer or The Introduction of Bookkeeping (Martin Luther und Thomas Münzer oder die Einführung der Buchhaltung*, 1970) analyzed the peasant revolt of the early sixteenth-century, showing reformer Martin Luther as a tool of early capitalism. Yaak Karsunke's *Peasant Opera (Bauernoper*, 1973), a comparably "progressive" didactic work, also focused on the peasant wars. Thematically, then, *Kohlhaas* embodied much of the mood of its time.

The Western and the *Heimatfilm*

The image of the horse is central to both the novel and the film. In Kleist's *Kohlhaas*, the horse represents the unifying formal symbol (*Dingsymbol*) from the specifically German novella tradition. Perhaps in allusion to this reading of the horse, Schlöndorff at one time had reportedly planned to call the film "Man on

7. *Michael Kohlhaas.* The hero and setting evoking the Western and *Heimatfilm* genres. Photo: Deutsches Filmmuseum Fotoarchiv.

Horseback" (Sandford 39). In the opening footage of the European prints, the director establishes an immediate reference both to horses and the contemporary radical student protests. Klaus Kanzog has pointed out how the imagery of policemen on horseback that occurs in the first few minutes of the film introduces the horse motif. It is a motif that continues until the very end (30–31).

What is more, Schlöndorff transposes the literary function associated with the figure of the horse onto an already established specific genre icon: the horse of the American Western. In so doing, this adaptation of Kleist's novella becomes the first of several Schlöndorff films that refer to the universe of the Western. *Kohlhaas* cites a second genre as well—that of the German *Heimatfilm*. The movie thus develops a network of overlapping genre references, one to patterns of imagery archetypally American, the other to what has almost exclusively been a German set of narrative conventions. (See illustration 7.)

Michael Kohlhaas's commercial potential was most probably based on the sudden popularity of the European Western at the time of its release in 1969. In particular, the series of Sergio Leone's Italian westerns, starring Clint Eastwood and beginning with *A Fistful of Dollars* (1964), achieved box office success.

Between the years 1963 and 1969, some three hundred Italian Westerns were shot (Frayling 256). Indeed, the genre has notable examples of overtly leftist political expression, especially in those scripted by Franco Solinas, a Communist party member and screenwriter whose work for directors Francesco Rosi (*Salvatore Giuliano,* 1961) and Gillo Pontecorvo (*The Battle of Algiers [La battaglia di Algeri],* 1965, and *Queimada,* 1969) is more famous. There was ample precedent for the genre being used for political comment (Frayling 217–44), which may account for the genre being particularly popular with German leftist intellectuals in the late 1960s (Rentschler, *West German* 111).

Sergio Leone has observed that the impetus for the Italian Western came in part from the box office success of a series of mid-1960s German Westerns directed by veteran filmmaker Harald Reinl, who drew inspiration from the Winnetou stories of the popular German nineteenth-century writer Karl May (Frayling 103–17). Given Reinl's connections to the cinema of the Third Reich, however, one imagines that Schlöndorff's choice of *Kohlhaas* for a subject was more a reaction against the Winnetou films than an extension of them. For the New German Cinema rejected the older generation of German filmmakers and deliberately sought out specifically German subjects. *Kohlhaas* would be a clear attempt to build on the popularity of a genre that characteristically involves horses, violence, and outlaw heroes while still giving that material a specifically German context.

In discussing how Schlöndorff's *Michael Kohlhaas* fits the characteristic patterns of the Western, we can consider three main aspects of it: its use of the outlaw hero, its embodiment of the classic dichotomy of nature versus civilization or wilderness versus garden, and its use of violence and vengeance as major narrative elements. Many of these qualities overlap with those of the *Heimatfilm.*

In his book *A Certain Tendency of the Hollywood Cinema, 1930–1980,* Robert B. Ray argues that one of the fundamental dichotomies of the American cinema has involved the tension between what he calls the "outlaw hero" (e.g., Davy Crockett, Jesse James, or Huck Finn) and the "official hero" (e.g., Washington, Jefferson, or Lincoln) (58–59). Where the outlaw hero traditionally distrusts the legal trappings of civilization, including marriage and the legal system, the official hero celebrates them and seeks to preserve them. *Michael Kohlhaas* thus portrays the transformation of its main character from a figure who embodies the ideals of the official hero—Kohlhaas is a law-abiding family man, a good middle-class entrepreneur with a strong sense of civic duty—to one who violently protests the inadequacies of the system.

This opposition between outlaw hero and official hero reflects in part what

Jim Kitses has seen as the broader opposition of wilderness versus civilization. The central visual motif of the film, horses, in itself reflects this dichotomy. The image that opens and closes the movie, that of horses running free, plays into the opposition developed in the narrative between horses as natural animals and horses as property. Nature thus becomes, on its positive side, an ideal that represents freedom and beauty, as opposed to the artifices of civilization. Yet this opposition, as in many classic Hollywood Westerns, is never simple and unambiguous. The film establishes Kohlhaas's domestic life, for example, as both natural and civilized. Still, what one might call the farmer's "natural civilization" remains opposed to what one might call von Tronka's "civilized barbarism," in the latter's use of his political and material power to exploit others, even while the Junker maintains a superficial pretense of being educated and cultured.

Nature has its negative side as well. Kohlhaas's violent retaliation against von Tronka becomes a surrender to animal instincts, a lawless inferno. If an opposite exists to the civilized farm, that opposite would be the battlefield, whose product—an animalistic violence—becomes even more terrible by means of technology. These contradictions between good and bad nature and good and bad civilization become evident in von Tronka's courtyard: a huge mechanical contraption hovers threateningly over the courtyard, suggesting both scientific advance and technological change. Yet the courtyard is also the scene of music, as seen when one of the students plays a lute. Nature is both orderly and ruthless; civilization is both cultured and exploitive.

This conflict between nature and civilization also happens to be the central structure of the German *Heimatfilm,* a genre with a long tradition in the German cinema, from the silent era through the 1950s. If the Western is defined in part by its deserts, mountains, and wilderness, the *Heimatfilm* constitutes itself as a genre in part by its Alps, heaths, and Black Forest. The opposition in the *Heimatfilm* has been described as being between country and city, with the former promising, in the words of Anton Kaes, "order, permanence and national pride," the latter "rootlessness, hectic activity, and transient, superficial values" (165).

As a genre characterized by nostalgia, sentimentality, patriotism, and traditionalism, the *Heimatfilm* enjoyed particular popularity in the immediate postwar era, when it provided its German public escape from the harsher economic and social realities. Rainer Ruther has argued that its appeal was particularly strong among those Germans displaced from eastern territories, like Silesia, lost after World War II (132). By one report, more than three hundred *Heimatfilme* opened in West Germany between 1947 and 1960, amounting to one fifth of the total film production output of those years (Rentschler, *West German* 108). One has to look only at a typical *Heimatfilm,* Helmut Käutner's *Jack the Skinner (Der Schinderhannes,* 1958), to see parallels to *Kohlhaas* in its story about a historical Robin Hood–like robber hero (Curd Jürgens): he lives outside the law, steals from the rich, shows compassion for the poor, and has a faithful woman by his side at the moment of his execution.

In contrast to the respectful Christian imagery of the traditional *Heimatfilm,* however, *Michael Kohlhaas* is filled with visual suggestions of blasphemy and anticlericalism, particularly in the scene in which Kohlhaas's men look for von Tronka in the nobleman's chapel. The men knock over artifacts, lay bare the altar in one or two quick strokes, throw a torch up into the organ, and cut off the toll collector's head right in the house of God. As a convent of nuns is assaulted in the subsequent scene, whose flashes of nudity may have been far more sensational in 1969 than they seem now, one senses that the values of the *Heimatfilm* are being turned on their head. Schlöndorff implies in these sequences the complicity between traditional religion and the oppressive social system. At the same time, however, the actions foreshadow how Kohlhaas's revolution is going out of control, how Kohlhaas's followers will ultimately defeat the values he set out to defend.

Michael Kohlhaas thus becomes, along with Peter Fleischmann's *The Hunters Are the Hunted (Hunting Scenes from Lower Bavaria, Jagdszenen aus Niederbayern,* 1968), one of the first of a series of what has sometimes been referred to as the critical *Heimatfilm* or new *Heimatfilm.* This phenomenon of the anti-*Heimatfilm* became especially prominent in 1970 with Schlöndorff's own *The Sudden Wealth of the Poor People of Kombach* and in 1971 with the release of Reinhard Hauff's *Mathias Kneissel,* Uwe Brandner's *I Love You, I Kill You (Ich liebe dich, ich töte dich),* and Volker Vogeler's *Jaider—The Lonely Hunter (Jaider—der einsame Jäger).* This genre revision has continued into the 1970s, 1980s, and 1990s (Rentschler, *West German* 109; Meitzel 133–34).

The Western hero, like the *Heimatfilm* hero, is traditionally associated with maleness and virility, with action and violence rather than reflection and gentleness. In its treatment, therefore, of students and women, two groups that contrast to the man of action, *Michael Kohlhaas* becomes particularly interesting. Schlöndorff's treatment of these two minorities attempts not only to update Kleist but also to revise the two genres to which the filmmaker refers. Schlöndorff constantly uses the students who join up with Kohlhaas's forces to bring to the fore both the ambiguities surrounding Kohlhaas's actions and the relevance of those actions to the student protest movement and counterculture of the 1960s. When the students join Kohlhaas, one of them offers the leader a religious icon pillaged from von Tronka's castle. Kohlhaas, who has time neither for religion nor for art, throws it away. At a later point in the film, the students and Stern go chasing after some young women and dally with them in a field. In the meantime, it turns out, the rest of Kohlhaas's followers have been fighting the governor's troops. The scene functions as a literal representation of the slogan, "Make love, not war"; but Schlöndorff challenges this simplistic thinking in the following scene in which the students leave their lovemaking to kill a fleeing soldier.

A number of critics, Raymond Bellour in particular, have emphasized the importance of the role of women in the Western, particularly as representatives of domestic and civilizing values (87). In this context, Kohlhaas's wife Elisabeth is central to the story. In the early scenes of the film, she becomes an idealized portrait of traditional womanly values—slanted, in part, toward 1960s sensibilities. Early shots in the film establish Elisabeth as the archetypal loving, hardworking wife and mother: she would be quite at home as the heroine of the typical *Heimatfilm.* We see her kissing her husband good-bye as he takes his horses to market; we see her involved with farm work and putting the children to bed. In one of the film's more modern and erotic scenes, she massages her tired husband's back with her feet, pulling up the weight of her body with the canopy-style frame of the couple's conjugal bed. Schlöndorff cuts to a medium close-up of Anna Karina's face, moving up and down in the frame as her feet supposedly soothe the husband's muscles. The image at once suggests both sexual intercourse and horseback riding, and the traditional analogy drawn between them, but in a decidedly indirect, nonvulgarized way. It is an image that refers back to the leitmotif of horses that structures the entire film and links Elisabeth's naturalness and beauty to that of the horses Kohlhaas first owns, then seeks, then finally frees.

As the film develops, this connection between Elisabeth and the horses becomes central to the narrative. Midway through *Michael Kohlhaas,* when Elisabeth optimistically seeks to petition the king for the return of Kohlhaas's horses, she is trampled by the horses in the king's party. The incident further extends the horse motif and foreshadows the way in which her husband will figuratively be crushed by the horses he has sought to have returned. With this scene, Kohlhaas's motives seem to change. What had been a legal concern with property becomes mingled with more passionate, less rational issues of vengeance. When Elisabeth's body is brought to Kohlhaas, Schlöndorff visualizes the scene as a kind of reverse Pietà, with the male Kohlhaas hovering over the female victim. It is with this scene that the focus of the film shifts from the issue of justice to the issue of vengeance, and with that shift comes the decline of Kohlhaas's revolution. The killing of Elisabeth becomes the destruction of a domestic ideal. The prostitute Katrina, who replaces Elisabeth as the woman most present in Kohlhaas's surroundings, comes to embody the negative result of unplanned revolution: selfish whoring, the debasement of female virtue. One may also see in the Elisabeth-Katrina opposition the traditional role opposition of women in the Western, that is, the domestic farm wife with the saloon girl.

To the extent that Elisabeth's death takes over as the primary dramatic motivator for Kohlhaas's actions, the hero's need for vengeance becomes the primary stimulus for the narrative, much in the manner of certain Italian spaghetti Westerns. With the death of the civilizing woman, the director replaces a thematic concern for civilizing justice with the less abstract, more easily visualized portrayal of wild and natural vengeance. As with the traditional Western, violence and spectacle allow Schlöndorff the opportunity to express dramatic conflicts in visual rather than literary terms. His depiction of war, as in the battle between the governor's troops and Kohlhaas's, is grisly and unheroic. We see primitive weapons, pitchforks, spears, chains, the first guns, all used with graphic bloodiness.

Schlöndorff likewise presents the raid on Wittenberg as a kind of descent into hell. We see the governor's head break through a window and get stuck in it. Children and animals flee through flaming streets. Looters revel. In the movie's most shocking scene, Kohlhaas's loyal servant Herse, having fallen off his horse and being pulled along by his leg, gets stabbed on his own huge scythe and dies near a huge tub of water in which another body is resting. Here Schlöndorff expressively creates the image of the grim reaper destroying himself with his own weapon. For the shot of the stabbing, Herse's face is suddenly made up in a death mask of ghostly expressionistic white.

Criticism from Left and Right

Few reviews of the time ignore the prominence of Schlöndorff's violent imagery. Conservative reviewers in Schlöndorff's native country measured the film against the Kleist novella and on this basis found the visual brutality gratuitous. German leftist critics such as Joachim von Mengershausen decried Schlöndorff's "fashionable sadism" (32). The same patterns appear in current criticism. Referring to the apocalyptic violence in *Michael Kohlhaas,* American critic Jonathan Rosenbaum has accused Schlöndorff of "a directorial excess that puts him in Ken Russell territory" (40).

But reaction to the question of violence was hardly the only issue for which Schlöndorff received a critical drubbing. A major attack from the New Left came from Dieter Prokop in the 1969 article *"Michael Kohlhaas* und sein Management" (*Michael Kohlhaas* and Its Management). Prokop, a University of Frankfurt sociologist, examined Schlöndorff's film in the context of mass communication and its commodity character in late capitalism. He used *Michael Kohlhaas* as a model to illustrate the relation of the artistic possibilities of the cinema to the laws of profitable production—and specifically to Hollywood motion picture aesthetics. For Prokop, the film exemplifies how directors censor themselves within this financing and production system by privileging "packaged," politically neutral imagery and philosophical values (e.g., horse, happy family, children, fighting) over socioeconomic insights and analysis of the patterns of class and power.

The responses of the conservative critics are far more predictable than those of their leftist counterparts. They voiced similar complaints about *Kohlhaas*'s supposed commercial vulgarization of Kleist, the movie's lack of structure, and its affinities to the Western. However, those critics raised most complaints in the context of the fidelity issue. For instance, one such faultfinder objected that "the film concentrates in a one-sided, voyeuristic manner on Kohlhaas's campaign of revenge against the rulers which amounts to no more than fully a tenth of the literary text" (Fink). Writing somewhat later, Rainer Lewandowski diagnosed *Michael Kohlhaas* as a questionable adaptation. The mere "lining up of the climaxes of the novella's plot" demonstrated to him that Schlöndorff failed "to place any value on accuracy vis-à-vis the novella." The fact that "such a significant figure as Luther is scarcely identifiable in the movie" serves as "circumstantial evidence for a very loose usage of the novella's material" (84). Just as Prokop falls into the trap of categorically assuming that *Kohlhaas* would have been a better film had it not been financed under a capitalist system, Lewandowski falls into the equally dangerous trap of assuming that *Kohlhaas* would have been a better movie if it had only stayed faithful to the book.

Criticism like Lewandowski's automatically assumes that the literary model always qualifies as a masterwork. It fails to ask if certain structural problems that weaken the movie originate, in fact, from the literary model. Even Kleist's contemporary Ludwig Tieck noted "the lack of true and specific scene-setting (*Lokalität*)" in the last quarter of the novella; to him it changed pace and direction, resulting in a much more abstract world (88). The difficulty with Kleist's narrative in terms of conventional dramatic filmmaking is that it puts all of the major action at the beginning of the story, as does Schlöndorff and Bond's compression of it. The narrative's initial moral problem—must an honest man resort to terrorism and violence to achieve justice?—can easily be posed through vivid spectacle in specific locations. Its talky resolution in the courts, however, is much less suited to presentation in visual terms. This results in a front-heavy structure, whereby the film moves from concrete physical action to more abstract legal interpretation of those actions. If anything, Schlöndorff has perhaps been too faithful to Kleist in this instance for having preserved in his film what may be a structural problem in the original.

Political Commentary and Precise Mise-en-Scène

When Schlöndorff is successful in *Kohlhaas* he creates scenes that achieve sophisticated historical and political commentary through precise mise-en-scène. Consider the scene of Elisabeth's death when she personally tries to bring Kohlhaas's appeal for justice to the Elector. Here Schlöndorff's changes from Kleist represent a major thematic shift in significance. Kleist describes Elisabeth's accident as follows:

> It appeared that she had made too bold an approach to the person of the king, and, through no fault of the latter, had received a blow on the chest from the butt of a lance, a blow that was the result of the rash devotion to duty of the bodyguard surrounding the ruler. (31)

What Schlöndorff shows us is something altogether different. On reaching the prince's castle, Elisabeth finds that she is but one of a crowd seeking to petition him. Reaching to give the petition to the prince as he rides past on horseback, she falls and is trampled by the horses around her. The implication is clear: the monarch has become isolated from his subjects and unconcerned about their welfare. Kohlhaas's and Elisabeth's problem is simply one among many. The system is no longer working. This scene visually speaks to the futility of individual rather than collective action. In an interview, the filmmaker emphasizes that "Kohlhaas fails because he wants to fight the system as an individual, something he would only be able to do in a collective" (Hopf, "Ein Individuum"). In a scene like this, Schlöndorff's political position becomes decisive and effective, if different from Kleist's more conservative one.

Consider also the sequence in the camp following the raid on Wittenberg. Schlöndorff clearly implies that Kohlhaas's fault—one might call it his tragic flaw—is not so much in his vengeful activities themselves, which one can excuse by circumstances. Rather, it is in his inability to control what he has started because he has joined forces with elements that by their nature doom the revolution to failure. When he orders Stern executed, one sympathizes with

8. *Michael Kohlhaas.* The unsuccessful revolutionary's execution. Photo: Deutsches Filmmuseum Fotoarchiv.

Kohlhaas's righteous fury, but at the same time the lack of any judicial due process stings with irony. Kohlhaas starts to become the kind of dictator he is fighting against; his revolution has been Stalinized. Schlöndorff underlines this idea with a touch strongly reminiscent of the famous robing scene in Brecht's *Galileo:* right before Kohlhaas condemns Stern to death, someone puts an elaborate robe, suggestive of royalty or high clergy, around Kohlhaas's shoulders. The action goes unexplained in the narrative but renders clear the filmmakers' ambivalence.

The final shots of Schlöndorff's film are a highly sophisticated cinematic transformation of elements from Kleist. As Kohlhaas is dying, Schlöndorff cuts to a shot of his children running at play and later to a shot of the two horses that come, in this context, to represent freedom. Kohlhaas dies in the hope that a free, unoppressed state can be passed to his children, and the movie suggests through this image a sense very close to Kleist's final words: "As recently as the last century, however, happy and sturdy descendants of Kohlhaas were still flourishing in Mecklenburg" (130).

By one report, Schlöndorff's original intention was to portray Kohlhaas as a Mother Courage–type character so that the audience would see, in his acceptance of his fate, that he had been brainwashed into accepting the ruling classes' definition of justice (Hopf, "Ein Individuum"). Such an ending would indeed be an ironic inversion of Kleist. Schlöndorff instead adopted a far more ambiguous approach, using almost mystical close-ups of David Warner's expressionless face as the character is tortured and executed. (See illustration 8.) Schlöndorff's critics would be correct in saying that the end result is neither faithful to Kleist nor politically focused. We are decisively deprived of any access to Kohlhaas's internal thoughts and feelings about his fate, and the audience is forced to read into Warner's features whatever it may choose. Such an ending would satisfy neither political activists nor literary purists, but it is distinctive and cinematic.

The debate about *Kohlhaas* remained largely limited to West Germany, since the film received no better than restricted theatrical release elsewhere. From all indications, *Michael Kohlhaas* was not released theatrically in the United States by the major company, Columbia, until June 20, 1980, after Schlöndorff's success with *The Tin Drum* during the same year (Canby, "16th-Century"). The negative reaction to *Kohlhaas* seems to have caused Schlöndorff subsequently to turn to a different mode of filmmaking, and *Kohlhaas* marks the end of what we describe as Schlöndorff's first period. The issues that it confronts, however, such as the relation of the serious filmmaker to the commercial system, the question of the viability of a political cinema that could be both popular and Brechtian, and the potential for the filmmaker to selectively and creatively use literary sources, all remain central to Schlöndorff's cinema that follows.

Part Two

**BRECHTIAN AND
PROFEMINIST SCHLÖNDORFF**

6

"Amphibious" Movies and Formal Experiments

After the critical and commercial failure of *Michael Kohlhaas,* Schlöndorff entered what one might describe as a period of retrenchment, a period that roughly parallels a transition in the New German Cinema in general. After the burst of activity of the Young German Cinema of the late 1960s, there was something of a lull before the more impressive achievements of the 1970s. Thus, during the first half of the 1970s, Schlöndorff worked exclusively on low-budget productions financed in association with German television. Although much of this period was a low-profile time for the director, it was also a productive one. The resultant movies, namely *Baal* (1969), *The Sudden Wealth of the Poor People of Kombach* (1970), *The Morals of Ruth Halbfass* (*Die Moral der Ruth Halbfass,* 1971), *A Free Woman* (*Strohfeuer,* 1972), *Overnight Stay in Tyrol* (*Übernachtung in Tirol,* 1973), *Georgina's Reasons* (*Georginas Gründe,* 1974), *The Lost Honor of Katharina Blum* (1975), and *Coup de Grâce* (1976), include several impressive successes.

The beginning of the second period is marked by Schlöndorff's founding, along with Peter Fleischmann, of his own production company, Hallelujah-Film, in 1969. The production company was for a period to be Schlöndorff's home base in working out production arrangements with West German television, and it operated until 1981. In 1973, Schlöndorff began, along with Reinhard Hauff, Bioskop-Film, for which much of his subsequent work has been produced. Both production companies were in Munich on the lot of the venerable "Arriflex," Arnold and Richter, camera works. After the collapse of the West German commercial film industry during the late 1960s, such independent production and distribution efforts became a trend, cresting in the 1971 establishment of the "Filmverlag der Autoren," a combined collective production and distribution setup.

Three major influences or factors shaped this period in Schlöndorff's work. As with all the New German Cinema, the institutions of West German television provided the filmmaker with his major production opportunities. Secondly, during this period Schlöndorff built upon the theories of the playwright Bertolt Brecht to create a body of work that strives to merge political commitment with formal innovation. Finally, Schlöndorff met and married Margarethe von Trotta, and developed a creative collaboration with her that combined his more professionalist, rationalist sensibility—albeit one open to protest and pop culture—with her more instinctive and feminist one. The resultant work is ambitious and intellectually substantive, both varied in its subject matter and consistent in its thoughtful rigor.

Schlöndorff and Television

Schlöndorff's transition to lower-budget films was brought about, in large part, by the 1968 revisions of the West German film-subsidy law, which essentially terminated funding for culturally ambitious filmmakers. At the same time, West German television became increasingly receptive to producing programming with an alternative, oppositional stance.

Serious historical discussions of the New German Cinema have had to confront the way in which German television has provided both a significant source of funding and a structure for project development for German filmmakers from the late 1960s to the present (Elsaesser, *New;* Collins and Porter). With a highly developed public television system, and with state production operations feeding into a federally organized structure, television production work often was and still is commissioned from or subcontracted to independent production firms. Both the virtues and limitations of West German film after the 1960s have arisen from this particular television production system that caters to a German population that has been not as enthusiastic about moviegoing as the French and Italians. Like all the filmmakers of the New German Cinema, including Fassbinder, Wenders, Herzog, and Hans Jürgen Syberberg, Schlöndorff's ties to television and its institutions have marked his work.

With the exception of *Georgina's Reasons* (which was part of a collection of Henry James adaptations produced for both French and German television), all of Schlöndorff's works from this period were produced in association with Hessischer Rundfunk, the Frankfurt-based television station. Even several of Schlöndorff's subsequent larger-scale international coproductions, such as *The Tin Drum, Circle of Deceit,* and *A Gathering of Old Men,* took advantage of Hessischer Rundfunk's production help.[1] Much of the resultant work falls into the category first described by Günter Rohrbach, that of the "amphibious film," referring to a kind of cinema that supposedly can be marketable and artistically successful both in theatrical venues and on television. In many ways, Schlöndorff may be considered the most successful amphibious filmmaker, at least during this era of the early 1970s.

Schlöndorff himself has expressed ambivalence about working within this smaller-format production context. On the one hand, the filmmaker has frequently championed the production within the German film industry of at least some high-budget, technologically advanced productions. Such films, Schlöndorff has argued, stretch the production capacities of the national film industry in a positive way, creating an infrastructure of facilities and technicians (Bronnen and Brocher 83). He has therefore complained about the way in which tiny television budgets restrict a filmmaker's options (Bronnen and Brocher 80–81). At the same time, however, Schlöndorff in 1972 described the benefits of working under the West German television system:

> Today I would be unable to realize any of my projects anywhere in Europe within the framework of the commercial feature film industry. . . . Only TV guarantees for me continual working on the basis of commissioned projects with an objective in view but without paternalistic meddling. For this reason, I prefer at this point television to a film producer as well as any of the existing film subsidy boards. ("Demnächst" 7)

Schlöndorff therefore repeatedly returned to Hessischer Rundfunk for help in making challenging works, some of whose commercial potential must have seemed exceedingly slender. This open, liberal climate was to continue through the mid-1970s, after which a conservative timidity surfaced.

Given the absence of commercial television in West Germany until the mid-1980s, the medium's institutional context comes close to that of public television in the United States. The high cultural values characteristic of the New German Cinema since its inception were indeed congenial to the German public broadcasting standards. Not surprising, we see in Schlöndorff's output during this television period a general conformity to this model of educational and cultural service—although his vision of such service proved frequently to be oppositional to traditionalist culture. *Baal* and *Georgina's Reasons* are literary adaptations, from Bertolt Brecht and Henry James, respectively; *The Sudden Wealth of the Poor People of Kombach* becomes a re-creation of a period from German history; *A Free Woman* is a topical treatment of issues of women's liberation, just as *Katharina Blum* treats the subjects of terrorism and yellow journalism. Only *The Morals of Ruth Halbfass* and *Overnight Stay in Tyrol* lack the respectability of literary or historical culture or social problem topicality, and these both are doubtless the least well received of Schlöndorff's works from this period. If in *A Degree of Murder* and *Michael Kohlhaas* Schlöndorff operated within a commercial and genre-oriented system of film production, his output from the early 1970s, although not without its elements of controversy and contentiousness, similarly suited the system of West German public television.

It is in this television period that Schlöndorff develops his most sophisticated applications of Brechtian theory to the cinema. Related to these applications is the way in which some of the works involved seem to move toward a blending of fiction and documentary. Although other influences surely come into play here, particularly those of the French New Wave, it is still provocative to speculate about why much of Schlöndorff's television work seems more Brechtian than most of the other work he has created. Let us therefore consider in more detail the full set of cultural influences and productive results surrounding Schlöndorff's attempt to incorporate the principles of the militant playwright and theorist into his cinematic vision.

Creating a Brechtian Cinema

Bertolt Brecht's aesthetics have had a major impact on filmmakers, men and women alike, of the New German Cinema. Motion picture directors, like playwrights and stage directors, struggled to develop an adequate vehicle for critical discourse, as was particularly evident in the West German student generation that protested the cultural regressiveness of the Third Reich and what it regarded as its Bonn afterlife. By the mid-1960s, both Brecht and his work had survived efforts at a cultural boycott by the well-entrenched political right in West Germany. The New Left was adopting scholarly attempts to reintegrate into the nation's consciousness the cultural contributions produced by those exiled during the Hitler years. Brecht was acknowledged as a central figure of "the other Germany," the anti-Hitler intelligentsia who, by moving abroad, outlived the Nazi regime. Brecht could claim a prominent position in poetry and belletristic literature, as well as in media theory. Henning Rischbieter, editor of the influential magazine for Central European stage criticism, *Theater heute*, reminisces: "Brecht . . . constituted the most powerful model for the changing of the German theater's working methods that started about the mid-60s" (Rouse 2). He was the towering force in the theater world, not just the Federal Republic.

The Brechtian stage promised aesthetic and social innovations. No wonder that forward-looking stage and film directors have drawn heavily on Brechtian aesthetics. At the examination for entrance to the DFFB, the German Film and Television Academy in Berlin, an examiner posed the following question to Rainer Werner Fassbinder: "In your opinion, what can Brecht give to anyone who wishes to make films?" Fassbinder, the student of both theater and film, replied: "the distancing effect which can be employed with such versatility in film" (Prinzler 60). Fassbinder was referring to the now famous cornerstone of Brechtian dramaturgy, the *Verfremdungseffekt*, which is translated variously as "distancing effect," "alienation effect," or "defamiliarization." By this term, Brecht meant the use of devices to remind the audience that what it is seeing is an artificial presentation about reality rather than reality itself.

Two years after failing the exam, Fassbinder himself was practicing Brechtian aesthetics, acting in the film version of *The Bridegroom, the Comedienne and the Pimp (Der Bräutigam, die Komödiantin und der Zuhälter)* as staged by the Munich "antitheater" troupe. The film's director, Jean-Marie Straub, advocated the Brechtian approach of instructing the actors to highlight the artificiality of their performances, rather than make them realistic. In the *nouvelle vague* France of an exiled Straub and a Godard (who admits to having schooled himself in Brecht's "Notes on the Opera *Mahagonny*")—the very France where Schlöndorff spent his apprenticeship years in film—Brechtian presentation principles had likewise begun to be adapted to cinema (Lellis 31–144).

This section proposes to identify Brechtian elements in Schlöndorff and the extent to which these elements were incorporated into his oeuvre during the years 1968 to 1978. In addition, we need to clarify the relations among the New German Cinema, the theater, and the ancillary medium of television with respect to the specific development of the Brechtian cinema. Many who worked in the New German Cinema set up for themselves the challenge of applying Brechtian aesthetics to film. Schlöndorff was one of the most important figures in this branch of the New German Cinema.

At the same time, we need to acknowledge that Schlöndorff's involvement with Brechtian aesthetics is not always complete or uncompromised. In keeping with the dialectics we have seen in his work between traditional and modernist values, between commercialism and artistic ambition, between the popular and the intellectual, Schlöndorff tempers leftist radicalism and dogmatism with humanism and flexibility. Schlöndorff seems pulled in contradictory directions, which puts him closer to the mature Brecht of the dialectic theater than to the younger dogmatic Brecht of the *Lehrstücke* (didactic stage plays).

Although Schlöndorff's work during the decade 1968 to 1978 is his most systematically politicized, one can find traces of "epic theater" and alienation tech-niques in the films that precede and follow this period. Schlöndorff had applied elements of Brecht's aesthetics even in *Young Törless,* where he attempts to cre-ate with the costumes a less-than-precise time and place ("Erwacht"). At the time of his 1968 adaptation of *Michael Kohlhaas,* Schlöndorff confided to an interviewer: "My original intention was to orient the film rather directly back to Brecht, including the effect on the viewer as well in narrative form and in the usage of intertitles" (Hopf, "Ein Individuum"). But when the filmmaker was unable to secure a production guarantee for his original *Kohlhaas* project, due to the collapse of German distributorships at the time, it was only as an American big-budget production via Columbia that the movie was made at all.

In later chapters, we pursue the Brechtian approach as it applies individu-ally to each film from this period. In preparation for these discussions, let us summarize some general concepts of Brechtian filmmaking. With these sum-maries, we do not mean to imply that every Schlöndorff film seeking Brechtian effects uses all of these techniques. Nor do we mean to imply that any time each of these techniques is used in a Schlöndorff film, or any film, a distancing effect is always intended or achieved. Rather, they become Brechtian when employed in the right context cumulatively and systematically. These techniques are:

1. Historification of plot elements, whereby stories are set in the past but par-allel the present, or deliberate anachronism forces the audience to compare past and present.

2. The narrator's voice, usually as a voice-over, forming the cinematic coun-terpart to the narrators and storytellers in Brecht's plays. This voice functions both as anti-illusionist commentary and as a way to provide for a dialectic between spoken word and visualized image.

3. Typed characters portrayed through the use of significant, selected actions and gestures that assign them a specific place in a social class system.

4. Subversions of commercial narrative conventions and cinematic genres, such as the Western, the *Heimatfilm,* the melodrama, or the film noir.

5. Citation of literary texts from outside the film, either through direct quo-tation or more indirect allusion. This technique defamiliarizes both the origi-nal text and the new context into which it is put. This is frequently combined with the practice of *Bezweiflung,* which involves analysis and demystification of commonplace ideological statements.

6. Preference for long shots over close-ups and extended takes and slow pans over traditional continuity editing—except when deliberate montage calls attention to the filmmaker's manipulation of material.

7. Nonsynchronous sound/image cuts (Bild/Tonschere). Here the image

sequence continues while the sound switches to the next scene. Or the sound, say of a dialogue, may continue, yet the editor has cut the visuals to the next scene. (The English term "sound advance cut" unfortunately indicates only half of the approach. While the first strategy occurs routinely in Hollywood films to create a smooth transition rather than an intentional disruption, the second, more alienating technique seldom does.)

8. Music, including songs, that works in counterpoint with the image rather than in simple support of it. Such music varies greatly from the predictable emotional telegraphing found in the mainstream genre film.

9. Title cards to interrupt the flow of the narrative, often used to introduce scenes.

10. Repetition or near-repetition of scenes to encourage reflection and analysis.

11. A string-of-pearls structure, i.e., loosely connected scenes and miniscenes as opposed to extended dramatic confrontations and a seamless narrative continuity.

12. Film-within-film, whereby the audience is reminded of the interventions of the very medium it is watching.

13. Characters or observers within the film whose gaze at the action of the film makes the audience aware of its own voyeurism.

14. Nonconventional cinematic endings, which promote a sense of irritation in viewers, generate protests, or at least cause them to ask questions, as opposed to the traditional "happy ending."

Many of the devices described above are applicable to both theater and motion pictures; others, such as voice-overs, gaze strategies, film-within-film sequences, and nonsynchronous image/sound cuts, are film-specific. The common denominator in all these effects is that they produce what Brecht called a "separation of elements," a dialecticism that activates the spectator. In lieu of unified filmic information, we see image, word, sound, music, light, framing, and acting technique. As separate information channels, they produce a heterogeneous, divergent, multidimensional presentation. Each functions as commentary to the other.

Related to this Brechtian approach is the theoretical notion of self-reflexivity, sometimes called self-referentiality. A self-reflexive or self-referential work of art is one which calls attention, within the artistic text, to the processes whereby the artist has produced it or the viewer consumes it. Many of the techniques listed above, such as the film-within-film approach or the use of gaze structures, are self-referential. In addition, we shall see, as we discuss Schlöndorff's Brechtian films, a frequent discourse on the roles of art and the mass media in society. In some cases, as in *The Morals of Ruth Halbfass* and *A Free Woman,*

Schlöndorff's self-reflexivity approaches self-critique of his own work as a middle-class commercial filmmaker.

To construct films according to this Brechtian and frequently self-referential model is experimental and not formally conservative. Perhaps one of the reasons why Schlöndorff's Brechtian strategies have gone so unrecognized is that they tend to be in the areas of a politicized dramaturgy and the structuring of sound-image relations. Within the individual photographic image, Schlöndorff maintains a realist or even illusionistic style. A movie like *A Free Woman*, for example, is photographed with a hand-held camera and location settings that suggest a semidocumentary. The blocking of actors and the presentation of sets and costumes are not areas in which Schlöndorff practices the alienation effect. Unlike Fassbinder's or Syberberg's, Schlöndorff's imagery contains little deliberate theatricality. In other words, what is in front of the camera in a Schlöndorff film is often "natural." The distancing effect comes through the manipulation of that seemingly natural image. This may mean that for some audiences and critics this Brechtian effect goes unnoticed.

"Antigone" of *Germany in Autumn*

We can see Schlöndorff's use of formal Brechtian principles in "Antigone," his major contribution to the 1978 omnibus film *Germany in Autumn*. Schlöndorff and novelist Heinrich Böll, his collaborator on the script, present a dispute between the programming board of German public television and the television film director engaged in adapting Sophocles' classical play. The board worries lest the viewership might draw potential analogies between Sophocles' classical drama and the political events of the German autumn of 1977. Sophocles presents Antigone's rebellion against king Kreon's refusal to allow her brother Polynices a proper interment. Likewise, German officials had objected to the public burial of the German anarchists. By this reasoning, Polynices becomes analogous to the German RAF terrorists, the "Rote Armee Fraktion" or Red Army Faction, who had mysteriously died in the Stammheim prison. Antigone's heroic defiance of state laws becomes justification to terrorist sympathizers. The board examines filmed footage of several versions of the program's opening and ultimately rejects all of them, fearful that none of the variants will keep the viewers from drawing parallels. (See illustration 9.)

Several Brechtian techniques here come to the fore. First, by putting ancient Greek tragedy into a modern context, Schlöndorff's "Antigone" alludes to classical literature. The episode mixes the mythical past with the topical present, allowing each to comment on the other. Viewing film footage from a fic-

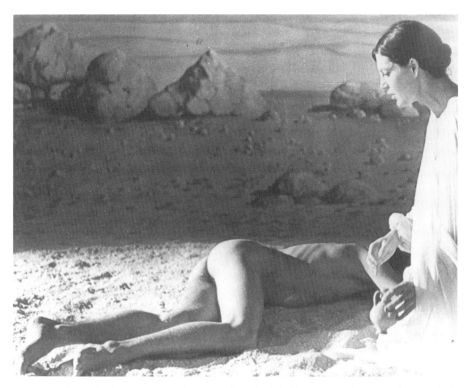

9. "Antigone" of *Germany in Autumn.* Angela Winkler as the classical Greek rebel, disobeying Creon's orders not to offer burial rites to her brother. Photo: New Line Cinema, with permission of Volker Schlöndorff.

tional television program makes us aware of medium conventions, just as watching the reviewers examine that footage increases our own sensitivity to the processes involved in viewing and responding to filmed images. The repetition of different versions of the same scene reinforces the previous two devices. And an obtrusive, jangling musical score emphasizes the harshness of Schlöndorff's detached and satiric point of view. Schlöndorff criticizes governmental hysteria and media censorship in a way that is both intellectually challenging and fun.

Why would a German filmmaker like Schlöndorff move into Brechtian filmmaking and thereby risk straying from the mainstream? An entire host of responses answers this question. Had the commercial West German production system not become economically impotent in the late 1960s, its practices still would have been ideological anathema to the New German Cinema directors. They were inclined to perceive it as the discredited continuation of Third

Reich film production. They likewise harbored mixed feelings about the dominant commercial film culture, Hollywood, because it institutionally threatened the very existence of an independent German cinema culture and because it became associated with what the student protest generation viewed as American neocolonialism during the Vietnam war. Post–World War II Germany has been described as a country missing its fathers, and with the cinema legacy of the Third Reich discredited, its young filmmakers felt culturally orphaned as well. Thus, the 1968 generation desperately searched for a filmic identity and media production conducive to sociopolitical change. At a moment in the mid-1960s, when German cinema was assumed to be passé, the New German Cinema filmmakers endeavored to reinvent it, employing a cutting-edge film language: Schlöndorff found himself in the company of Alexander Kluge, Rainer Werner Fassbinder, and others from Munich. In Berlin, a second group of filmmakers, including Christian Ziewer, also engaged in Brechtian experiments. They built on philosopher Ernst Bloch's utopian vision of worker pride and solidarity to revive the *Arbeiterfilm,* or proletarian film. Soon following them was the newly emergent German women's film by directors ranging from Helma Sanders-Brahms to Helke Sander. They would likewise explore Brechtian screen forms and vocabulary toward feminist ends.

Critics have debated whether television provides a more or less friendly medium for post-Brechtian drama. Some have suggested that its merger with television is a natural one, given television's customary use of interruptions, intertitling, and breaks in the unity of time (Mathers 96–97; Stam 37). The argument is questionable, not only because television so often lends itself as a medium to uncritical, couch-potato viewing. In addition, the "distanced" New German Cinema, in works like Kluge's *Yesterday Girl* (1966) and *Artists under the Big Top: Perplexed* (*Artisten unter der Zirkuskuppel: ratlos,* 1967) or Straub and Huillet's *The Bridegroom, the Comedienne and the Pimp* (1968) and *Othon* (1969), predated the "TV period." Finally, given that the New German Cinema was an intellectualist movement and that television throughout the 1970s tended to be held in a low esteem by West German intellectuals on both the Left and the Right (Kreuzer), what we seem to have had is more a marriage of convenience.

Most important, parties central to the New German filmmakers' realization of a Brechtian cinema were so predominantly involved with the theater, and the contemporary theater of the 1960s was so overwhelmingly dominated by Brecht, that Brechtian plays and stagecraft first and foremost qualified as the model of the corresponding cinema. Straub and Fassbinder have been mentioned here. Another central representative of the Brechtian film, Michael Verhoeven, likewise functioned as a stage director. Syberberg and Egon Monk, in fact, studied stagecraft under Brecht at his East German Berliner Ensemble theater. Television officials may have been swayed into granting space to this innovative type of film because they were familiar with and appreciated its corresponding mode of presentation on the stage. In 1960, the very Egon Monk, former assistant to Brecht, assumed control of the "TV Play" section of the then central NDR radio and television broadcasting network. As its longtime head, he promoted—and personally actively contributed to—the production of Brechtian films.

The Brechtian mode of cinematic aesthetics is characteristic of the 1970s and represents an optimistic continuation of 1960s activism, not only in West Germany but also internationally. As a rationalist form of discourse, it stands at variance to the mainstream cinematic model that Hollywood has cultivated: the film as the mass audience's collective dream, loaded with action, interwoven with special effects and wish-fulfilling fantasies. By the end of the 1970s, Hollywood, inspired perhaps by increased box-office attendance attributable no doubt to economic recession, found ways to breathe new life into old formulas and produced big successes like *Jaws* (1976), *Star Wars* (1977), and *Close Encounters of the Third Kind* (1977). This historical shift was accompanied and even promoted by a technical reinvigoration of American film due to new special effects, computerization, and Dolby sound systems.

During the Reagan 1980s, canons of taste even among the protest generation of 1968 began to move in a less oppositional direction. By the time Umberto Eco labeled "the crisis of reason" as the mid-1980s zeitgeist, an analytical aesthetics such as Brecht's could not but be affected by the vogue of postmodernism and poststructuralism (531). This crisis of the second enlightenment, as so termed by Jürgen Habermas, also occasioned a crisis in Brechtian film aesthetics.

Starting with his 1979 *Tin Drum* adaptation, Schlöndorff was to move in a somewhat different direction. Seen from a perspective of two decades later, Schlöndorff's second period is one in which the filmmaker is remarkably prolific, making about a film a year, and resourceful, working with a broad range of subjects, in a variety of styles, but always with that edge of awareness sharpened on the stone of Brechtian theory. In his later films, Schlöndorff became interested in different aesthetic issues, such as creating intensely vivid dreamlike experiences, producing powerful emotions, and exploring mythological motifs. The concept of cinema as dream would begin to encroach upon the Brechtian notion. "Cinema and opera . . . —in contrast to the stage play—appeal to the unconscious, to a dream dimension," Schlöndorff would state in the early 1990s, explaining his change in orientation (Krekeler). But he also periodically has returned to themes, dramatic structures, and defamiliarizing techniques, all of which show that the lessons of epic theater have not been forgotten.

Von Trotta and Feminist Perspectives

If Schlöndorff's interest in Brecht is a logical outcome of his empathy with and participation in the protest generation of 1968, then it is not surprising that the preoccupations of the newly expanding feminist movement would become part of his interests. According to one source, von Trotta and Schlöndorff met at the 1969 premiere of Peter Fleischmann's *The Hunters Are the Hunted* and in February of 1971 they got married (Nemeczek). During the next decade, the careers of both partners were to become strongly entwined. At the height of their creative involvement, that is, their codirecting of *The Lost Honor of Katharina Blum,* they presented themselves as equal partners in collaboration. Von Trotta's influence on Schlöndorff seems to have pushed him in the direction of acknowledging and treating women's issues, and in some ways Schlöndorff may be seen as a precursor to the group of German women filmmakers who have adopted Brecht's theories and aesthetic model and applied them to sexual politics. Ironically, however, von Trotta may also have eventually pulled Schlöndorff away from the systematically Brechtian strategies he had used in the earlier part of this period: her own work as a director makes only occasional reference to Brecht.

Von Trotta's earliest work as an actress involved not only her major role in Schlöndorff's *Baal,* acting opposite Rainer Werner Fassbinder, but parts as well in early Fassbinder-directed films from 1969 and 1970 *(Gods of the Plague [Götter der Pest], The American Soldier [Der amerikanische Soldat],* and *Beware of a Holy Whore [Warnung vor einer heiligen Nutte]).* Schlöndorff was to use her and Fassbinder again in *The Sudden Wealth of the Poor People of Kombach* (1970), but here she would also serve with the director as coscriptwriter.

Her screenwriting and performing with Schlöndorff continued with *A Free Woman* (1972) and *Coup de Grâce* (1976). For both *The Sudden Wealth of the Poor People of Kombach* and *A Free Woman,* von Trotta sorted through libraries and collections of materials as preliminary work for the screenplay. Then in some cases, each partner took over single episodes, as in *Kombach,* so that the individual imagination might first unfold in unedited fashion (von Trotta, "Husbands" 36). In other cases, both partners wrote all parts of the scenario together, as in *A Free Woman.*

A Free Woman was the couple's most personal early collaboration, and the film may be read in some ways as von Trotta's biography; von Trotta herself plays the lead. We may note parallels between von Trotta's divorce and that of the character Elisabeth Junker, as well as the battle for custody each has for her son. Moreover, we may note the self-deprecating analogy between

Schlöndorff and the character Oskar, whom Elisabeth later marries. The film's female protagonist is comparable to von Trotta in that both strive to realize themselves in art, seeking to define the coordinates of a new self in this sphere. The film may possibly be read as a mental rehearsal for an unrealized pessimistic life scenario; in real-life, von Trotta achieved custody of her son, became a successful artist, and presumably married a man sensitive to her needs and career.

The most harmonious form of collaboration between von Trotta and Schlöndorff seems to have been screenplay writing. When they attempted codirecting in their next work together, *The Lost Honor of Katharina Blum*, tensions set in. In general, the more private the form of communal creation, the less tensely the collaboration tended to proceed; in the public eye, when they codirected, frictions appeared. In von Trotta's view,

> when we write together and visualize a film, the purely organizational conflicts, which are not necessarily competitive, are relatively easy to solve. The public ones . . . when we appear in public together, for example, wherever we are filming or with journalists, are hard, they may be impossible to solve, they are absolute, these are power struggles. ("Gespräch" 30)

This contrast between intimate and socially externalized collaboration is illustrated, according to von Trotta, by the example of the *Katharina Blum* film. It was relatively easy to write the screenplay together, following Böll's model; they were alone. But the moment they began filming, von Trotta would often have to step back: "I had my own ideas. But he was the main director because he already did ten films" (Schlöndorff and von Trotta, Video interview). It was difficult for them to appear in front of the crew and make clear to everyone that both directors were of equal standing. Also, problems arose regarding competitiveness. They finally decided that von Trotta should primarily control the work of actress Angela Winkler, Schlöndorff the other functions and the camera. On the promotion tours for the finished film as well, it became evident how difficult it was to appear in public as equals. Thus, they later conducted these tours separately ("Gespräch" 32). As von Trotta began her own solo career as a filmmaker, she found herself a leader and figurehead for women's film both in West Germany and internationally. After her first solo feature, *The Second Awakening of Christa Klages* (*Das zweite Erwachen der Christa Klages*, 1977), von Trotta followed up with *Sisters* (*Schwestern*, 1979) and the even more successful *Marianne and Juliane* (*Die bleierne Zeit*, 1980), both films in which the relations between biological sisters serve to illuminate various forms of bonding and role playing among women in general. Von Trotta's subsequent features, including *Sheer Madness* (*Heller Wahn*, 1983) *Rosa Luxemburg* (1984), *Three Sisters* (*Fürchten und Lieben*, 1987), *The African Woman* (*Die Rückkehr*, 1990), *The Long Silence* (*Il lungo silenzio*, 1993) and *The Promise* (*Das Versprechen*, 1995), have tended to be somewhat more coolly received than her first efforts.

In the 1980s, von Trotta and Schlöndorff went their separate ways professionally, and the situation for German film production required both to internationalize their activities. After Schlöndorff began to work in the United States, von Trotta in 1988 chose Italy as a base of operations. With this geographical separation came their eventual breakup in 1991 (Freyermuth 58). In 1993, she introduced as her "partner" the Italian journalist Felice Laudadio who was later her collaborator on the script of *The Long Silence*. After a divorce in the same year, Schlöndorff remarried. Since then the couple has maintained professional collegiality, and von Trotta's *The Promise* was a major production under Schlöndorff's supervision at the Babelsberg Studios.

For the period when they were together, Schlöndorff and von Trotta had iconic significance within the New German Cinema, and the period of their most visible association almost precisely coincided with the zenith of the movement. Schlöndorff's integration of his wife into his professional activities became a kind of symbolic welcoming of women into the New German Cinema. It also validated a principle of film production as collective political activity. In this way, Schlöndorff's early works with von Trotta in the 1970s herald the German women's film movement that was to develop shortly thereafter.

By at least some standards, many of Schlöndorff's works from this period qualify as feminist, even if one grants that the word "feminist" has become a slippery one and that it is probably more accurate to talk about "feminisms" in the plural, as some film theorists have done (Pietropaolo and Testaferri). Consider the criteria offered by Gudrun Lukasz-Aden and Christel Strobel in their introduction to *Der Frauenfilm:*

> Women's films—that means for us . . . motion pictures which critically examine woman's role in society and family and present it in a differentiating way, provide impulses for reflection and alternatives. Films which unmask traditional role behaviour, uncover and "metaquestion" mechanisms, and point to variants of dropping out of traditional women's roles. . . . Such films need not necessarily have been made by women . . . for men, too, have confronted this subject matter cinematically. (8–9)

In the pages that follow, we see how, at least by these standards, most of Schlöndorff's works from this period could be considered women's films. In his second period, Schlöndorff produced his most concentrated body of work on women's issues, but we also observe how even in later decades, the filmmaker returned, in movies like *The Handmaid's Tale* and *The Legend of Rita,* to gender-related themes.

What problematizes Schlöndorff's feminism is his tendency to present women as victims, even as he sympathizes with their oppression. Often his women fail in their resistance to the patriarchy, and often they show a certain naïveté or lack of awareness of their own situation. But one might counter that Schlöndorff's male characters are no more successful or admirable than his women. He tends to draw political lessons from failure whether the films are made with von Trotta or by himself.

Von Trotta's personal influence is probably inseparable from the influence of feminist politics on Schlöndorff's work in the 1970s.[2] Together with the television production system and Brechtian theory, these politics form the three primary colors with which Schlöndorff paints his oeuvre of the decade.

7

Baal

As an adaptation of Bertolt Brecht's first play (first written in 1919 but revised several times after that), Schlöndorff's 16-mm television film *Baal* (1969) is a bow to German cultural tradition and in particular to the anarchism of late expressionism and Weimar culture. Drawing once again from the stylistic approaches of the French New Wave, *Baal* unites these German and French sources to map a path forward to the New German Cinema of the 1970s. The film is at once a highly literary presentation of the Brecht text and an exploration of the newer, freer film vocabulary that had emerged from the international young cinema movements of the 1960s.

The film follows Baal, a young, ingenious, and unstable poet-balladeer with a scandalous zest for life, love, and liquor, through multiple sexual encounters and cruel, shocking personal adventures that end with his premature death. Baal qualifies as a male counterpart to Frank Wedekind's Lulu—equally manipulative, equally fascinating to both sexes, but more dissolute, depraved, deviant, and even outright criminal. In normal narratives, Baal would be a villain, but the character acquires quasi-mythical dimensions and associations to French poets François Villon and Paul Verlaine. The hero becomes a kind of hedonist demigod who reverts to simple mortality as his lonely death approaches. In the role of Baal, Schlöndorff cast Rainer Werner Fassbinder, whose strident productions had made him a controversial figure in the Munich underground theater.

Brecht for Hippies

One motivation for Schlöndorff to adapt *Baal* appears to have sprung from the comparable sense of hedonism and anarchism that the youth culture of the late 1960s shared with Brecht's figure. Brecht's Baal is a hippie before his time, a dropout who both profits from and disdains middle-class society. The updating is a natural one, for the spirit of the time had given the play new relevance. The New Left of the student protesters and their intellectual sympathizers, including filmmakers like Schlöndorff and Fassbinder, was discovering Brecht and adopting him as one of its political and cultural father figures. In the special case of Schlöndorff's adaptation we can, however, trace the specific affinity for the young poet-bard Brecht, the anarchist of 1919—as opposed to the late 1920s doctrinaire *Lehrstücke* didacticist and the mature post–World War II playwright. A play like *Baal*, much like Schlöndorff's *A Degree of Murder*, could thus be shocking to both the puritan Old Left and traditionalist conservatives. It radiated the sensualist vibes of the 1960s counterculture.

Thematically, this shock value makes the film *Baal* a logical extension of both *A Degree of Murder* and *Michael Kohlhaas*. In terms of style and production values, however, the Brecht adaptation represents a venture into ultra-low-budget filmmaking. Schlöndorff has commented on this change:

> I wanted to get out of the structures of the film economy after I had just failed with the large-scale American production of *Michael Kohlhaas*. In protest I shot *Baal* with a hand-held 16mm camera, almost with a lay cast, without recognized actors—Fassbinder was not yet a known quantity. ("Nett" 102)

It was a change made possible by the structures of West German public television in the late 1960s.

Schlöndorff's film becomes an exemplary document from German television history. Since the establishment of the West German noncommercial television network of ARD in the 1950s, theater-oriented programming, whether live or filmed, constituted nearly 65 percent of its scheduled fiction broadcasting (Canaris 184–85). Into the 1960s, only the middle class, the social stratum favoring the theater, was able to afford expensive PAL-format television sets; hence, theater adaptations remained a West German specialty. Catering to a select audience that had doubtless sampled Brecht on stage, such programming could also include the daring language of *Baal*. Schlöndorff saw this production as occupying a kind of middle ground between cinema and theater. He stated, "It is neither staged and performed in such a way that it also could take place on stage (as is the case with the usual television play) nor filmed in such a way that it could fill movie screen and house, but rather at best a living room" (*Baal* press materials 4).

The production of *Baal* is a fascinating and deliberate antiestablishment experiment. The presence of Rainer Werner Fassbinder in the lead—a figure who has always embodied a blend of slickness and bluntness—establishes the tone and manner of the entire work. Seen from the perspective of the first decade of the twenty-first century, Schlöndorff's Baal appears as a prophecy of the legendary Fassbinder persona that was to develop in the 1970s immediately after the film's production. Fassbinder's infamously cruel personal relations, his renowned abuse of drugs and alcohol, and his untimely death now give to his Baal an odd blending of real person and fictional character. The tactlessness, the brashness, the Bohemianism, the psychosexual range of lifestyles, as well as the genius behind the unappealing exterior—all appear in real-life Fassbinder as much as in the film.

"Antitheater" Distancing

Stylistically, *Baal* is close to Fassbinder's work both in theater and film. Fassbinder's theater work prior to *Baal* involved an approach known as "antitheater." It featured a communal group largely composed of lay enthusiasts whose lack of professionalism allowed them to develop an alternative, stylized presentational method through cooperative self-instruction. This method borrowed from Brecht, minimalism, and early performance art. It paralleled American groups like the Living Theatre, the Judson Poets Players, and the Café La Mama troupe. To describe it in Schlöndorff's words: "It was an ensemble that acted differently and spoke differently from standard stage practice. It was cinema on stage" ("Nett" 100).

The majority of the roles of Schlöndorff's *Baal* are cast with members of the "antitheater." Two exceptions, Günther Kaufmann and Margarethe von Trotta, were to join the troupe immediately after. A third exception, Sigi Graue, was a hippie cult figure and so much an amateur actor that his inabilities caused Fassbinder to urge Schlöndorff to fire him ("Nett" 102). *Baal*'s mixture of polished and crude performances is part of its aesthetic strategy, a strategy characteristic of the late 1960s' avant-garde, including the "antitheater." This strategy questions what a "good" or "bad" stage or screen performance is.

This mixture of acting styles is only one of a number of tactics Schlöndorff uses in his first systematic and successful attempt to create a Brechtian cinema. The very structure of the play, divided into more than twenty short scenes, is of course typical of the playwright. Schlöndorff highlights this discontinuous structure by introducing each scene with a graphic title, with the number of the scene filling the entire frame. This same technique was previously used by Jean-Luc Godard, most notably in *Masculin-féminin* (1966). Like Godard before him, Schlöndorff employs the technique to subvert the cinema's natural tendency to

10. *Baal*. Rainer Werner Fassbinder as the title figure, in a self-reflexive image of theatrical illusion making. Photo: Deutsches Filmmuseum Fotoarchiv.

present material in a smooth, continuous flow and to reflect cinematically the episodic progression found in the original play.

Schlöndorff devises alienation techniques in *Baal* that are different from those that would be employed in the theater; they are instead cinema-specific. (See illustration 10.) The most fundamental of these would be in the juxtaposition that Schlöndorff achieves between Brecht's highly theatrical text and the movie's very natural and unstagy locations. The filmmaker noted

> the language is recited in such a manner that it has the effect of a written text. The settings and actors, however, are as realistic as possible. . . . A tension emerges between a landscape or a face and the text. And this tension (or brittleness), not the written poetry, makes the film poetic. (*Baal* press materials 5)

A scene like Schlöndorff's thirteenth in *Baal* exemplifies the effectiveness of using real-life locations as settings for stylized dialogue. Brecht presents the trio of Baal, the poet Ekart, and Baal's current lover Sophie in an intense argument. Where Brecht specifies the setting as "the plains, sky, evening," Schlöndorff realizes the scene during the day by the side of the German autobahn, creating an effect that could never be achieved on stage and that recontextualizes the play for 1970. Similarly, when Fassbinder reads his poem about Johanna, the young woman Baal has driven to suicide, he does so in an old junked bus. Schlöndorff's setting suggests that Baal's amorality is part of the decadence of post–World War II industrialized Germany.

This tactic of setting an older literary text in a contemporary environment is one Schlöndorff shared with Jean-Marie Straub and Danièle Huillet. Like Schlöndorff, the filmmaking couple availed themselves of the Munich "antitheater" troupe for their 1968 short *The Bridegroom, the Comedienne and the Pimp*. This film also updated a stage play, Ferdinand Bruckner's *The Sickness of Youth* (*Krankheit der Jugend*, 1929). The filmmakers' version of the Corneille play *Othon*, enacted in twentieth-century Rome, was also shot in 1969 with an odd variety of actors, creating a similar sense of dislocation. Although Schlöndorff's *Baal* is not nearly as extreme as the work of Straub and Huillet, it shares with them—and with some of Fassbinder's work to come—a fascination with the possibilities of a pared-down, minimalist cinema.

In contrast to Straub and Huillet, however, who have always maintained an intense commitment to using directly recorded sound, one of *Baal*'s most distinctive stylistic traits is its use of postsynchronized sound. Although this practice may have been due to economic necessity on such a low-budget production, it also produces aesthetic effects consistent with the film as a whole. One can even see the postsynchronized sound as a central component of Fassbinder's performance. Fassbinder reads his lines in a quiet, nontheatrical, often affectless voice but one recorded with full, bright immediacy. Similarly, the slight mismatch in lip synchronization and resonant vocal quality of Sigi Graue's line readings makes the character of the Bohemian composer Ekart more otherworldly, even angelic (e.g., Schlöndorff's scene 4). The break between individual scenes is emphasized all the more by the way in which Schlöndorff gives each scene a distinctive ambient sound, sometimes even allowing the sound effects to compete with his dialogue. A clock ticks loudly in Baal's attic, a chain saw buzzes in the forest, cars whoosh by on the autobahn, birds chirp in the fields, a baby cries among quarrelsome drinkers. Although one might argue that these sound effects reinforce illusionistic image making, they are also intrusive and obvious and sometimes subvert those same illusions.

Various productions of *Baal* in the 1920s already showed application of Brecht's ideas about how music should be used in the theater. The play's songs often function as analogy to and commentary on Baal's life. "The Chorale of the Great Baal" (Schlöndorff's scene 1), for instance, compares to the previews Brecht would later employ to lay out entire works or scenes at their outset. This particular chorale highlights in song Baal's life under the firmament until his death in the woods. Schlöndorff handles this chorale as a nonsynchronous sound commentary separate from his images. In the first scene, we hear Fassbinder perform the chorale as a traveling camera follows him walking along a country road. The camera sometimes hovers behind him, sometimes stays alongside him, sometimes pulls ahead to face him from the front. The effect is to create an aural-visual metaphor whereby the road on which Fassbinder walks becomes Baal's life. The effect is striking, in part because Klaus Doldinger's music with its folk-rock style unifies the film's hippie-dropout ethos with Brecht's stylized poetry. Schlöndorff echoes the movie's opening scene in his scene 18 in which we hear Fassbinder singing "Death in the Forest" as we see Baal and Ekart walking through a harvested field into the sunset. In both scenes, Fassbinder half sings, half speaks the lyrics in antioperatic cabaret style. With this device, Schlöndorff has found an effective cinematic counterpart to Brecht's use of stage songs.

In both cases, the length of the song dictates the length of the scene. In a comparable way, the rhythm of most of Schlöndorff's *Baal* becomes very much dictated by the rhythm of the spoken original text. Schlöndorff's aim is not to have enacted scenes come alive as any kind of reality but rather to use the words in almost musical counterpoint to a camera that casually hovers and floats around the actors. Consequently, although Schlöndorff varies his editing patterns at different points in *Baal*, this work differs stylistically from his other films in its frequent and intense use of uncut takes. This gravitation toward a restricted film vocabulary links *Baal* both to the minimalism of Straub and Huillet and to the comparable style Fassbinder used in his films around 1970, a style that has also been associated with the cinema of Andy Warhol. More so than Fassbinder and Warhol, however, Schlöndorff, as well as Straub and Huillet, employs stasis to emphasize poetic language. Schlöndorff engaged as cameraman for *Baal* Dietrich Lohmann, who had already photographed Fassbinder's *Love Is Colder than Death* (*Liebe ist kälter als der Tod*, 1969), which may explain why *Baal* resembles works by the early Fassbinder. By the same token, however, Schlöndorff provided a scenario idea for Fassbinder's *Rio das Mortes* in the same year (Limmer 157). Clearly, influence went in both directions.

Fassbinder's work has always had one foot in parody and pastiche, and Schlöndorff's *Baal* shows a similar visual facetiousness in the periodic use of Vaseline shots that create an out-of-focus halo around the periphery of the image. This citation of a turn-of-the-century romanticist photography fits, because *Baal* is in part a parody of a comparable literary heritage (especially Hanns Johst's "The Lonely One" [*Der Einsame*, 1916]), and becomes an ironic deconstruction of that tradition. A historicized photographic device is overlaid on contemporary imagery, which in turn is overlaid on a fifty-year-old play whose intent was to debunk the myth of the suffering poet-genius.

Whether for similar parodistic purposes or simply for distancing, Schlöndorff, in line with other New German Cinema filmmakers, also occasionally employs color distortions achieved with the use of filters or tinting. For example, Schlöndorff uses a blue tint for scene 10, perhaps in homage to the silent film convention of presenting nighttime scenes in blue. The scene is an exemplary one for both Brecht's and his screen adaptor's tactic of mixing the romanticized with the everyday (a technique known as *Stilbruch*). In the original text, Brecht sets up a tone of tenderness cast in poetic imagery. Baal says to his lover, Sophie, for example: "The whirlpool of love tears the clothes off one's back and, after one has seen skies, buries one, naked, under the corpses of leaves." A few lines later, however, Brecht undercuts this mood by having Baal say to Sophie: "Now I'll pull up your undershirt again." The play continually bounces back and forth from elevated to common language.

Schlöndorff's staging of this scene makes it even more outrageous. He places the lovers outside in a soaked corn field, a touch that becomes more pointed when one realizes that Germans grow corn almost exclusively for fodder. As Baal and Sophie exchange their words of ecstasy, Sophie rolls over into the mud, grasping it passionately with her fist. She is unconcerned that Baal strokes her breast and neck with his filthy hand. The scene is short, photographed in a single take, with the camera perched in a high-angle shot as though from the point of view of an intruder. The *Stilbruch* verbal oppositions have thus been heightened by Schlöndorff's visualization.

This confrontation echoes the more fundamental opposition between nature and culture that we have already discussed in connection with *Michael Kohlhaas*. Baal is a figure who straddles both universes, being both a vulgar, earthy sensualist and a poet. (See illustration 11.) His vitality comes out of the combination. If *Baal* can be seen as a quasi road film, then its progression would run from the society party in Schlöndorff's scene 2 to Baal's solitary death in the forest. Brecht's imagery constantly compares Baal to a tree, so it is fitting that Baal should die among woodcutters. Baal has his most direct confrontation with death in the forest when in Schlöndorff's scene 11 he takes a dead woodman in his arms—albeit to steal the man's liquor. The montage sequence that opens the scene amplifies the image of Baal as a tree about to be felled. Here,

11. *Baal.* Baal, the poet and vulgar sensualist, in one of his encounters. Photo: Deutsches Filmmuseum Fotoarchiv.

the director cuts from Baal walking into the forest to huge cut trees quickly falling. In his progression, however, from an urban salon to his ultimate forest resting place, Schlöndorff's Baal, unlike Brecht's, must pass by junk heaps and roadside eyesores. Where Brecht presents a simple city-country opposition, Schlöndorff suggests that the former is contaminating the latter. Perhaps Baal's problem is that he belongs in neither place. Indeed, Schlöndorff's visualization of *Baal* deliberately avoids idealized landscape imagery. In the world of this film, nature is a concept rather than an experienced reality—we see trees being cut down but never standing as entities in themselves.

Shocked Reactions

Fassbinder's Baal rarely embodies the all-growing, all-devouring, all-dying, all-recycling force of nature that Brecht's textual Baal does. In place of this inverted pantheistic myth, Schlöndorff, knowingly or not, was to substitute the Fassbinder myth—a myth that includes Fassbinder's bisexuality and that turns *Baal* into one in a series of Schlöndorff films that discreetly raise the issue. The narrative motif of a male lover's violent attack on his partner calls to mind the Rimbaud-Verlaine relationship, one that Schlöndorff later was to consider presenting in an adaptation of Christopher Hampton's play *Total Eclipse*. Indeed, Hampton's play also dates to the hippie era and exploited similar parallels to a previous generation.

Because *Baal* was a work in part calculated to shock, it is not surprising that a significant number of viewers responded negatively. A number of stations registered protest calls, and West German TV guides such as *Funk-Uhr* received letters to the editor complaining of "impudence" and "smut." Nevertheless, after its television premier on the Hessian hr television channel Third Program on January 7, 1970, Schlöndorff's film was broadcast for a second time on the ARD national West German television channel on April 20, 1970. With an "Infratest" rating of 26 percent of viewers, it garnered a respectable portion of the audience. Journalistic reviews ranged from respectful to hostile to uncomprehending ("Hit der Woche"; Wirsing; Weigend).

Some professional critics seemed to miss the point altogether. A reviewer for *epd/Kirche und Fernsehen*, for example, complained in the early part of his review that Schlöndorff did not use conventional Brechtian distancing techniques in his film (hy 13). A paragraph or two later, however, he faulted the film for "the dissonance between image and word" and for the further "dissonance" between lay actors and professionals. A more understanding view was presented by Georg Hensel of *Fernsehen + Film*. Although Hensel found that Schlöndorff's film sometimes undercut Brecht's poetry with banal images, he also admired the intensity and consistency of the production, as well as the way it successfully avoided expressionism and highlighted the text (41).

The reaction of the Brecht estate was predictably negative. The play itself was problematic for East German ideology, and Schlöndorff's adaptation showed far more reverence to the spirit than the letter of the play, not to mention the production's connection to the presumably decadent "antitheater." This negative "official" reaction by the play's copyright holders may explain why the film has been subsequently screened only on rare occasions. On the other hand, two subsequent television versions of Brecht's play demonstrate its continued fascination to directors in the image media. In 1978, Edward Bennett realized a British Film Institute production, and in 1982, Alan Clarke cast David Bowie as Baal in a television adaptation accomplished jointly with John Willett.

Baal is thus an important if underrecognized film, central to the careers of both Schlöndorff and Fassbinder and, consequently, to the New German Cinema in general. It was Schlöndorff's first adaptation of a stage play and thus relates to his television version of *Death of a Salesman* that was to follow some fifteen years later. Schlöndorff was later to report that for Fassbinder the experience of watching his professionally trained colleague was an important one. Schlöndorff writes:

> I wanted to leave the structures of mainstream moviemaking. . . He, however, was on the reverse path: it was his ambition to find a large-scale international distributor and to open his next film in Munich's biggest movie house. . . . He observed accurately what I did and how I did it—from the camera and lighting to the sound, from the shooting script to the production schedule. He attended the rushes and forced his entire troupe to watch the various rough cut versions. It was a paid workshop; he took what he could get. ("Nett" 102)

For today's viewer, *Baal* remains perhaps most fascinating as a document of Fassbinder, one that becomes richer with hindsight. It is a document as well of the late 1960s culture from which the New German Cinema of the 1970s was to spring. As such, it represents a convergence of sensibilities that were soon to separate as Fassbinder and Schlöndorff pursued different paths. *Baal* is, in Schlöndorff's words, "a critical memorial to the last anarchist solo-fighter" (*Baal* press materials 7). Equally well, it became a comparable memorial to Fassbinder.

8

The Sudden Wealth
of the Poor People
of Kombach

The subject matter of Schlöndorff's next film, *The Sudden Wealth of the Poor People of Kombach* (*Der plötzliche Reichtum der armen Leute von Kombach,* 1970), is similar to that of *Michael Kohlhaas.* Both films treat incidents from German history that involve unsuccessful rebellion against oppressive authority. In many ways, Schlöndorff corrected what can be seen as the problems in *Kohlhaas.* Where *Kohlhaas*'s big budget may have weighed down the production, *Kombach*'s more modest conditions of shooting clearly encouraged invention. Where the earlier film's specifically German qualities were diluted through the use of an international cast and multilingual shooting, *Kombach* is a thoroughly German project. Where *Kohlhaas*'s political message was ambiguous and not clearly articulated, the discourse of the later film is precise and lucid. Where Schlöndorff never realized his original vision of Kohlhaas as a character modeled on Brechtian dramaturgy, *The Sudden Wealth of the Poor People of Kombach* is the most systematic application of Brecht's theories of all of the film director's works. The movie's initial and continuing success with critics and audiences indicates that Schlöndorff got it right the second time.

The film marks a historical juncture in the New German Cinema. *Kombach*'s excellent critical reception acknowledged that a real film movement was taking form rather than just a series of isolated individual successes. Schlöndorff here collaborated with four major figures of the cresting new wave: Reinhard Hauff plays the soldier Heinrich Geiz; Margarethe von Trotta, his common-law wife Sophie; Rainer Werner Fassbinder, a peasant; and critic Joe Hembus, a courtroom scribe. This casting documents for cinema history the communality and united purpose of a real movement.

The story of *Kombach* was taken directly from an early-nineteenth-century chronicle (Franz). *Kombach* deals with a group of rural workers and peasants who rob the duke's stagecoach in Hesse. After a series of bungled near-attempts, the group eventually seizes the treasure. Most of its members are caught, however, because the very act of such poor men spending money signals their guilt to the authorities. By the end of the film, two men have committed suicide, four have been hanged, and only one has escaped. As a narrative, *Kombach* focuses on the robbery as a collective act, without privileging any particular character's point of view. Schlöndorff clearly means this story to be not about mere criminals but about humans acting for their own survival in a protorevolutionary way.

This chapter examines how Schlöndorff fashioned a film that deals with concrete historical realities but with literary sophistication and a Brechtian sense of the politically dialectical. Schlöndorff analyzes nineteenth-century German attitudes and their effects, alluding to his own epoch in the process. He criticizes the period's public illusions—its superstitions, its wish-fulfilling dreams and utopian fantasies, and especially its idolization of America. In an interview of 1972, the director stated that he approached his film project with a twofold concept: "On the one hand, I wanted to explain why a peasant of the period in no way could comprehend the concept of revolt. On the other hand, I wanted to develop why the exploited subject could not easily grasp that he was being exploited" ("Entretien" *Cinéma* 138). The *Kombach* film, then, teaches a history lesson about an evolving human society that is steered largely by economic factors and needs improvement. It portrays dissidents and involves acts of suppression, refusal, liberation, persecution, and failure. Nevertheless, it is not completely pessimistic, because it encourages the active spectator to learn from the historical mistakes of predecessors.

A Learning Play for the Screen

If the movie *Baal* is inspired by the early Brecht, Schlöndorff orients *Kombach* toward the later, more mature Brecht. Let us look at four elements of the "epic theater" that Schlöndorff transforms into cinematic terms in this film. First, Schlöndorff systematically types all characters. Second, he employs multiple commentaries that present and analyze the same events from different points of view. Third, the filmmaker constantly refers—often with heavy irony—to previous literary sources. Fourth, small incidents and details become social gests that illustrate mechanisms of class suppression. (Here we use the word *gest* to translate Brecht's term *gestus*, following John Willett's translation of

Brecht's theoretical writings.) Through these devices that defamiliarize history, Schlöndorff achieves a remarkable synthesis between a pointed rhetorical message and poetic techniques that impressively support it.

The film's title refers not to an outstanding hero or single protagonist but to the people of Kombach—father and sons, family and extended family, and nameless social participants like scribe, gooseherd, pastor, and soldier. Characters whom Schlöndorff does not immediately signify as types from their names—as with *Bauer* (farmer or peasant), *Acker* (acre), and David (Jew)—he identifies as representative in other ways. For instance, consider the scene in which Heinrich Geiz depressedly drags himself home after the peasant gang's third failed attempt to seize the ducal equivalent of the Wells Fargo money coach. In fact, the group had almost attacked an empty coach. At that very moment, the voice-over commentary metamorphoses Geiz from an individual into a representative of his social class. The voice informs us how one-tenth of the population of Hesse, the German state encompassing Kombach, had emigrated to the New World during the nineteenth century. We learn that entire towns had migrated. In this way, the commentary places character, narrative, and context in a precise historic context.

The film offers additional levels of commentary. Characters from within the narrative provide observations that work in counterpoint to the enacted story. As peddler David Briel wanders, in the penultimate scene, from the foggy background to the forefront of the frame, he articulates his analysis of the German peasantry. Both the objective voice-over that unifies the film and the peddler's commentary frustrate the viewer's expectations about conventional film practice. The first voice is female, in direct opposition to the tradition of the male "voice of God" found in the standard documentary. The second speaker's comments begin as what seems to be a voice-over. Only as Briel nears the camera do we see his lips moving. As his image grows from a tiny dot to a near close-up, his voice hovers throughout at the same strong volume. Schlöndorff both violates traditional sound perspective and the canon of realism that holds that such a character would not say those words aloud to himself.

Just as Schlöndorff employs verbal commentaries that are somewhat jarring in their use of unfamiliar or inappropriate elements, the director deliberately uses music that is out of character with the images. The syncopated beat that accompanies even the initial run of the peasants through the forest originates from an entirely different zeitgeist than that of the early nineteenth century. On occasion, the score is ironic, as in the scene in which the "successful" robbers run gleefully into the valley, accompanied by musical motifs whose excessive lyricism reflects for the audience the unsophisticated innocence of the characters.

Even where the director had planned to place less anachronistic music, he was thinking, as he planned his original script, of music by Hanns Eisler, Brecht's longtime musical collaborator whose film scores have featured spare, dissonant orchestrations that often jar with the images they accompany (Schlöndorff, *Der plötzliche* Filmtexte 41). Instead he worked with Klaus Doldinger, a prominent jazz clarinetist whose film scores became a standard feature in productions of the New German Cinema, including Schlöndorff's previous *Baal*.

Such counterpoint among image, score, and verbal commentary achieves what Brecht termed separation of elements. The filmmaker creates a similar effect of defamiliarization or alienation by comparing and contrasting images from different time frames, breaking, as Brecht often did, any strict unity of time. With the film's opening shots, the spectators view several minutes of the final execution of the robbery, although what viewers have seen will not be clear to them until much later in the film. The first half of *Kombach* uses a musical structure in which each false start to the robbery repeats a similar situation with a different variation. Each variation tells us something more about the peasants' naïveté and ineptitude in a way that dampens any real suspense about the ultimate outcome. Time elements are further manipulated when, at the end of the film, viewers hear, from the voice of the female commentator, a description of the peasants' execution before the condemned quartet arrives at the site of their beheading. Peddler David Briel, moreover, in his early-nineteenth-century hymn to America, praises New World cities and states before they were even settled. One recognizes temporal shifts that play with and deconstruct conventional narrative time.

Commentary and achronology, music and sound track become separated and polarized signifiers in the *Kombach* film. This fundamentally dialectic method applies as well to equally complex strategies of quotation and cultural reference in the film. We shall see how quotation, whether from sayings, popular tradition, or literary works, is drawn into the dialectic as part of the tactic of *Bezweiflung,* literally "doubt production." This technique goes a step beyond irony in both making a statement and subverting it. We can see this technique in the simple and folksy opening illustration of the idyllic church and village that overlies the credits. Schlöndorff establishes a pastoral ideal, only to have the audience watch it dissolve under scrutiny.

A Critique of *Heimat* Idealization

Schlöndorff also accomplishes this dissolving of the pastoral ideal by referring to genre elements and then undermining their traditional operation. Obvious models for the director include the Western, the *Heimatfilm,* and perhaps the tradition of the caper film in which a crew of disparate types works together to pull off a heist, only to see their success disintegrate after the big job. Indeed, Schlöndorff himself in an interview acknowledged in *Kombach* aspects of the Western, emphasizing, however, not a "folkloristic" Western but a "dialectic (and didactic) one" (Schlöndorff, "Entretien" *Cinéma* 139). As a variant on the *Heimatfilm*, *Kombach* becomes the major representative of a new genre, sometimes referred to as the anti-*Heimatfilm*, already mentioned in the *Michael Kohlhaas* chapter.

Like Brecht, Schlöndorff displays skepticism and opposition against existing clichés about *Heimat* in general and the countryside in particular—clichés that arose with the industrialization of the nineteenth century. On behalf of the new *Volksstück*—a genre of play that focuses on popular subject matter, emphasizing country life—Brecht raised the "call for a new realistic art" ("Anmerkungen" 119). He himself responded to his own theoretical call in poems such as "Der Bauer kümmert sich um seinen Acker" ("The Peasant's Concern Is with His Field"; *Poems* 212–13) and his play from the 1940s, *Master Puntila and His Servant Matti (Herr Puntila und sein Knecht Matti)*. His poem "Die Literatur wird durchforscht werden" ("Literature Will Be Scrutinized") applauds

Those who reported the sufferings of the lowly
. . . .
With Art. In the noble words
Formerly reserved
For the adulation of kings.

(Poems 344, trans. Patrick Bridgwater)

This politicizing of attitudes toward provincial life is a progressive tradition initiated in German literature by early-nineteenth-century German dramatist Georg Büchner. *Kombach* takes a bow toward Büchner as well as to Brecht in a number of quotes and shared motifs. In Schlöndorff's *Kombach*, as in Büchner's *Woyzeck*, a commoner soldier lives in abject misery and is too poor to afford marriage and thus legitimize his bastard child. Schlöndorff's soldier Geiz, dismissing the need for religious ceremony, employs Woyzeck's very words, "Dear God will not examine the worm for whether the 'Amen' was said over it before we made it." In addition, many of peddler David Briel's lines are adapted from Büchner's play. Other phrasings and plot developments, such as the one whereby compliant peasant informers turn in their rebellious peers, relate the film to "The Hessian Country Messenger," a pamphlet authored by Büchner jointly with his fellow revolutionary, Ludwig Weidig (Schlöndorff and von Trotta, Video interview). Hesse is the region where both Büchner and the film's peasants undertook their revolts. Darmstadt, Büchner's hometown, houses the court of the film. *Kombach* finally shares Büchner's insights into the conservatism of Central Europeans and particularly of German peasants who appear incapable of genuine revolution.

In his film, Schlöndorff's strategy is to attack folklore and edifying literature. He confronts stereotypes with an empirical perception of reality, thereby raising questions and doubt in the viewer. The young maid guarding the geese, for instance, insists on prospects for her future with, "I have been told many stories of how a gooseherd became a queen." Ludwig Acker deflates such expectations, pointing out how her current job has lowered her status permanently and predestines her for a life of low wages and imperious treatment. While seeking refuge from an unexpected rain shower, the same goose-girl elsewhere tells Acker that in a May rain one should make a wish. He counters: "I know a wish, with which one can fulfill all one's desires." An abrupt cut promptly produces the image of the ducal money coach on the screen. In a dialectic structure, the film presents a hard reality that is antithetical to folkways and superstition.

Schlöndorff similarly attacks the type of literature that has historically enforced social conformism and affirmed the dominant ideology. The people of Kombach are bombarded with pious readings and verses that misrepresent their social reality. Examples include an excerpt from Jeremias Gotthelf's moralistic story "The Broommaker of Rychiswyl," Bible passages, quotations from Luther, and last but not least, Christian Fürchtegott Gellert's verses entitled "Contentment with One's Own Status" (269–70). A young, wreath-crowned girl recites at soldier Geiz's wedding: "Never does status, never do goods/Present man with satisfaction. The true calm of the mind/Is virtue and self-sufficiency" (269). The early-nineteenth-century country reality of Kombach, where Heinrich Geiz is unable to marry without the money from the robbery, speaks a different language. Schlöndorff thus combines criticism of both *Heimat* clichés and proestablishment verse making with an understanding of the economic realities of historical country life.

America: A Utopia or a Nonalternative?

If *Kombach* deconstructs the idealized *Heimat* idyll and deflates literary stereotypes, in the same manner it also undermines the utopian image of America. During the economic depression of the early nineteenth century, suffering craftsmen and populations in the countryside began to view the New World as the way out; waves of emigration established a panacea to domestic problems for Germans. Even among German intellectuals of the 1960s there was a tendency to focus attentions abroad, in this case on Third World problems, rather than at home. In response, other intellectuals, novelist Günter Grass in the forefront, rallied to the cry of "hiergeblieben" or "Let's remain here and solve our problems at home" (Grass, *Über das* 218; Brode 122). Can *Kombach* then be seen as incorporating this very message about the lack of focus on domestic problems? Does Schlöndorff in 1970 anticipate the broken U.S. image of Werner Herzog's 1977 *Stroszek* and Wim Wenders's *The American Friend* (*Der amerikanische Freund,* 1977) and *The State of Things* (1982)?

At any rate, the New World initially assumes fairy tale–like traits in the eyes of the Kombach peasants; this image is later placed on a more realistic and limited footing. In a forest scene, David Briel reads an emigrant's letter to his coconspirators:

> Here in America milk and honey are flowing. . . . Swarms of bees can be found in abundance in hollow trees. Buffaloes stick their heads into windows . . . and only await to be shot. The peasant can share being master here. We drink more coffee and wine than you do water.

The United States are transformed into a sheer fairy-tale America, a location comparable to that in the German story of *Schlaraffenland,* a fantasy place in which all desires for food and drink are effortlessly satisfied. The film's peasants frequently intone the 1832 emigration song "Wir ziehen nach Amerika" or "We Are Moving to America" (Verleih Neue Filmkunst 6–7). This song claims that in the United States:

> Potatoes aplenty, like marzipan,
> Three bushels ripening on every twig.
> Coffee grows on each shrub . . .
> The Turkish wheat is healthy
> With the head often weighing up to ten pounds
> The largest carps known
> One catches there with bare hands.

(6)

In response to the fanciful hyperbole of the letter, one of David Briel's conspirators objects that "paper is patient," meaning that one can write falsities on it. Fairy tale elements, then, also draw contradictions and protests.

Similarly, in the period around 1970, when the film was released, Central European society showed little inclination to continue its idealization of the

United States as it had done during the immediate post–World War and Kennedy eras. America could offer no real solution to the internal German problems that Schlöndorff addressed—neither those of the peasants of Kombach nor of the filmmaker's contemporaries. Schlöndorff evidently wanted to communicate his conviction that one has to change a society that allows its own members to suffer like the peasants in Kombach. In this light, America can only present an individual way out that fails to reform Kombach. Without a change of consciousness among the oppressed classes, *Kombach* ultimately implies, there can be no change of the human condition. By contrast to the peasants, David Briel is more open-minded and flexible and can therefore escape. His success, however, is that of an individual rather than a society.

Internalization of Authoritarian Ideology

We have seen how by typing characters, establishing multiple layers of commentary, and citing cultural and literary texts, Schlöndorff applies Brechtian theory to his subject. Let us consider a fourth technique whereby Schlöndorff uses small details of human behavior to explain why the Kombach rebellion is choked. Schlöndorff employs the Brechtian performance tactic of the social gest, that is, the use of significant statements, postures, gestures, or facial expressions to designate class relations (*Brecht on Theatre* 104–5, 139). (See illustration 12.) The very first dialogue within the film is a classic example of this strategy. The audience sees the character Jacob Geiz, a day laborer, cutting the grass of the postmaster with a scythe. Looking on, the boss criticizes Geiz for leaving the grass too long and is unimpressed when his worker explains that cutting it shorter would risk damaging his tool. In a single scene, Schlöndorff encapsulates the social relations that drive his narrative, one of poor men in a double-bind situation that drives them to criminal activity. In the conversation that immediately follows the grass-cutting scene, David Briel proposes attacking the coach to Jacob Geiz. The first scene motivates the second: suppression by the empowered classes makes violence against them appealing to those oppressed. Most striking in the Briel-Geiz conversation is the almost total lack of affect in the actors' delivery of their lines, an approach that initially seems stylized and even mannered. As the narrative develops and Schlöndorff repeats these tactics of gestic scene construction and emotion-free performance, we come to understand these as devices to further produce audience reactions that run against the grain of both the character's feelings and conventional dramatic expectations.

Such social gests further demonstrate mechanisms of oppression like authoritarian conditioning, nonemancipatory teaching and Lutheranism. During the

12. *The Sudden Wealth of the Poor People of Kombach.* A robber turned would-be aristocrat and a peasant, whose respective styles of clothing highlight the arbitrary nature of
class distinctions. Photo: Museum of Modern Art / Film Stills Archive.

first robbery attempt, the conspirators stand ready in ambush . . . and the
money cart passes unmolested. The conspirators fail because they await the signal of father Geiz to attack in accordance with their patriarchal upbringing. Yet
he, himself accustomed to being an underling, likewise awaited the command
of a higher-up. Father Geiz, like pastor, judge, and duke, remains one cog in the
wheel of the authoritarian system.

The rural pedagogy is another significant cog in the mechanism of suppression. The countryside instruction of the children takes place at the foot of
Geiz's hillside field. Geiz and his kin are cultivating their acre with extreme
strain. The ground is so barren, rocky, and hilly that daughter and son-in-law
must join the bony family cow in pulling the plow. In the same scene, the village teacher is drilling the students by rote in the verses of the medieval epic
Meier Helmbrecht. As the class gets to the line "For many a fair lady . . ./Thanks
her beauty to your work," we see the face of the wrinkled, worn-out Mrs. Geiz
passing more closely in front of the camera. The scene mixes quotation with
social gest, which confronts the edifying literature with the serfs' reality.

Juxtaposed with the peasants' misery, Schlöndorff's presentation of the ped-
agogical drill appears cynical to twentieth-century viewers, stirring up their
criticism, protest, and resistance. In terms of Brechtian aesthetics, the approach
here is one of working against the grain of conventional psychological identification, of trying to stimulate in the audience emotions counter to those experienced by the characters. An appeal for humanity and against injustice arises
in the spectator who watches these human beings become degraded to function as beasts of burden and, what is more, degrade themselves by accepting
their situation as right and appropriate.

This against-the-grain mode of presentation reveals sociopolitical injustice; it visually demonstrates the cruel internalization process that holds
together an undemocratic order. In the hillside classroom scene, Schlöndorff
illustrates this internalization procedure with children. In the more physically brutal incarceration scenes, he demonstrates it among adults. In the
dungeon, when Heinrich Geiz rejects the pastor's communion because it
affirms the feudal system's "justice," Jacob Geiz and Ludwig Acker hold
down their coprisoner. Father Geiz attempts to beat him into submission.
In a moment of black comedy, the torturers compete to outdo one another in
praise of a social and religious system that allows them to suffer in extremis.
The observant viewer understands that the more vehemently Jacob Geiz and
Acker repent, the more they deny their real humanity in response to religious
and authoritarian brainwashing. The ultimate irony is that their compli-
ance in no way affects the final outcome: all four men will die anyway. (See
illustration 13.) Only the soldier Heinrich Geiz maintains any consciousness
of the injustices the feudal order has inflicted on them. The subjects have
been taxed to the bone to provide a splendid marriage ceremony for the
duke's daughter. Yet if they take some of those funds to improve their lives
or to allow Heinrich Geiz to marry his common-law wife, they are doomed
by the system.

The *Kombach* screen story demonstrates how difficult it has always been for
Germans to effect political change. And Schlöndorff clearly wanted to draw
analogies to the situation of the late 1960s and early 1970s. The filmmaker confirmed to a French interviewer in 1972:

> Don't forget that in Germany there was no 1789. Later, the endeavor of 1848 did
> not push things any further. The Frankfurt School (with Adorno) offered an auda-
> cious thesis: the premises of our first revolution were not posited until 1968. What
> interests me and numerous young German filmmakers . . . is to know why there
> was no revolution in my country after 1789. ("Entretien" *Cinéma* 139)

13. *The Sudden Wealth of the Poor People of Kombach.* The rural rebels on their way to the execution. Photo: Museum of Modern Art/Film Stills Archive.

Kombach appropriated the disappointment of the New Left about the restoration of the status quo after 1968. Again, we can see adopted and applied Brecht's strategy of "transposing into the past."

Kombach enjoyed decisive critical success (*Munzinger Archiv.* 13049). Respected critics both nationally and internationally appreciated the film as one of Schlöndorff's best works—a "masterwork," in Ulrich Kurowski's evaluation (Kurowski, "Junger" 72; Tichy 2: 506; Amiel 136–37). Eric Derobert, in a 1992 sampling of the editors of the French film journal *Positif* as to the ten best films ever made, included *Kombach* in his ranking ("Les 10 films" 27). In 1995, the editors of the German *Reclam Filmklassiker* collection of critical reviews included the film in their canon as among "the most significant examples of the 'critical *Heimatfilm*' produced . . . in the Federal Republic" (Hickethier, *"Der plötzliche"* 225). As for broader audience reception, the film attracted an extensive television viewership during a period when German-language films had problems reaching their audience in the Federal Republic because of a weak domestic distribution system. Bronnen and Brocher recorded "eleven million spectators . . . bordering on a broad mass reception" (79); the "Infratam" rating, a German counterpart to the Nielsen ratings, recorded a high 29 percent. Almost a full decade after the film's German opening, film critic Peter Harcourt concluded his 1980 American review with, "In its quiet way, it is an extraordinary film. It deserves to be better known" (63).

The same critic assessed *Kombach* as "one of the finest examples of a Brechtian *Lehrstück*" (Harcourt 61). However, the film rejects simplistic didacticism. Instead, it adapts an historical chronicle and analyzes the apolitical stance of oppressed Hessian peasants. It expresses Schlöndorff's sentiments about the political situation after 1968. Through its presentation by contradictions, it appeals to the viewer's resistance against unjust political conditions. If it were possible today to ask Brecht whether this early-nineteenth-century story still held topical interest, the dramatist would surely have answered in the affirmative, using the very words he employed to affirm the relevance of his own popular play *Puntila:* "Because one does not only learn from the struggle, but also from the history of struggles" ("Ist ein Stück" 1175).

9

The Morals of Ruth Halbfass and *Overnight Stay in Tyrol*

Volker Schlöndorff based his next film, *The Morals of Ruth Halbfass* (*Die Moral der Ruth Halbfass*, 1971), on a rather spectacular murder case that involved a rich Düsseldorff industrialist's wife, Minouche Schubert. The case was the stuff of tabloid newspaper exposés, and to some extent *The Morals of Ruth Halbfass* was a calculated attempt by Schlöndorff to win over a popular audience. The movie's central situation smacks of cliché: a wealthy, superficially glamorous couple, united in a loveless marriage, tolerate one another's joyless extramarital affairs until attempted murder complicates things. On close inspection, however, there is a lot more complexity to *The Morals of Ruth Halbfass* than immediately meets the eye. Schlöndorff uses the movie's familiar narrative framework as a context in which he makes a number of serious observations about contemporary German life and culture. He also undercuts usual genre expectations by using unsympathetic characters whose comportment always keeps the audience conscious of their place in a larger social system. Let us examine *Ruth Halbfass,* and, as a kind of footnote to it, *Overnight Stay in Tyrol* (*Übernachtung in Tirol,* 1973). This television film from two years later is perhaps the least significant of Schlöndorff's works but one that shares with *Halbfass* a number of similar aesthetic strategies.

The "Trivial" Film

The spirit of Claude Chabrol hangs over both *The Morals of Ruth Halbfass* and *Overnight Stay in Tyrol.* The French director, with his love of contrived plots, decadent bourgeois settings, caricatured acting, morally ambiguous themes, and a constantly mobile, probing camera style, had always fascinated the new German filmmakers. He represents a major connection between the French

100

New Wave of the 1960s and its later, German counterpart. A number of commentators have immediately suggested affinities between *Ruth Halbfass* and Chabrol's work, with one going so far as to call it the German version of Chabrol's *La femme infidèle* (1968), in which a wealthy middle-class husband murders his wife's lover (Montaigne).

Not only is Schlöndorff's portrayal of a grotesque, cynical, jaded bourgeoisie very much similar to Chabrol's universe, but one can see in *Ruth Halbfass* an almost perfect illustration of the ideas the French *cinéaste* sets forth in his famous essay "Little Themes." In "Little Themes," which Chabrol published in *Cahiers du cinéma* in 1959, Chabrol argues that the filmmaker who shapes his narrative out of familiar, conventional, or everyday elements often stands more of a chance of producing a work of substance than the filmmaker who chooses a topic that announces itself as important. A quarrel between neighboring farmers, he suggests, is not by definition a less profound topic than nuclear holocaust; rather it is the treatment of a subject that can make a mundane filmic situation meaningful, or, by contrast, an extraordinary topic banal (Chabrol 73–77). Schlöndorff's own statements about *The Morals of Ruth Halbfass* reflect exactly this same attitude. In a newspaper interview following the release of the film, Schlöndorff argued:

> The word "trivial" is often overused and misunderstood. People consider those who commit suicide, for whatever reasons, as trivial, and show in the same breath Lady Macbeth as a figure of art. The true trivial story doesn't exist, for Büchner made a work of art out of a Woyzeck. For me that means that one has to approach these so-called trivial stories with the same sophistication as those things we consider higher. In this respect the tragedy of industrialism is of more importance than a classical royal drama. (Lotz)

For all its possible Chabrolian influences, *The Morals of Ruth Halbfass* is by no means just a German knockoff of a French product. There is a major difference between Chabrol's characters and Schlöndorff's and thus a major difference between their work. Where Chabrol regards his characters in moral terms—as good or evil, sincere or hypocritical, loving or selfish—Schlöndorff gravitates toward more solemn social critique. Schlöndorff's is a predominantly political world rather than a moral one (despite the film's title), and his characters do not so much struggle with questions of conscience or guilt as they are trapped by an environment that seems to stifle sincerity and pervert whatever remnants of integrity they may possess. Chabrol's attitude (as Schlöndorff's colleague Rainer Werner Fassbinder has observed) is far more conservative and religious in that the Frenchman criticizes immorality and hypocrisy within the social system rather than the system itself ("Insects"). By contrast, Schlöndorff, who saw the newspaper scandal surrounding the Minouche Schubert trial as something of a witch hunt, has claimed that he means *The Morals of Ruth Halbfass* not as a portrayal of the Schubert case but rather as a demonstration of how a woman like Minouche Schubert is simply a product of her society (Lotz).

Schlöndorff, like Chabrol, uses the conventions of the crime melodrama but also employs two main techniques to subvert and ironize his material: first, he deprives us of any conventional identification with the film's characters, emphasizing instead environment over characterization in a way that suggests the two are totally indissoluble; second, he toys with parody throughout, undermining certain conventions even while he uses them. The end result is a film in which every action in some way resembles a Brechtian social gest. That is, gestures in acting become motivated not by internal psychology but rather by an understanding of that character's particular place in the economic system (Brecht, *Brecht on Theatre* 104–5, 139).

Unsympathetic Characters, Cluttered Settings

One of the most obvious things about *The Morals of Ruth Halbfass* is that there is no one in the film with whom we sympathize; no one represents the audience's point of view. Everyone's behavior is essentially selfish, hypocritical, and cold, devoid of honor, nobility, and even good taste. We are thus denied any Manichaean pleasure of identifying with one person or another in the narrative's conflicts. Even the character of the cheated husband, who is more appealing than any other, is comic and pathetic rather than strong or virtuous.

The Morals of Ruth Halbfass opens with a pastoral interlude in which Franz Vogelsang (Helmut Griem), a high school teacher of about thirty-five, is reading from Ibsen to his lover, Ruth Halbfass (Senta Berger). The camera pans from a brook, across grasses, to the lovers sitting under a tree. It is only when the couple returns to her car that they start to make love, forming an embrace that is broken when they realize the lateness of the hour and Ruth's need to get back to her husband. Schlöndorff makes the moment comic, for it is only when Franz's hand is right on Ruth's breast that he notices his watch. Their interrupted lovemaking, which by the conventions of the romantic melodrama should suggest an almost savage link to nature, takes place instead in the modern, mechanized shelter of an automobile. And it is the mechanized nature of modern life that causes the interruption. In the context of this theme of corrupted nature, Franz's last name, Vogelsang ("Birdsong"), takes on an ironic sense, especially given the cheated husband's love of music.

Just as the peasants of *Michael Kohlhaas* or *The Sudden Wealth of the Poor People of Kombach* are trapped in an oppressive world of poverty and economic exploitation, the bourgeoisie of *The Morals of Ruth Halbfass* have unknowingly imprisoned themselves by accepting the conventions of their own social class and station. Ruth's husband, Erich (Peter Ehrlich), had once longed to be a singer but instead is now the comfortable director of a women's lingerie factory. The constant images of women in underclothing that pervade Erich's office reinforce a sense of everyone in the film having a hidden, sexualized existence under the surface. Erich plays, over and over again, recordings by his favorite artist, Richard Tauber, and spends his evenings at the opera and at concerts. Ruth herself, longing for independence, wants to open a combination boutique and art gallery yet gets the money to do so only on the basis of her husband's credit rating. Her lover Franz must depend on Ruth's money to maintain the kind of affair that would suit her. They drive her car (she lets him off at a tram station after their opening tryst); she tries to set him up in an apartment that she pays for; he ultimately feels too poor to win her total commitment.

Schlöndorff's mise-en-scène manages to make wealth and elegance seem stifling, trivial, at times even threatening. A heavy iron gate separates Ruth's home from the outside world, electronically opening and closing to form a metaphoric prison whenever one of Schlöndorff's shots of it lingers. The home itself is filled with overstuffed chairs, Romanesque arches, marble floors, crystal, silver, fine china. (See illustration 14.) Ruth's hairdresser is in a building filled with elaborately baroque ornamentation that looks fake and contrived. Yet the alternative environments Schlöndorff proposes are no more inviting. When Ruth enters her teenage daughter's room, it is similarly cluttered with trivial objects; they are simply brighter in color and made of plastic rather than fine materials. The apartment that she leases for her lover is spare and modern, with stark white walls. While it avoids the clutter of the other locations, it is in a sterile, high-rise building and is no less depressing for being in marginally better taste than the other places.

The emphasis Schlöndorff puts on objects, decor, and clutter within Ruth's environment links him to a certain tradition of the Hollywood film. Thomas Elsaesser has described this relation between decor and people in the melodramas of directors like John Cromwell, Douglas Sirk, or Vincente Minnelli:

14. *The Morals of Ruth Halbfass.* The title figure (Senta Berger) and her husband (Peter Ehrlich), surrounded by signs of their wealth. Photo: Museum of Modern Art/Film Stills Archive.

. . . the more the setting is filled with objects to which the plot gives symbolic significance, the more the characters are enclosed in seemingly ineluctable situations. Pressure is generated by things crowding in on the characters, life becomes increasingly cluttered with obstacles and objects that invade the characters' personalities, take them over, stand for them, become more real than the human relations or emotions they were intended to symbolize. ("Tales" 530)

This substitution of objects for human feeling can be seen further in two scenes between Ruth and Franz. When the lovers first go to the apartment, Ruth brings champagne but no glasses. The pair exultantly drink the champagne from their hands, having momentarily found that natural freedom they have been longing for. A few minutes later Franz chides her for not having bought sheets for the bed. He can only take so much of the primitive life.

Possessions become an obstacle to love and spontaneity. During a later argument in which she declares that she should give up her wealth for him, Franz goes to an expensive vase and shatters it on the floor to test her commitment. Her response is to slap him, demonstrating where her priorities still really are.

If the peasants of *Kohlhaas* or *Kombach* have no ready way out of their oppression, Schlöndorff offers no way out of that of contemporary Germany either. In their own respective ways, *Ruth Halbfass*'s characters look to culture and the arts for spiritual liberation or escape. By having them do so, Schlöndorff overlays onto *The Morals of Ruth Halbfass* a harsh critique of postwar German culture. In contrasting Franz and Erich and emphasizing Ruth's choice between them, Schlöndorff suggests a rather unacceptable range of cultural choices.

On the one hand, Erich represents an impotent, outdated, ultimately silly traditionalism. The weepy, operatic Richard Tauber tunes that Erich plays suggest a sensibility locked in the past, but one is struck by how appropriate a metaphor they are for the cuckolded husband's situation. If the full-bodied, operatic voice suggests passion and masculinity, Erich's recordings embody a past masculinity, perhaps his own past masculinity. It is a masculinity linked not to the world of business, but to the world of art, a world in which Erich can participate only vicariously. Playing against clichés of both cruel husbands and fat capitalists, Schlöndorff makes Erich relatively sympathetic. He is as trapped and victimized as either of the other, supposedly more liberated lovers. Erich's love of art may be silly, but at least it is sincere, and while he has a mistress, there is little evidence of unfairness in his relations with Ruth.

By contrast, Franz represents a world of modernist culture, one that rejects traditional values but one, Schlöndorff suggests, that is just as empty in its effects. For all of Franz's idealistic citing of Ibsen, he remains entrenched in comfortable, complacent behavior. Why else indeed would he be attracted to Ruth? When Ruth furnishes their love nest, she is careful to supply Franz with his favorite books and records, but one feels that she reduces them simply to further objects of luxury, simply another kind of furniture. For her there may indeed be little line of distinction between the boutique and the art gallery.

Franz openly embraces popular culture, remarking in one scene that the rise of the trivial in art approaches the discovery of truth. According to him, "[t]he most simple murder mystery treats its readers more as intelligent beings than an opera. The headline of a boulevard sheet reveals more reality than a drama by Ibsen." He is temporarily arrested near the film's end during a class lecture on a "trivial" genre of literature, the detective story, an ironically self-referential touch in a seemingly trivial film.

Schlöndorff pointedly emphasizes the way in which the system has corrupted the world of art and aesthetics. Franz goes to an art dealer to buy a gun; the dealer has a whole collection of presumably illegal firearms carefully hidden among his paintings, sculpture, and antiques. The message is clear; culture is simply a cover-up for the violence underlying German society. Schlöndorff amplifies this theme in a key scene that follows, one in which Ruth and her husband attend a lecture on contemporary art that Franz is giving. In it, Franz talks about the relation between modern art and violence in the contemporary world, arguing that art can give only an abstraction of violence. Making his audience uncomfortable by carrying a rifle to Ruth, he asks her to shoot at a balloon that turns out to be filled with red dye. As a kind of happening, a piece of performance art, the presentation emphasizes for the audience within the film its own discomfort at seeing even harmless images that suggest violence.

The scene performs two functions for *The Morals of Ruth Halbfass*. It underscores Franz's hypocrisy, since it reflects the violent murder of the husband that the art teacher is planning. It also acknowledges, perhaps, Schlöndorff's own feelings of uncertainty about the efficacy of even his own art to produce social change. Schlöndorff extracts from the scene what might be seen as the ongoing critique by the left of German culture: Franz's love of art is no more consequential to his personal life than the love of presumably ennobling classical music was to the prevention of the atrocities of National Socialism.

On a self-referential level, then, *The Morals of Ruth Halbfass* presents Schlöndorff's reflections on this aesthetic tug of war. Erich's records suggest in their way a musical analogue to the genre of movie, dealing with passion, infidelity, and murder, on which *Ruth Halbfass* would superficially be modeled. Yet genuine love or real passion is exactly what Ruth and Franz's relationship lacks. The values of a modern world preclude the kind of sincerity that make an authentically operatic sensibility viable. Schlöndorff implicates his own tastes in this dialectic on aesthetics and character, as his sound track music is in distinct opposition to Erich's musical preferences. Sparsely orchestrated and Stravinsky-like at first, it moves near the end toward more jazzlike rhythms and instruments, like flute, trumpet, or xylophone. It is music from a 1970s generation that can no longer respond to romanticism with Erich's spontaneous pleasure.

That Schlöndorff seems aware of the film as a reflection of his own cultural dilemma is further evident in the character of Ruth's daughter Aglaia, who rather mindlessly runs about making home movies of the goings-on about her, including, it would seem, the incident in which the killer harasses Ruth at her front gate. Aglaia's thoughtless filming suggests yet one more unacceptable, contemporary cultural option, another empty alternative sensibility. Film needs to be more, Schlöndorff implies, than just technological doodling.

Comic Social Gests

Instead of straightforward storytelling, Schlöndorff fills *The Morals of Ruth Halbfass* with touches that smack of parody, ambiguity of tone, and the use of black humor. The opening credit sequence reflects this indirectness. We see a portrait photograph of Senta Berger enclosed in a cameo-like oval, with smaller ovals of the two men in her life on either side of her, all set against an old-fashioned wallpaper pattern. The image both suggests and mocks Ruth's bourgeois world and that of the sentimental melodrama. In an early scene in the film, Erich is swimming in his pool at home. As he gets out, Ruth brings him his robe, and he awkwardly slips his bathing suit off under it and gives it to her. The wealthy millionaire momentarily becomes awkward, bumbling, comic, falsely modest; his wife's subservience borders on obsequiousness. When Franz overcomes Ruth sexually on the parlor floor after the vase-breaking incident, it seems less like a presentation of genuine lust than an ambivalently regurgitated convention of the romantic film of passion.

When Ruth applies to the bank for a loan to start her boutique, she is dressed in a kind of grotesque variant of formal business clothing—a rather flashy, black-and-white lady's suit, worn with a little tie and a white fedora. Similarly, when the hairdressers (who are the would-be hit men supposedly hired to murder Erich) go to the husband's office to blackmail him with a check written by Ruth but given to them by Franz, Erich takes the check from them and throws them out of the office. The two thugs nonetheless address him deferentially as "Herr Director" even as they leave.

All of these elements point to a story that is organized around social relations rather than interpersonal psychology. Almost every action or behavior in the film relates to the characters' place in the class system, to aspects of the general society of which they are a part.

Although *The Morals of Ruth Halbfass* is not a fully systematic Brechtian film, one can relate its approach to character and acting to the Brechtian notion of gestic acting. Selected behaviors show each character to be a type and suggest his or her place in the economic system. And the actions they perform—Erich's being driven to the opera in a chauffeured car; Ruth's buying books and records for her love and her assumption that opening a combination boutique and art gallery will be both good economics and good aesthetics; Franz's uneasiness about being seen with Ruth by his students—all point to a specific relation between culture and money. When we see Ruth has returned to the security of her husband in the end, the implication is clear: middle-class culture is dictated by economic freedoms and limitations. Perhaps the only thing that keeps the film from being overtly political is that there is no real class *struggle:* only the middle class is presented in encased isolation, as a closed system, a dead end.

The closest Schlöndorff comes to portraying the proletariat in *Ruth Halbfass* is through the characters of the hairdresser Francesco and his sidekick Bonaparte, the two pseudo-gangsters who ineptly try to exploit Franz, Ruth, and Erich. Despite their being doubly marked as outcasts from German society, being both homosexual and Mediterranean rather than Nordic in background, their model is clearly to imitate that same society. Like Erich, they attend the opera, as we see from their presence at the production of the "bourgeois" *Fidelio.* "Who's going to pay for the Porsche now?" Bonaparte complains to Francesco after they have been tossed out of Erich Halbfass's office. If there is latent in *The Morals of Ruth Halbfass* the archetypally Brechtian analogy that capitalists are like gangsters, Schlöndorff extends the analogy to suggest that, in postwar Germany at least, art professors are also very much like capitalists— all three are acquisitive, self-interested, self-deluding, and ultimately impotent.

For all its use of genre elements, *The Morals of Ruth Halbfass* never falls comfortably into a single Hollywood category. Its plot elements of murder and extramarital lust suggest Hitchcock (and Chabrol's variants of Hitchcock), but the movie is singularly lacking in suspense and is thematically unconcerned with issues of guilt, innocence, or personal morality. Its use of decor and its central character suggest the traditional "women's film" melodrama, but we laugh at rather than weep with its suffering heroine. Where a different sort of director might have turned the movie's main plot elements into a film noir, exploring a moral universe of corruption and evil, Schlöndorff largely avoids noir stylistics: *The Morals of Ruth Halbfass* is for the most part brightly lit, suburban rather than urban in setting, and preoccupied with daytime banalities rather than nighttime intrigue or exoticism.

In this sense we can see *The Morals of Ruth Halbfass* as a work that both uses and parodies the codes of familiar film genres. It thus grows out of its predecessors in the French New Wave, such as Truffaut's *Shoot the Piano Player* and almost all early Godard and Chabrol, not to mention Schlöndorff's own *A Degree of Murder.* This semiserious toying with elements of the American crime melodrama makes *The Morals of Ruth Halbfass* akin to the early anticinema of Rainer Werner Fassbinder (in, for example, *Gods of the Plague* and *Whity*) or Wim Wenders (in *The Goalie's Anxiety at the Penalty Kick [Die Angst des Tormanns beim Elfmeter]*), all similarly made in that same period, 1969–71. All of these movies have in common an interest on the part of their respective directors in making movies about filmic conventions, in exploring the structures and signifying practices of previously established cinema. *Ruth Halbfass*'s constant self-reflexive elements—Aglaia's home movies, Franz's discourses on popular culture, the hairdresser's references to Michael Caine and Charles Bronson heroes—all underline the artificial nature of Schlöndorff's efforts. The consummate irony of *Ruth Halbfass* is that the film, derived as it is from a case history, is Schlöndorff's most *synthetic* work, in both senses of the word. It both unites and commingles various cinematic conventions and themes and provides for a movie that is fully meaningful only in the context of these conventions despite its deliberate comment on social reality.

Schlöndorff's efforts may well have been somewhat too complex to find an appreciative international audience. The film has had no commercial release in French- or English-speaking countries, and at least some German critics have judged it to be a cynical attempt by Schlöndorff to go commercial (Donner, "Himbeerwasser"). Even critic Rainer Lewandowski, who clearly understands what Schlöndorff is trying to do, finds the movie unsuccessful. He writes

> It was Schlöndorff's objective to 'ironize' trivial film with the means of the trivial film genre. It does not become clear, however, where he wanted to reveal the known clichés, and where he fell for them, i.e., where did the cliché prove to be stronger and more resistant against the means of irony than he thought? Schlöndorff does not succeed in getting beyond his take-off. . . . [T]he ironic postulation of the Josef Schmidt lied "Es wird im Leben" is too little because it only described the situation that is to be commented on, but does not exaggerate it. . . . What remains is a trivial film, even as an art form. (139)

One might argue instead that Lewandowski misses the point or that Schlöndorff has been a bit too subtle for his tastes. For *The Morals of Ruth Halbfass* is a little film with an archetypally Chabrolian "little theme," one that need not obviously hammer home its ironies to quality as significant. While *Ruth Halbfass* is not one of Schlöndorff's most famous films, it is one of his most precisely structured, careful works, in which every element works to support a coherent whole. As such, it may be no less substantive than the director's later attempts to tackle "big themes"—terrorism, police brutality, fascism, nuclear war. Schlöndorff subverts a conventional crime melodrama by making all of the characters grotesque or ugly, by presenting all of their actions ambiguously, by connecting every element of the film to a carefully constructed discourse on the relation between wealth and art. A story of presumably passionate love, *The Morals of Ruth Halbfass* is a movie based almost entirely on artifice and contrivance. Its virtues lie not in its realism, but rather in its caustic critique of a society whose values—about family, culture, love—have all become perverted and mechanical.

Overnight Stay in Tyrol

Schlöndorff was to use many of the strategies of *Ruth Halbfass* once more in *Overnight Stay in Tyrol*, a made-for-television film for which, after the hiatus of *A Free Woman*, he collaborated again with Peter Hamm on the scenario. What *Ruth Halbfass* was to the crime thriller, *Overnight Stay* tries to be to the *Heimatfilm*, a parodistic deconstruction of conventions and stock characters.

Overnight Stay's narrative involves a group of five upper-middle-class travelers who, due to a car accident, are forced to spend time in an isolated alpine village. Both the tourists and the villagers are clichés. Among the former are a doctor (Reinhard Hauff) and a wife (Margarethe von Trotta) whose marriage is threatened by boredom and failure of communication; their son seems like an accessory, like the BMW the physician has managed to strand on a precipice. Along with them is an equally vacuous, uncommitted couple, a photographer and a model. In the village these five meet characters who are unreformed *Heimatfilm* archetypes: the drunken schoolteacher, the innkeeper's wife, card players, and village idiots. They also encounter Strupp, a philosophy-spewing painter specializing in avalanche scenes—and an apparent parody of the central figure of Austrian writer Thomas Bernhard's novel *Frost* (1963)—who tries to seduce and eventually rapes the physician's wife.

After the strong feminist statement of *A Free Woman*, *Overnight Stay* seems like a temporary step backward into a narrative in which women are not that important and rape is no big deal. In terms of content, it is difficult to sense exactly what Schlöndorff and Hamm are getting at, with both city values and country values equally hypocritical. On a formal level, Schlöndorff's most interesting idea is the construction of the story around a series of mistaken perceptions. We see this when the physician's wife, thinking her husband dead, mistakes him for a ghost or when both she and other characters assume that a corpse found near the church is her missing husband, when it is really the schoolteacher.

This kind of humor tends toward the blunt and deadpan, and it was perhaps due to the presence of Herbert Achternbusch in the role of the teacher. Achternbusch, a Bavarian writer and dramatist of idiosyncratic and highly metaphoric comic tales, here initiated a comic film persona that he continued immediately after *Overnight Stay* with *The Andechs Feeling* mentioned earlier. This 1974 Achternbusch film was the first of a series of self-devised clownlike screen vehicles for himself, which established him as a filmmaker in his own right. It was produced by Schlöndorff's Bioskop. In it, Achternbusch used himself, von Trotta, and Hauff as his leads, the same performers as in *Overnight Stay,* and he continued, indeed with much more success than Schlöndorff, in this mode of parodying *Heimatfilm* conventions.

Although *Overnight Stay in Tyrol* is undoubtedly Schlöndorff's least well known film, it was successful in achieving a television audience share of 53 percent for ARD, then West Germany's largest network (Infratam). It was coolly received by the majority of critics and has since fallen into oblivion.

10

A Free Woman

At first glance, *A Free Woman* (*Strohfeuer*, 1972) represents a definite break from Schlöndorff's earlier work. At least superficially, it is his most optimistic, upbeat movie up to this time, one that constantly tries to please the audience by being genial and ingratiating. This optimism is due to its main character, Elisabeth, who is so different from Schlöndorff's other main characters from the preceding period. Unlike Baal or Ruth Halbfass, she is likeable; unlike Törless, she tends to be active rather than passive; unlike Michael Kohlhaas or the poor people of Kombach, she does not fail completely. Stylistically, *A Free Woman* is much more open and spontaneous than its predecessors, substituting an almost documentary-like lightness and immediacy for the oppressive, Fritz Lang–like determinism of the director's usual mise-en-scène.

A closer look, however, reveals in *A Free Woman* elements of content, structure, and style that expand and amplify aspects of Schlöndorff's previous films. As Marcel Martin has pointed out, Elisabeth is, like all of Schlöndorff's other main characters, in unsuccessful revolt against the constraints of society (*"Feu"* 68). And like *The Morals of Ruth Halbfass*, *A Free Woman* achieves much of its substance and complexity in its examination of contrasting forms of cultural expression. Like the earlier movie, it contains a pervading message about the interaction between aesthetic practice and political oppression. And again like *Ruth Halbfass*, it can be read two ways—on a straightforward narrative level and on another that undercuts and questions our first reactions to its more conventionalized elements. *A Free Woman* is built around contradictions: a contradictory main character who both liberates herself and resists her own liberation and a contradictory dramatic structure that mixes genre sentimentality with ironic self-criticism.

Based on Margarethe von Trotta's own experiences after the collapse of her first marriage, *A Free Woman* shows the difficulties of an attractive, middle-class woman in trying to succeed on her own. The movie appeared in 1972, when feminism was still a relatively novel subject and is now clearly one of the key works in the emergence of a feminist cinema in the 1970s, both nationally and internationally. By Schlöndorff and von Trotta's own admission, however, *A Free Woman* is not a militant film, and commentators are far from unanimous in assessing its success as a politically correct portrayal of feminist political struggle (Schlöndorff, "Entretien" *Écran* 69.)

A Woman's Story, A Women's Film

A Free Woman's opening shots, of Elisabeth on her motorcycle going to divorce court, characterize the woman's situation. She is free and mobile, like her means of transportation, but the experience is also a bit dangerous and threatening. The cars are larger and more powerful than she, and she clearly needs to be alert and assertive to get along. In subsequent scenes we see Elisabeth struggle with a series of new jobs—as a tour guide, in a fur shop, and finally with an art gallery. We see her confront the problem of getting custody of her young son. We see her fall in love with and eventually marry an attractive, kind, sympathetic man. The story is straightforward, simple, and accessible in a way that makes it an anomalous film among Schlöndorff's, one possibly shaped as much by the input of his wife, von Trotta, who also plays the lead.

Schlöndorff and von Trotta clearly mean Elisabeth to be an exemplary figure, one intended to illustrate typical problems of women. At the same time, Elisabeth is clearly not always a positive example. Much of what she does shows how her efforts to free herself are subverted by her own misjudgment and lack of political awareness. The filmmakers raise the question, To what extent is Elisabeth her own worst enemy?

Not particularly trained for the job market, as demonstrated when an employment counselor asks her about her knowledge of computers or medical technology—Elisabeth must find a way to use her education and intelligence. She begins to take singing and tap dance lessons but evidently is only modestly talented, without much realistic hope of career success as an entertainer. What is more, her dream of being a star plays right into an image of herself as objectified woman, one appealing to men on the basis of physical qualities like looks and voice. The first thing she does upon getting her divorce is to buy herself a rather unflattering wig. We see her fuss with her appearance to impress men, and Schlöndorff's camera more than once eyes von Trotta's body less than innocently. In one long take, for example, it travels up her bare legs to her buttocks and then back down again. How, ultimately, should we feel about Elisabeth's frivolous career expectations and complicity with the way a male-dominated society objectifies women?

Most questionable from a feminist standpoint is the way in which Elisabeth resolves the problems in her life by relying on a man, Oskar (Martin Lüttge), to rescue her. By marrying him, Elisabeth no longer need prove that she can earn a substantive living in order to keep custody of her child, after she has refused to let mutual friends say damaging things about her ex-husband in the custody hearing. Feminist critic Marjorie Rosen has particularly objected to the wedding that gives the movie its nominally happy ending, arguing that

> by marrying again she makes a peculiar trade—surrendering her independence, her most precious freedom, out of disproportionate concern for friends' momentary discomfort. This suggests that her passivity is simply due to ambivalence, or that at bottom she never wanted the burden of freedom in the first place. (11)

Rosen may well miss the point of the ending, which, while optimistic and happy in its physical images, undercuts this mood in the song on the sound track, whose stirring lyrics describe the feelings of an embittered woman who has been asked all her life to wait for what she wants. The song concludes with the verse:

> Hence I have been a good girl,
> as they told me to be, have read a lot,
> have avoided violence,
> have accomplished nothing and am old.

Schlöndorff himself has commented on this ambivalent ending. He argues that such an ending, which shows how Elisabeth is still manifestly burdened by existing social structures, is preferable to a militant conclusion in which Elisabeth would simplistically solve all of her problems by joining in organized struggle as part of the women's liberation movement. Rather than suggest that everything will be all right through either the right-wing fantasy in which marriage cures all problems or the left-wing fantasy in which political commitment solves everything, Schlöndorff offers a pessimistic but purposefully consciousness-raising end ("Entretien" *Écran* 69).

This ending suggests the way in which Schlöndorff in *A Free Woman* carries on preoccupations and aesthetic strategies similar to those found in *Ruth Halbfass*. As Rosen has pointed out, Elisabeth's rescuer Oskar is a simplistically drawn, unconvincingly virtuous character. Through him, Schlöndorff and von Trotta play on the conventions of the Hollywood romantic comedy, and indeed the filmmakers claim their work to be modeled on the cinema of Ernst Lubitsch ("Entretien" *Écran* 68–69).

In this context we must acknowledge that *A Free Woman* contains a strong streak of sentimentality, an element almost totally absent from Schlöndorff's earlier work. Consider, for example, Schlöndorff's use of Stanley Myers's background music. Where most Schlöndorff films contain scores that tend toward complexity and ambiguity, *A Free Woman*'s background music, apart from its several songs, consists of a single lyric melody inserted periodically for dramatic emphasis. It resembles very closely Michel Legrand's music for Jean-Luc Godard's *My Life to Live* (*Vivre sa vie,* 1962) and *Band of Outsiders* or Georges Delerue's theme for François Truffaut's *The Soft Skin* (*La peau douce,* 1964). Schlöndorff uses short bursts of a pleasant, slightly wistful tune to underline selected scenes. The first introductions of this theme in *A Free Woman* are for piano. The theme pops up orchestrated for strings, milking even more sentiment from it, at a key dramatic moment in which the husband forces Elizabeth to return her son to his father's home. Only at the end of the film, when the harsh words of the song betray the filmmakers' true feelings, does Schlöndorff turn this melodrama into irony, allowing us to put the sentimentality into perspective.

In terms of emotional response and the manipulation of sentiment, *A Free Woman* was Schlöndorff's most calculated and atypical film to date. Our strong identification with Elisabeth, our enjoyment of her successes, makes her husband's inflexibility about child custody all the more intolerable to us. The film's two emotions feed one another; our joy at seeing Elisabeth's moments of strength and assertiveness only intensifies our anger at the obstacles that remain for her. The tension of her repeated difficulties collects and is released through her inevitable anger—particularly in the scene in which she calls for her husband at his office and proceeds to beat him in a furious outburst. This release of anger, in turn, immediately precedes the "happy" ending. *A Free Woman* partakes of the rise and fall of emotional temperature so characteristic of domestic melodrama.

Gender Aesthetics and Politics

In other words, Schlöndorff and von Trotta construct *A Free Woman* in a way that allows us to enjoy its comic, conventionalized, and sentimental aspects even while the filmmakers critique some of these same conventions and modes of representation. *A Free Woman* thus contains an important subtext about the relationships among art, work, and culture and particularly about men's domination of the world of aesthetics.

While nothing comes directly out of Elisabeth's singing and dancing lessons, they demonstrate an authentic sensitivity to art that probably went undeveloped during her marriage. She receives somewhat more encouragement from her dancing instructor than her singing teacher, though even the former tells her it will be two years before she is really in shape. It is clear to the audience from what we hear that her voice is far more suited to her rendition of "I Can't Give You Anything but Love" than a Mahler lied. The contrast in this scene between the pop song and Mahler, between popular culture and established culture, sets up an opposition that the film carries through systematically.

The movie constantly suggests that established artistic institutions are male dominated. Both Elisabeth's husband and her new lover work in publishing, for example, and early in the film she and her husband have a fight about which of their books she can take with her. He wins: the man who controls the books controls the culture.

The scene that in Schlöndorff's eyes sums up the theme of the movie, although it is not terribly relevant to the narrative, shows Elisabeth accompanying Konrad Farner, an art historian who plays himself in the work, to the Alte Pinakothek, Munich's renowned art museum (Even 13). In talking to her about the paintings, Farner describes how the portrayal of women has changed from the idealization of early Christian art, an idealization linked to subservience to men, to erotic objectification in later, more secular painting. (See illustration 15.) Men have thus for centuries dominated images of women. This same art historian, for all his seeming political awareness, admonishes Elisabeth, as they say good-bye, to stay pretty.

The scene takes on a number of meanings. The art historian suggests, perhaps, von Trotta's own father, who was a painter. Indeed, at one point Elisabeth affectionately tells him that she would love to have had a father like him (a statement that takes on added resonance if one is aware that von Trotta's father never married her mother). Through this sequence, Schlöndorff links his film to a tradition of German critical thought by choosing Farner, a Marxist exiled in Switzerland since 1923, noted for his defense of Bertolt Brecht against the Stalinist critiques of Georg Lukacs. The sequence ultimately asks, How does one go from theory to practice? What images of women must replace those that oppress either by misplaced idealization or eroticization? How can women succeed in their struggle when even politically aware men can't avoid being partner to a culture of sexism?

In contrast to all the men around her—her husband, Oskar, Farner, the art gallery owner, a cello-playing former boyfriend with whom she considers trumping up a false paternity claim—Elisabeth is clearly a creature of popular

15. *A Free Woman.* Art historian Farner suggesting to Sophie (Margarethe von Trotta) that images of women have traditionally been dominated by men. Photo: Deutsches Filmmuseum Fotoarchiv.

culture. She sings popular music better than classical and tap-dances better than she sings, and this affection for the popular seems to put her in touch with other women in the film. At the dance school, another of the students, a rather young girl, talks of her desire to imitate Joan Crawford and go on to become a big star. The suggestion is clear: Hollywood has offered more appealing images of women and more cause for optimism for women than more supposedly respectable forms of art. But the trade-off is also clear: one must pay for Hollywood's brand of strength and assertiveness by accepting conventional, sex-object models of behavior.

In the movie's only major fantasy sequence, Elisabeth imagines Oskar coming into the fur shop in which she is at the moment working. He rejects all of the glamorous models in their furs in favor of her, picking her out, Cinderella-style, from a corner. The scene turns into a pseudolavish musical comedy number, with Elisabeth singing the lead. The scene merges Elisabeth's dreams, for both her personal and her professional life. The sequence shows Schlöndorff's technical skill to great advantage, for although the scene conveys a pleasing sense of mobility and kinesthetic appeal, it is actually shot rather simply, obtaining its dynamism from a series of carefully edited rack focus shots rather than any elaborate camera movement. If the film is indeed an autobiographical one for von Trotta, the sequence becomes a celebration of *A Free Woman*'s itself being a fulfillment of dreams. Von Trotta has become a movie star in a film based on her own life.

In two other places in the film, the actress sings songs on the sound track: during the romantic interlude in Italy with Oskar and at the end of the movie during the wedding. Noteworthy about these musical numbers is that von Trotta sings charmingly but hardly perfectly. Her vocal gifts are for spontaneity, sincerity, and warmth rather than precision, polish, or complexity. In the system of oppositions the movie sets up, this emotion is where Elisabeth's talents may well lie. We see her encouraging her son with painting and with learning to play the piano. Such encouragement and the love of aesthetic values it embodies may be as important to the cultural life of a society as formal professional achievement.

Seen in this light, Elisabeth's seemingly impractical stabs at a show business career suggest an extremely positive side of her personality: she has the strength to hold out for a job that is rewarding, fun, nonalienating. In this context, her presence at a secretarial school near the end has an ominous ring to it: is it a step forward in her maturing or a compromise, like her marriage may be, toward conformity?

Schlöndorff himself, in commenting on the way in which *A Free Woman* was shot, as a collaborative effort in which performers and technicians both had input into the work, has said, "Filmmaking should be a non-alienating trade. Since it is a hand craft, one can achieve this more easily than on an automobile assembly line" (Even 13). Elisabeth's forms of expression—imperfect, spontaneous, personal, popular—suggest an alternative, childlike, nonalienating practice of art. They suggest art made not as a commodity but for personal pleasure, a form of work that becomes a protest against the restrictions of a postindustrialist culture.

Elisabeth's success at her art gallery job is due directly to her knowledge of Italian, since she becomes important to her boss as an interpreter. *A Free Woman* plays consciously on the stereotyped perception of Italians as spontaneous, open, sincere—exactly the qualities Elisabeth possesses. Appropriately, then, the romance between Elisabeth and Oskar blossoms in Italy. In one shot during the Italian episode, the camera looks at an old man riding on a dilapidated, creaky bicycle, pans with him as he rides, and comes to Oskar's car parked by the side of the road. As the panning continues over into a field, we just barely see Elisabeth and Oskar, hidden among the flowers of the field, making love. Italy becomes a place in which Elisabeth can find refuge from an overly rigid society. The point is ironic, of course, since she has gone to a country in which, at least according to stereotype, sex roles are more rigidly set than West Germany. A further irony is that Oskar has come from Germany to rescue Elisabeth from the sexual harassment of her boss.

Collaborative Dialectics

If one returns to the question of autobiography—and to this opposition between male-dominated, Germanic, institutionalized, formalized art and female-oriented, Italianate, spontaneous, popular art—one wonders at the extent to which Schlöndorff and von Trotta are commenting on their own artistic collaboration. In *A Free Woman*, in Schlöndorff's words, "She acted, I filmed, but the relationship was one of confidence, not of authority" (Even 13). Von Trotta's background as an actress would presumably emphasize those instinctive, affective qualities that much acting embodies; Schlöndorff's inclinations would lie in the direction of the more rationalist construction of screenplays and images.

Stylistically, Schlöndorff's camera in *A Free Woman* seems busier than von Trotta's in her later solo films, his editing trickier and tighter. He fills *A Free Woman*, for example, with tiny sound overlaps that pull us out of scenes and into the next ones. At the same time, we can only admire Schlöndorff's clear recognition that a major strength of *A Free Woman* lies in von Trotta's performance and his skill at never allowing *A Free Woman*'s camera work or editing to overshadow the sense of sincerity and spontaneity that von Trotta conveys. Uncharacteristically for Schlöndorff, the shooting of *A Free Woman* relied heavily on improvisation, and the sequences with the music teacher and with Farner reportedly are the result of editing down a much larger amount of footage (Schlöndorff, "Entretien" *Écran* 69). The final effect, given the film's calculated structure, is one of deliberation and conscious thought.

This opposition or tension between "feminine" emotion and "masculine" intellect is not without its ambiguities. When Elisabeth is leaving her art gallery job because its seeming lack of security supposedly makes her a poor risk to be able to support her child, the gallery presents her with a print by the artist Niki de Saint-Phalle. Konrad Farner comments on the print's image of woman—underdeveloped in the head or brain, overdeveloped in the body, heart, and breasts. It is an image of woman not at all flattering in a feminist context but one that has been created by a woman artist herself. Modern art comes in for a critique in an earlier sequence as well, in Italy, when her boss looks at some photographic documents of a work of performance art, a semipornographic happening in which unclothed women are presented in degrading and subservient actions.

A Free Woman works constantly on two levels. On the one hand, it draws from the personal experience of its makers; on the other, it acknowledges an awareness that the movie itself is a part of the process of creating images of women that may contain all manner of ideological content. In his television film, *A Scenario for Passion* (*Un scénario pour passion*, 1982), in which he discusses principles of script writing and filmmaking, Jean-Luc Godard described all cinema as involving a meeting ground between reality and abstraction. *A Free Woman* is consistently animated by this same dialectic made articulate and manifest, of film images being both recordings of a specific reality and a discourse about that reality.

Critical reaction has been almost unanimous in acclaim of Schlöndorff and von Trotta's success at capturing the surface qualities of Margarethe von Trotta's experience. But is the movie a fair abstraction of the problems of modern women? Schlöndorff and von Trotta refer directly to their German title, *Strohfeuer,* in a scene in which Elisabeth visits her lawyer. The German title literally means "straw fire," and other English translations—the movie was called *Summer Lightning* in Britain and the title *Flash in the Pan* has also been suggested—come closer to this meaning than the American title, *A Free Woman,* does. Elisabeth's lawyer, herself a woman, compares her struggles for freedom to a straw fire—a release of energy that will burn quickly and brightly and fast die out.

Schlöndorff and von Trotta leave ambiguous whether we must see Elisabeth's efforts as a flash in the pan or as a start on her way to becoming a free woman. On the one hand, her moves toward conformity near the film's end suggest the impossibility of undoing the effects of years of social oppression. On the other hand, von Trotta's personal success as a feminist filmmaker contradicts the semidownbeat ending she has given her fictionalized autobiography. Whether an audience finds this portrayal of Elisabeth's sometimes misguided feminist strivings positively realistic or negatively antimilitant, it cannot deny that the filmmakers have been thoughtful in their approach to the problems, one that links a specific realist portrayal to questions of how society should think of and portray women.

11

Georgina's Reasons

Schlöndorff's next film, *Georgina's Reasons* (*Georginas Gründe*, 1974) would appear to be a rather routine television assignment. It is on the surface a conventional, rather straightforward adaptation of a story by Henry James made as part of a series of five James adaptations coproduced for French and German television, with the other episodes directed by Claude Chabrol, Paul Seban, and Tony Scott (Appel). Schlöndorff worked from a script by Peter Adler, but on close inspection one sees that *Georgina's Reasons* picks up two major motifs that run through Schlöndorff's other work: the impossibility of love in a society that offers too many constraints and the problem of being a free-minded woman in that same repressive society. In adapting this Henry James story to television, Schlöndorff has deliberately turned a detached, third-person narrative into a subjective, first-person drama. He has, either by instinct or design, created a work in which the patterns of his mise-en-scène duplicate for the television viewer the patterns of looking and desire that operate within his own fictional narrative. In portraying a man's desire to possess an unresponsive woman, Schlöndorff employs mechanisms of voyeurism, of a male gaze directed at an idealized woman, to create a visual analogue to the character's internal state. In giving a story of female resistance an uncomprehending male point of view, he strengthens the woman's mystery and power. At the same time, this treatment may become problematic from a feminist viewpoint, in its adoption of strategies similar to those of patriarchal traditional cinema.

Georgina's Reasons is the story of a young woman from a good New York family who marries a young naval officer, Raymond Benyon (Joachim Bissmeyer), against the will of her parents. Georgina Gressie (Edith Clever) keeps the marriage a secret and makes her husband swear not to reveal the marriage until she permits. She has a child, which she goes to Italy to deliver, still keeping the marriage from her family. After virtually abandoning her baby, she marries again but still refuses to free her first husband to remarry legally.

Inversion of Victorian Conventions

Set in the nineteenth century, the movie relates to Schlöndorff's earlier work in raising issues about the emancipation of women, but for both James and Schlöndorff the title *Georgina's Reasons* is clearly ironic. We never learn Georgina's reasons directly, and the movie's fiction is perhaps best seen as a deliberate reversal of the conventional Victorian narrative (seen in one of its most famous variants in D. W. Griffith's *Way Down East*) whereby the man exploits a woman, impregnates her, then walks out on her and the child. Here it is the woman who uses the man, becomes pregnant, then walks out on both father and baby. Georgina reverses the traditional double standard; the film becomes a kind of antigenre film. Schlöndorff uses this antigenre structure to suggest that Georgina, like so many other Schlöndorff heroines, is a woman whose odd behaviors arise out of the conditions of the society in which she lives. Her unarticulated reasons are ultimately political and feminist.

Despite its deceptive simplicity, *Georgina's Reasons* is not simply an impersonal, academic literary adaptation. Rather, it reveals Schlöndorff's understanding of those qualities in the original story that make it highly suitable to visualization. *Georgina's Reasons* explores the ability of the filmic medium both to reveal and conceal the interior thoughts and feelings of characters. The movie opens to us Benyon's thoughts and feelings while we at the same time share his ability to read Georgina's internal motives for her externally eccentric behavior. As Schlöndorff constructs the film, the actress who plays Georgina, Edith Clever, becomes an object of our fascination and admiration. Much as Benyon has done, we scrutinize her beauty and try to decipher her motivations. *Georgina's Reasons* is a film about sexual frustration, about Benyon's desire for Georgina and his inability to fulfill it, and about his inability to remarry and so fulfill any sexual desire. Benyon's frustration becomes analogous to the way in which the audience is both tantalized by Edith Clever's beauty and similarly can neither act on it nor even fully understand the reasons for the fascination. (See illustration 16.)

Schlöndorff is faithful to the events of James's narrative. Shifts of point of view, tone, emphasis, and detail, however, make the filmmaker's visualization a significantly different work. Schlöndorff's most striking departure is his use of a flashback structure whereby we first see Benyon at the end of the story reflecting on events that we are about to see. Schlöndorff presents Benyon in close-ups, talking to himself (but by extension, because he is looking at the camera, to the audience). The director externalizes what would otherwise be an internal monologue. By using close-ups and frequently cutting back to Benyon

16. *Georgina's Reasons.* The bigamist title figure (Edith Clever) with Captain Benyon, the narrator (Joachim Bissmeyer). Photo: Deutsches Filmmuseum Fotoarchiv.

talking in the film's present, Schlöndorff allows us to identify all the more with the man's point of view: we get to see the past through his eyes. Third-person narration in James becomes first-person monologue in Schlöndorff.

An obvious result of this difference is that Schlöndorff strengthens Benyon as a character. In addition, the filmmaker eliminates the slightly deprecating qualities James uses to describe him. Schlöndorff's Benyon no longer stutters and stands a full head taller than Georgina rather than slightly under her. If James's tale is more a comedy of manners dissecting nineteenth-century morals and etiquette, the movie is darker, more personal, more tragic, all as a result of this shift of point of view. Where the actor who plays Benyon, Joachim Bissmeyer, is appealingly modest and subdued, the character of Georgina becomes stronger and more heroic than in James largely through Edith Clever's presence as an actress. Schlöndorff deemphasizes the story's minor characters, like Georgina's father or Mrs. Portico, the family friend with whom Georgina goes to Europe, in favor of a more intimate, more direct struggle of wills between the equally sympathetic Georgina and Benyon.

A major quality of the close-ups of Benyon narrating is that they exclude other people from the frame and set up a system whereby for much of the film there is a separation between an admirer and the woman admired. Apart from a couple of shots early in the movie, we rarely see Georgina and Benyon together in the same frame. Those few scenes following the wedding in which we do see the couple framed together represent short, unpleasant moments of conflict after the couple has been intimate. Schlöndorff's emphasis on one-shot close-ups also excludes from the film a strong sense of visual setting or environment. In this sense *Georgina's Reasons* is a more personalized, more psychological exploration of human sexual relations than works like *The Morals of Ruth Halbfass* or *A Free Woman*. This emphasis may be due to a need to work within a small television budget, one that would exclude expensive set construction or location shooting. But the end result fully supports the effect of eroticism Schlöndorff has created. Television-style close-ups keep the story within the realm of intimate personal conflict.

What is more, the Benyon who narrates the movie is a slightly different Benyon from the one early in the film, in that Schlöndorff designates the passage of time by having him grow a mustache. This changes his image from that of a somewhat naive young man to that of a sexually mature sea captain. Schlöndorff sets up a system whereby Benyon, like the audience, is removed from the action of the movie, thus linking Benyon's desires and our own: the fulfillment of Benyon's desire would come, in effect, in our being able to see the mature Benyon and Georgina together in the frame. The audience senses that the eventual return of Benyon into the action will be satisfying, for it will reunite the desired object, Georgina, with a desirer with whom we identify, Benyon. One suspects this inscription into the film of a male point of view works the same way for both male and female viewers.

Georgina's Reasons thus becomes a kind of exercise in perversity; like voyeurs or fetishists, we take pleasure in a substitute for the real thing. Schlöndorff takes from James a situation in which an idealized woman is both present and unattainable. She is both possessed (married to Benyon) and impossible to possess (apart from him). The distance between Benyon and Georgina metaphorically becomes the same separation as that between the audience and Edith Clever. How appropriate it is, therefore, that Benyon's rediscovery of Georgina and her second marriage should come about because of his stumbling across a painting that looks like her in an Italian museum. The painting is an image, a substitute. It sparks comments about Georgina from Benyon's companions, who do not realize he knows her. The picture, though not of Georgina, is Georgina's image, and Benyon contemplates it as a work of art, again like the audience's contemplation of Edith Clever. One wonders indeed whether the image of Georgina is not more important to Benyon than the reality. The Italian critic Alberto Cattini describes Schlöndorff's Benyon as a man who "loves not the true woman, but the idea of woman, and therefore his greater wish to possess her legally, and abstractly" (84).

Medium-Specific Mise-en-Scène

The discovery of the painting and the revelations about Georgina's where-abouts that result from it lead directly to the climactic scene in the movie in which Benyon confronts Georgina. He wishes to be freed of his promise, so he can marry Kate Theory (Margarethe von Trotta), an American woman he has met in Italy and who has returned to the United States. In this confrontation Georgina has also matured sexually: Schlöndorff gives her the artificial, Hollywood accoutrements of glamour—a flowing, red, bare-shouldered dress, bright red lipstick, ostentatious jewelry—that at once idealize her and make her more unattainable. The filmmaker conflates the mechanisms of Hollywood star worship with the narrative structure of the unrealizable desire. The star is out of reach to the audience just as Georgina is unattainable to Benyon.

The confrontation contains an unusual amount of sustained drama for a Schlöndorff film, perhaps because Georgina is one of Schlöndorff's most active women characters. We get the excitement of potential sexual contact between the mature Benyon and Georgina, while at the same time that desired contact never occurs. We get, instead, anger, recrimination, hostility—not the desired emotions but substitute ones that are still expressive, appropriate, and satisfy-ing to the audience. It is rare in a Schlöndorff film from the 1970s to find a scene with such cathartic follow-through, and the confrontation finally brings Georgina to tears. The audience's desires are satisfied, if not quite in the way anticipated, and much of the encounter has been photographed in two-shots, allowing us finally to see the former couple together in the frame.

After Georgina's tears, however, Schlöndorff returns in the scene to putting the characters in single-head close-ups, particularly once her second husband enters. The state of sexual frustration that has dominated the film returns as an unresolved problem. After Benyon leaves the house, we get a close-up of Georgina alone, followed immediately by a close-up of Kate Theory. Theory stands alone at her sister's grave, about to be rejected by Benyon, who prefers to fulfilled love the strict honoring both of his word and the bond of legal mat-rimony. Schlöndorff visually transfers the situation of separation and sexual frustration from one woman to another. Indeed, in that Kate Theory has pursued Benyon more aggressively than may have been customary for the time, Benyon seeks to trade, as one critic has suggested, one emancipated woman for another (hmb).

Schlöndorff has thus constructed *Georgina's Reasons* around a system of close-ups whereby the director opposes single, talking-head shots to more emotionally charged two-shots on which the audience can project feelings of intimacy and emotional involvement. The critic David Head has argued that the close-ups of Benyon in which he seems to address the audience directly show a perceptive understanding on Schlöndorff's part of the nature of television as an individual rather than a communal experience ("West German"). Schlöndorff himself has commented on what he set out to do in *Georgina's Reasons:*

> This is the way I envision it: one evening an isolated, solitary television viewer (is there any other kind?) turns on his set and there on the screen sees someone speaking to him. A man sitting on the deck of a ship in the gray light of morning raises his head and begins to tell him the story of his life. To be more accurate: he reflects on his relationships with women, he's thinking aloud, and the viewer shares his thoughts and experiences. It is as if he had opened a book and were having a conversation with the author. Isn't the experience of watching TV much more similar to reading a book than going to a play or a movie? (Pflaum, "Adler")

In the final image of the movie we see Benyon tying his tie (a signifier of repressing masculine sexuality) and setting sail for sea. These images suggest a gap between the sexes, between a masculine world of militarism and heterosexual deprivation and a feminine world of security and domestic pleasure. If Schlöndorff forgoes direct social criticism here, neither does he suggest that masculine and feminine psychologies are fixed and unchanging. Rather, the society creates parameters that limit human behavior or sometimes make it take surprising forms. Who indeed is more restricted in *Georgina's Reasons*—Georgina, because she has to go to such lengths to live as she wants, or Benyon, because he allows himself to accept uncritically society's rules? Rainer Lewandowski has argued that both of Georgina's husbands—Benyon, because he remains tied to his honor, and her second husband, who would be ruined if it became common knowledge he was married to a bigamist—are prisoners of the very social system they epitomize. "Georgina's freedom or liberty," Lewandowski writes,

... consists in the fact that she reinforces the dependency relationship for her partners by ensnaring them into their own social net. That is an almost dialectical reversal of prevailing conditions, the attempt to construct a woman's personal liberty in opposition to the rules of society. That is what Georgina manages to do; those are the reasons for her actions. However, all of this can succeed only because both parties are held strictly to social conventions. In that respect her way can't be a model for modern attempts at emancipation. Georgina conducts a social experiment which is tied to her historical period, and was radical for her time, because it uproots the conventions of her social environment to her own advantage. (185)

To the extent, however, that Schlöndorff invites us to observe Georgina's actions from a present-day perspective, her motives suggest the historical roots of the dissatisfaction felt by many contemporary women. Schlöndorff's originality lies in his ability to have seen the inherently cinematic nature of the story, to weigh, as one critic has suggested, the nineteenth-century perspective of its male protagonist equally against the twentieth-century point of view of its heroine (hmb). Benyon's desire and dilemma parallel the audience's experience of watching a television movie. James's story is about the ways in which erotic attraction is often based on the most superficial qualities, qualities that in turn may disguise any number of inner motivations. By so carefully emphasizing Benyon's point of view and linking it to the audience's through *Georgina's Reasons*'s structure of flashbacks and subjective close-ups, Schlöndorff is able to explore in his drama the nature both of physical desire and of fantasized, cinematic desire. By adapting a socially relevant Henry James story and allowing its ambiguities to surface effectively, Schlöndorff achieves that lucid form of literary adaption that is at once a presentation of its original author's fictional world and an analysis and interpretation of the work and the society that produced it.

12

The Lost Honor of
Katharina Blum

In both Schlöndorff's development and that of the New German Cinema, *The Lost Honor of Katharina Blum* (*Die verlorene Ehre der Katharina Blum*, 1975) marks an important stage. The mid-1970s saw the West German new wave achieve firm international status, reaching a high point at the New York Film Festival of 1975 where Werner Herzog's *Kaspar Hauser*, along with Schlöndorff and von Trotta's *Katharina Blum* and Fassbinder's *Fox and His Friends (Faustrecht der Freiheit)*, dramatically conquered new cinéaste audiences. This foreign prestige provided encouragement for a New German Cinema that had as yet engendered little interest in its country of origin. Indeed, in West Germany, the New German Cinema was barely surviving in an art film ghetto. It was to the credit of Schlöndorff and von Trotta's *Katharina Blum*, as well as to *Lina Braake*, Bernhard Sinkel and Alf Brustellin's sociopolitical low-budget comedy of the same year, 1975, that the walls between the wider German audience and the New German Cinema were cracked by unexpected popular successes.

The movie hooked audiences with its story of a somewhat naive, idealistic woman, Katharina Blum (Angela Winkler), who becomes brutalized by the law and the press immediately after she falls in love. At a relative's Mardi Gras party Katharina becomes infatuated with a stranger, Ludwig Götten (Jürgen Prochnow), who she does not realize is an army deserter. Götten and Katharina have a one-night stand, which the entire West German justice-police-and-press apparatus reads as terrorist contact between a wanted anarchist and the female who has sheltered him. The authorities who have stalked Götten are all the more convinced of Katharina's guilt as they watch him escaping from her apartment. In league with the police, the yellow press totally vilifies Katharina until her reputation is shattered. It is at this point that she shoots the press reporter, Tötges (Dieter Laser), when he arrives at her apartment to suggest intercourse before working jointly on articles about her secret amorous "underground life."

The positive response of the West German public to the film was all the more remarkable because it was overtly political. It directly confronted the mid-1970s issue of what to do about supposed terrorist sympathizers. What the political right viewed as the justified prosecution of citizens who had sheltered criminals, the left saw as a political witch-hunt of radical protesters. The film also supported women's liberation, both in its critique of an institutionalized patriarchy and in the public acknowledgement of how Schlöndorff and von Trotta equally shared directorial responsibilities.

Katharina Blum also provides us with another example of Schlöndorff's literary adaptations. Not only did Nobel novelist Heinrich Böll approach the directors with his book prior to its publication, he also closely supervised their revisions of the script, and Böll himself suggested actors Angela Winkler and Mario Adorf for the roles of Katharina Blum and police inspector Beizmenne (Stoll; Holetz). Böll, Schlöndorff, and von Trotta held a common political and aesthetic orientation, and the adaptation shared with the book the West German culture's same historical moment and ideological context. The personal involvement of the author turns any issues of fidelity into ones of medium specificity—issues that merely compare the literary model with its specifically cinematic adaptation. This angle has been pursued successfully by other scholars such as Joan and William R. Magretta and Petra Schubert-Scheinmann.

Our task here is to lay out the film's historical background to show how *The Lost Honor of Katharina Blum* functioned as a political film for its time. On the one hand, critics have conceived of the work as a mass audience film, casting it into the thriller genre, featuring as it does a single, sympathetic victim as its protagonist. On the other hand, Schlöndorff and von Trotta's adaptation uses modernist techniques such as self-reflexivity, complex positioning of the spectator, and ironic genre subversion, resulting in a sophisticated rewriting of Böll's literary strategies. This combination raises several questions. Why did the filmmakers use the conventions of the thriller to adapt an ironic, pseudo-documentary novel? Why did Schlöndorff and von Trotta resort to a seemingly simplistic dramaturgy involving a distressed heroine who is victimized by a threatening patriarchy? Where does this dramaturgical choice place *Katharina Blum* in relation to feminist filmmaking? How do the filmmakers lead the audience to reflect on its own voyeuristic exploitation of Katharina Blum? Finally, how does the movie comment on the machinery of the media in general? In addition to these questions, we also examine those strengths of the work that have stimulated artistic echoes and cinematic "offspring" both at home and abroad.

1970s Terrorism Hysteria

To understand *The Lost Honor of Katharina Blum* adequately, we must first place it into historical context. The political climate of 1970s West Germany was overshadowed by internal strife. When Willy Brandt stepped down after the Guillaume scandal in 1974, Helmut Schmidt, a more conservative Social Democrat, took over as chancellor of West Germany. Afraid of continued anarchist incidents, the federal government introduced laws that restricted government employment to "loyal" citizens *(Berufsverbot)*. These laws were in specific response to terrorist acts committed by the Baader-Meinhof group and the Red Army Faction, radicalized offshoots of the 1960s student protest and anti-Vietnam movement. From 1972 to 1975, the violent gangs' actions caused bloodshed and headlines when they attacked the 1972 Munich Olympics and the West German Stockholm Embassy and kidnapped chief judge Gustav von Drenkmann and Berlin conservative CDU party chairman Peter Lorenz.

The Axel Springer press had been one of the most outspoken West German news media sources that attempted to define this terrorist uproar in the rightwing terms of the establishment. For decades, West Germany's William Randolph Hearst had dominated nearly a third of the daily press's output, controlling the largest urban print news markets, such as Hamburg and West Berlin, with a two-thirds share (Noelle-Neumann and Schulz 227–28). Springer's *BILDzeitung*, a yellow press prototype rivaling the *National Enquirer* in libel trials and smear campaigns but—with its five-million circulation—comparable to that of *USA Today* in the United States, fanned political hysteria. Jointly, the Schmidt government's actions and its media coverage spearheaded by the Springer press empire initiated a general political swing in West Germany toward conservatism.

If *Bild*—as the sensationalist press closely allied with the right-wing CSU party—promoted West Germany's conservative establishment, the younger generation of the 1960s opposed that establishment as reactionary. West German students and New Left alike viewed this alliance, in part in its acceptance of American counterinsurgency policy in Vietnam and elsewhere, as a tradition related to Germany's fascist past. In the extraparliamentary opposition activities of the second half of the 1960s, politicized students and members of the New Left voiced their anxiety that the Social Democratic Party had also turned its back on its antifascist past by joining the "Grand Coalition" with the post-Adenauerian Christian Democratic party. As the student movement's activism gave way to attitudes of dissolution and resignation *(Neue Subjektivität* and *Neue Sensibilität)* around 1970, the radical Baader-Meinhof fringe developed.

The historical paradox in these developments lies in two political adversaries—the Left and the establishment—fighting each other in the name of antifascism. The majority of the West German intelligentsia, including the radical filmmakers of the New German Cinema, still perceived the actions of terrorists like Ulrike Meinhof and Gudrun Ensslin, daughters of Protestant theologians who had been involved in church resistance circles during the Third Reich, as legitimate extensions of their fathers' commitment. The extent of support that the Baader-Meinhof group and the Red Army Faction enjoyed was remarkable. A survey of West Germans conducted in 1971 by the Allensbach Institute of Public Opinion indicated that one of every twenty citizens was then willing to harbor illegally one of the terrorist fugitives for a night, even at the risk of serious consequences; in northern Germany the figure was one in ten (Aust 154).

Schlöndorff himself was seen as a supporter of terrorists, as was Böll. In September 1976, Springer's flagship daily *Die Welt* attacked Schlöndorff as a "Baader-Meinhof-Sympathisant"—the term "terrorist sympathizer" being one of the most abusive labels during the political controversy over the anarchists. In addition, during the making of their film, Schlöndorff and von Trotta, under threat of court action from the Springer publishing house, had to agree not to run in West Germany an ironic disclaimer that refers literally to *Bild. Die Welt* further demanded that the Social Democratic Party withdraw the filmmaker from his role as the party's official delegate to the administrative council of the "Filmförderungsanstalt," the national foundation for film subsidy (Vielain). And the party did drop the filmmaker once a further denunciation complicated his position (Schlöndorff, *Die Blechtrommel: Tagebuch* 48). One is not surprised then to learn that the conservative press was outraged by *The Lost Honor of Katharina Blum,* with one critic comparing it to anti-Semitic Nazi propaganda, writing, "Schlöndorff's *Katharina Blum*-Film belongs to the most evil propaganda reels of the present. . . . A leftist *Jew Süss*" (Habe).

Schlöndorff, of course, inherited the stigma of "sympathizer" for collaborating with Böll in a screen adaption of a novel that the writer employed as a literary response both to the *Bild* tabloid's red-baiting and the harassment it directed at him personally. In an open letter to the West German news magazine *Der Spiegel,* the novelist had censured the tabloid for its "naked fascism" of unsubstantiated reporting and irresponsible rabble-rousing ("Will Ulrike"

199). In addition, scores of police with submachine guns invaded and searched the houses of Böll and his extended family, at times even posting sharpshooters on the roofs of adjoining houses. The first raid of this kind took place on June 1, 1972, and Böll continued to report such harassment as late as September 1976 (Schlöndorff, *Tagebuch* 44). Indeed, Böll, writing with hindsight in the mid-1980s, confirmed that his *Katharina Blum* is "a pamphlet, a broadside, invented, designed, and executed as such, . . . and occidentals in particular . . . ought to have known that pamphlets belong to the finest Western traditions" ("Zehn" 260).

Political Thriller, Patriarchy, and the Female Victim

The novelist and filmmakers did not forget to temper their personal rage and political commitment with formal control. While Böll, Schlöndorff, and von Trotta shared their topical concerns in the writing and making of their respective versions of *Katharina Blum*, each decided on suitable medium-specific strategies. To oppose public hysteria in print, Böll, the pioneer who invented the story, created a detached omniscient observer who is given to verbal arabesques about the sources, research, and artful presentation of his "facts." The irony of this device lies in part in the observer's insistence on objectivity while he himself progressively assumes more partiality toward Katharina Blum.

In contrast, the filmmakers—in keeping with Schlöndorff's creed that his medium remain responsible to the mass audience—turned toward the popular genre of the thriller. Of course, such medium-specific transformation from book to screen had its consequences. The filmmakers had to reposition the novel's narrative point of view—absorbing the playful, almost dawdling observer-narrator's figure into the suspense mechanisms and storytelling conventions of the thriller. The result provoked some critics, such as R. W. Kilborn and John Sandford, to cite Schlöndorff and von Trotta's method as "the deliberate reduction of a complex literary text" (Sandford 37).

Cinematic genre codes foreground the threatened heroine and reshape her world. From Fritz Lang's *Dr. Mabuse* to Alfred Hitchcock's *Psycho,* "the model of all directors active in this genre" (Tichy 3: 667), thrillers have cultivated the cinematic art of totally involving the spectator in a movie's plot to the point of physical reaction—the thrill. The suspense genre generates fear and anxiety by creating spectator identification with the hero, who is frightened by events of a threatening nature, through mystification and the specters of murder and annihilation as the core motifs. Heroes or heroines—whether Katharina Blum or Indiana Jones—must fight as individuals against an entire system, a whole

evil world, often without a clear overview of their enemy. The central figure—
along with the spectator who is equally mystified—first must overcome the
general disorientation in the given situation.

In the 1970s a specifically European genre of the "political thriller"
emerged, involving works that used the suspense mechanisms of the commercial cinema to deal with topical issues of the day. We have mentioned in
the context of Schlöndorff's relations to IDHEC the subgenre's most famous
practitioner, Constantin Costa-Gavras. But the genre also found Italian representation in the works of Francesco Rosi (*The Mattei Affair [Il caso Mattei]*, 1972)
and Elio Petri (*Investigation of a Citizen above Suspicion [Indigane su un cittadino
al di sopra di ogni sospetto]*, 1970), who mixed leftist politics with popular filmmaking formats. That Schlöndorff and von Trotta's film became a midseven-
ties box office success should thus come as no surprise, nor should the way it
shares with its French and Italian counterparts a certain stridency and tendency toward caricature.

The thriller film version of *Katharina Blum* must involve the spectator in a
way completely different from that in which Böll's literary original does its
reader. The adaptation replaces Böll's analytical literary plot structure with a
story of suspense. The spectator only gradually discovers the whole person
and full situation of Katharina Blum. Suspense reigns everywhere, from the
police surveillance at the outset of the film to details such as the two car chases
on dark and wet roads or the undercover agent costumed as a sheik. More significant are the many questions that hover over the filmic narrative: How did
Katharina's lover Ludwig escape, and when, where, and how will the police
apprehend him? Will Katharina crack under inspector Beizmenne's pressure?
Will the police trap snap shut when the detectives tap and record the lovers'
telephone conversation? The thriller also repositions the narrative point of
view; it eliminates the omniscient observer-narrator and, simultaneously, the
comfort he affords the Böll reader, in favor of the mystifying, emotionally
exciting cinematic cosmos of crime, detection, and shifting points of view.
Transported intermittently and increasingly into the heroine's mind frame, the
movie spectator shares more immediately Katharina Blum's anxieties and
tremors.

One striking aspect of *Katharina Blum* is the way in which the filmmakers
identify the movie's terrorizers as masculine and its terrorized as feminine. This
is, of course, a major convention of the thriller, that of the threatened woman in
distress who must either be rescued by a man (the case in more classic versions)
or fight back (the case in more modern variants). Schlöndorff and Trotta emphasize Katharina's vulnerability from being a woman in love. They underline

17. *The Lost Honor of Katharina Blum.* The police moving in on the vulnerable domestic (Angela Winkler). Photo: Museum of Modern Art / Film Stills Archive.

sexual politics through a network of militaristic, phallocentric images as well as through a special psychological pattern of aggression and blame. Here we only need to refer the spectator to the sight of the high-rise apartment building immediately before the police phalanx prepares for its invasion of Katharina's flat. In its gigantic phallic shape, it contrasts effectively with the fragility and defenselessness of the woman, Katharina, alone in her intimate domestic space. (See illustration 17.)

Joan and William Magretta first examined (286–87) this pattern of aggression and blame, the recognition of which can help sensitize the spectator to the film's gender politics. The Magrettas noted that *Bild* reporter Tötges continually blames Katharina for things of which he is far more guilty: he calls her a slut, when he himself is sexually unprincipled; he blames Katharina for the death of her mother, when he himself was the source of the mother's fatal stress; he blames Katharina for pursuing men with Porsches, which is exactly the car he drives (286). Similarly, the district attorney and Beizmenne both downgrade Katharina for running around scantily dressed, when it is in fact the police who have stormed her apartment and invaded her privacy. Even in the final "Epilogue," the eulogist defines Tötges as a political victim—echoing the motto on the funeral wreath—when in reality it is he who victimized Katharina.

Certain viewers may object to the film by claiming that the figure of Katharina is overly idealized or that the filmmakers went too far in their victimization of the heroine, as seen in one hyperbolic shot that presents Katharina lost in the vast meadow at Sträubleder's summer home among police cars and armored vehicles. Indeed, much of the negative criticism of *Katharina Blum* has centered around the use of a single protagonist whose essential purpose in the film is to be victimized. Each of the adversaries Katharina encounters becomes a personification of a specific societal force in Germany in the 1970s—police, legal system, church, business, press. Two critics, scholars Petra Schubert-Scheinmann and Jack Zipes, find the filmmakers' approach simplistic and inadequate because goodness and evil are personalized as a single virtuous woman and a multitude of male fascists. By contrast, Wolf Donner in his review takes roughly the same critical approach but turns the argument around, transforming these very objections into the very merits of the film. *Katharina Blum,* according to Donner

> tells a concrete case, quite sensibly, and thoroughly emotionally. This cinematic figure Katharina Blum, a seductive invitation for identification, plausible and touching, a woman who energizes our entire feelings, makes us so concerned because she imparts to us immediately the two depressing truths of her story: first, the same could happen to each of us, with the same brutal logic, leaving us equally as hurt, destroyed, and defenseless; secondly, violence as counter-violence arises in this way, pushed against the wall to this degree, one must defend oneself and has no choice but to turn radical. ("Der lüsterne Meinungsterror" 44)

Like Donner, critic Günther Rühle agrees with such aesthetics in the film, for,

> thus, in private reality, institutional reality, too, becomes visible. This is what makes this movie . . . so significant; it concerns problems of a democratic society whose institutions after all are also supposed to be outward manifestations of humanity. ("Die vier")

Gaze Structures and a Self-Reflexive Media Critique

The Lost Honor of Katharina Blum provides a single point of view through which the audience can see and assess a number of West German institutions. We witness Schlöndorff and von Trotta applying a strategy used repeatedly in their earlier films from the 1970s. In *Ruth Halbfass, A Free Woman,* and *Georgina's Reasons,* elements of a familiar genre or the use of a sympathetic heroine, or both genre and heroine together, work in dialectic with playful underminings of genre expectations and self-referential discourses about the place of art in society. In a similar way, *Katharina Blum,* which could otherwise be mistaken for a "one-dimensional" film, tempers its audience-friendly thriller elements and its appealing heroine with the skillful and systematic use of self-reflexivity.

Schlöndorff and von Trotta introduce two strategies that put *Katharina Blum* beyond the realms of mere entertainment or unthinking political polemic. First, they systematically use gaze structures that create a narrative in which we not only see the world through Katharina's eyes but also get a sense of how that world sees and exploits her. Second, the filmmakers constantly and carefully juxtapose black-and-white with color images, to remind the audience of the extent whereby a media-filtered reality may be the reality that most people experience. Let us consider each of these strategies in more detail.

As a film, *The Lost Honor of Katharina Blum* strongly emphasizes the role of the look in human intercourse. Throughout the film, the looks of others focus on Katharina and those dear to her. The directors make clear their understanding, implicit in countless Hollywood films but brought to the surface here, that to look at another human is to experience power over that other and to be looked at is to be vulnerable. The glances of others can drive Katharina to desperation. For instance, as the heroine is taken to her second interrogation, Frau Pletzer and the policeman temporarily lead her into a closed, bare white room. A woman, probably another renter in Katherina's apartment building, enters and stares at her. Moments later, while the lady is taken away to testify, a male enters the room. Again, Katharina's move toward social intercourse yields nothing but his protracted stare. Her reaction shows that she is visibly shaken; she almost attempts to flee and is prevented from doing so only by opening the door to a room filled with police costuming themselves as carnival revelers. (See illustration 18.)

If others seem to be empowered by their ability to look at Katharina, she herself wants to claim power by looking as well. She insists on reading the hate mail from which her aunt wants to shield her. She assertively requests to view her mother's body as it is being prepared for a funeral. In the scenes of her

18. *The Lost Honor of Katharina Blum.* The victimized woman being overpowered by males at the interrogation. Photo: Museum of Modern Art/Film Stills Archive.

interrogation, the sense of ebb and flow in her power struggle with the police is precisely linked to who is looking and who is being looked at: when Katharina stares at police inspector Beizmenne, she seems to take command. Finally, in talking to Blorna, her employer, about her plans to give an interview to Tötges, she says: "I want to know what such a man looks like." Her will to look embodies her urgent need to fight back.

The next connection in the film's web of looks is apparent in that characters observing Katharina function as stand-ins for the film's spectator. We see this in the scene that immediately follows Katharina's first interrogation at the police headquarters. When she declines to share Beizmenne's lunch, she indicates her preference to be taken to a cell, where she cannot be seen. Escorted there by two police officers, Katharina has to pass through the anteroom, a room with a special function in the scheme of looks that the filmmakers have set up. As Blum passes the glass partition to the anteroom, two observers face the oncoming Katherina, their backs toward the audience. As Blum moves forward, the camera gradually travels closer to the back of a women's head, one of the two anonymous "stand-in" spectators. The woman's gaze and that of the audience gradually align in looking at detainee Blum.

A second scene reinforces this reading. As Katharina leaves the interrogation after Beizmenne's examination of the fifty thousand surplus kilometers on her Volkswagen's gauge, she again passes the anteroom. Again the camera retreats before the oncoming suspect. On the left side of the frame, the back and the turned-away head of the same stand-in of the previous paragraph merge into the frame and are joined by those of another anonymous stand-in spectator. The camera draws back further while Blum moves nearer to the foreground. This particular scene ends with those onlookers already in the room and the spectators in the movie house forming a circle of curious and insistent viewers who stare at the suspect. (See illustration 19.) Similar scenes occur at other points in the film.

As important as the familiar anonymous couple and other human bystanders is another essential ingredient of this gaze scheme—a nonhuman medium, the glass panel, which alters the spectator's perception of Blum. Repeatedly, when Katharina moves to and from her interrogations, she passes a filtering glass partition, a semitransparent wall that borders the anteroom. What the spectator sees, which includes Katharina as she moves past the other side of the glass panel, no longer appears in color but approximates black and white, creating a connection to her objectified representation in the police film. The filmmakers thus give the spectator the opportunity, first as a covoyeur with the stand-in characters, then through the filtering, quasi-photographic interpolation of the glass panel, to perceive Katharina as a degraded object. The spectator's conspiratorial function is implicit as early in the film as during the very first shots when the audience shares the plainclothesman's view through the focal cross hairs of the surveillance camera. Subsequently, the film viewer also "sits in" on the screening of this agent's recording at police headquarters.

In addition to the thriller genre's encouragement of identification with action and heroine, *The Lost Honor of Katharina Blum* offers an alternative invitation for the spectator to contemplate his own conspiracy in the victimization of the young woman. Is the spectator, in this scheme, then only a detached observer or a covictimizer? In seeking an answer to this question, one is reminded of the same question suggested in similar cinematic form about Törless, in Schlöndorff's film of the same name, when he is sitting at the edge of the frame observing Bazini's brutalization by fellow students Reiting and Beineberg. It is characteristic of Schlöndorff to pose complicated relations in such complex visual forms. Like Törless, we can opt out of any responsibility or we can com-

19. *The Lost Honor of Katharina Blum*. The stand-in voyeur couple gazing at the heroine emerging from behind the glass panel. Photo: Deutsches Filmmuseum Fotoarchiv.

mit ourselves to respond actively to the victimization at hand. As in the scene from *Young Törless*, we must remember that in *Katharina Blum* we are confronted not with a purely imaginary scene but a discourse about a specific historical reality concerning the Federal Republic.

The glass panel mentioned above already suggests the intervention of a lens-like medium that allows for the transformation of Katharina Blum, the person, into Katharina Blum, the image that can be misused for propaganda and fear mongering. The film's second self-referential strategy is constantly to underline the disparity between the real Katharina Blum and mediated images of her. Earlier critical studies have observed how this theme is developed through mechanisms that involve patterns of looking and a monochrome-color opposition (Friedman; Head, "Autor"; Schubert-Scheinmann). Schlöndorff and von Trotta use black and white, in particular, to construct a relationship between police and *Bild*. Schubert-Scheinmann, partially basing her argument on an earlier comment by David Head ("Autor" 259), puts forward this view, "for a photograph of Katharina from the *News*, as well as the pictures by the press photographers, and the surveillance films of the police have been photographed in black and white" (171). The modulation between black-and-white and color, as we have shown, establishes visual links between law enforcement and journalistic institutions, each decisive in shaping a person's public image. Although earlier critics have noticed this relation, few have commented on the frequency, mass, and pervasiveness of these links. There are more than a half dozen film-within-the-film sequences. Similarly, more than a dozen black-and-white photos or groups of photos maintain the pattern established decisively in the first half of the film and continued with many further reproductions from the *Bild* paper, including close-ups of Katharina's face used as title-page illustrations.

When joined with the voyeuristic system of looking, the contrast of the two images of Katharina—the positive Katharina in color versus the negative Katharina in black and white—doubly implicates the voyeuristic spectator in the police-justice-press complex. Even more significant is the clash with the established notions of the medium of truth. Schlöndorff and von Trotta signal an inherent contradiction: we have been socialized to equate black and white—regardless of whether in press photos or film-within-the-film—with the documented or documentary truth. Here, however, this medium of authenticity is manifestly associated with distortion and stigmatization.

In this ironic reversal of audience expectations, the film version achieves the same end as Böll in leading the audience toward political commitment. Within the limits of their chosen film genre, the thriller, Schlöndorff and von Trotta set up an irony comparable to that which Böll, in his own literary *Katharina Blum*, generates through the omniscient author figure. Both the novelist and the filmmakers interrupt their narratives to remind us of artistic production and medium. Böll chose to point to sources by means of authorial intrusion. The filmmakers, for their part, expose newspaper, surveillance, and screen images as a discourse by those who determine and view their content. Both novelist and filmmakers label textual elements medium-specifically—whether they be print pages or newspaper or film-within-the-film images—as no more than patterns of or codes about thought, media, and politics, rather than factual reality. In "this specific cinematic means of contrasting and estranging," Schubert-Scheinmann reluctantly acknowledges, "the adaptation . . . undoubtedly established an unambiguous analogy to its literary model" (171). This accomplishment of the medium-specific transformation of Böll's irony to the screen should be fully recognized.

The Lost Honor of Katharina Blum has the reputation of being a conventional, commercial crowd pleaser. In a deeper, more significant way, however, it appears closer to the works of Fassbinder, Reitz, and Kluge than to conventional motion pictures. The important link resides in the film's self-reflexivity and voyeur structures that resemble those employed in Fassbinder's *The Bitter Tears of Petra von Kant* (*Die bitteren Tränen der Petra von Kant*, 1972) and *Ali: Fear Eats the Soul* (*Angst essen Seele auf*, 1973). Fassbinder, with *Petra von Kant's* Marlene and *Ali's* snooping neighbor, similarly evokes and indicts the spectator's voyeuristic fascination with the on-screen events. Both Marlene and Schlöndorff and von Trotta's anonymous surrogate couple perform this function as silent figures. As with Fassbinder, identification in *Katharina Blum* serves more as a means to an end. A viewer, say a feminist-oriented woman, may elect to identify directly with the victimization of the heroine. With their conclusion in the cemetery, however, the filmmakers eliminate potential identification and direct the spectator toward confronting society rather than empathizing with the heroine alone. Schlöndorff and von Trotta could have ended the film with the lovers' prison encounter or with Katharina's arrival at the scene that follows Götten's arrest. Instead, they added the satirical episode of Tötges' burial to direct the spectator's attention to the ongoing collaboration among media, law, and the state, one that disregards individual civil rights. Schlöndorff and von Trotta's study of female victimization is a highly successful film employing an entertainment genre for a serious discussion of the status of women, individual rights, media, and political culture in West Germany. The film's self-reflexive and subversive structures refute critical charges of pure illusionism, one-dimensionality, and neglect of Böll's irony.

Success and Spin-Offs

In *Katharina Blum*, Schlöndorff and von Trotta have provided one of the few influential models in the New German Cinema for publicly accessible political art. The reader may judge from examples of this film's artistic offspring. Among spin-offs from *The Lost Honor of Katharina Blum*, first mention should be made of Margarethe von Trotta's 1976 stage play of the same title (von Trotta; Moeller 6–7). This theatrical dramatization, like the cinematic one, replaces Böll's analytical plot structure with a linear one. Further down the line of general descendants from the film are two musical compositions. After scoring the film, Hans Werner Henze extended his composition into an independent concert suite for orchestra in six movements with the major theme of "Katharina's Klage." In addition, Tilo Medek composed the opera *The Lost Honor of Katharina Blum*, which had a May 1988 premiere at the West German Musiktheater im Revier, Gelsenkirchen ("Opera *Katherina Blum*").

Among the more specifically cinematic descendants that should be mentioned first is more work by von Trotta, Schlöndorff's coscenarist and codirector on the film. Her first directorial project after *Katharina Blum* and at the same time her debut as independent filmmaker was *The Second Awakening of Christa Klages* (1977). That film shares with *Katharina Blum* references to the life and case of Margit Czenki, a Munich child care worker who held up a bank to finance a day care center. The two films have in common the motif of terrorism and a female protagonist. However, in our context, their most significant joint angle may be a formal one, namely the employment of the popular thriller genre to enliven political debate via a publicly accessible movie.

A CBS made-for-television remake, *The Lost Honor of Kathryn Beck* (1984), produced by and starring Marlo Thomas, emphasized the personal over the political. It demonstrated that the effectiveness of the German film depended much on a specific political context and that the presence of Kris Kristofferson as the fleeing terrorist was not enough to make up for this absence of political relevance. One need not fully grasp the self-reflexivity and the medium-within-the-medium structure of *Katharina Blum*, absent in the remake, to appreciate that Marlo Thomas's *Kathryn Beck* is the more illusionistic and consumerist of the two versions.

In comparison with *Kathryn Beck*, Reinhard Hauff's *Knife In the Head* (*Messer im Kopf*, 1978) and *Stammheim* (1986) occupy a different branch of this cinematic family tree. Besides the same production company, Schlöndorff and Hauff's Bioskop, they share with Schlöndorff and von Trotta's *Katharina Blum* chiefly the quality of being publicly accessible movies that address the problem of protest and alternative politics in the context of West German terrorism. The filmmakers of *The Lost Honor of Katharina Blum* had planted a seed for a type of political film that grew into a German film genre about terrorists.

This crop, it appears to us, contradicts Robert Fischer and Joe Hembus's claim regarding *The Lost Honor of Katharina Blum* that "despite the unbelievable success of this movie, its formula found . . . little imitation" (112). On the contrary, it did spin off descendants; it substantiated the epithet of Wolfram Schütte's early review calling the film the "breakthrough" of the West German cinema; and it did lead the way for other West German films that, toward the end of the 1970s and in the 1980s, aimed at overcoming the New German Cinema ghetto of the intellectual film. No matter how difficult the market position of the West German cinema, it turned to a more internationally directed production in the aftermath of *The Lost Honor of Katharina Blum.* This special position in the history of the West German cinema may have induced Peter Cowie's *International Film Guide 1988* to evaluate Schlöndorff and von Trotta's film in a retrospective as one of the ten German best of the period from 1962 to 1987 (189). And Günther Rühle, starting his review of *Katharina Blum* in 1975, was right when he said that it would "lift the long discussion about the German cinema to a new level."

13

Coup de Grâce

Despite its modest claims, Volker Schlöndorff's twelfth film, *Coup de Grâce* (*Der Fangschuss*, 1976), can be considered a jewel among his creations.[1] This film brings the 1920s heritage to life, thanks to quilted jackets, frozen landscapes, impersonal firing squads, uniformed soldiers folk dancing at war-ravaged estates: images, sound, and texture evocative of revolutionary Russia (Grélier 70–71). In addition, actress Valeska Gert, 1920s exponent of avant-garde pantomime, expressionist dance, and women's liberation, graces the screen in one of her final performances. It marks, at the same time, Schlöndorff's return to and recapitulation of his own cinematic methods from *Törless* and *Kombach*. It presents Margarethe von Trotta, here also Schlöndorff's screenwriter, in some of her most convincing scenes as an actress. It carries on the portrayal of rebel women in the line of *A Free Woman* and *Katharina Blum*, though in more spartan visual style. In all its simplicity, this is a key work by a pivotal literary filmmaker of Young and New German cinemas (Cattini 103).

Coup de Grâce places the reader or viewer in conditions of near civil war that raged in the Baltic provinces near Riga in the early twenties, with a confusing array of alliances and coalitions, similar to that of Beirut in the 1980s or the former Yugoslavia in the 1990s. Radical Bolsheviks, Estonian and Latvian nationalists, German Junkers, and White Russians, as well as fortune hunters and volunteer militias, attack each other. One reactionary stronghold is the castle Kratovice, ancestral home of Konrad von Reval (Rüdiger Kirschstein), who returns as an officer and finds his sister Sophie (Margarethe von Trotta). She falls in love with his comrade Erich von Lhomond (Matthias Habich), also a childhood friend. She politically sympathizes with village Bolsheviks, and when Erich does not return her love, she moves to the communist camp. When her troop falls to Erich's unit, Sophie insists that he personally execute her.

This chapter introduces and provides critical exegesis of this less well known Schlöndorff film: how does it relate to its 1939 literary model, *Coup de*

144

Grâce, by French Academy member Marguerite Yourcenar? How does it compare in narrative style and point of view? How does Schlöndorff find cinema-specific means to enact the narrative, express the themes, and parallel the terse elegance of Yourcenar's prose? How does this literary adaptation relate to the previously established motion-picture genres of the war film and the love story? How are the themes of intimacy, love, and sex presented? How does *Coup de Grâce* extend Schlöndorff's earlier 1970s efforts to create a cinema of analytical detachment?

War from a Woman's Point of View

In his study *Marguerite Yourcenar,* Jean Blot outlines "the form of the novel" *Coup de Grâce:* "The hero narrates, and realizes himself through his narration . . . but at the same time he pleads his case and establishes his morals" (129). Erich commands more prominence than Sophie in the novel, if only because he, as narrator, continually reports both events and their implications and pushes himself closer to the reader. In addition, this particular narrator keeps the reader aware, by means of his obvious prejudices, not only that he is speaking but is speaking *pro domo.* Like Nabokov's literary Humbert Humbert in *Lolita,* he enjoys commenting on his report and addressing his audience. One can see the novel as a monologue by Erich, in which the hero-narrator relates past events and his attitudes toward them.

This practice is in keeping with the nature of the novel as a literary genre, as Wolfgang Kayser has observed, in which a narrator by definition "faces the object of his concern . . . as something past" (207). In the literary medium, the reader of *Coup de Grâce* thus encounters the past at a temporal and spatial distance. A film is quite different. André Bazin has observed that photography characteristically documents events in present time. And François Truffaut maintains that film has "nothing in common with those art forms which permit a return to the past as does literature" (qtd. in Kurowski, "Rückblende" 139). Hans Günther Pflaum remarked in an early review of *Coup de Grâce* that although the film presents Erich's memories, it does not have the effect of conjuring up the past. "The narrative stance is not that of a person who remembers but that of an observer who himself is still unsure about which position he should take vis-à-vis these events, who is too close" to them (Pflaum, "Jagdfest"). The immediacy of the film medium shifts emphasis here.

This shift assigns a new significance to the character of Sophie. "Sophie gains an importance which she, as perceived by the narrator, could never have," Alain Garsault states in his review in *Positif* (63). Schlöndorff has, in fact, reconfigured the point of view within the narrative situation: as the material changes from book form to the film medium, Sophie turns into Erich's coprotagonist.

This change proves useful to Schlöndorff's personal set of themes, since instead of an officer and his memories, a woman moves to the forefront along with the conflicts of her emotions, her epoch and environment. She has the courage to admit her feelings, to break with her aristocratic background and finally to join up with the revolutionary Bolsheviks. She tries to take the first step in her relationship with Erich von Lhomond and confesses her love for him. Her powerlessness is in constant juxtaposition to male authority. Men surround her with a hopeless war, force her to do battle with her lover Erich. The masculinized military cosmos denies her femininity, first through rape and finally—and absolutely—through being shot by Erich. The officer, who in accordance with the old order sees himself as Sophie's protector, betrays himself as her executioner. The movie presents a constellation of women's issues.

In the adaptation process, Schlöndorff has set up an unusual narrative structure. On the one hand, he is taking a book that features a male point of view and evokes the genre of the war film, a genre usually characterized by a male point of view. On the other hand, the very shift away from a first-person male narrator represents here a subverting of the war film's unusual masculine perspective. One of the traditional observations about the war-film genre is that it is almost impossible to make a pacifist war film. That is, the very structures of narrative that require the presence of good and evil forces undermine any oppositional stance to the conflict: if both sides are bad, you have no story, but if one side is good, the war becomes justified (Hughes). Schlöndorff provides an unusual solution to this dilemma, making the conflict in his war film not between the two sides in the fighting but between traditional masculine warrior values and their feminine domestic inverse. (See illustration 20.)

Schlöndorff implies that the values involved in the war are not to be given absolute priority. *Coup de Grâce* shares this thematic thrust with other films of the New German Cinema such as *The Trip to Vienna* (*Die Reise nach Wien*, 1973), an almost unrecognized Edgar Reitz and Alexander Kluge collaboration presenting the comic experiences of two wives left behind in the province while their husbands have gone off to the front. Another such antiwar film is Helma Sanders-Brahms's *Germany Pale Mother* (*Deutschland, bleiche Mutter*, 1980). Here, World War II burdens a young woman, who raises a child alone and survives with her infant the hardships of the flight from the eastern provinces. Jointly, these films reexamine twentieth-century war from the perspective of women.

20. *Coup de Grâce.* Sophie von Reval (Margaretha von Trotta) among the military men. Photo: Museum of Modern Art/Film Stills Archive.

An Inverted Love Story

Schlöndorff's *Coup de Grâce* has in common with these New German Cinema films that it is an inverted war film; but it also combines this subgenre with an inverted love story. Schlöndorff's film *Coup de Grâce* develops its love-story narrative in parallel to its war-film narrative. This strategy in itself would not be that unusual, in that it is standard for the Hollywood film to set a narrative of romance against a backdrop of military conflict. In Schlöndorff's case, however, both here and in the later *Circle of Deceit,* the love story becomes a way to explore an array of contradictions involving an individual's personal background and behavior and the broader political implications of that behavior. In *Coup de Grâce,* Sophie's intertwined expectations for meaningful relationships, personal happiness, and sexual fulfillment are at odds with the largely male-created universe of militarism. Schlöndorff creates a world of intimacy without sex, of sex without intimacy, and of both without happiness. In terms of film genre, the movie asks whether the traditionally configured love story can survive if the woman seeks to be the man's equal and strives to propagate values counter to repressive masculine ones.

In *Coup de Grâce*, Schlöndorff employs two stylistic devices, both of which undermine traditional Hollywood practice, and both of which complement the social system of inverted values that he presents in realizing Yourcenar's narrative. First, he has devised a drama in which intensified sound and loudness indicate not importance nor significance but rather the opposite: the most meaningful moments of *Coup de Grâce* are deliberately its most quiet. Second, Schlöndorff reverses usual mechanisms of suspense to dedramatize much of his narrative. These two approaches are related and skillfully subvert the warlike good-bad oppositions of the classical narrative. As we look at the movie's treatment of intimacy, love, and sex, let us do so with an awareness of these unconventional structures. In place of the traditional loudness-equals-meaning equation and the unquestioned good-bad values that allow suspense mechanisms to operate, Schlöndorff uses a complex system of mise-en-scène devices and patterned echo structures or leitmotifs to push the viewer into actively constructing meaning from the presentation rather than passively witnessing it.

Schlöndorff uses careful visual design first to suggest the potential compatibility between Sophie and Erich, then to deny that compatibility in a series of scenes spread throughout the movie and performed with a quiet, close, whispered style of acting. As the two former friends renew their relationship, the camera's position suggests they are potential partners who seek each other's company. In the salon, for example, in the shot from Erich's location where he is seated at the piano, Schlöndorff shows Sophie approaching. Shot and reverse-angle shot reveal Sophie's developing interest and Erich's apparent responsiveness.

Their relation is, however, destabilized by the presence of Sophie's brother Konrad, Erich's soldier friend. On the one hand, Konrad brings Erich and Sophie together. In the scene at the piano, as Erich and Sophie exchange glances, Sophie snuggles up to her brother in a way that suggests a kind of interchangeability between the two men who, as indicated by Yourcenar, look very much alike. On the other hand, the movie eventually reveals that Erich and Konrad have a homosexual relationship. We learn about this, however, only somewhat before Sophie does, and the film in no way exploits a suspense mechanism of "When will she find out?" Rather, the revelation to Sophie of her brother's attachment to Erich is simply one in a series of disappointments that collectively suggest the impossibility of love.

In two scenes early in the film, both of which feature the previously mentioned conspicuous quiet, Sophie becomes seductive toward Erich. In each, she smokes a pipe. In the first scene, which takes place in Erich's office, Sophie forwardly asks him if he has a mistress. Much of the encounter is portrayed through a shot that presents Sophie in profile at the extreme left of the screen with Erich reclining at the extreme bottom right. There is maximum space between them, with an emotional gap emphasized through an empty center composition. Sophie's assertive vertical complements Erich's passive horizontal.

In the second scene, in a glass pavilion, Sophie assumes an almost aggressive role in declaring her love for Erich. His reaction, as unemotional and reserved as Sophie's offer, is to respond as though it were a marriage proposal, indicating his unsuitability and questionable prospects. Schlöndorff organizes this scene into a relatively conventional series of reverse-angle shots, moving in for close-ups only with the very last line of dialogue, of Erich to Sophie, "With you it's always serious." This restraint only plays up the spareness and stillness of the scene.

The film employs a pattern of creating and frustrating erotic tension. Erich periodically encourages Sophie, as when he approaches and distracts her from reading to talk about the dangers of her going into town or, later, when he asks her to walk with him during his patrol duty. In *Coup de Grâce*'s most sensuous scene, Erich and Sophie find themselves in a hunting cabin with their clothing soaking wet from rain. As they dry their clothing by the fire, the combination of close quarters and bare flesh raises expectations of sexual activity in both Sophie and the audience, but Erich again dampens any sparks in the relationship. (See illustration 21.) A similar pattern occurs in a later scene in which the couple begin a fight prompted by Sophie's carelessness in maintaining a nighttime blackout. The conflict and division between the two find an objective correlative in the airplane outside that threatens to bomb the estate. Sophie accuses Erich of being afraid to die, at which point he pulls her up and takes her out on the balcony, their lit lamp making them a sitting target. When a bomb hits the stables nearby, they rush back into safety, embrace, and then fall to the floor to begin lovemaking. Quickly, however, Erich changes his mind and storms off. Here, Schlöndorff uses raised voices and noises of war to suggest negative, destructive human relations. Erich seems to have acted only because Sophie dared him to, not out of sincere feeling.

Perhaps the most striking encounter between the pair occurs near the end of the film when Sophie goes to Erich's room and once more declares her love for him in a barely audible whisper. He talks to her through the door and asks her to wait until after he returns from a military operation. The door separating the two partners in this sequence of three reverse-angle shots reveals their

21. *Coup de Grâce*. A seduction scene between Sophie and Erich von Lhomond. Photo: Museum of Modern Art/Film Stills Archive.

isolation and imprisoned feelings. Schlöndorff sets up the scene clearly to evoke a Roman Catholic confessional. Only at the conclusion of this scene do we see Konrad sleeping in the bed near Erich, the movie's first conclusive evidence of their sexual bonding. The scene is constructed for surprise rather than suspense.

Such scenes of frustrated desire set *Coup de Grâce* apart from contemporary love stories and films. It stands in unusual opposition to post-1960s Hollywood conventions of sexual freedom; the pair's frustrated intimacy is heightened even more when offset by Sophie's sexual episodes with soldiers. Sophie is open, while Erich, to conceal his tenuous hold on reality, clings to orthodox formalities and appearances. She is self-disclosing, Erich evasive and even duplicitous. Schlöndorff tantalizingly conceals Erich's motivations (in a situation that involves the gender-inverse of Georgina's concealed reasons in Schlöndorff's film of the previous year). We are never sure whether his feelings for the contessa are sexual, fraternal, or controllingly paternalistic. This ambiguity throws audience identification all the more onto the side of Sophie. Unfulfilled desire and the complex relationship of the protagonists in *Coup de Grâce* characterize both the inverted love story and, thereby, the specific quality of the film.

When Schlöndorff postpones revealing conclusively Erich and Konrad's homosexuality, he wisely steers the narrative away from being a mere love triangle. Instead, Schlöndorff's handling of the relationship parallels the open-ended, elliptical, and indirect narrative approach of the novel but proceeds through formally different and highly visual allusions and leitmotifs. On Christmas morning, Konrad clambers up a castle garden tree to pick mistletoe. In an earlier scene, Erich and Konrad had been roughhousing in the snow under the same tree. Now Erich quickly rushes to the tree and improvises a ladder from a garden table and chair to help his friend down. This scene clearly harks back to another early scene in which Sophie stands on a ladder to decorate the topmost branches of a Christmas tree. Among those in the room was her current lover Volkmar von Plessen (Mathieu Carrière), who rushed to help her down. The symmetry of the two scenes suggests that Erich's relation to Konrad is like that of Volkmar to Sophie.

Another leitmotif, an additional index of the film's indirect narrative technique, draws attention to political aspects. It cinematically establishes a close link between the contessa and a captured rebel. The latter is not present in Yourcenar's novel and thus becomes a cinema-specific addition that multiplies meanings through visual echoes and parallels. Both are not only interrogated by Erich but are asked expressly, in a way that may suggest Schlöndorff's German point of view, whether they have relatives living in Germany. Although both are of German extraction, they join Bolsheviks and wear the characteristic quilted jackets. For both, the last cigarette symbolizes giving themselves to death with inner composure. Both are executed according to martial laws. Understood in a broader sense, the film actually offers two "coups de grâce." In both cases, the business of the execution is cold and efficient; the executioners have little time. Nor does the camera allow the viewer much chance to sympathize, because both "coups de grâce" are photographed from a distance. Both times, executioners shamelessly leave corpses behind, like piles of trash. Variations on the theme of death (the killing of the Darmstadt rebel; Franz's dying; Sophie's losing her dog Texas, risking typhoid at bedsides of dead soldiers, and narrowly escaping during an air raid) culminate in Sophie's own execution. At the same time, one minor detail during Sophie's execution creates a troubling image. Throughout the early part of the film, Sophie has worn her bobbed hair with conspicuous bangs. At the time of her execution, however, her hair is combed to one side, in a way that echoes Erich's similar hairstyle. The metaphoric result is a suggestion that Erich is somehow killing part of himself.

Issues of Realism

Such characteristically delicate touches caused a number of critics to comment on how different *Coup de Grâce* was from its immediate predecessor, *Katharina Blum*. They have noted the more reserved, artistically quieter approach of the former, as compared to the emotional charge of *Katharina Blum* (Canby, *"Coup"* C15; Jeremias). Among more scholarly observers, however, the reception was in many respects similar. Timothy Corrigan's extensive analysis in *New German Film* takes the position that *Coup de Grâce* fundamentally conforms to the requirements of commercial realist narrative. Implicitly, Corrigan positions the work as inferior to films by Fassbinder and Syberberg that are more directly subversive. As with much of the reception of *Katharina Blum*, Corrigan's analysis misses many of the ways in which Schlöndorff provokes activated viewing and audience reflection on what it is watching.

In response to Corrigan, we argue that Schlöndorff assembles an array of alienating strategies that operate subtly and scrape against the grain of a superficially realist narrative. We have already established how *Coup de Grâce* inverts both war-film and love-story conventions, as well as traditional structures of suspense and dramatic emphasis. We have also analyzed shots and scenes in which gender role reversals between Erich and Sophie raise issues of sexual politics. In addition, as numerous critics have noted, the movie's narrative contains many gaps and ellipses, as well as many places where, with characterization developed only through externalized behavior, motivation is implicit or ambiguous; all of these require an alert viewer to fill in what is missing (Jaeggi). Although Schlöndorff is careful to maintain period consistency, he nonetheless has created a narrative that an intelligent viewer cannot help but relate to events that followed: Erich clearly becomes a fascist prototype, just as Sophie embodies a privileged woman, not unlike an Ulrike Meinhof, who rebels against and challenges a repressive system. Rather than draw us closer to Erich, his voice-over commentary only makes him less sympathetic to us. The title card at the film's conclusion, after Schlöndorff shows us Sophie's collapsed corpse, laconically reports Erich's final comment from the presumed vantage point of years later: "One is always caught in a trap with such women." The character of Grigori's mother, the seamstress-midwife, presents further irony in her constant treatment of Sophie in a deferential, caste-based manner that runs completely counter to the class warfare in which she is involved. A comparable contradiction can be seen in Grigori's gift to Sophie of a book of Georg Trakl's poems inscribed with the words "Always follow the voice of your heart." The dedication, which is nowhere found in Yourcenar, can only force the attentive spectator to question the narrative's constant tensions between the personal and the political.

In addition, Schlöndorff incorporated into *Coup de Grâce* results of research into the place and period, such as the notice that all citizens were required, under pain of death, to report Bolsheviks to authorities. Schlöndorff strove for a tension between his documentary and fictional elements:

> I find it fascinating when completely documentary scenes or moments occur in a purely fictional story with the quality of a chamber drama that could take place in a closed space, perhaps even in the theater. Then a particular tension arises, similar to when one suddenly places among extremely professional actors a non-professional, and the thing assumes a new dimension, whereby the viewer can become more strongly conscious that the film is a fiction behind which real history is hiding. (Schlöndorff and von Trotta, "Melville" 58)

In all of these examples, we perceive small applications of Brechtian theory but, as is typical with Schlöndorff, more in the areas of structure, characterization, and narrative inflection than in obvious areas of mise-en-scène. As with *Katharina Blum*, they are easily overlooked.

Because of its Brechtian bent and Sophie's character, the screen version of *Coup de Grâce* stands between profeminist films by male filmmakers of the seventies, such as Schlöndorff's own *A Free Woman*, Alexander Kluge's *Part-Time Work of a Domestic Slave* (*Gelegenheitsarbeit einer Sklavin*, 1975), and Rainer Werner Fassbinder's *Effi Briest* (*Fontane Effi Briest*, 1974), and feminist films, such as Jutta Brückner's *A Totally Depraved Girl* (*Ein ganz und gar verwahrlostes Mädchen*, 1976) and von Trotta's *The Second Awakening of Christa Klages*. All are political films in an extended sense.

In her introduction to the *Coup de Grâce* novel, Marguerite Yourcenar insists that her intentions were not to side with any political group or party but rather to present a "study in character and emotion." Schlöndorff achieves something different. Although it is clear that his political sympathies are not anti-Bolshevik, he never establishes whether his drama should be interpreted personally or politically and so challenges the viewer to resolve the tension between the two. Indeed, as with his earlier *Michael Kohlhaas* and his later war film, *Circle of Deceit*, Schlöndorff was attacked by German critics on both the left (Jansen) and the right (Deschner). At the same time, it is clear that conflicts between the sexes, women's themes, rebellion, and politics, as well as German history, offer points of contact between Schlöndorff's film and Yourcenar's novel. What is most remarkable in Schlöndorff's adaptation is the way in which, despite changes in structure and point of view, the two works remain strikingly aligned in mood, meaning, and final effect. Each shows an elegant crafting of its respective medium and a certain formal precision, and yet neither indulges in stylistic excess for its own sake. To the film's admirers, *Coup de Grâce* brings Schlöndorff back to the qualities that first made him successful, exhibiting "effortlessly," as Hans Günther Pflaum wrote, "the stylistic economy" of *Young Törless* ("Jagdfest").

Part Three

THE INTERNATIONAL SCHLÖNDORFF

14

A German Consciousness for an International Audience

With the production of *The Tin Drum* (1978–79), Volker Schlöndorff moved into a new phase of his career, a third period in his work that we call his international period. This period comprised two other major features, *Circle of Deceit* (1981) and *Swann in Love* (1983), as well as documentaries and contributions to omnibus films. Schlöndorff's feature work during this period grew out of far more international production structures than before, was somewhat more stylistically conservative than much of the preceding efforts, and involved a move away from the earlier films' feminism and confrontational activism. Although the three features still have critical elements to them, much of Schlöndorff's oppositional energy shifted to the small-scale, less mainstream films. With this period, Schlöndorff began to work increasingly for the opera, and although we do not examine in depth the director's output in live theater and opera, we consider it in the context of his film production.

Schlöndorff's new international status had much to do with both the more restrictive film production situation beginning to unfold within the Federal Republic and the positive reputation of the New German Cinema by the end of the 1970s. We have discussed earlier the dependency on state and public television funding that the New German Cinema had developed. With the emergence of a more conservative political climate in the wake of the fall 1977 climax to the terrorist crisis, institutional subsidy of alternative filmmaking became far less reliable. Of equal or even greater importance was the near desperate situation of German film exhibitors. The number of filmgoers in West Germany had steadily declined from 320 million persons in 1965 to 128 million in 1975 and to 104 million in 1985. "The hardest hit were Germany's small movie entrepreneurs who do culturally ambitious programming . . . and, what is more, relate strongly to the German film" ("Jetzt hilft" 233). This economic situation was leading to the decline of the *Programmkino* as an institution that could be relied upon to bring adventurous German moviemaking to a domestic audience.

On the bright side, West German film producers were to see foreign business triple between 1979 and 1981, amounting then to nearly 62 percent of total turnover (Deutsches Institut 91). Clearly, the future of the New German Cinema lay in the international market. This change was due largely to the international prestige and box office clout generated in the late 1970s by works like Herzog's *Stroszek* (1977), Wenders's *The American Friend* (*Der amerikanische Freund,* 1977), and Fassbinder's *The Marriage of Maria Braun* (*Die Ehe der Maria Braun,* 1978). Schlöndorff himself was quite aware of this situation, which he saw in 1980 as comparable to that of the Weimar period: "At that time, as today, the German cinema could only survive through exportation" ("Der Wille" 248).

The first step in this process of internationalization would be the shooting of works in English, which occurred with Fassbinder's *Despair* (1977), Herzog's *Nosferatu* (1978), Wenders's *The State of Things* (1982), and Peter Lilienthal's *Dear Mr. Wonderful* (1981–82). In other cases at this time, German filmmakers have even shot in Portuguese (Lilienthal's *The Autograph* [*Das Autogramm*], 1983–84) and the Philippine native language, Tagalog (Werner Schroeter's *The Laughing Star* [*Der lachende Stern*], 1983), in order to continue working. Perhaps because *The Tin Drum* was both Schlöndorff's most successful film to date and one of his most distinctively German, Schlöndorff lagged behind these colleagues in making the transition to English. One can, however, understand through this inhospitable domestic context why he might choose to shoot his next fiction feature in Beirut and to follow that with a French-language *Swann in Love.*

This international production context is distinctly echoed in the films themselves. To an extent not seen in Schlöndorff's earlier work, cities take on a symbolic function, starting with *The Tin Drum.* The cosmopolitan and metropolitan emphasis grew noticeably between *The Tin Drum* and *Swann in Love* at the expense of what is regional and ethnic. Matzerath's Danzig embodies, besides the site of the historic German-Polish conflict, the locale of Kashubians, shop owners and petite bourgeoisie. In contrast, Swann's much more homogeneous Paris can claim—as Schlöndorff remarks in his production notes—to be "the essence of all cities" ("Notes on Making" 3). In all three films, the relationship between setting and central role can be described in the terms used by the filmmaker for *Circle of Deceit:* "The leading role in the film besides Laschen is the city of Beirut. . . . In my film there is correspondence between the setting and the character" ("Oskar Matzerath im" 12).

The progressively increasing familiarity of the cities used as settings goes with a tendency toward cultural mediation, often in the sense of an "international reconciliation." *The Tin Drum* mediates between Poles and Germans, *Circle of Deceit* between Germans and the residents of Beirut in particular and citizens of the Third World in general; *Swann in Love* mediates between French high culture, especially its higher literature, and interested parties internationally.

A Male Point of View

In contrast to this sense of intercultural mediation, we see Schlöndorff continue his exploration of the theme of the mismatched couple who cannot communicate. Although this narrative motif is relegated to minor characters in *The Tin Drum*, it comes to the fore in both *Circle* and *Swann*. In these two works, we see rather passive men in love with independent women. Indeed, these men are victimized by them, and one cannot help but be struck by the shift in Schlöndorff's sensibility from a feminist bias to a more male-centered consciousness.

One can speculate here about whether this reorientation may be a result of the filmmaker's increasing professional separation from his wife. It may also have to do with the blossoming of the West German women's film movement in the late 1970s: with women filmmakers finally able to speak for themselves and other women, there was perhaps no longer need for Schlöndorff to be their advocate. In any event, all three features from this period center around male protagonists who, unlike the heros of *Georgina's Reasons* and *Coup de Grâce*, are not in struggle with their female counterparts to provide for the audience's point of view.

Indeed, all three works are drawn from fictional sources that emphasize the extreme subjectivity of a male narrator or author. For all, Schlöndorff has created first-person narratives in which he has set up for himself the challenge of converting fictions centered around thoughts, memories, and emotions to an entertainment medium that conventionally emphasizes action and physical conflict. Schlöndorff renders these stories cinematic by emphasizing the voyeuristic qualities of his heros. They are always looking and observing, and derive sexual and ego-enhancing pleasure from doing so.

With this new emphasis on subjectivity comes something of a loss of the political partiality in Schlöndorff's earlier work. These new heros are not political rebels seeking social change. Even the high-spirited Oskar Matzerath does not qualify as an activist, and he is a grotesque figure, meant as much to be read as a metaphor or symbol than as a real character. Georg Laschen is a journalist whose job is to report on what he sees, not to change it. And Swann is merely solipsistic, a figure of bourgeois decadence. Yet all are also sympathetic characters who thereby position the audience's point of view.

As a result, some observers have seen in these movies a retreat from Schlöndorff's previous political engagement. If so, that retreat is hardly total, for *The Tin Drum* surely addresses political and cultural issues surrounding fascism, *Circle of Deceit* raises major questions about journalistic ethics and responsibility, and *Swann in Love* contextualizes Proust's narrative with observations about class and sexual politics. In terms of form, none of these three films follows up in any systematic way on the Brechtian strategies of Schlöndorff's previous period. At best, all three movies offer elements of self-reflexivity, use episodic structures, and draw political analysis through typed minor characters. But Schlöndorff holds back somewhat from the conscious mixing of political content with alienating form.

If one is to look for confrontational activism and radical form during this period, one will find it more easily in *Germany in Autumn*'s (1978) analysis of the aftermath of terrorism, *The Candidate*'s (1980) acid portrait of right-wing Bavarian politician Franz Josef Strauss, and *War and Peace*'s (1983) pessimistic observation of militarism. Made without state or television subsidies, these films represent attempts by the new German filmmakers to intervene in significant issues of the time. All are collective efforts, and Schlöndorff's contributions to them are varied. Related to this documentary and agitprop work but far less directly political is Schlöndorff's documentary study *Just For Fun, Just For Play—Kaleidoscope Valeska Gert* (1979).

This third period in Schlöndorff's filmmaking career represents a bifurcation into an even more issue-specific activism than ever before and the simultaneous establishment of himself as a specialist in adapting to cinema what might be considered unfilmable texts. This latter literary side connects to the economic issues discussed above. To increasingly skeptical and politically and socially cautious subsidy boards, a recognized literary source becomes protection against accusations of bad decision making. In commercial terms, Schlöndorff's projects increasingly become Hollywood-style packages in which a literary property or topical tie-in to the Lebanon war provides for immediate audience recognition, a set of bankable stars contributes to box office potential, and a brand-name director becomes the ribbon that ties it together. Schlöndorff's detractors would argue that this new positioning makes for the worst of both worlds, with the result being a cinema that has neither the energy and vitality of popular culture nor the intellectual depth and challenging structures of important alternative art.

Our position in the pages that follow is far kinder. It is probably simplistic to see this new direction in Schlöndorff's work simply as opportunistic and compromising. One may admire Schlöndorff's more aggressively radical works without necessarily taking as insincere or totally reactionary his attempts to extend more conventional cultural traditions. Indeed, part of the pleasure of a film like *Swann in Love* is its ability to embrace very real contradictions about society and aesthetics. The films deserve to be judged on their individual merits, not on the production system out from they arise.

Work for the Opera

Schlöndorff's ambivalence about the traditional arts shows up in somewhat different form in his acceptance of directorial assignments for the opera. Schlöndorff's involvement with opera begins somewhat prior to this period, in 1974, with his staging of Leoš Janáček's *Katia Kabanova* for the Frankfurt/Main Opera, and has continued into the 1990s for a total of seven productions. Despite this overlap of periods, let us here briefly consider Schlöndorff's opera career, for it can perhaps throw some light on the director's attempts to work within established institutions in positive and progressive ways.

Schlöndorff's involvement with opera has exemplified a pattern also exhibited by several of his colleagues in the New German Cinema, such as Werner Herzog and Werner Schroeter. Because the opera is an institution so central to German culture, it should not be surprising that so many German filmmakers should both work in the medium and use it as a subject for film, as in, for example, Werner Schroeter's portrayal of and shorts about Maria Callas (1968), his *Eika Katappa* (1969) and *The Death of Maria Malibran* (*Der Tod der Maria Malibran*, 1971), Jean Marie Straub and Danièle Huillet's *Moses and Aaron* (1975), Werner Herzog's *Fitzcarraldo* (1981), Hans Jürgen Syberberg's *Parsifal* (1982), and Alexander Kluge's *The Power of Emotions* (*Die Macht der Gefühle*, 1983). We have already discussed Schlöndorff's ambivalent presentation of the opera-loving industrialist in *The Morals of Ruth Halbfass*.

The appeal of creative activity with the opera would have several aspects. Schlöndorff himself has commented on the pleasure of working within the well-subsidized system of European opera companies ("Der Filmregisseur"). Particularly after the decline of state film subsidies during the Kohl era, to enjoy the significant resources of German and French opera houses became, according to Schlöndorff, a chance to recharge his creative batteries ("Avec l'opéra"). In addition, opera for Schlöndorff "has to do with child-like fantasy" (Methner).

The operas Schlöndorff has committed to have tended to be twentieth-century works, although he has directed Henry Purcell's *Dido and Aeneas* (1981, Montepulciano, Italy) and Giacomo Puccini's *La Bohème* (1984, Frankfurt). His second effort at twentieth-century opera renewed his collaboration with both Hans Werner Henze and Edward Bond, who wrote the music and libretto, respectively, for *We Come to the River,* which Schlöndorff directed in Berlin in 1976. That same year, he was involved with Matthieu Carrière in presenting Thomas Jahn's *Zoopalast* (Montepulciano, Italy), a production broadcast on television as *Der zoologische Palast* in 1978. He returned to Janáček once again with the version of *From the House of the Dead* staged for the Paris Opéra Comique in March of 1988. Dimitri Shostakovich's *Lady Macbeth of Mitsensk* is a similar modernist creation that Schlöndorff put on stage for the reopening of the renovated Bavarian State Opera in Munich in 1993. Clearly, Schlöndorff has favored challenging, unusual works, not mere fodder for mindless fans. He has also indicated a rejection of the Wagnerian tradition with its "enclosed universe" ("Avec l'opera" 87).

The Henze, Janáček, and Shostakovich works are grim, serious operas that emphasize collective oppression. In the case of both *Katia Kabanova* and *Lady Macbeth of Mitsensk* we also find protofeminist heroines, the latter of whom is, like Katharina Blum or Kate in *The Handmaid's Tale,* willing to kill to escape her oppression. As Shostakovich himself has said of his female protagonist, "her crimes are an expression of protest against that form of societal existence in which she lives, against the sinister and choking atmosphere of the world of merchants during the previous century" (Schostakowitsch 39). These modernist operas are thematically of a piece with Schlöndorff's film work.

By contrast, Schlöndorff's choice of *La Bohème* at first seems out of place. The director himself, however, has admitted to the difficulty of staging Puccini without cheap sentimentality and saw it as his challenge to get to the authentic emotion in the work ("Notes on Making" 3). As a device to focus on *La Bohème*'s emotions, Schlöndorff devised a staging that involved the creation of a second framing rectangle within the proscenium stage, a visual strategy immediately evocative of the cinema. Critics have found other filmlike aspects of Schlöndorff's opera stagings. The visual look of both his *La Bohème* and *From the House of the Dead* has been compared to that of a black-and-white film (Engelhard; Beuth). The elaborate stagecraft of *Lady Macbeth* involved the use of scrims and multilevel playing areas to allow for presentation on stage of simultaneous actions and fluid movielike transitions. In keeping with Schlöndorff's Brecht-influenced side, however, we see a counterbalancing of operatic emotion with devices that produce detachment. In the last act of *Lady Macbeth,* for example, Schlöndorff uses a low-lit, darkened stage, which he pierces with a roving spotlight that calls to mind both a prison searchlight and a hand-held camera.

Critical reception of Schlöndorff's opera activity has been mixed, and some traditionalists have been upset with his attempts at innovation. Reviews have been most positive for *Katia Kabanova* and, particularly, *La Bohème*. The mix of opinion is not surprising, for we can see in Schlöndorff's opera work the same synthesis of contradictions that characterizes his work in film. On the one hand, he has worked within a cultural system of the establishment. On the other, he has gravitated toward substantive, often noncommercial work that challenges the cultural clichés of virtuoso divas, vocally acrobatic arias, and knee-jerk emotional responses. He seems to be striving in the operas, as in his films, for both an appealing, dreamlike world and analytical objects of cultural reflection.

As we look at Schlöndorff's third period, let us bear in mind this bipolar pull in his work between working with the establishment and rebelling against it.

15

The Tin Drum

The Tin Drum (*Die Blechtrommel,* 1979) holds a key place in Volker Schlöndorff's career. As a multiple prizewinner, *The Tin Drum* represents, along with Rainer Werner Fassbinder's *The Marriage of Maria Braun* (1978), the apotheosis of critical, popular, and commercial success of the New German Cinema. This adaptation of Günter Grass's 1959 international best-seller of the same title was Schlöndorff's first foray since *Michael Kohlhaas* into comparatively high-budget, international filmmaking. It cemented Schlöndorff's reputation as a director who could successfully bring to the screen works of great literature that would ordinarily be considered "unfilmable."

A sure-footed, intense cinematic adaptation of a literary masterwork, Schlöndorff's *The Tin Drum* is a political statement for its time. In examining the film, we will consider both its rhetorical and poetic strategies. On the rhetorical level, both the original novel and the film are direct attempts to bring about a reconciliation of Polish-German tensions that emerged with World War II. Both analyze fascism and its relation to class issues. On the poetic level, the central, freakish character of Oskar Matzerath is a metaphoric figure whose meaning in both novel and film constantly shifts as the narrative progresses. In adapting Grass's novel to the screen, Schlöndorff finds cinema-specific ways to express Grass's ideas, feelings, and attitudes, all of which the novelist had articulated through words alone. Schlöndorff presents differing points of view; renders grotesque the novel's main character; allusively cites other movies, literary genres, and cultural points of reference; and employs cinematic leitmotifs that both echo and elaborate on the literary motifs in the novel. Finally, we consider Schlöndorff's filmic reworking of *The Tin Drum* as an updating to the 1970s, one that extends forward Grass's critique of the 1950s generation to include a parallel appraisal of the disenchanted post-1968 generation.

Let us first, however, summarize the narrative strands of Schlöndorff's Central European epic. *The Tin Drum* is a story as highly specific to the East

European city of Gdansk and its region as it is to the three ethnic groups who lived there into the first half of the twentieth century: the Poles, the Germans, and the Kashubians. An older, smaller, mostly rural and somewhat oppressed Wendish-Slavic population, the Kashubians are considered indigenous to the area. The screen *Tin Drum* begins and ends with powerful images of a mythic Kashubia. Seated by a fire in a potato field, hefty Anna Bronski (Tina Engel) is resting from harvest work as a little man comes running toward her across the fields, imploring her to provide a hiding place; her wide skirts are the only refuge. (See illustration 22.) While the two policemen in pursuit interrogate the peasant woman, Joseph Koljaiczek impregnates her with a daughter, Agnes Koljaiczek. As a nurses' aid, Agnes (Angela Winkler) in the post–World War I years takes a liking to both wounded German soldier Alfred Matzerath (Mario Adorf) from the Rhineland and Jan Bronski (Daniel Olbrychski), her cousin. She marries Matzerath but continues seeing Bronski, and either one of these two may have fathered Oskar Matzerath in 1924.

At a party to celebrate his third birthday, Oskar (David Bennent) elects to "drop out" of the human world in general and this parental triangle in particular. He engineers a fall down the cellar staircase that stunts his growth. In the body of a three-year-old, forever hammering on his tin drum, he experiences the 1930s and 1940s, that is, the Nazi era. The dwarf not only possesses the intellect of an adult but also a high-pitched voice that enables him to shatter glass. Escaping from the shop of Jewish toy dealer Markus (Charles Aznavour), the ever-friendly replacer of the dwarf's used-up instrument, Oskar locates the hourly-rate hotel where his mother Agnes and Jan Bronski enjoy their regular Thursday encounter. He climbs to the nearby bell tower and, facing the lovers' meeting place and the city theater, raises his voice, causing a cascade of bursting window panes.

Visiting a circus, he is attracted to lilliputian Bebra, who, after Oskar's demonstration of his vocal talents, extends to him an invitation to join his act. During their conversation, Bebra issues to him a warning that he had better become an actor rather than remain a spectator in an upcoming era of political rallies and an ideology that will preach the downfall of the likes of them. Soon Oskar not only witnesses a gathering of the newly enthroned Nazi party but also, from under the grandstand, employs the magic of his drum to totally confuse the flashy brass-filled Hitler Youth band, leading them rhythmically into a three-quarter tact that drives Hitler Youth girls and brownshirts to waltz until a cloudburst ends the entire event.

Good Friday 1938 finds Oskar's mother, Bronski, Matzerath, and the tin drummer wandering along the beach of the Baltic Sea. At a breakwater they

22. *The Tin Drum.* Oskar's grandmother hiding his grandfather-to-be from the police under her mythical skirts. Photo: Volker Schlöndorff.

chance on an angler who employs a horse's head to fish for eels. Subsequently, Oskar's mother starts stuffing herself with any and all fish until she suddenly passes away. Toy dealer Markus kills himself during the 1938 Crystal Night pogroms. Bronski also loses his life, a victim of the German attack on Danzig/Gdansk's old Polish post office. Maria (Katharina Thalbach), a Kashubian girl from the countryside, starts helping with Matzerath's retail store and with Oskar. He "courts" her by pouring fizz powder into her hand and activating it with his saliva, and even crawls into her bed. An unspecified coupling within the new triangle of Matzerath, Oskar, and Maria generates Oskar's brother Kurt.

Oskar joins Bebra's lilliputian troupe, entertaining the German military at the Normandy fortifications. He falls in love with colleague Roswitha but loses her during an artillery bombardment. Returning home at the end of the war, he finds Russian troops occupying his home and sees them shoot his father. He blames himself for the death. At his father's graveside, Oskar resolves to grow up beyond the body of a three-year-old. Maria, Kurt, and Oskar begin their trip to the west of Germany on a freight train that passes a potato field where an old Kashubian peasant woman in her traditional black dress with wide skirts is busy fanning the fire. Schlöndorff ends his narrative much earlier than Grass does, and we discuss later the political and aesthetic effects of this dropping of Grass's book III, or about a third of the novel.[1] Schlöndorff at some time considered directing a sequel, but the project was never realized ("Schlöndorff, Herzog" 26; Thomas 6).

Toward a Reconciliation of Poles and Germans

The novel and film are thus about Polish-German relations and the dramatic shifts that have occurred in how the two peoples have regarded one another, with the book in particular representing a direct and successful attempt at cultural intervention to correct wrongs of the past. A century and a half ago, democratic Germans, like dramatist Georg Büchner, respected Poles as dauntless freedom fighters (Storznowski 7). Yet the nineteenth century witnessed a profound alienation between the two peoples, one further deepened by Hitler's invasion of 1939, subsequent "Germanization" policies, and the atrocities of the SS during World War II. In the years immediately after the war, Germans resented the loss of eastern territories, including the port city of Danzig/Gdansk, and blamed Poles for the sufferings of Germans displaced from East Prussia and Poland. The result was hostility in both directions. The Allied Agreements of the 1945 Potsdam Conference acknowledged the new Polish state; her borders with Germany, however, were left to be resolved in a future peace treaty with Germany. The GDR, or East German Democratic Republic, soon after its creation recognized the new Polish state in the Warsaw Declaration of June 1950. But not until after the superpowers' policy of detente in the 1960s and the 1969 changeover to the social-liberal coalition in the Bonn government did a West German reorientation take effect. This *Ostpolitik*, a new policy toward the East Block that put greater emphasis on negotiation and conciliation, recognized de facto—though not without certain legalistic reservations—the new post–World War II German-Polish border. On this basis diplomatic relations were finally established in September 1972.

Grass's 1959 novel was one of the forces behind this political revision of West German opinion. As Freimut Duve states in his article "Moral des Friedens" ("The Ethical Lesson of Peace"), "The *Ostpolitik* of Willy Brandt was a large and liberating step forward to which Germany's intellectuals from Günter Grass to Karl Steinbuch contributed. It was not an accomplishment of the staff of the Foreign Office alone" (5). Grass published *The Tin Drum* novel in 1959, midway between 1956 and 1962, a time when those West Germans opposed to relinquishing the claims to the eastern provinces now under Polish rule fell from 73 percent to 50 percent, that is, by nearly a fourth (Kellermann 208). In what way can the novel *The Tin Drum* be seen as contributing to reconciliation of the Germans with their Polish neighbors, and to what extent does Schlöndorff continue this process?

As political discourse, these works of art deal with German-Polish relations in a fresh, frank, and enlightened manner. The very setting of the first two-thirds of the novel has an impact of its own, because it centers on the long-disputed Eastern ex-territories of Germany, specifically in Danzig. With the reading and watching of *The Tin Drum*, the German spectator is involved in a final celebration of the Danzig region and its people, one that rekindles memory, stimulates grief, and provides a final catharsis. In the film as in the book, episodes like the battle for the Polish Post Office in Danzig and the occupation in 1945 of this Baltic port city by Soviet forces stand squarely in the foreground. Grass and Schlöndorff here give testimony to a regional culture and mourn its loss.

Against this ethnically mixed backdrop, Polish, German, and Kashubian characters are forced to choose either the Polish or the German side, and Schlöndorff periodically uses Grass's words from the novel to establish these relations. A glance at what the literary and cinematic Oskar calls "the trinity that brought me, Oskar, into the world" can help clarify the political thrust of *The Tin Drum*. Grouped with Oskar's Kashubian mother, Agnes, are Jan Bronski, her relative who sides with the Poles, and Alfred Matzerath, a German

Rhinelander. In the aftermath of World War I, Matzerath wants to deemphasize all political distinctions in the city he has chosen for a new beginning after his war injury. Turning to Bronski, he assures him: "Germans, Poles, Kashubians, we all live together in peace." The old divisions and tensions, nevertheless, reappear within a decade or so. Matzerath, after joining Hitler's storm troopers, the SA, criticizes Bronski for subscribing to a Polish newspaper and indirectly attacks his position at the Polish Postal Service. His in-law steadfastly replies: "I am a Pole." Even the toy shop owner, Markus, urges Oskar's mother to avoid contact with her cousin, Bronski, because "he's in the Polish Post Office. He's with the Poles, that's no good. Don't bet on the Poles." Bronski's death during the taking of Danzig by the Germans in September 1939 tragically proves Markus right. Both novel and film make the Agnes-Bronski-Matzerath triangle a metaphor for both the three ethnic groups' cohabitation and subsequent conflicts. And both novel and film see beyond the conflict between the individual Pole and German: as we shall see, reconciliation is, if not the little tin drummer's tune, then at least the novelist's and filmmaker's.

It is clear that Schlöndorff, through his principles of visualization, selection, and composition, wishes to emphasize the political relationship among the Poles, Germans, and Kashubians, as well as the reconciliatory tendency of *The Tin Drum*. First, the filmmaker emphasizes the triad of Kashubian (Agnes Matzerath, born Koljaiczek), German (Alfred Matzerath), and Pole (Jan Bronski) in his mise-en-scène. When, in the film rendition of Oskar's birth, the infant first perceives his mother, Bronski, and Matzerath, Schlöndorff's composition forms a spatial triangle. This triangle becomes a visual leitmotif, most markedly at Oskar's first "vitricidal" act, as he shatters the glass of the grandfather clock. Schlöndorff clearly appreciates, moreover, how Grass used the number three to configure *The Tin Drum*'s political and ethnic mix in a tightly integrated formal, magic organization. Oskar fixates on the same number: on his third birthday, he turns into a permanent three-year-old and later returns for the third birthday of Kurt, his "son"; Agnes eats three eels and dies in the third month of her third pregnancy. Schlöndorff represents a magic numerological principle within a formal pattern to produce a political metaphor.

Yet it can also be said that Schlöndorff emphasizes the Polish-German-Kashubian scheme much more strongly in the film's ending than did Grass in the novel. The filmmaker's choice and manner of ending his movie with the conclusion of the novel's "Book II" deserves attention here. In the first place, Schlöndorff suppresses the details of the Matzeraths' departure from Danzig/Gdansk and omits their trip through postarmistice Poland in the chapter entitled "Growth in a Freight Car." Schlöndorff's cutoff point for the motion picture highlights that the Poles are the new rulers, the Kashubians the old underlings, and the Germans the departing losers. The film's history lesson thus establishes an ongoing obligation for the Poles, and no less for the German audiences of *The Tin Drum*, to remain aware of the Kashubes, the victims of their strife. The image of the old Kashubian grandmother left behind as the train takes the Matzeraths to Germany suggests that the role of the Kashubians has in no way changed.

Fascism and the Petite Bourgeoisie

Nevertheless, Schlöndorff's appeal to a common ground for reconciliation also has a specific political bite. For *The Tin Drum* is of course not only a history of the animosity between Poles and Germans: it is also an examination of that relation in light of the rise and fall of fascism. How do Grass and Schlöndorff here explain this complex historical phenomenon? Our answer, of course, cannot cover all aspects of this problem; let us be content with asking in what social strata—military or technocrats, industrialists or working class, landowners or bourgeoisie, intelligentsia or petite bourgeoisie—the novelist and the film-maker, rightly or wrongly, locate the roots of this ideology. Evidently, the circle of friends and the neighborhood of the Matzeraths consist predominantly of small shopkeepers such as Greff, the vegetable dealer; Scheffler, the baker; and Matzerath, the grocer. Fascism flourishes here in the petite bourgeoisie but also extends to some Danzig nationalists and military men. This focus on petite bourgeoisie and its embrace of fascism, while perhaps a simplification, is a carryover from the novel. In an interview with John Hughes, Schlöndorff said of his source,

> Grass shows Nazism deriving from the banality of middle-class life aspiring to become something else. For Grass, these people aren't very innocent. They wanted to feel important, to feel like generals in control of history. And this is a very dangerous energy because it has certain legitimacy. That's what fascism is built on: *making everybody in the street feel important. . . .* They claimed to be controlling history while in reality they left all decisions in the hands of their *Führer*. ("*The Tin Drum . . .* 'Dream'" 5)

The baker's ejection of the Jewish toy merchant, Markus, from the site of Agnes Matzerath's burial; the SA's rampage during the *Kristallnacht* of 1938; the shopkeepers imagining, over their dinner goose, the destruction of Moscow and entire East European populations; Matzerath's first hanging and then removing the portrait of Hitler—these are concrete manifestations of such perverse aspirations that appear in both book and film. Schlöndorff earlier, in his *Young Törless* of 1965, had seemed to identify a protofascist element in the Austro-German intelligentsia or the tradition of Austro-German military academies. Grass, likewise, in his 1961 novel *Dog Years (Hundejahre)*, extended his own theory of fascism to the upper classes. In *The Tin Drum*, however, the focus is on the petite bourgeoisie.

Oskar: Metaphor, Point of View, and the Grotesque

The true stroke of genius in both *Tin Drum*s can be found in the figure of Oskar. In many ways, Oskar represents the most unfilmable part of the novel. A three-year-old who speaks and behaves like an adult would be almost impossible to portray, except perhaps through animation. Grass once abruptly ejected from his house a producer who offered him a promising opportunity to make a film of the novel precisely because his guest had dared to inquire whether one could not simply refashion Oskar into an adult ("Wie Literatur in Bildern"). Schlöndorff's solution to the problem is achieved with such confidence that audiences are willing to overlook its inherent contradiction. By having selected a small, growth-impeded, twelve-year-old actor to play Oskar, Schlöndorff maintains Grass's general conception of an adult in a child's body (Schlöndorff, *Die Blechtrommel: Tagebuch* 24). The result becomes the image of a child of almost indeterminate age, and the audience becomes thrown off balance about whether to see this person as innocent or evil, sincere or duplicitous, naive or wise. Oskar becomes a multivalenced metaphor, a "person" whose freak form can be read in at least three contradictory ways:

1. It is a protest against his sociopolitical environment and as such is a passive protest against fascism. He is so angry at the adult world that he decides to become a midget. It is Oskar, the purposefully rebellious child.

2. It is a part of Nazi Germany, that is, a freakish but willful deformation of Germany's own nature. Hitler was also known as the "drummer." It is Oskar, the infantile, self-gratifying child.

3. It is a product of strained German-Polish relations and the resultant alienation. It is Oskar, the hurt, powerless child.

These three aspects of Oskar are not at all fully compatible. Nevertheless, they collectively signify a paradoxical embodiment of the sometimes contradictory impulses in the Danzig region at that given historical moment. Oskar's grotesque "person" embodies the very human contradictions that make untenable any simple, polemical extrapolations by readers and viewers. To read

Oskar's human form with sensitivity is automatically to move beyond the reduction of persons to one-dimensional political symbols. So, in the very multivalence of Oskar we are supposed to discover the grounds of a reconciliatory tolerance. In short, Oskar can serve to accommodate equally well a number of nearly opposite metaphoric statements.

This accommodation may explain why the novel hardly created political controversy in the Adenauer era. Oskar, the child-man, never fully becomes involved in the questions of Pole or German, Nazi or anti-Nazi: he is, physically, a three-year-old. He is able to blend in with persons defending the Polish Post Office, but he can also get away on the arms of a brownshirted SA man. He may well be hiding in the basement of Matzerath, now an enemy for the Russians when they occupy Danzig. But for the Ivan who takes Oskar into his arms from his mother's lap, he's just an innocent child. Both times, Oskar is sheltered while driving his two fathers to the fatal consequences of their chosen political options. Oskar, as the grotesque narrator of *The Tin Drum*, is thus an apt medium through which to process and blunt the directness of political polemics, to take the edge off counterarguments. Schlöndorff carries this indirectness over into the film.

In *Die Filme von Volker Schlöndorff*, Rainer Lewandowski perceives in the cinematic figure of Oskar a shortcoming that flaws the unity of the film work from the very start:

> Oskar, the true gnome, inmate of a mental institution: this is the narrator of the book. His childhood is told from this perspective, as well as his decision to halt his growth. Schlöndorff steers clear of the figure of the narrator. He has little Oskar speak directly, consequently robbing the figure of his indispensably artificial element. The Grassian device of the grotesque narrative perspective does not enter the motion picture and is rare even in its visuals. (267–68)

There are in Lewandowski's critical commentary two cardinal issues. The first involves the question of how Schlöndorff handles narrative point of view through both voice-over narration and mise-en-scène. The second concerns the role of the grotesque in *The Tin Drum*, especially the disparity between Oskar's physical immaturity and his mental capacity. Let us consider each in turn.

In part for reasons of length, Schlöndorff chose to omit the third book of the novel from the motion picture. Thus the film leaves Oskar in his twenty-first year. In the novel, Grass lets him grow to be thirty and has him tell his life as he looks back from that stage and from the vantage of an insane asylum. With the elision of the last part of the book, this pseudoautobiographical framework could never have been built into the film. Autobiography traditionally places some distance between writers and their childhoods after they have acquired an objective relation to their younger selves. Clearly, the twenty-one-year-old tin drummer had to be a different kind of narrator, for he is less apt than his thirty-year-old self to view his earlier, boyhood existence as that of another person.

Medium specificity further restricts the use of the novel's pure verbal power: the literary Oskar is able to enjoy flirting with words and reams of paper to an extent his cinematic twin cannot. Nevertheless, Schlöndorff does address the issue of narrative point of view in the context of his medium and its potential. He gives us a changing perspective by shifting from Oskar, the third-person commentator, to the first-person Oskar, who lives out the experiences. In addition, Oskar sometimes refers to himself in the third person. In a parallel way, Schlöndorff alternates between objective third-person shots of Oskar, a spectator observing the action in a detached way, and highly subjective shots from Oskar's point of view inside his environment. There is, in short, a multiplicity of Oskar "stances" and "voices" in the film. Oskar-the-commentator, moreover, tends to stand out more by means of a declamatory tone rather than the normal spoken child's voice of the first-person speaker Oskar. Schlöndorff reinforces the double concept of his hero with visuals. In one shot, Oskar watches Agnes and Bronski's foreplay from a closet whose mirror on the door reflects the image of the voyeuristic son, creating a second Oskar (Schlöndorff and Grass 85).

Clearly, Schlöndorff has striven to make Oskar a character that embodies several points of view. This narrative cubism leads to a grotesque element in the screen figure of the tin drummer, one that Lewandowski fails to appreciate. Adult knowledge is grafted onto a child's body from the start of Oskar's life. Himself a member of the post–World War I generation, Oskar is, at the Hitler takeover in 1933, chronologically nine—while a three-year-old in size. During the Nazi grab for Danzig and Poland in 1939, he is fifteen—and a three-year-old in size. Finally, at war's end, he is twenty-one—and *still* a three-year-old in size. Oskar's dual character should be obvious from the scene of his birth early in the film—the audience observes his birth while he gives a running commentary of the proceedings. Other examples abound of this unnatural child-adult hybridization. Take only the shots of Oskar observing Matzerath and Maria having intercourse on the family couch. The postadolescent mind of Oskar perceives the couple with obvious sexual jealousy. Moments later, he responds with child-like behavior in his attempt to win back Maria during her postcoital douche; in

23. *The Tin Drum.* The double Oskar—the observer and his reflection—in the closet.
Photo: Deutsches Filmmuseum Fotoarchiv.

all innocence, he sprinkles fizz powder in her hand. Or consider the rally
episode, to be analyzed in detail shortly, and it becomes clear that the child's eye
supplies the perspective. Contrary to Lewandowski's critique, Oskar's disapproval of the rally, however, is a manifestation of the critical faculty of an adult.
The point here is that the film retains the grotesque figure of Oskar, as well as
the separation of the point of view of Oskar, the critical observer, from that of
Oskar, the child protagonist. (See illustration 23.)

As portrayed by Schlöndorff, Oskar was to retain an ability to shock and
offend. Long after the film's initial release, an Oklahoma judge responded to a
citizens' group's request by ruling the film obscene. Local police seized video
copies of *The Tin Drum,* causing a controversy about free speech. Apparently
Oskar's half-child status was confusing to a judge who, sensitive to issues of
child pornography, admitted he had not seen the film in its entirety
("Oklahoma Police"). A federal court later ruled that the seizures were uncon-
stitutional and that the sexual portrayals did not meet the standard for child
pornography ("Oklahoma Judge" 3).

Citation and Leitmotif as Adaptation Strategies

We have addressed two important issues of content: the positioning of the narrator's point of view and the grotesque nature of Oskar's child-adult convergence. Part of the brilliance of Grass's novel, however, lies in his playful use of language through puns, metaphors, and free associations. Consider, for example, the following passage. Oskar is in the Catholic church observing the statue of Jesus while his mother is absorbed in confession.

> At every step I had the feeling: he is looking after you, the saints are looking after you, Peter, whom they nailed to a cross with his head down, Andrew whom they nailed to a slanting cross—hence the St. Andrew's cross. There is also a Greek cross, not to mention the Latin, or Passion, cross. Double crosses, Teutonic crosses, and Calvary crosses are reproduced on textiles, in books and pictures . . . The Moline cross is handsome, the Maltese cross is covered, the hooked cross, or swastika, is forbidden, while de Gaulle's cross, the cross of Lorraine, is called the cross of St. Anthony in naval battles. . . . Yellow cross is poison, cross spiders eat one another. At the crossroads you crossed me up, crisscross, cross-examination, cross purposes. (Grass, *Tin Drum* 140)

The syllable and image "cross" here unfolds a suggestive formal power. On the surface, this may appear to be only an exercise in punning. It also reflects, however, both Oskar's fascination with language and the author's involvement with automatic writing, a characteristic of those twentieth-century novelists who work with mental processes rather than external action. Words and literary images contaminate one another in a free fall of associations.

How can the filmmaker find an equivalent for this kind of passage? Schlöndorff has not attempted to imitate directly such passages in the film, but he has developed his own visual equivalents for the multistylistic verbal richness of the novel. Where Grass combined the picaresque, Döblinian montage, Dadaism, and many other literary genres and styles, Schlöndorff blended cinematic genres and personal styles. German film critic Hans C. Blumenberg identifies quotes and conventions from such diverse genres as the horror film—seen in Oskar's birth, the horse's head on the beach (and one should add both Oskar's attack on the pregnant Maria's belly with scissors and Matzerath's burial, with the corpse's hand protruding from the coffin); the *Heimatfilm* regional homeland film—seen in the Kashubian plain (and to tack on a supplement, in the burial of Oskar's mother, Agnes); the heroic drama—seen in the Post Office episode; and even the Italo-Western finale à la Sergio Leone—seen in the freight train slowly moving toward the horizon ("Das war" 206) (and, to expand on Blumenberg, in the failed attempt of the mounted policeman and his colleagues on foot to capture Koljaiczek) .

Drawing on the stylistic treasure chest of the cinema, Schlöndorff gives the film a variety similar to that of the novel by patterning many episodes after other directors' personal styles. Sometimes, personal styles and genres may even overlap. Thus, the initial footage of the screen version of *The Tin Drum*—realized with an Askania silent film camera (Schlöndorff, *Die Blechtrommel: Tagebuch* 57)—suggests Chaplin and the Keystone Cops, the typical slapstick foils of the cinema's silent film era. Similarly, the initial shots of the Danzig party rally, filmed in color but then bleached and tinted to approximate black and white, offer an uncanny illusion of archival newsreel material before the film returns to full color. At the same time, the exaggerated close-up image of the speaker's mouth is reminiscent of Chaplin's *The Great Dictator* (1940).

Still more clearly identifiable is the specific documentary-like directorial style behind both Schlöndorff's Danzig party rally and the additional episode entitled "Hitler in Danzig" in the filmmaker's list of sequences in his published *Tagebuch einer Verfilmung*, or *Diary of an Adaptation*. The camera moves from the close-up of the speaker to an ornamentally arranged mass of party followers that Albert Speer could not have orchestrated better. The model is obviously Leni Riefenstahl, and the resemblance is not merely due to the inclusion of such clichés as the brownshirts, the Hitler Youth playing the Badenweiler March, the arrival of the leader by open motorcar, and the presentation of a bouquet of flowers by a young girl. Even more revealing are the shifting camera angles and the rhythm of the film editing: a long shot down the aisle toward the speakers' platform showing the back of the prominent brownshirted leader and three comrades moving forward; a side-aisle view of these leaders goose-stepping down the center aisle framed by the masses; a frog-eye shot upward toward the area commander on the platform prepared to welcome these guests; finally, an extreme overhead shot down onto the moving brownshirt quartet. In the scene following the German occupation of the Polish Post Office, the camera, mounted on a traveling open automobile, films the files of passing jubilant spectators while a uniformed arm saluting in *Führer*-like posture statically stretches its salute into the frame: the heroic style of Riefenstahl.

What is, of course, not visualized in Riefenstahl's glorifying party documentaries, such as *Triumph of the Will (Triumph des Willens)*, is Oskar's glancing through the knothole and his observations behind and underneath the grandstand. He interacts musically with the Hitler Youth band whose military beat is interrupted by his drumming, which gradually transforms their march rhythm into a three-four waltz time that in turn seduces the entire gathering. Nor would Riefenstahl have shown the low-angle shot of the boots of the party bosses correcting their step to the three-four beat of the waltz as they come down the aisle. Where, in Grass's portrayal of the Nazi rally, a debunking of fascist culture is achieved through comic elements, some of which Schlöndorff retains, the filmmaker adds to this a level of cinematic parody. Schlöndorff's parody often independently follows codes of cinematic rather than literary tradition. As he draws on one of the traditions of Nazi cinema, the satirical punch of his sequence achieves savage immediacy.

On the other hand, the stylistic quotations by no means constantly strive for a satirical effect. They may, for instance, be subtle, appreciative—bows to the model. French movie critic Jean de Baroncelli aimed at Louis Malle's influence when he wrote that Oskar was, to him, something of a "Zazie chez les Polacks" ("Le jour"). In an interview, Schlöndorff confirmed that his midget scene under the Paris Eiffel Tower (a full twenty years after his work with the French director on the same location) "became a tribute to *Zazie* and the Tower in Malle's film" (*"The Tin Drum . . . 'Dream'"* 4).

Schlöndorff's citations may simply represent an affinity, shared with other moviemakers, for a grotesque film language bent on grasping at reality by means of a deforming and distorting style that resembles the literary idiom of Grass. The stylistic parallel mentioned most frequently is that of Italian filmmaker Federico Fellini. Eckhart Schmidt of the German weekly *Christ und Welt*, for years one of Schlöndorff's most persistent conservative critics, censures the filmmaker for depicting the midgets of Bebra's theater at the front by "suddenly resorting to images à la Fellini" ("Oskar" n. pag.; cf. also Baroncelli, "Sous les yeux"). Hans C. Blumenberg, by contrast, perceives a *"Satyrspiel,"* or comedic interlude, rather than stylistic dependency on Fellini ("Das war" 207). The analogous effects may partially derive from common third contributors or sources. Thus, Schlöndorff in his journal pays tribute to his *Tin Drum* collaborators, Rino Carboni and his assistant Alfredo Titeri, makeup artists with years of experience working with Visconti and Fellini (*Die Blechtrommel: Tagebuch* 64–65). In addition, in the German filmmaker's view, Fellini "is very influenced by Grass, as you can see from the fish at the end of *La Dolce Vita*" (*"The Tin Drum . . . 'Dream'"* 5). At the same time, Schlöndorff compliments the Italian director's treatment of political infantilism, in particular the way this is achieved in *Amarcord*: "Fellini shows the way the adolescent dependencies of Italian men provided fuel for the growth of fascism" (*"The Tin Drum . . . 'Dream'"* 5). Critic Henri Plard has also noted this relation to *Amarcord*: "If a work could have inspired Schlöndorff [in *The Tin Drum*], it is . . . Fellini's *Amarcord*" ("Sur le film" 82).

Schlöndorff's imaginative independence in unfolding creative cinematic equivalents to Grass's own literary play on styles works simultaneously with other adaptation strategies that hold particularly close to the prose source. In particular, Schlöndorff's use of leitmotifs demonstrates how the filmmaker can adhere closely to his literary model. Of the many objects and symbols handled in leitmotif style, such as the moth, the queen-of-hearts playing card, and the grandmother's skirt, we analyze only the example of the fish or eels.

The fish in *The Tin Drum* are tightly associated with Oskar's parents, although they also allude to more general themes. Early in the film, Agnes, Matzerath, and Bronski pass by the fishmongers' stands in the marketplace, a sequence that also begins to develop their triangle relationship. The implicit sexual aspect is overtly emphasized in the scene in Tischlergasse. As Oskar stares up at the hotel room where Agnes and Bronski engage in intercourse, he causes a fishmonger to fall from his bicycle and spill his slippery wares all over the pavement. The cyclist had ostentatiously balanced his eels—an obviously phallic symbol—in his hands. Clearly, however, in the disquieting beach scene where eels writhe out of the decomposing horse head, there is not only an allusion to the sensualism of Agnes and Bronski. There is, even more, the linkage between life and death—the eels, according to the fisherman, never grew as thick as during the war, especially after bloody naval encounters nearby. At the same time, eels and physical lovemaking cannot be separated, as Bronski keeps fondling Agnes even while she cannot hold her food and the eels keep issuing from every orifice of the horse's head. Agnes, it is true, refuses to eat from the dish that Matzerath prepares from the eels. But she does not refuse Bronski's subsequent sexual massage, even while assuming the pious pose of the Mary Magdalene portrait over her bed. When Agnes soon afterward begins to stuff herself with sardines and every other possible variety of fish found among the shop's wares, this act again carries by association a reference both to birth or pregnancy and to death. For she herself is pregnant and will die soon thereafter. The association with birth, life, and disease had of course been already established in the scene in the office of Oskar's physician Dr. Hollatz: among the collection of glass containers that Oskar shatters with his voice are snake and reptile specimens approximating the eel's shape.

Fish, especially eels, in the psychological imagery of Grass and Schlöndorff, stand not only for Agnes Matzerath's moral weakness and adultery. They are also connected with the larger issue of the process of sex, birth, growth, and death. This reading is confirmed by the fuller literary text that connects Agnes's corpse and embryo to a little chunk of eel, . . . eel flesh . . . from the . . . Neufahrwasser breakwater, . . . from the horse's head, possibly eel from her father Joseph Koljaiczek who ended under the raft, a prey to the eels, eel of thine eel, for eel thou art, to eel returnest." (Grass, *Tin Drum* 163–64)

The religious puns in the statement, like those cited earlier in the passage dominated by the syllable "cross," only tend to heighten its archetypal and mythical significance. The spectator understands full well that a drastic change is taking place in Frau Matzerath's life and that it is connected with her refusal to continue cooperating with a world dominated by the biological cycle of life and death. The filmmaker, through this central leitmotif chain, has remained loyal to the core of the novel.

Cross-Generational Associations

To their credit, both author and filmmaker of *The Tin Drum* have tried not to let the leitmotifs and the genre parodies become ends in themselves. They prefer instead to subordinate them to political ideas, as when the eels are associated with naval warfare and when the stylistic allusions to Chaplin's *Great Dictator* and Riefenstahl debunk Nazi leaders. An additional political association is evident in Schlöndorff's and Grass's attempts during the adaptation of *The Tin Drum* to update the material, to make its sociopolitical attitudes more topical or applicable to the contemporary situation. From the perspective of the 1970s and 1980s, the main theme of *The Tin Drum* is that of noncooperation with the establishment, or "*Verweigerung.*" The 1959 *Tin Drum* novel embraced the first impulses of social refusal: Oskar's urge to remain in his mother's womb as well as his resolve to stop growing, physically, at the age of three. The intent in the film was to make the metaphor of *The Tin Drum* even more encompassing: to expand Grass's implicit identification of the pre-Nazi mentality and the apolitical attitudes of the 1950s to political attitudes of the 1970s and 1980s. (See illustration 24.)

   That one can read the cinematic Oskar as a dropout from society provides for a cinematic echo of the way Grass reflects the 1950s "*ohne mich,*" or silent generation stance, in the last third of his novel—with a minor reinterpretation in light of the 1970s posture of noncooperation with a perverted society. In contrast to the direct activism of the 1960s, the 1970s was, for many Europeans, a decade in which people retained sympathies with previous leftist commitments but slipped into passive introspection. According to Schlöndorff, "The

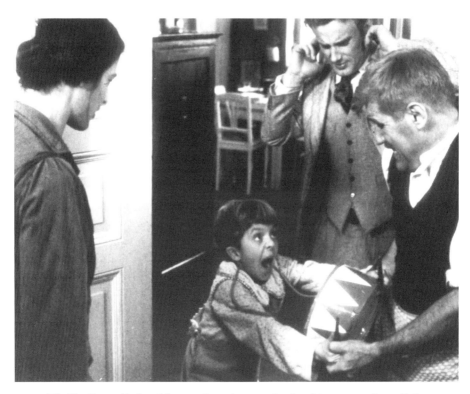

24. *The Tin Drum.* Father Matzerath trying to take the drum away from Oskar, suggesting in its way the struggle between generations. Photo: Museum of Modern Art/Film Stills Archive.

best analysis of the film's treatment of Oskar was given by Ludwig Marcuse" (*"The Tin Drum . . .* 'Dream'" 7). In Marcuse's view, "[t]he reason the film is an international hit is the character of Oskar. You have taken a very contemporary type and have inserted him into the Nazi era. The film works on both levels simultaneously." Silent generation and disillusioned postprotest youth thus are being linked; according to Schlöndorff, the film attempts to give new life to the novel by bringing Oskar up to date (*"The Tin Drum . . .* 'Dream'" 7; cf. Grass and Schlöndorff, Interview 186). Critics have concurred that the motion picture presents a cinematic iconography inspired by post-1968 attitudes (Piccadilly). The connection between generations is more of a poetic association than direct political discourse, but it creates a rich analogy whereby viewers can consider and process questions about individual responsibility and collective societal guilt.

This update no doubt forms a fundamental reinterpretation of *The Tin Drum* novel and raises the question of whether Grass approved of so bold an extension of the story's metaphoric reach. Evidently, Grass agreed with the new consensus of media scholars that "adaptations are always—nondiscursive—interpretations" (Knilli et al 12). On the occasion of a June 1979 cycle of discussions with writers and filmmakers at the Berlin Academy of Arts (called "How Literature Learns to Move in Framed Images") Grass postulated on the "inherent laws" of cinematic adaptations. He agreed with fellow German novelist Siegfried Lenz's view: "When one attempts . . . to make an adaptation . . . of a literary text, he is dependent on . . . rendering it into another medium, to modify it . . . every author ought to proceed from the premise that . . . the literary original by necessity has to be modified" ("Wie Literatur" 171). This insistence on the specificity of media indeed characterized Grass's own conditions for approving filmmaker Schlöndorff's adaptation. In an interview broadcast over Bavarian Television, Grass stated:

> Not until I perceived that Schlöndorff was someone who has . . . the imaginative power to adapt a literary original . . . on the basis of the aesthetic norms of the filmmaker, was my mind at rest. If it had been someone . . . trying . . . to produce a dull cinematic imitation of the novel, I would not have granted my approval. (Schlöndorff, *Die Blechtrommel: Tagebuch* 24)

It is legitimate, then, to view the film, which Schlöndorff did not only with Grass's blessings but also with his assistance on the dialogues (23), as Grass's way of adding another possible interpretation to his own novelistic oeuvre, of suggesting an updated contemporary applicability.

In conclusion, Grass appears not only to accept a contemporary revision as a revitalization of his novel but to have desired an adaptation of the kind that approached his text on the terms of its medium specificity. During the process of adaptation, both Grass and Schlöndorff consciously employed the novel's politicocultural metaphor for the stance of noncooperation. The versions in both media still allow the German people to draw a lesson from their political history. In addition to stimulating aesthetic pleasure, Schlöndorff's motion picture thus continues the endeavors of the New German Cinema to establish a political public countersphere, an arena in which a mass audience can address intelligently important issues. It reminds Germans of the need for neighborly relations with Poland. It warns them both of the freakishness of a culture that turns fascist and of the state of political dwarfs that can arise if generations adopt the posture of the "great refusal." In this sense, one can speak of coming to grips with both the past *and* the 1970s present in Schlöndorff's updating adaptation of Grass's *The Tin Drum.* To come to terms with past and present—the Third Reich's so-called Thousand Years, the *ohne mich* or silent generation, and the post-1968 years—together in one film is a bold stroke.

16

Just for Fun, Just for Play—
Kaleidoscope Valeska Gert,
The Candidate, and
War and Peace

If Schlöndorff in his international period moves in the direction of large-scale international productions, he also takes periodic breaks from bigger budget filmmaking through involvement with more modest documentary projects and contributions to collective filmmaking efforts. We have already mentioned his "Antigone" episode in *Germany in Autumn,* which becomes a kind of bridge between the second and third periods in the director's work. "Antigone's" Brechtian satire looks back to Schlöndorff's 1970s sensibility, but at the same time its content—a jaundiced observation of working within the self-censoring West German broadcasting establishment—is a commentary on the very situation that was to encourage Schlöndorff to seek more international production situations. In this chapter we consider the nonmainstream output of Schlöndorff's third period: *Just for Fun, Just for Play—Kaleidoscope Valeska Gert (Nur zum Spaß, nur zum Spiel—Kaleidoskop Valeska Gert,* 1977), *The Candidate (Der Kandidat,* 1980), and his episodes in *War and Peace (Krieg und Frieden,* 1983). Together these form an alternative tributary in the river of Schlöndorff's professional career, one marked most strikingly by a strong, assertive antimilitarism and a use of free-form, collagelike structures. Aspects of this alternative cinema provide a good sense both of certain German cultural traditions and of the West German political climate of the time.

Just for Fun, Just for Play—Kaleidoscope Valeska Gert

Although some of Schlöndorff's earlier work had been inspired by true-life incidents and journalistic *faites diverses, Just for Fun, Just for Play—Kaleidoscope Valeska*

Gert, a movie about the then seventy-seven-year-old actress and dancer, was Schlöndorff's first full-scale feature documentary. It grew out of Schlöndorff's experience working on *Coup de Grâce* with the actress, whom he had admired ever since seeing her early films at the Cinémathèque in Paris ("Zu meinem Film" 2). He describes in his documentary how he became so fascinated with the stories and experiences she recounted while they worked together that he decided to make a film about her. In its connection to *Coup de Grâce* and Brecht, *Valeska Gert* looks back to Schlöndorff's early 1970s attitudes; but in its involvement with irrationality, emotion, the grotesque, the German exile tradition, and indeed something of a revisionist attitude toward Brecht, it signals many of the changes that were to follow it in Schlöndorff's creative production.

Gert was an avant-garde performer of the 1920s and 1930s, one who shocked audiences with a mode of dance and pantomime that was impolite, blunt, outspoken, and harsh in its portrayal of reality. Schlöndorff's *Valeska Gert* is a collage film that edits together various footage—interviews with Valeska Gert; performances by the actress herself (both drawn from archival materials and done for Schlöndorff's camera); performances of her works by her younger protégées; and other materials documenting her past. The movie's format and eclectic sources suggest the kaleidoscope of its full title, but the picture is nonetheless carefully structured. After introducing us to Valeska Gert and some aspects of her art, *Valeska Gert* takes a more or less chronological approach to reviewing the main periods and stages in the woman's career.

Schlöndorff is clearly interested in Gert and her career, but from the material he takes about Gert, one can see emerge in the film two other preoccupations: death and the cultural heritage of the German Left. These are, in effect, the thematic abstractions that Schlöndorff draws from his specifics. The filmmaker clearly wanted to record Gert for posterity before her death, an event that occurred a year after he made the movie. Gert comments early in the film that she doesn't think of herself as old. "I may be old by the newspapers," she says, "but inside I'm young in spirit." Yet Schlöndorff's image is clearly that of a very old woman talking.

When Schlöndorff begins his survey of Valeska Gert's career, he asks her how she became a dancer. She describes a moment as a teenager when she was struck with the consciousness that she was going to die; she took up her art as a way of leaving something behind. Schlöndorff immediately moves to a performance of Gert's "dance of death," in which she dies in one long movement and which Schlöndorff photographs with the dancer in a black sweater against a completely black backdrop. The filmmaker then dissolves from Gert's final death mask to a photograph from her younger days. The movie becomes, in this way, an almost perfect illustration of André Bazin's famous essay, "The Ontology of the Photographic Image," in which Bazin argues that a primary purpose of the visual arts is to serve as a kind of preservation of images of how people looked against the ravages of time and death (1: 9–16). At another point in *Valeska Gert,* Schlöndorff lingers on the few remaining pieces of movie footage documenting Gert's 1920s performances, thus reinforcing the impression that Schlöndorff's recording of later performances may be just as valuable in decades to come.

Part of Schlöndorff's fascination with Gert is, without doubt, his interest in the prewar German cinema, and we see in *Valeska Gert* clips from Gert's work in the cinema of that time. Gert's comments about the era shed light both on her work and on Schlöndorff's. She tells of her annoyance at being called an "expressionist" actress and talks instead about observation as the basis of her work. She created dances, for example, based on various sports, such as boxing, tennis, and skiing, and we see in the movie her attempt to re-create with a student her boxing number from the 1920s. She describes a dance she did about a prostitute, for which she studied a real prostitute—the way she would walk, sit, hold her legs, through the various aspects of the pickup, until she finally rid herself of the client. She characterizes her art as a process of creating symbols drawn from life and experience—"not bloodless abstractions" but abstractions all the same.

In interviewing her, Schlöndorff is quick to ask about her relation to Bertolt Brecht, and the implication is clear. Would not her "abstractions" be attempts to draw generalizations about human behavior in a way comparable to Brecht's notion of "epic theater"? Would not her dances be a kind of gestic acting? Gert leaves the door open for such an interpretation, saying simply that Brecht and she never discussed his theories and that it was always he who asked for her ideas, not the other way around.

If Schlöndorff's method as a filmmaker is to move, however, from the particular to the general, then *Valeska Gert* becomes a portrait not just of an individual woman but of a generation. Schlöndorff documents Gert's emigration to the United States during the Hitler era, her lack of success in Hollywood and on Broadway, and finally her unexpected success in opening the Beggar Bar in Greenwich Village, where she performed her nightclub acts to widespread acclaim. He describes her homecoming to a Berlin that never could return to what it was before the war. One finds in Schlöndorff's tracing of her career not only a sense of nostalgia but also a desire to find a positive cultural heritage to continue.

Schlöndorff ends with Gert performing an antimilitarist song, one that ridicules war and an entire war-oriented culture. Gert clearly represents for

Schlöndorff an artist who epitomizes many of his own aesthetic standards as someone who can take positive elements from both high art and popular art, as a feminist role model, as a creator who can react emphatically against middle-class aesthetics.

The Candidate

By contrast, Franz Josef Strauss is a public figure whom Schlöndorff would have disdained not only as an individual but also as a representative of a political and cultural tradition. *The Candidate*, produced to coincide with the 1980 electoral contest between centrist Social Democrat Helmut Schmidt and rightist Strauss of the Bavarian Christian Socialist Union, represents the second in a series of German-produced collective films about current social issues. *Germany in Autumn*, a response to the issue of terrorism, preceded it in 1978; *War and Peace*, about nuclear armaments policy, followed in 1983. Unlike these two other films, however, *The Candidate* is more of a piece; it forms much more of a coherent whole. Where *Germany in Autumn* and *War and Peace* are episodic in structure and contain segments easily attributable to one director or another, it is far more difficult to determine which filmmaker did what parts of *The Candidate*. German critics credited Kluge with "incalculable collage technique," Stefan Aust with "data-obsessed TV journalism," and Schlöndorff with "patient documentarism," calling him "a brilliant documentarist" (Blumenberg, "Deutsche") and noting, as well, the "precise and empathetic recording of human beings and politicians" (Nagel 252).

The Candidate is not a wildly propagandistic film. The late Bavarian prime minister Strauss was a brilliant ideologue of the Right, a charismatic orator, a machine politician with absolute control of the Bavarian electorate, a nationalist who also favored a strong anticommunist West, and a lifelong advocate of the military; he also was associated with an aftertaste of corruption. As such, Strauss would be an easy target for leftist filmmakers. Some critics have, however, praised the reticence and fairness with which Schlöndorff and his colleagues went after their target. Hans C. Blumenberg of the conservative weekly *Die Zeit* perceived "no flaming assembling [*Appell*] of the troops" ("Deutsche"). Ronald Holloway of *Variety*, recognizing that the filmmaker's "research has been so accurate," cites the film's "non-polemical approach" (Holl.). While the movie is clearly not pro-Strauss, it hardly glamorizes Strauss's eventually successful opponent either. Rather, it goes beyond the immediate political situation to see Strauss as not so much a problem in himself as a symptom of larger problems in West German politics.

Given the political touchiness of the subject, *The Candidate*, like *Germany in Autumn* and *War and Peace*, but unlike almost all of Schlöndorff's other projects, received no state subsidy nor funding from West German television. Rather, the filmmakers produced the movie themselves and constructed it largely from materials received from foreign television stations. A touch of vengeance may be involved in the production: Filmverlag der Autoren, which coproduced and distributed the movie, had been since 1977 financially controlled by majority shareholder Rudolf Augstein, publisher of the magazine *Der Spiegel* (Eder, "Starfighter"). As the secretary of defense during the 1962 "*Spiegel* affair," Strauss had ordered a journalist of the news magazine arrested for allegedly leaking military secrets. Augstein, too, was temporarily imprisoned. Strauss finally was forced to resign when his lies to parliament about the affair were uncovered (Grosser 157).

The general structure of *The Candidate* is similar to that of *Just for Fun, Just for Play—Kaleidoscope Valeska Gert*. After a section that introduces Strauss and the general themes of the film, we see a chronological presentation of the statesman's past. This chronology includes Strauss's rise to fame in the years that followed World War II, first as a special advisor to Konrad Adenauer on defense and West German rearmament, then on nuclear warfare, and later as minister of defense. *The Candidate* documents the scandals that later hit Strauss, ultimately forcing his resignation. It goes on to show Strauss's gradual rebuilding of his power base from 1963 through the 1970s, including his 1966 appointment as treasury secretary. The filmmakers intercut past events with present consequences, the candidate's history with his current campaign. And in terms of themes and preoccupations—its antimilitarism, its concern for finding a continuity between past and present German culture, its attack on a certain bourgeois complacency—we can see *The Candidate* as a kind of anti-*Valeska Gert*. It does with a negative example what the earlier film did with a positive role model. Its closest American equivalent would be something like Emile de Antonio's *Millhouse: A White Comedy* (1971), which compiled newsreel footage of Richard Nixon to create a partisan caricature of him.

The Candidate begins with striking images of the Rhine River in Bonn, its tranquil twilight beauty marred by the intrusion of surveillance helicopters. This image encapsulates what is to come. The German government, the filmmakers seem to be saying, is dependent on military strength to maintain its power, and military power represents an intrusion on an idyllic natural order. The filmmakers follow these shots of Bonn and its official buildings with footage from the Hitler era—specifically that of the Führer's 1938 meeting with Neville Chamberlain on the nearby banks of the Rhine, which resulted in the

Third Reich's annexation of Czechoslovakia. The documentarists then return to the present to show us today's political leaders entering the halls of power and meeting with the press. Having established the physical context of power in West Germany, Schlöndorff and his associates show us Strauss in some detail, at a political rally in Passau.

In surveying Strauss's career, the filmmakers often break from their chronological material to insert other footage that first seems extraneous or digressive but which ultimately works back into one of the film's major statements: militarism permeates the whole of German culture. Shots of nuclear explosions establish the context of the 1950s; newsreel footage shows world leaders proclaiming the benefits to come from the use of nuclear power. Later footage from Three Mile Island dampens the optimism expressed in the previous decade, until finally we see a meeting of the radical, pro-ecology Green Party. The progression suggests that this contemporary phenomenon is a logical outgrowth of the militarism of the Adenauer era. The filmmakers show a seemingly innocuous merry-go-round outside a building where a Strauss rally has taken place. As the camera inspects it carefully, we see that half of its images, of soldier boys and drummer boys, suggest war, already indoctrinating the young into militaristic thinking. Schlöndorff and his codirectors are clearly as interested in the context of Strauss's political success as they are in the man himself.

One of the images that *The Candidate* returns to more than once is indeed that of a mirror. At the end of the movie's introductory prelude, we get an image of Strauss looking into a mirror. With the Grimm fairy tale words of "Mirror, mirror on the wall" heard on the sound track, Strauss is positioned as the wicked stepmother in *Snow White*. This becomes a pun referring to the *"Spiegel* affair"—the word *Spiegel* means "mirror" in German. Schlöndorff and his associates, however, clearly also see Strauss himself as a reflection of the society that produced him.

If one thinks of a mirror as a medium, a mediator between a reality and an observer, then the image of Strauss looking in a mirror also suggests an image of someone very much conscious of his media image and very much willing to manipulate that image. In a scene at the Passau rally near the movie's beginning, we see Strauss's aides maneuvering at his table to replace what looks like a champagne bottle and glass with a paper cup filled with water. The former would presumably be bad for his image, especially considering past publicized incidents of excessive drinking. We see Strauss gleefully signing autographed pictures at the rally. *The Candidate* frequently contrasts newsreel or video images of Strauss with footage photographed in color for the movie, in a manner comparable to similar techniques in *The Lost Honor of Katharina Blum*. In one particularly interesting Eisensteinian edit we see a "live" shot of Strauss entering a building cut in continuity with a video image: Schlöndorff and his associates keep us conscious of the degrees of mediation that our knowledge of Strauss is dependent on. If we see *Valeska Gert* as a work that comments on the medium of film as a way to preserve the truth of the past, *The Candidate* suggests something opposite: a mirror that can distort or conceal the truth.

The end result of *The Candidate* is not readily clear. While it offers any number of reasons for the West German voter not to vote for Strauss, it does little to suggest reasons to vote *for* anyone else. *The Candidate* strikes an odd balance. On the one hand, it is clearly made out of deep partisan political conviction; on the other, it avoids overly facile ridicule or heavy propagandizing. On the one hand, it aestheticizes its materials—with ironic music, with clever editing, with unexpected documentary materials, with some rather dazzling color photography, with a crystal-clear sound track recorded to maintain the intimacy and intensity in its softly spoken narration (at the expense of the occasional intrusion of brightly hissing sibilants). On the other hand, it gains its real strength and credibility simply from the thoroughness of its research and documentation.

War and Peace

War and Peace is yet a third topical film Schlöndorff made collectively with several of the same colleagues involved in *Germany in Autumn* and *The Candidate*—Alexander Kluge, Heinrich Böll, and Stefan Aust—as well as with Axel Engstfeld. The new work was shot largely in 1982 and, after a "work-in-progress" preview at the 1982 Hof Filmfest, received its official premiere at the Berlin Film Festival in February 1983 (Kluge and Schlöndorff 3; Pflaum, "Ein vergebliches"). In it, the politically committed filmmakers attempt to treat the issue of war in general and nuclear war in particular in specific response to the proposal to use West Germany as a launch site for the Pershing II missile. Like *Germany in Autumn* and *The Candidate, War and Peace* is thus a film interested both in a specific political issue and in more general principles of political thought and action.

War and Peace reflected the broader anxieties and conflicts around 1980 that gripped Central Europe more than any other region of the globe as the Cold War reached a new height. The Soviet Union had introduced a new generation of SS missiles, and NATO—under American leadership and with the consent of the German chancellor Helmut Schmidt and, later, his successor Helmut Kohl—campaigned for a new push to keep up in the armaments race *(Nachrüstung)*. This issue became particularly sensitive for the Germans.

War and Peace is involved as well with the process of collective filmmaking, represented in other works from the time, such as the feminist movie *Out of the Blue* (*Aus heiterem Himmel*, 1982). Many critics have responded to *War and Peace* as a rather disorderly patchwork of episodic footage, and by the filmmakers' own admission, they were not fully clear about what they intended to accomplish. They shot only about half of what was originally planned, and the death of Rainer Werner Fassbinder deprived the project of a contribution from him (Kluge and Schlöndorff 8). The problem is all the more ambiguous for American audiences in that the prints shown in the United States were a good half hour shorter than the version shown in West Germany and ordered the movie's materials somewhat differently.[1]

Schlöndorff's part in *War and Peace* consists of two major contributions to the work: he directed three short fictional episodes, written by Heinrich Böll, about the aftermath of nuclear war, and he photographed and edited footage of the 1982 Versailles summit conference.[2] (He would also shoot a similarly formal 1981 East German meeting of Helmut Schmidt and the GDR's state and party boss Erich Honecker, which Alexander Kluge later integrated into his own *Odds and Ends* [*Vermischte Nachrichten*, 1987] ["Register"; "Gill" 124].) The fictional and documentary styles represent almost totally different filmmaking strategies. One involves planned, scripted, and acted storytelling, the other postproduction editing of spontaneously shot documentary footage.

Perhaps the most audacious of Schlöndorff's episodes is the playlet entitled "Kill Your Sister," a title deliberately intended as an ironic variation on "Love Thy Neighbor" (Kluge and Schlöndorff 13). Although its effect is blunt and by some standards even inept—one critic called it "embarrassingly staged and acted" (*"War and Peace"* 322)—the episode in several ways epitomizes the strategy of much of *War and Peace* as a whole. In this short sequence Angela Winkler plays Margot, a woman who has temporarily survived the initial effects of a nuclear holocaust. Having successfully dragged herself through the resultant rubble, she reaches the entrance to a fallout shelter owned by her brother Albert. He refuses to let her in and instead produces a small, toy-sized tank that shoots at her and kills her. Schlöndorff's mise-en-scène for the episode is stylized to the extreme: an eerie red light bathes much of the clearly artificial studio set. Expressionistic music adds to the spookiness of it all.

The extreme stylization of "Kill Your Sister" works as an acknowledgement that any film about nuclear war must not only think the unthinkable but portray the unportrayable. One must ultimately resort to speculation, to fantasy, to childlike play. Böll and Schlöndorff's toy tank immediately reminds one of American artist Chris Burden's antiwar works from the 1980s, such as *Tale of Two*

25. *War and Peace.* The director on the set with the Russian astronaut. Photo: Museum of Modern Art/Film Stills Archive.

Cities, in which the artist assembled some three thousand small war toys in a three-dimensional tableaulike staging of military action that the gallery-goer could look at through binoculars (Gambrell 83–87; Crary 77–79; Handy 39).

Schlöndorff's sick joke picks up again the theme, introduced in *The Candidate,* of the way in which militarism permeates our whole culture, including the toys innocent children play with. In the second of the Böll-Schlöndorff episodes, two Russian astronauts manage to talk by radio to two American spacemen as both circle about an earth that has been blown to destruction in a nuclear holocaust. Behaving with the kind of intelligence Schlöndorff characteristically gives the military, the two teams of men proceed to argue seriously about who won the war. Militarism, Schlöndorff implies, reduces humans to argumentative youngsters interested only in some vague concept of winning. (See illustration 25.)

It is no surprise, then, that when Schlöndorff changes genres and gives us his documentary footage of the Versailles summit conference, he succeeds in making the world leaders all look like so many children playing at being important: the palace of Versailles becomes their playhouse. By repeating similar shots of helicopters landing and red carpets being rolled out, Schlöndorff pokes fun at empty diplomatic protocol. A few moments later, Margaret Thatcher, displeased with some of her accommodations, refuses to take a boat ride on the Seine. Later we see Ronald Reagan look miffed when François Mitterand criticizes the then-current Israeli military action in Beirut. Throughout the episode, Schlöndorff implicitly emphasizes how the world leaders, self-important and eager to play their parts well, seem oblivious to the militaristic culture that so thoroughly surrounds them. Soldiers in military dress stand at attention; France honors its visitors with cannon salutes; the rooms of Versailles are named "Salon de la Guerre" and "Salon de la Paix." If the purpose of such a conference is to produce world peace, why do the leaders seem so comfortable with an excess of military tradition? Nuclear war becomes the outcome of this militarism.

To render this episode more than simply comic, Schlöndorff intercuts into it footage from the war in Beirut that was going on while the NATO participants talked and fussed. He contrasts the world of real political conflict, of real war, with the near fantasy world in which the leaders operate. Schlöndorff calls on us to be less removed from reality than they.

Schlöndorff's contributions to *War and Peace* are minor in and of themselves, but they become more interesting when seen in context with the offerings by Kluge, Aust, and Engstfeld in the same film. The latter filmmakers provide, among other things, a short history of war and the representation of war in art and on film; a short history of nuclear war; some poetically calm footage featuring a woman in a kitchen seconds before a nuclear blast; reportage from the Bonn antinuclear demonstrations; an interview with Sam Cohen, inventor of the neutron bomb, at his home in the southwest United States;[3] and views of the German town of Hattenbach, ground zero in the event of a nuclear attack on the Federal Republic.

In its dialectic between fantasized images and concrete reality, *War and Peace* becomes a significant alternative to predigested news broadcasts. It becomes a kind of "antinews." Stefan Aust has commented that he joined the project because he "wanted to do what you cannot do (or cannot do any longer) in television, to try new forms, to sharpen the content, to become involved in the pressing political problems of the day, take a position, and demonstrate connections" (Kluge and Schlöndorff 17). Its tactic is, in the words of H. G. Pflaum, one of *Verweigerung*, or "refusal," for as Pflaum puts it "the current film dramaturgies are more serviceable to war" than they are to peace ("Ein vergebliches").

The most immediate difference between *War and Peace* and the conventional news broadcast is the film's emphasis on personal discourse rather than objective reportage. In commenting on the collective nature of *War and Peace,* Schlöndorff has said,

> A standardized imagery would at once be an anonymous film language. I believe that each expression should be a personal one, for that makes the images human. You should never claim that everybody in a collective film swears to a common language. Rather it means that you come to terms with one another. . . . Day by day we have looked at one another's products and discussed them, but we've made sure that each person retains his own "tone of voice." (Kluge and Schlöndorff 23)

If one looks more closely at Schlöndorff's Versailles sequence, one can see how idiosyncratically Schlöndorff has ordered and shaped his material. He contrasts, for example, the public Versailles spectacle, which the traditional media would simply swallow whole, to images of how that spectacle was devised. We can see, for example, the fountains of Versailles being turned off *after* the guests have departed. The commentator remarks that the order in which the heads of state arrive corresponds directly to the gross national product of each country. What the news takes for granted Schlöndorff chooses to show and state while also pointing to the summit conference's real economic agenda (Kluge and Schlöndorff 2).

Much of the negative criticism of Schlöndorff has characterized the filmmaker as an opportunist who cannibalizes good literature without necessarily making good cinema. The historical awareness of *Valeska Gert,* the rhetorical pointedness of *The Candidate,* and the macabre playfulness of *War and Peace* all present a somewhat different director, and whether one finds them fully successful or not, one cannot but recognize a certain integrity. They deserve to be more widely seen, not only for their intrinsic merits but also for the other side they reveal of their maker. The dialectic between the disparate elements and styles in *War and Peace* is not unlike comparable dialectic in Schlöndorff's work as a whole.

17

Circle of Deceit

After the success of *The Tin Drum* and the change of pace of *The Candidate,* Schlöndorff planned to direct another film written by Günter Grass. The general subject of *Kopfgeburten (Headbirth)* was to have been the relationship between developed nations, such as West Germany, and the Third World. Grass and Schlöndorff planned to have the script grow out of a trip they took to Egypt, India, and Indonesia, but Schlöndorff was dissatisfied with what Grass finally wrote because of its lack of character or story. It was, in Schlöndorff's words, "a scenario in the form of an essay which would have made, under other circumstances, a very good Godard film" (*"Le faussaire"* 41).

Grass published this script in 1980 as the novel *Headbirth or The Germans Are Dying Out* (*Kopfgeburten oder Die Deutschen sterben aus*), which he dedicated to Nicolas Born, a German writer who had just died. On reading Born's *Die Fälschung* (translated in English as *The Deception*), a novel published in 1979 and set against the ongoing war in Lebanon, Schlöndorff found in Born's novel many of the themes and preoccupations present in the *Headbirth* project. Both works presented prosperous but anxious West Germans faced with economically poor but confident and decisive members of the Third World. The filmmaker determined to adapt Born's work instead of film Grass's screenplay (Schlöndorff, *"Le faussaire"* 41).

The film version of *Die Fälschung,* called *Circle of Deceit* in English-speaking countries, might at first glance be called one of Schlöndorff's most commercial projects up to that time. It makes superficial concessions to popular taste, providing for a scenario that contains elements of adventure and romance in exotic settings. On second glance, however, one sees that *Circle of Deceit* is a film containing specific discourses about both politics and philosophy. As a political film, it is a critique of journalistic sensationalism, an exposition of the complexities of the Lebanese political situation, and an examination of the gap between developed nations and the Third World. As a philosophical essay, it brings into question three adjacent issues: the complex relations among words, images, and the realities they can portray; the moral problem of the responsibility of a bystander toward the events he observes; the tension within the reflective individual between drives toward personal pleasure and those involving political commitment and responsibility.

Circle of Deceit's twin discourses, political and philosophical, permeate the movie. We keep both in mind as we consider the production history of the film and the aesthetic decisions the filmmakers made, the content of the film itself, and the mixed critical reaction it received. We include in our analysis in particular a discussion of the climactic scene in the film in which the German hero kills an anonymous Moslem, for it is in this scene that the multiple themes of the work converge. Finally, we see that beneath the film's political and philosophical discourses is a psychoanalytic subtext, one that may or may not consciously be put there by Schlöndorff, about voyeurism and masochism.

A Topical Film

Circle of Deceit takes place during January 1976, a period of significant escalation of the conflicts between the Moslem-Palestinian and Christian forces in Lebanon. On January 13, Moslem and Palestinian fighters laid siege to Damur, a Christian stronghold some twelve miles south of Beirut. In response to these leftist assaults on Damur, the Lebanese air force bombed gunmen who had attacked a government military convoy on its way to the town. The air attack was made despite directives against it from the country's prime minister, Rashid Karami, the only strong Moslem representative within the government, who resigned later that week. The attack was the first instance of air fighting since the previous April, and the fighting that ensued resulted in the closing of the Beirut airport and temporary suspension of international telephone and Telex communication (Markham, "Lebanese Planes").

In retaliation against leftist successes in the Damur struggle, rightists claimed to be "liberating" the Karantina and Maslakh slum sections of Beirut by transporting hundreds of Moslem families to more solidly Moslem areas in the city. Finally on January 20, Damur fell to the Moslem and Palestinian forces. An estimated two hundred combatants and civilians were killed in the last day of the struggle, and about six thousand refugees evacuated the city (Markham, "Beirut Ex-Premier"; Markham, "Strife in Lebanon"). The struggles for Damur, Karantina, and Maslakh and the bloodshed that accompanied them form the immediate political context for Born and Schlöndorff's narrative.

Schlöndorff's original plan for shooting the film had been to reconstruct

Beirut in Algiers, where Schlöndorff had worked with Louis Malle on a television documentary about the Algerian War some 20 years earlier. In connection with this original plan, one cannot help but remember Schlöndorff's political involvements in France during the Algerian conflict and his activism in calling for an end to the use of torture by the French (Schlöndorff, "A Parisian-American" 45). One recalls that Schlöndorff's first short, *Wen kümmert's?*, was a work about Algerian war protestors. One may note, too, at least the superficial similarity between the senseless murder central to *Circle of Deceit* and the one in Albert Camus's *The Stranger*. In this respect, then, one finds what may be the earliest sources of *Circle of Deceit*'s political and philosophical concerns in Schlöndorff's formative French experiences.

Schlöndorff's plans changed when he visited Beirut for background information and was struck by the strong visual quality of what he saw there. Finding both the leftists and the rightists willing to cooperate, he decided to shoot the film there. Schlöndorff has said that his purpose in using real locations was to prick the viewer's conscience, to undermine any complacency the spectator might have from seeing anything but the real places where such suffering had occurred (Vinocur). At the same time, Schlöndorff wanted *Circle of Deceit* to be clearly designated as fiction and consciously avoided handheld cameras and grainy film stock that might have lent the work an excessively documentary air. Schlöndorff chose to work out carefully the elements of composition, camera movement, and color, again with the intent of playing against any illusion of the film being a documentary (Schlöndorff, *"Le faussaire"* 41–42). In the director's own words, "of course the film *Die Fälschung* is again a *Fälschung* [deception]" (Schlöndorff, "Oskar" 6). This deliberate confrontation of reality with aesthetic artifice is in keeping with the approach of Born's novel, which uses a self-consciously literary, nonjournalistic writing style to deal with the Lebanese war.

Jacques Rivette has commented that the circumstances by which a film is shot ultimately dictate its real content, and *Circle of Deceit* becomes a demonstration of Rivette's thesis ("Entretien" 19; Bergala, "Rivette" 5). Reports about the production describe it as having been besieged with problems: the physical discomforts and dangers involved in shooting in a war-torn city, difficulties in obtaining permissions to film, Schlöndorff's continual mind changing when faced with measuring a preconceived script against a real-life setting, problems with actors (Nasri 48). From a screenplay that reportedly began as being partisan and sympathetic to the Moslem-Palestinian cause, Schlöndorff wound up filming a movie that reflected his own confusion on seeing things firsthand.

To at least some extent, the guilt, indecision, and anguish felt by the film's hero, Georg Laschen, reflect Schlöndorff's own feelings in trying to portray honestly the Lebanese war. Indeed, Schlöndorff has indicated that, on reading the book, he identified strongly with Born's hero on the basis of the German director's own journalistic experience in Algeria ("Oskar" 17). Both Schlöndorff and the fictional Laschen would represent politically committed men attempting to act responsibly even after their political convictions have been shaken (Schlöndorff, "The Limits" 47). Schlöndorff's decision to shoot on location became, in effect, a putting of himself in the same position as Laschen, making Schlöndorff himself a reporter covering the Beirut war and increasing the potential for physical danger and moral confusion. In this respect one might see *Circle of Deceit* as a small-scale counterpart to movies like Joseph L. Mankiewicz's *Cleopatra* (1963) or Francis Coppola's *Apocalypse Now* (1979), works in which one can find striking similarities between elements of their fictional plots and their disastrous conditions of shooting (Comolli; Le Pavec).

Contradictions of the Lebanese War

In trying to respond to questions of political and moral responsibility in the Lebanese conflict, Schlöndorff combines two approaches: first, he refuses to take sides but rather presents the struggle in all its contradictions; second, his film constantly questions the truth and falseness of media image making and is consistently self-referential. There is, Schlöndorff suggests, a certain affinity between the photographic image and atrocity. Schlöndorff asks the political question, How can a comfortable, prosperous Westerner most fairly understand the war in the Middle East? He asks the philosophical one, How do those who represent events relate to the reality they portray?

The picture begins with Georg Laschen (Bruno Ganz), a journalist, leaving Germany to cover the war in Beirut. He has been quarreling with his wife, Greta, particularly about his objections to her career. By leaving his home and family life in Germany, he is leaving a world in which he participates for one in which his job is simply to observe. He will become a spectator, a voyeur, a nonparticipant.

In Beirut, Laschen finds that most of the fighting is done at night and that his comfortable, luxurious, somewhat garish hotel is in no-man's-land, between the two fighting forces. After watching a street vendor get shot during the daytime, a native tells him that the way to stay alive in Beirut is to keep moving, never to be a sitting target. The war is, in other words, like a movie. A movie takes place in the dark (and usually at night), is seen from the sometimes tackily

elegant surroundings of a movie theater, and in effect dies—gets burned up—
if it ceases to be a moving image.

After a bit of street fighting during the day, some Lebanese wheel a dummy
out into the street to see whether anyone will shoot at it and test thereby the
advisability of going out. As with the movies, we use the imaginary, the fake,
to test the real. Later in the film, a minor character takes her supper on the
balcony of her house every night so as better to watch the entertainment of
the fighting and explosives. The war, Schlöndorff seems to be saying, is both
terrifying and fascinating, and this combination of terror and fascination is
comparable to that same terror and fascination we seek in the cinema. More
than one character says, in the course of the movie, that he or she has never felt
safer than in war-torn Beirut, that the experience has created for them a feeling
of security.

Throughout his attempts to observe, Laschen tries not to become involved,
yet the disengagement he seeks becomes difficult. During some street fighting,
a man gives him a gun to defend himself, and he must in turn give it back. Later,
a woman tries to pull him into an argument; he resists, but moments later gunmen force both him and the lady into a truck. Simply being on the street makes
him suspect. To avoid becoming involved or taking sides is a constant challenge.

If acting to release tension, to reduce frustration, or simply to blend in with
one's environment becomes increasingly attractive, acting from thought-out
political conviction becomes increasingly impossible. In visiting a leader of the
Christian forces in the city, the pro-Palestinian Laschen asks intimidating questions and angers the leader. Yet when he goes to the Palestinian camp, he witnesses at Damur a cruel execution of captives that he is unable, in his somewhat
naive attempts, to stop. As he tries to write reports on the war for home,
Laschen admits that he exaggerates to give readers something sensationalized,
but as he sees more and more, he finds it harder and harder to write about what
he sees. At one point he says, "All I do is entertain." Schlöndorff acknowledges
the ambiguity of his own situation. He is surely making a fiction movie to entertain, but he wants to do something more with his film than simply amuse.

Georg Laschen discovers, then, that there are two wars going on in Lebanon,
a war of flesh and blood and a war of images, and it is the war of images he is
already a part of. Hoffmann (Jerzy Skolimowski), the photographer who
accompanies Laschen, complains that he cannot get pictures because all of the
fighting is at night or because charred bodies and burnt-out buildings all look
alike after a while. Laschen and Hoffmann discover a Palestinian who has studied music in Germany; Hoffmann poses him at a piano, his machine gun resting on top of it—to make the kind of sensational image he is looking for.

Pictures, propaganda, public relations, exploitations, all become as much a part of the war as the flesh-and-blood fighting. Schlöndorff's adaptation personalizes Laschen's journalist colleagues far more than Born's book does and types them according to their varying sensationalist or sober approaches: creation of media images of the war becomes for Schlöndorff more emphatically an issue of personal responsibility.

Schlöndorff emphasizes his point about the image war through the character of Rudnik (Jean Carmet). Rudnik is a French arms vendor who has been profiteering from the situation and who becomes an embodiment of both wars together. On the one hand, he traffics in arms, but he also has atrocity pictures to sell to the Western press: the two have become interchangeable. Laschen jokingly calls the latter "[d]irty pictures to look at in clean places." Making his message even more obvious, Schlöndorff has Rudnik comment that the reporter should have brought over some porno pictures from Germany: "You can trade them for anything," he comments.

Warfare and Eroticism

The comparison of atrocity photos to pornography may at first seem simply like a facile metaphor, but taken in context, it establishes a link to an entirely different discourse in the movie. Schlöndorff returns in *Circle of Deceit* to his ever-present theme of the impossibility of love, linking it to the question of warfare, images, and pornography. Laschen, unable to get along with his wife at home, has an affair in Lebanon with Ariane Nassar (Hanna Schygulla), a German consulate employee who has been married to a wealthy Arab. As a simple narrative turn, the affair fits the conventions of the standard adventure film, providing for a bit of eroticism to balance the action. (See illustration 26.) In much the manner of the classic Hollywood film, danger seeking becomes associated with sex, as when the couple decide to stay above ground and make love during a bombing, while everyone else has fled to the cellar.

Circle of Deceit's treatment of love and eroticism is complicated, however, by a single set of shots that occurs early in the film and that gives all of the work's subsequent images a thoroughly new context. One of the first images in *Circle of Deceit* involves Laschen's daughter, Else, accidentally seeing her parents begin to make love. This event does not occur in Born's novel and is one of Schlöndorff's few significant additions to the film. The event occurs right after we have seen Laschen pack in his suitcase the knife he will wear hidden, strapped to his leg, throughout the movie and with which he will kill an anonymous Moslem near the story's end.

26. *Circle of Deceit*. Reporter Laschen (Bruno Ganz) and embassy employee Ariane (Hanna Schygulla), with a wry comment on the nature of their love. Photo: Museum of Modern Art/Film Stills Archive.

Placed so early in the film, this image of the child establishes certain leit-motifs that Schlöndorff carries on throughout it—of voyeurism, intrusion, lack of participation, a combination of interest and fear on the part of the person looking. The image is, of course, one that relates directly to the Freudian notion of the primal scene, the traumatic experience, real or fantasized, whereby the jealous child watches his parents making love. We need not digress to recapitulate Christian Metz's well-known theories of the primal scene as an organizing metaphor for the film medium itself (63–65). One can nonetheless see in this prelude to the main action of the film the eroticization of its central theme: the civilized German becomes a metaphorical pervert, a voyeur who prefers watching to performing. Schlöndorff himself has compared Laschen's voyeurism to that of Oskar Matzerath in *The Tin Drum* ("Oskar" 11). Indeed, Schlöndorff's play in this film with powerful gaze structures extends not only those patterns found in *The Tin Drum* but also those of earlier films, from *Törless* to *Katharina Blum*.

This suggestion of the primal scene, whereby the witnessing child is excluded from the parents' lovemaking, occurs again in the sequence in which Laschen discovers Ariane's affair with a Palestinian lover. Having decided to leave his wife and remain in Beirut to be with Ariane, Laschen returns to Ariane's house uninvited. Just as Laschen approaches, Ariane emerges from the house with Ahmed. Laschen crouches, unobserved, behind a car. He watches the lovers embrace, then slips off as the car drives away. He becomes, in effect, the intruding little boy, unable to compete with the masculinity of the father.

This incident is Laschen's most intense experience of a symbolic primal scene, and the evident frustration he feels after the incident gives rise to the climactic moment in the film in which the passive reporter progresses to participation rather than observation. During a shelling in which Laschen is confined to a crowded shelter, he falls to the ground with a number of local men in the almost totally darkened room. When an anonymous Moslem man leans or falls against Laschen during the confusion, the reporter pulls out the knife he has been carrying strapped to his leg and stabs him.

The stabbing scene is supremely ambiguous. Although the British critic Tom Milne has argued that the scene is "so clumsily staged that it is not clear whether the Arab was attacking him, simply panicking, or pressed against him by the milling crowd" (85), one suspects that Milne misses the point: Laschen doesn't know why the Moslem is on top of him—nor even, one might add, if his body is alive—and neither are we supposed to know. A check back to Born's novel is no help here; Born's description is fully from Laschen's confused point of view (*The Deception* 203–4).

Furthermore, Schlöndorff gives little clue as to Laschen's motives for the act—if, indeed, Laschen himself knows them. On the one hand, one senses in Laschen a generalized rage at having lost Ariane to a Palestinian. In addition, Schlöndorff withholds, through elliptical editing, the full enactment of the stabbing until a later flashback, as if to suggest that it is only later that Laschen fully realizes what he has done. The effect is one of a kind of psychological censoring: we see the man atop Laschen, then later the knife in his back, but Schlöndorff withholds for some minutes the image of its actual insertion.

The imagery of the scene as a whole peculiarly suggests a love scene, one that in its own way echoes the earlier image of Laschen and Ariane crawling along the floor during the earlier bombing. The scene inverts the primal scene leitmotif and continues the movie's use of motifs of light and dark. To observe, one must have light, distance, rationality. To participate, one can be surrounded by darkness, in enclosed, crowded spaces, ruled by impulse and emotion. The more one reads the image, the more its meanings multiply and its psychoanalytic levels merge with others. To kill the Moslem is

1. to kill the symbolic father, who has claimed Ariane, the symbolic mother (the latter metaphorical position made all the more obvious by Ariane's efforts in the film to adopt a child);
2. to act on a certain irrational, perhaps instinctive, combative homosexuality;
3. to reject reason in favor of emotion, observation in favor of participation;
4. to war not with images but with physical contact;
5. to reject the passive role of the masochistic, guilty observer, in favor of an active role of sadistic aggressor;
6. to reconfirm the fundamental dominance of the Third World by the First.

Laschen's experience of murder proves to be cathartic but terrifying: it frees Laschen from his inaction, but now, having committed a crime as senseless as all the others around him, he must live with guilt. In the scene immediately following the murder, Laschen steps into the shower in the hotel room and tries to wash blood off his clothes. Stripping, he tries to cleanse his body, too. The sense Schlöndorff conveys is one of liberation, even if that liberation may be temporary. Laschen can at last experience real guilt—not the passive, ambiguous, uncertain guilt of the bystander who watches violence and does nothing about it. As is the pattern with much Hitchcock, guilt is decisively transferred to a formerly innocent bystander.

Like so many Schlöndorff films, *Circle of Deceit* is a labyrinth with no real exit. Returning to Germany, Laschen quits his job but still must face his wife and marriage. The circle of the film's English title refers, ultimately, to the movie's circular structure. Only at the end of the film do we realize that the image that began it, of Laschen approaching his home in a car surrounded by a blinding rainstorm, is really from the story's conclusion.

A Negative Reception

If *Circle of Deceit* is a movie whose discourse operates on two planes, the political and the philosophical, one can categorize critical reaction to it according to each. On the more purely political plane, Schlöndorff pleased neither side in the Lebanese conflict, and various critics have found the film biased, perhaps unintentionally, toward one side or the other. John Vinocur notes that the pompous, aristocratic Christian whom Laschen interviews is the only political leader we get to see directly. Given this unflattering portrayal and that of an equally obnoxious pro-Christian journalist in the film, Vinocur finds *Circle of Deceit* pro-Palestinian by default (33). By contrast, pro-Palestinians have objected because Schlöndorff shows the Phalangist atrocities against them only secondhand, through videotapes seen within the film, while presenting the bloody execution of the Christian village much more directly, as something Laschen witnesses (Nasri 50).

West German critics by and large received *Circle of Deceit* cooly and accused Schlöndorff of exploiting a horrible political situation for the purpose of making an essentially self-indulgent film about personal discomfort. The film also fared poorly at the box office there (Vinocur 33). The same complaint, and comparable lackluster box office performance, characterized the movie's American reception. Andrew Sarris, for example, accused the work of having a pro-Palestinian and subtly anti-Israeli bias, charged Schlöndorff with hypocrisy, and saw the film as representing "a new dream of the third world, a dream in which the guilt-ridden intellectuals of the West can find relief through self-flagellation" (45).

John Powers, writing in *American Film* with a far more leftist orientation, attacked the work on somewhat different grounds. Lumping it with other movies from the 1980s about the Third World, like *Missing, Under Fire,* and *The Year of Living Dangerously,* Powers argued that Schlöndorff's work joins the Hollywood tradition by reinforcing racist stereotypes, portraying Third World peoples as exotic, inscrutable, mysterious, and scary. Like the directors of the other films cited by Powers, Schlöndorff supposedly opts for dramatically potent images of confusion and chaos, images that distort, simplify, and trivialize Third World problems, all for the sake of telling an engaging story (38–43). (See illustration 27.)

Schlöndorff upset an entirely different set of critics on philosophical grounds. Several writers in England and France have been far more concerned with the implications of Schlöndorff's strategies of mise-en-scène and in particular with the issues of realism it raises. Even a critic favorably disposed toward the film, David Shipman in *Films and Filming,* argued that one should ignore Schlöndorff's claim that the film is a fiction and consider the film "as the documentary about war that it isn't supposed to be" (*"Circle of Deceit"* 32). Several French critics have been similarly interested in the film's semidocumentary nature and have questioned in particular Schlöndorff's use of real locations in the movie. In an especially negative review, Gaston Haustrate ridiculed the situation that occurred whereby Schlöndorff persuaded the warring factions to cease fighting in a certain quarter so he could use it as a location to portray fictionally the same fighting that would resume as soon as he was finished. The result of grafting a fictional story onto these persuasive locations was, to Haustrate, "a somewhat false simplification which adds to an already extreme confusion" (104–5). Marcel Martin reflected a similar attitude

27. *Circle of Deceit*. Laschen standing in the rubble of Beirut. Photo: Museum of Modern Art/Film Stills Archive.

in writing, "Is not Schlöndorff himself behaving like a *forger* in trying to pass off his filmic verisimilitude at the cost of making it an alloy with documentary truth?" (*"Le faussaire"* 25). A parallel view is offered by German critic Thilo Wydra's comment:

> The "real reality," if not adequately suitable cinematically and screen compatible, is being produced by French pyrotechnicians. And when one needs charred human remains at the beach of the "death city,". . . and Schlöndorff has these especially flown in from Cinecittà, a 12-year old boy comes to them, asking why they would use such artificial material. He could provide the genuine stuff for them. The next day he stands there—with the genuine bones and skulls. These were not used in the movie. (Wydra 143–44)

In the final analysis, most negative reviews of the film, if not partisan in their reactions to the film's political discourse, express the critics' discomfort at Schlöndorff's mixture of elements—of documentary with fiction, of politics with existential anguish, of exotic, unfamiliar locations with more familiar narrative conventions (Canby, "Mankind's Folly"; Kifner).

The unity with which *Circle of Deceit*'s various elements are assembled is perhaps its most problematic aspect. In this regard, one may usefully compare the finished film to a book Schlöndorff published with Bernd Lepel and, posthumously, Nicholas Born, simultaneous to the film's release in West Germany. *Die Fälschung als Film und der Krieg im Libanon* includes the screenplay for *Circle of Deceit* but goes far beyond being simply a published screenplay, for it juxtaposes, collage-style, several materials: the movie's script, frame enlargements and production stills from the film, other photographic documentation of Lebanon and the war, excerpts from Nicolas Born's writing, and a series of reproduced newspaper articles, dating from 1975 to 1981, that describes the events against which *Circle of Deceit*'s story is set and against which its shooting took place.

Schlöndorff could easily have made a film in some ways equivalent to Laschen's killing of the Arab, a cinematic stab in the dark whose sole purpose would be to reduce the anxiety of the stabber. *Circle of Deceit* is an expression, perhaps even an exorcism, of anxiety, but Schlöndorff's choices have been tempered by his characteristic rationalism. Particularly in the book drawn from the film, Schlöndorff invites critical speculation about the correctness of his choices. By inscribing into *Circle of Deceit* Laschen's reportorial dilemma, the movie invites its own critical reading. In such self-reflexivity lies *Circle of Deceit*'s intelligence, modernity, and ultimate integrity.

18

Swann in Love

For his next assignment, Schlöndorff signed onto a project that had previously daunted such film artists as Luchino Visconti and Joseph Losey—an adaptation from Marcel Proust's multivolume novel *Remembrance of Things Past (À la recherche du temps perdu)*. The German filmmaker's *Swann in Love (Un amour de Swann)*, shot in France in the summer of 1983, takes a single volume from Proust and spins it out into a feature-length film that only alludes to the larger work as a whole. As narrative, *Swann in Love* is a wisp of a story. It is about Charles Swann (Jeremy Irons), an upper-middle-class dandy who has social access to the late-nineteenth-century French aristocracy but who sacrifices his social standing by becoming obsessively infatuated with a capricious demimonde, Odette de Crécy (Ornella Muti). Schlöndorff's film describes how Swann pursues the only intermittently responsive Odette, only to see desire evaporate as soon as its realization becomes possible. The movie ends with Swann as an old man, reflecting on a life that he has all but thrown away on an evanescent flirtation.

Critical reception of *Swann in Love* was not particularly warm. Both popular reviewers and literary scholars found the film a rather flat adaptation of only a portion of Marcel Proust's sprawling *Remembrance of Things Past*, and few film critics have argued that the film successfully stands alone as a work of film art. Audience reception was comparable. Although the film broke opening week house records in its New York premiere at the Paris theater in fall of 1984, its box office grosses declined precipitously in subsequent weeks, indicating mediocre word of mouth (Coursodon 22–23).

Subsequent scholarship has been no more positive. Perhaps the most stinging academic attack on the film has been by Phil Powrie, who argues skillfully that the film is a mere transformation of a work of literature into a commercial property, designed to turn Proust into a cultural commodity for international bourgeois audiences. Schlöndorff's involvement in the project was to be merely a way to legitimatize large-scale monetary investment. Similarly, the presence of international stars like Irons and Alain Delon becomes part of an industrial package that gets wrapped up with lavish sets and costumes and pretty photography by renowned Swedish cameraman Sven Nykvist. For Powrie, *Swann in Love*'s few social concerns are superficial and ultimately hypocritical. He labels the film "static, vacuous, dehistoricized spectacle" (33).

We would like to propose a qualified defense of *Swann in Love*. It is not that Powrie is totally wrong: *Swann in Love* was certainly marketed as a cultural commodity, and Schlöndorff's prestigious reputation as an adapter of "impossible" literature was no doubt a comfort to investors. There is no question that, had its script been proposed without the context of Proust's literary classic, the film might never have been made. But we would also assert that the whole issue of adaptation has so clouded the reception of *Swann in Love* that a number of its particular subtleties have gone unnoticed. Schlöndorff has constructed *Swann in Love* around three central, interrelated metaphors whose sources may be less in Proust than in Schlöndorff's approach to cinematic narrative and audiovisual expression. These metaphors involve the movie's twenty-four-hour structure, its dominant images and sounds, and the symbolic nature of its sexuality. Seen in the light of these metaphors, *Swann in Love* takes on a limpidity, coherence, and cinema-specificity that critics have ignored. Schlöndorff has transformed Proust into something different—not necessarily something as important or as rich as its literary antecedent but neither something to be immediately dismissed.

Metaphor One—The Day and the Lifetime

In accepting the *Swann in Love* assignment from producer Nicole Stéphane, Schlöndorff retained a structure that had been devised for the film when Peter Brook was at the helm of the project: the condensation of the movie's main action to a single day, with a filling in of necessary material through flashbacks and an epilogue. Some critics, such as Anne Tarqui, have seen this as a major betrayal of Proust. Tarqui argues that "Proustian writing consists exactly of minimizing the singular to emphasize the habitual, the repetitive. The Proustian formula is not 'once upon a time' but 'often.'" The result, the argument goes, is that the telescoping of sequences flattens the interior life of the characters and the novel's subjective richness (Tarqui 53).

What Tarqui misses is the different sort of thematic interest that this temporal condensation gives the film. For one thing, it allows the afternoon-to-afternoon cycle that makes up the film's circular structure to become a metaphor

for the birth-to-death cycle itself.[1] Swann's initial rising at noon is, quite simply, the beginning of a progression toward eventual sleep. Swann's separation
from sleep at the beginning of the film becomes a metaphoric birth, a separation from the mother. By contrast, Swann's death is evoked by his words to
his friend Charlus (Alain Delon) while still in bed the following day, right
before the latter pushes Swann to admit that he plans to marry Odette de Crécy:
"This morning when I woke up, I knew I was free of Odette." Given that Swann
has twice before claimed that he would cease to exist without his love for her,
the scene marks the end of love and, by extension, the end of life.

Schlöndorff retains implicitly the cyclical quality of Proust by giving his film
the sense that we are seeing not just a day in the life of Swann but Swann's
entire life crystallized in a single day. As a result, any given moment in the film
may work on more than one level—as an event in the particular day the movie
presents, as a metonym for some broader aspect of Swann's whole life, and
intertextually as a metonym for broader, unadapted sections of Proust's novel.
What may have begun as a device to give dramatic shape to a loosely structured work of literature acquires its own kind of complexity.

More important, *Swann in Love*'s afternoon-to-morning progression provides
for a temporal structure that emphasizes Swann's confinement by time as a
major theme. By setting his film's action in a specified, limited present,
Schlöndorff underscores Swann's inability to return to, hold on to, or possess
the past, except perhaps through art. This sense of temporal confinement as a
major motif in the film becomes obvious in *Swann in Love*'s final scene. Swann
and Charlus, amid the automobiles and hubbub of a more modern Paris, sit at
the Tuileries and reflect on their past. Swann, who has found out that he has
only several more months to live, describes thinking of his life as like looking
at a collection consisting of the loves he has had. (See illustration 28.) The biological limitations of life itself are the ultimate confinement: we have only the
moment we are currently living. We have only, in a manner of speaking, the
madeleine before us.

Metaphor Two—The Physically Visual and the Spiritually Aural

If our first metaphor establishes temporal confinement as a major structural
device of the film, the movie's mise-en-scène constantly reinforces a sense of
spatial confinement. *Swann in Love* takes place predominantly in interior settings, and the material world it presents is at once comfortable and oppressive.
As in the melodramas of Douglas Sirk, the characters' lavish, cluttered interior surroundings restrict and imprison them at the same time this lush envi-

28. *Swann in Love.* The older Swann and Charlus contemplating their past from a park bench. Photo: Museum of Modern Art/Film Stills Archive.

ronment impresses the viewer with its style and richness. By contrast, Swann's interior life is indicated through the sound track, both by means of Swann's voice-over narration and especially through music, which comes to signify transcendence and spirituality.

With the exception of the final scene in the work, virtually all of the exterior scenes in *Swann in Love* present people in transit from one indoor place to another. The conversations in the Bagatelle Gardens, in which Swann meets Odette after the musical reception at the Guermantes', involve the characters going to and from the restaurant where they have chocolate. When Swann goes to meet Odette after the opera, we see mainly his search for the restaurant where she will be. Once separated from her again that same evening because she has chosen to ride home with Fourcheville in Madame Verdurin's carriage, Swann wanders the streets aimlessly, only to resolve his anxiety by knocking at Odette's window. Only in the last scene of the film do the two men, outside in the park, have nowhere to go, a situation that is both liberating and suggestive of death.

The tenuous story line in *Swann in Love* hinges on Swann's simple desire to be alone with the woman he loves, which is translated imagistically into a kind of mild agoraphobia. Swann exudes anxiety whenever he is outdoors or in what one might call the movie's public interiors, the various salons and restaurants in which Swann's society meets. When Swann is finally alone with Odette in her rooms, we sense momentary relief and comfort. The physical atmosphere becomes intimate and secure, although Swann's jealously and petulance spoil what satisfaction he might get from it. Similarly, a flashback of Odette's visit to Swann's apartment is idealized in its intimacy and warmth.

Although most of *Swann in Love* has a pretty, picture-book image track, Schlöndorff and his composer, Hans Werner Henze, often undercut these pleasant images through the use of spare, mournful, anxious musical motifs that cue us to Swann's discomfort. Schlöndorff and Henze suggest through sound the turmoil underlying the superficial pleasure and prosperity of the environment. The movie's imagery is, in effect, the banally polite, genteel exterior that masks both passion and despair.

At the opening of the work, we hear a pen scratching, a sound that at once acknowledges the literary source of the story and suggests Swann as the source of the narrative in an implicit first person. On the sound track, however, Schlöndorff and Henze bring up a rather strident melodic line for violin: the scratching of the bow and the scratching of the pen soon merge and overlap in an aural analogy between the two art forms. We then hear Swann's first voice-over narration. His second sentence, "My love for Odette goes beyond the bounds of physical desire," sets up a fundamental opposition of the movie between flesh (expressed through images) and spirit (expressed through sound).

Music becomes for Schlöndorff's film a kind of analogue to memory and the mental processes involved with memory. Where painting, by contrast, is physically linked to the material world and objects and possessions, music, as it drifts from room to room, can transcend immediate spatial boundaries. To the extent that a melody exists in the head of the listener and is perhaps even more easily remembered than a visual image, music suggests escape from temporal confines as well. The listener can, in effect, carry with him the work of musical art even after the concert or recital is over.

Although Swann compares Odette physically to a work by Botticelli, it is the "Vinteuil Sonata" that better reflects the Swann-Odette romance. Here Schlöndorff both shows his own intelligence and respects his audience's. Hans

Werner Henze's realization of the "Vinteuil Sonata" puts an emphasis not on a recognizable, hummable melody that the audience can immediately recognize but rather on loosely constructed, chromatic musical lines, much in the manner of Debussy (whom some observers see as Proust's model for Vinteuil). Where a filmmaker seeking the residual benefits of record sales could easily have made the "Vinteuil Sonata" a sentimental love theme for Swann and Odette, Schlöndorff and Henze choose instead to give us a sonata that deemphasizes repeated motifs and is not easy to follow on first hearing. If music becomes the analogue to love and memory, the lack of melodic resolution in Henze's "Vinteuil Sonata" suggests something intensely experienced in the present but elusive to exact memory. Far from missing the opportunity provided by the sonata, as some critics have suggested, Schlöndorff makes of it not a cheap theatrical effect but a more complex analogue to Swann's state of mind.

One of the few critics to have appreciated Schlöndorff's use of music in *Swann in Love* was Wilfried Wiegand, who has argued that "[o]ne misunderstands this film if one does not also comprehend it as a musical work." Wiegand writes that the music

> is in the history of film music one of those rare compositions which not only interprets the action as mood painting, but turns into an element of the action itself. . . . Not only the music, but the entire action at such moments assumes a hallucinatory quality: one no longer feels like one is viewing an objectively existent exterior world, but the lovesick Swann's worlds of desire and delusion.

Schlöndorff's staging of the scene in which the sonata is first played solidifies the film's thematic associations. As the pianist begins to perform it at the Verdurins' postopera soirée, Odette deliberately moves to sit next to Swann. Where up to now the Verdurins' party has been marked by its vulgarity and dilettantism, Schlöndorff frames Odette and Swann from the back in a tight two-shot in which their intimate words suggest a closing off from a banal material world. Their intimacy is later recaptured when Odette somewhat clumsily plays a portion of the sonata while she and Swann are alone in her chambers, just prior to their making love. In both cases, the sonata helps the couple achieve a kind of idealized confinement.

One eccentric feature of Henze's score is his use of a single soprano voice that emerges on the music track at several key points in the movie. We hear it first during Swann's interrogation of Odette about her suspected lesbian experiences, later when Swann goes to her apartment at night to rap on the window, and finally at the end of the film, accompanying the final image of Odette some twenty-five years later, still strikingly beautiful. Like Swann's voice-over nar-ration and unlike the other voices in the film, this voice belongs to the realm of art. This additional, intruding voice suggests an almost spiritual presence, a body we never see. This voice seems somehow liberating in its ability to tran-scend space and time.[2]

Metaphor Three — Odette as the Mother

Whose voice is this? Let us propose a third metaphor central to *Swann in Love*, one that requires a psychoanalytic interpretation of the narrative. *Swann in Love* is filled with images and incidents that point to Swann's search for Odette as a search for the mother, an absent mother who indeed may be calling through the disembodied voice that recurs on the sound track. Given Proust's own with-drawal into reclusion after the death of his own mother, such an interpreta-tion of Swann's debilitating dependence on Odette would indeed be a reasonable autobiographical interpretation of the source material.

If Swann's rising in the morning is a metaphoric birth, then his bed is ana-logically a womb, and his all-consuming desire to take Odette to bed is in effect a desire for a return to prenatal bliss. Swann's immediate thoughts on awak-ening are of Odette, and we see the first of several flashbacks to the carriage scene, with its famous cattleyas. In our first view of the carriage, however, we see nothing of Odette's face, only her bosom, and Swann's sexual attachment to her breasts in no way contradicts what may be also an image suggestive of mothering. Swann's search for Odette becomes in turn a search for maternal love, for youth, for life itself. Consider, too, Swann's words of love to Odette during the "Vinteuil Sonata" scene, words evocative of childbirth, not to men-tion Plato's cave: "I existed in a dark void, then suddenly saw the world bathed in a new light."

One of the more controversial aspects of Schlöndorff's *Swann in Love* has been its two sex scenes, one with Swann at a brothel, the other between him and Odette. In the former, Swann, with only his pants removed, presumably sodomizes a young prostitute, a cigarette stuck in his mouth the whole time. In the latter, when Odette finally invites him to bed, he enters her from behind in a way that deliberately echoes the preceding scene. The scenes become a locus for several meanings. Jean-Francis Held has speculated, for example, that this is Schlöndorff's way of indicating Proust's homosexuality and the set of expe-riences from which he drew the *Remembrance of Things Past* (19). Schlöndorff himself has indicated that Swann needs to objectify Odette, to control her, and hence can never really love her (Buck 392). These scenes, however, both portraying sexual penetration from behind, form a direct contrast to the cattleya flashbacks. In this other scene of *remembered* sexual action, Swann approaches Odette's breasts from the front, in a way that suggests infantile pleasure rather than sophisticated disengagement. (See illustration 29.) Schlöndorff makes a parallel point when the young Jewish man whom Charlus had picked up at the park restaurant leaves Charlus's carriage, rejecting the older man's sexual advances. The carriage-womb suggests a place of idealized loving contact, but the contact is elusive—quickly lost and hard to regain.

Swann's quest thus becomes an impossible one because Odette can never be his mother; the movie takes on an archetypal quality in which the idealized woman, the Odette whose image is found in the Botticelli fresco, must ultimately be contradicted by carnal, flesh-and-blood reality. The idealized Odette is destroyed as the relationship is consummated; the relationship ends as it leads to marriage. As Schlöndorff himself has put it, *Swann in Love* is a movie about futility (Blume 5). Odette has been both the mother and the whore. Each relationship is an impossible one for Swann, and both roles are incompatible with being a wife.

In this context, *Swann in Love* fits both classic notions of Oedipal sexuality and more contemporary revisions and variations of the Oedipal scheme. In Freud's system, guilt over sexual desire for the mother produces homosexual desires for the father as a form of self-protection against castration. Hence, one can see in the character of Charlus, Swann's homosexual alter-ego, the consequence of Swann's sexual desire for the Odette-mother. If one follows the alternative structure proposed by Gilles Deleuze and Gaylyn Studlar, the child experiences ambivalence toward the mother. He sees her as both a nurturing love object and a manipulative threatener, qualities Odette takes on by turns. This ambivalence can result in either sadism, in which the subject destroys the object he loves through physical, orgasmic contact, or masochism, in which the subject takes painful pleasure in his separation from the love object (Studlar 6–8).

We can see in Swann elements of both this sadism and this masochism. With the latter, Swann becomes a standard Schlöndorff hero—sensitive, suffering, and ambivalent toward women. He joins Franz of *The Morals of Ruth Halbfass*, Benyon of *Georgina's Reasons*, and Laschen of *Circle of Deceit*, all definitively masochistic protagonists, and all, from an auteurist standpoint, suggestive that Schlöndorff's body of work has substantial thematic unity despite the disparate literary sources from which he draws.

Swann in Love is surely not the fully satisfactory adaptation of Proust that some might have hoped it would be. Taken purely on its surface, as a linear story, the film is rather static and at most only modestly successful.

29. *Swann in Love.* Swann (Jeremy Irons) and Odette (Ornella Muti) in a moment of idealized tenderness. Photo: Museum of Modern Art/Film Stills Archive.

Nonetheless, the recognition of Schlöndorff's metaphoric strategies—his use of a day to represent a lifetime, of furniture and clutter to suggest the banality of physical existence, of music to suggest transcendence, of Swann's relation to Odette as an analogue to an Oedipal mother attraction—may well be a prerequisite to appreciating its below-the-surface pleasures. The complexity, cinematic specificity, and coherent interrelation of these metaphors make *Swann in Love* a film that goes beyond the sort of simplistic and empty literary adaptation some critics have called it.

Part Four

**THE AMERICAN
SCHLÖNDORFF**

19

A German Filmmaker in the United States

After the completion of *Swann in Love*, Schlöndorff traveled to New York, where his brother Detlef had been living and where he had originally planned a three-month sojourn to seek a change of scene (Siclier 10). The stay became an extended one. With the production of *Death of a Salesman* (1985) at the then recently renovated Astoria film studios in Queens, Schlöndorff began his fourth, American period. It extends through his subsequent two features, *A Gathering of Old Men* (1987) and *The Handmaid's Tale* (1989), both of which were shot in the American South. With these projects, Schlöndorff joined and extended the tradition of German émigré and exile filmmakers.

Schlöndorff's reasons for staying in the United States doubtless had to do with the further deterioration of the film production situation in the Federal Republic. When a rightist Christian-Liberal (CDU) government under Helmut Kohl replaced the Social-Liberal one led by Helmut Schmidt in 1982, the film subsidy process underwent a radical reorientation. The New German Cinema has sometimes been regarded as the cinematic creation of the Social-Liberal government. By contrast, governments under CDU leadership have constantly favored the old-guard, commercially oriented film. Interior Secretary Friedrich Zimmermann sent a decisive signal of this new conservative policy in the summer of 1983. He rescinded previously granted funding for counterculture filmmaker Herbert Achternbusch's film *The Ghost* (*Das Gespenst*, 1982) due to alleged blasphemy (Horak 2; Pflaum, "Konzertierte" 24–28). This government intervention not only indicated an ideological reversal but also marked a shift in film funding. No longer was it a system based on cultural merit; now it was one based on industrial and economic models. Only a few large projects guaranteeing "entertainment value" would be funded in the future, according to Zimmermann. When Schlöndorff learned of the interior secretary's new directives while he was working on *Swann* in Paris, he drafted an open letter of protest entitled "Zimmermanns Hinrichtungslinien," a pun converting *Richtlinie* or "rule" to "execution policy." He regarded Zimmermann's new edict as one "designed to prevent in the future such projects as my Proust adaptation" (91). The tenor of his protest demonstrates an expectation of censorship and a barring of all funding opportunities for any ambitious intellectual or literary cinema.

The restrictive political climate soon extended to a West German public-interest television system that began to fall increasingly under conservative control. This development only exacerbated the thematic timidity and conformism of West German filmmaking that had first taken hold during the second half of the 1970s, with the period's mood of terrorist hysteria. In addition, a fundamental reorganization of the federal broadcasting system further limited film funding opportunities from television. The first commercial West German television stations were licensed in the mid-1980s. RTL, Sat 1, and other stations began to take larger market shares from public television, thereby limiting the funds available to film production and forcing the public broadcasters into more entertainment-oriented programming. Moreover, the rapid expansion of the cable television system, which had been established by the German postal service in the early 1980s, resulted in diminished production and broadcasting of German films. All of these changes in the electronic arena, referred to in Germany as the *Neue Medien* or "New Media," had the practical effect of limiting funding and distribution of the domestic independent film.

Other factors contributed to a decline in the morale of the New German Cinema. With the death of Rainer Werner Fassbinder in 1982, one of the driving forces of the German New Wave came to a halt. Although Wim Wenders was to win the Golden Palm at Cannes in 1984, disagreements over the release strategy for *Paris, Texas* caused a falling out and a bitter lawsuit between Wenders and Filmverlag der Autoren, the collective distributor most associated with the new German filmmakers (Wenders 100–101). At the same time, a new Reagan-Kohl–era audience was turning away from the culture of the 1960s and helping to turn the conventional Hollywood narrative into an economic and cultural monolith.

Schlöndorff found the professional opportunities in New York far more inviting than those in Germany. Unlike Wim Wenders around 1980 and Wolfgang Petersen in 1986, Schlöndorff moved not to Hollywood but to the East Coast. There he pursued independent film projects in coproduction with television. In a transatlantic variation of West German models, whereby television broadcast and theatrical release were carefully coordinated, he was able to profit from a combined, "staggered" exploitation of television and movie theater releases. Both *Death of a Salesman* and *A Gathering of Old Men* were shown first on American television, then released theatrically in Europe. Though its results are often mixed, the American made-for-TV movie is a genre known for addressing public issues and social problems often ignored in Hollywood theatrical fare. With both *Salesman* and *Gathering,* Schlöndorff was to find here a production system in which he could have a degree of artistic and political maneuverability. Of course, some U.S. projects remained unrealized. In 1985, he had planned to make "The Last of the Saints" ("Der letzte Heilige"), the story of a German religious fanatic migrating to Utah in an attempt to establish his cult there. In 1986, he worked on a political satire in which Steve Martin was not only to star as "The Most Powerful Man in the World" ("Der mächtigste Mann der Welt") ("Schlöndorffs Requiem" 223) but, according to Gundolf Freyermuth, also to collaborate with the filmmaker on the script (98). In 1988, finally, he pursued jointly with Donald Westlake an adaptation of Eric Ambler's novel *Passage to Arms,* which again fell through (Westlake 13).

Schlöndorff has spoken positively about his East Coast experience: "I do not have the impression of there being a break with my European film work. The place is different, the human truth is the same" (Siclier 10). It is indeed possible to see continuities in Schlöndorff's American films with his German work and the tradition that surrounds it. In each film, however, the emphasis is somewhat different. In *Death of a Salesman,* for example, it is the theatrical style that emphasizes the play's links both to the expressionist tradition and Brecht's distancing.[1] In *A Gathering of Old Men,* the connection comes in the construction of a leftist-leaning drama about class rebellion. And finally in *The Handmaid's Tale,* we get both antifascist and profeminist messages embedded in a story about a woman's resistance to social and sexual oppression. All these films are based on significant works by North American writers.

The denominator common to the three works is that each deals with the American Dream: the disillusionment with and nonachievement of that dream in the first and last movies, and its success and fulfillment in the case of *Gathering.* In *Death of a Salesman* and *A Gathering of Old Men,* Schlöndorff seems to break new ground by moving from what one might call a narrative-based structure of short, carefully linked episodes to a more traditional, dramatically oriented mode of expression in which extended scenes are deliberately begun, developed, modulated, and brought to a theatrical climax. Such a classic structure, grounded in identification and actor-centered mise-en-scène, is new to Schlöndorff's oeuvre and represents a pulling away from the more detached, emotionally cold ambience of the director's earlier, more challenging German work. With *The Handmaid's Tale,* however, the filmmaker readopts many of his earlier stylistic qualities, which may account for the film's colder critical reception in the United States in comparison with those of the previous two.

The only noteworthy European interruption of Schlöndorff's American artistic period continues the theatrical sensibility of *Death of a Salesman* and anticipates stylistic properties of *The Handmaid's Tale*. After *A Gathering of Old Men*, Schlöndorff was to adapt a Böll work again, this time for the stage, with a theatrical version of the late writer's last work, *Women in a River Landscape* (*Frauen vor Flußlandschaft*, 1985), a dramatic "novel in dialogues and soliloquies." The piece premiered at the Munich Kammerspiele in January of 1988. Set in the Bonn capital of the Federal Republic, the work has a satiric focus dealing with, in Schlöndorff's words, "politicians, their wives, their lovers, their family members, their aides, as well as the bankers and industrialists who finance them" ("Warum *Frauen?* "). The novel and play's point of view is feminine, viewing the government scene from the perspective of leaders' wives and female companions. (One character, Katharina Richter—a 30-year-old maid who studies on the side and is the confidant of her female boss—echoes Katharina Blum.) Set design for the Munich stage production was by the American painter Jennifer Bartlett, who was to collaborate as a visual consultant with Schlöndorff on his American *Handmaid's Tale* as well.

In coming to the United States, Schlöndorff left behind certain aspects of his work, such as the thematic emphasis on troubled couples and direct political activism. But when we look in detail at *Death of a Salesman, A Gathering of Old Men*, and *The Handmaid's Tale*, we find an extension to an American context of the filmmaker's leftist commitments, professional skill, and interest in the creative process of adaptation.

20

Death of a Salesman

Now how all this will translate on film we don't know. This is an experiment. I think I'll only try and help how best we can what has been so successful on stage put on film. See that these walls don't quite fit. It is not so much that we wanted to make an economy but to make clear from the beginning and all the way through that this is not a real house. Because if you have that much reality, you don't need that many words any more. This being a play, a reality should be created through the words. If the reality is there anyhow in front of the camera, they don't need to talk that much and it doesn't fit together then. You will contribute greatly by creating reality through your performances. Everything should be fake except for the emotions. They'll be real. And they'll be what we'll be moved by.

> —Volker Schlöndorff, addressing the cast of *Death of a Salesman*
> (from *Private Conversations*)

*D**eath** of a Salesman* marks a departure for Volker Schlöndorff. It was his first film made in the United States from an American subject, his first English-language production since *Michael Kohlhaas,* and his first screen adaptation of a play since *Baal.* The production, presented on U.S. television on September 15, 1985, was an enormous critical and popular success, racking up ratings twice as good as those for the last television presentation of the play almost twenty years earlier ("'Death' . . . Doubles 1966 Audience"). With the noted exception of his cinematographer, Michael Ballhaus, Schlöndorff used a largely American crew. Yet despite the new ground broken, *Death of a Salesman* bears some similarities to Schlöndorff's other works: it was a faithful adaptation of a literary classic; it was made with an aesthetic awareness that its primary use would be on television; and it has a theme typical of Schlöndorff, namely, the damage wrought to human relationships as a result of capitalism.

Schlöndorff's *Death of a Salesman* was in part an attempt to translate to film the successful Broadway revival of the Arthur Miller play that opened in May of 1984 and ran for some 250 performances. The production starred Dustin Hoffman as Willy Loman, the proud but despondent, physically and psychologically ailing salesman who has difficulty communicating sincerely with his loving wife, his emotionally distanced sons, and his sympathetic neighbor. *Death of a Salesman* was, like *Swann in Love,* a project into which Schlöndorff entered relatively late. Working from a determined script and with almost all the actors from the stage production and using a set that derived from the one used on Broadway, Schlöndorff took on the role of *metteur en scène*. If in the publicity that accompanied this filming of *Death of a Salesman* Schlöndorff often took backseat to Miller and Hoffman, that very inconspicuousness and self-effacement may well be the director's triumph, for it is a movie that intentionally showcases Miller's text and Hoffman's performance to maximum degrees. (See illustration 30.)

In discussing *Death of a Salesman,* we consider three major issues. First and foremost is the issue of adaptation, for in many ways *Death of a Salesman* is an exemplary film adaptation of a theatrical work. Related to this is Schlöndorff's particular and deliberate use of space, both to enhance the play's theme of freedom versus confinement and to provide for a mise-en-scène closely associated with the play's dialogue. *Death of a Salesman's* use of space is, in short, one built around the spoken word. Finally, we treat the question of emotion in *Death of a Salesman* to inquire as to how Miller and Schlöndorff's manipulation of the audience's affective responses relates to the production's aesthetic and political effects.

Adaptation and Theatricality

In considering *Death of a Salesman* as a theatrical adaptation, two things stand out. For one thing, Schlöndorff adapts the play with scrupulous faithfulness; for another, his adaptation confronts the theatricality of the play itself, acknowledging and emphasizing its artificiality and departures from realism. Let us consider these issues in relation to the writing of two theorists of film and theater, André Bazin and Yann Lardeau.

One of the most famous essays on the subject of theater-to-film transformations is André Bazin's two-part essay, "Theater and Cinema." One cannot read the French critic's discussion of the subject after seeing *Death of a Salesman* without being struck by how perfectly Schlöndorff has followed Bazin's prescription for successful filming of a theater piece. Bazin calls on the film director not to digress from the theatrical origins of the adapted play but rather to empha-

30. Arthur Miller *(left)*, Schlöndorff, and Dustin Hoffman during filming of *Death of a Salesman*. Photo: Museum of Modern Art/Film Stills Archive.

size them—to let the preexisting text, with all its inherent theatricality, dictate the style of the production. The practice of "opening up" a play by using different, varied, and authentic locations dooms the film to failure, he argues. Describing an unsuccessful adaptation of *Le médecin malgré lui*, Bazin argues that "The text of Molière only takes on meaning in a forest of painted canvas and the same is true of the acting" (1: 86). In short, unlike the process of adapting a novel to the screen, "[o]ne is no longer adapting a subject. One is staging a play by means of cinema" (1: 93).

One can immediately see that *Death of a Salesman* fulfills the qualities Bazin describes. It follows Miller's text with only minor cuts, slight transpositions, and occasional rephrasing of lines, and Schlöndorff deliberately stylizes the production so that one is always conscious of the movie as a filmed theatrical presentation even while one is caught up emotionally in its dramatic action. Although Schlöndorff skillfully uses cinematic techniques, he remains substantively faithful to Miller's text and its inherent theatricality. Indeed, Miller has commented that one of the reasons he approved of Schlöndorff as the film's director was that Schlöndorff understood the play's roots in the German expressionist movement of the 1920s (Shewey 23).

One can compare Bazin's comments to those of Yann Lardeau, which in their own way suggest that Schlöndorff's deliberate use of artificiality and falseness shows a decided understanding of the nature of the two media. Lardeau writes in his essay "Le décor et le masque":

> The theater puts a man in a stage setting and shows the different kinds of relations that exist between this man and this setting. The cinema puts a man in a frame and shows the different connections that can arise between this man and this frame. But the decor of the stage is abstract, artificial, made of signs and symbols; only the actor is true, whereas the cinematographic frame is comprised of traces of a real environment, whether it be a setting created especially for the film or whether it's a case of natural settings, of exteriors. In theater an actor lends his body to a representation. (10)

Thus, although an occasional critic has complained about it (Shipman 155), Schlöndorff's use of a set for the Loman home that features incomplete walls, revealing the houses and world outside it, makes perfect sense: it plays up to the tension between the two media. The openness and unreality of Schlöndorff's set only underline the nature of the decor as consisting of "signs and symbols." And although Miller's dreamlike, free-association structure suggests a cinematic approach to space and time, that structural freedom only makes the physical confinement of the stage all the more metaphoric for the psychological confinement of the characters.

There is one scene in which Schlöndorff's deliberate acknowledgement of the theatrical is most prominent. Not far into act 1, when Willy and Linda have been talking in their bedroom, Willy complains about the lack of fresh air in the room. Linda tells Willy the windows are open, and Willy decries "[t]he way they boxed us in here. Bricks and windows. Windows and bricks." He talks about the crowding in the neighborhood and begins to reminisce about how the neighborhood used to be, with its lilacs and wisteria, peonies and daffodils (Miller 17).

For the first part of the scene, Schlöndorff frames the actors through the window, with the camera on the outside—a shot that has no correlation with any character's point of view. Rather, the use of the window as a framing device calls attention to the place of the audience as voyeurs; we sense how Willy and Linda have been placed within the frame of the window for our aesthetic appreciation, in much the same way that the drama as a whole might be placed on a proscenium stage or is framed by the movie camera. As the shot progresses, the camera creeps forward to make for a tighter framing. Schlöndorff then switches to a high-angle shot of Hoffman, who says, "There's more people! That's what's ruining this country! Population is getting out of control. The competition is maddening! Smell the stink from that apartment house! And another one on the other side . . ." (Miller 17). As Hoffman delivers this speech, the camera pulls up and back on a crane to reveal the artificial, constructed, ceilingless set on which Dustin Hoffman and Kate Reid are performing.

These shots come at a key point in the text, for here Miller establishes a major theme of the play. He starts working with motifs of nature versus civilization, country versus city, liberating outdoors versus confining architecture. One can see in Willy's two sons the two sides of Willy himself. Biff (John Malkovich), on the one hand, claims he wants nothing more than to be outdoors with his shirt off. Happy (Steven Lang), on the other hand, pays lip service to Biff's ideal of freedom but remains resolutely in the city, waiting, in his own words, for the merchandising manager to die, trying to make it in the business world. Both sons, like their father and mother, are trapped—as emphasized by the shadowy, low-ceilinged, gable-roofed bedroom where they sleep. Only Willy's millionaire brother Ben (Louis Zorich), as a ghostlike apparition who appears periodically throughout the play, is free to float in and out at will.

A Mise-en-Scène of Confinement

The theme of psychological confinement, as represented metaphorically in physical confinement, is a common enough one in Schlöndorff's work, ranging from the boarding school in *Young Törless* to Swann's overfurnished rooms in *Swann in Love,* but it is particularly well underlined in *Death of a Salesman.* To have "opened up" Miller's play through the use of in-the-street locations would have been to undermine visually the play's theme of domestic and professional oppression. Schlöndorff's mise-en-scène thus creates both an artificial space and a tight, restricted, confined space.

When Schlöndorff takes us away from confining interiors, the spaces provided nonetheless continue both the artificiality and the restriction established elsewhere. The lighter-toned flashbacks that take place in the Lomans' backyard are like the outdoors in the concluding funeral scene, set against a painted backdrop: the freedom of open air is only an illusion. The opening shots of the film that occur under the credits, of Willy driving his car at night, are of patent studio illusionism. The old Chevrolet sways in place in the dark, with flashing lights suggesting the movement through suburban streets. We are conscious of the dark lighting and tight framing used to conceal halfheartedly the trickery involved. Yet far from destroying our belief in the story, the fakery simply cues us to look elsewhere if we want authenticity.

One of the most terrifying shots in the film creates a feeling of claustrophobia in an exterior location. We see Willy leave the office building where his boss, Howard Wagner (John Polito), has just fired him. He walks out into the pedestrian traffic reciting a half-crazed monologue to a crowd of people who pay no attention to him. In his play, Miller asks for the monologue to be recited offstage, with traffic noises to indicate Willy's walk from one office building to another. Schlöndorff shows the street but frames Hoffman in a tight shot and has him walk against the flow of traffic, making the street seem more confusing and more threatening than anything we have seen in Willy's home. We sense Willy being crowded out all the more by the city and his need for fresh air becoming all the more acute.

Much of *Death of a Salesman* is thus characterized by a style that juxtaposes theatrical coding, which establishes the artificiality of the setting, with cinematic coding, which underlines the authenticity of the human performers and which pushes the illusionism toward a suggestion of the real world. In this respect, the film partakes of what may be a major shift in film aesthetics in the 1980s. Alain Bergala has argued that the year 1980 may well mark the end of an era in film history, begun around 1955, when the question of the relation between film and truth was the major force behind the conception and practice of cinema ("Le vrai" 4–9). With the 1980s, Bergala reasons, citing filmmakers like Jean-François Beineix, Nagisa Oshima, André Tarkovsky, and Raoul Ruiz, directors begin to start from a premise that the nature of photography is to produce falseness and deception rather than truth and authenticity. The payoff in this delight in the false has been a rediscovery of the pleasures of the theatrical and a playing with exactly the kind of flip-flopping between the patently artificial and the persuasively true that one experiences in the Schlöndorff film.

Emotion Versus Detachment

Death of a Salesman is clearly a film designed to produce an intense response in its audience. That in itself marks it as a break from Schlöndorff's other work in film in that so many of his earlier movies are characterized by detachment, irony, and *Verfremdung*. In watching Schlöndorff's other motion pictures, one often feels that the dramatic climaxes are suppressed, rerouted, or implied. In *Death of a Salesman* (and in his subsequent U.S. film, *A Gathering of Old Men*), one senses Schlöndorff making an about-face, departing from the distance and dour coldness one associates with so much of the New German Cinema. If films like *Baal, The Sudden Wealth of the Poor People of Kombach,* and *A Free Woman* are filled with deliberately Brechtian and politically explicit elements, *Death of a Salesman* appears to lean toward a mode of theater Brecht would despise: the realistic domestic drama that focuses on specific individuals and in which the audience's emotions are manipulated by playwright and performers to produce psychological catharsis.

Yet the issue is not quite so simple. For in at least some correspondence with the Brechtian theater, the Loman family is a family of types, very much representative of the effects of capitalism and its ideology on the individual in general. Miller constantly underlines the roots in economic status issues of just about all of their actions. And the play's refusal of complete illusionism does, perhaps, encourage a certain amount of reflection or critical distance. As we have seen, in considering Willy's bricks-and-window speech, framing the characters through the window—as in comparable framings in Fassbinder's films or in *Katharina Blum*—invites awareness of both the gaze and the viewers' voyeuristic activity. Where the play and the film are resolutely non-Brechtian, however, is in the area of emotional identification, for frequently throughout the work we share in one or another character's feelings. Can we make a case for *Death of a Salesman* as a specific synthesis or hybrid, that is, an attempt to blend the discourse of a politically committed theater with the emotional operations of the traditional tragedy or domestic melodrama?

Let us recall Schlöndorff's statement, "Everything will be fake except the emotions." This concern with analyzing, indeed exposing, how dramatic works produce emotions is one that Schlöndorff shared at that time with his colleague in the New German Cinema, Alexander Kluge. A one-page text by Kluge from his prose collage *Die Macht der Gefühle (The Power of Emotion,* 1984), is prominently cited in the Frankfurt Opera program for the production of *La Bohème* that immediately preceded the *Death of a Salesman* project ("Über Gefühl" 5). Both Schlöndorff and Kluge, and to a certain extent Fassbinder, too, seem drawn to the idea that you can simultaneously provoke and analyze the production of emotions through dramatic means. When Schlöndorff describes his filming of *Death of a Salesman* as an experiment, one senses that he means it in a fairly deliberate sense of the term, that he wants to stimulate the emotions but not necessarily at the expense of rationalist analysis. Miller ultimately demonstrates that one of the evils of capitalism is its depersonalization, its reification of people, its coldness. If this is true, can a true alternative be achieved by the suppression of human feelings on the stage or in the cinema?

The last two major segments of *Death of a Salesman,* one at Frank's Chop House and the following final confrontation in the Loman kitchen, demonstrate

Schlöndorff's mastery of the film medium at the service of emotional expression. We see in these two sequences a striking shift of emphasis in Schlöndorff's visualization away from Willy and toward Biff, an emphasis that reflects Biff's increased importance near the end of Miller's script. The son Biff becomes the audience's point of identification, for he is able to reconcile his personal conflicts in a way his father cannot. The play's emotional effectiveness comes from the audience's sharing in that reconciliation.

Miller has constructed the restaurant scene around multiple parallels and analogies among the characters. Biff's revelation of having stolen Bill Oliver's fountain pen parallels Willy's that he has been fired. Biff's failure in the job-seeking situation parallels his flunking of math as a senior in high school. The less than reputable women in the bar seem to provoke in Willy memories of his mistress in Boston. The scene represents a coming together, without resolution, of the characters' failures.

The most immediate stylistic impression one gets from the restaurant scene comes from the dominant use of the color red, and all of that color's connotations suit the scene: danger, sexuality, violence. The red walls of the restaurant (and the red dress of the Miss Forsythe that Happy picks up there) contrast with the drab neutral and earth tones that we have seen everywhere else. The mood is one of confusion. As Biff and his father begin to argue, they circle around the room, almost like boxers in a ring. As the scene builds, Schlöndorff intensifies the sense of confusion by increasing the amount of camera movement and framing his subjects so tightly that we lose any full sense of the geography of the room. Schlöndorff also creates a layered sound track in which the dance music from the bar is dissonantly mixed with more theatrical music. Voices and sounds from the past (the hotel operator ringing Willy's room and then paging him and Biff's knocking at the hotel room door) mix with sounds from the present (father and son arguing, the waiter knocking at the bathroom door to check on the babbling Willy). At its richest, *Death of a Salesman*'s sound track has a striking aural complexity in its mingling of times and places, motivated and unmotivated music.

Although all of these effects derive from Miller's script, the scene represents *Death of a Salesman* at its most cinematic, from the point of view that it uses framing, camera movement, editing and complex sound mixing to its most untheatrically fluid advantage. Schlöndorff also draws on the expressionist tradition whereby external aspects of environment—the red walls, the honky-tonk music, the swirling camera—come to reflect characters' internal states. Because we are aware of Willy's growing confusion, we identify the growing aural and visual confusion in the scene with Willy's state of mind. The delirium and anxiety that the scene portrays allow us to share in Willy's delirium and anxiety.

Reflecting the play's portrayal of Oedipal competition, a competition Willy is doomed to lose, Biff becomes increasingly the focus of attention as the sequence develops. In the hotel room flashback, for example, after Willy's mistress has left the room, a specific pattern of mise-en-scène accompanies the father and son's dialogue. Biff is repeatedly in close-up, his father in medium to long shot, with Biff at the left of the screen, Willy at the right. The dominance of Biff's close-ups weights the exchange in his favor, and we sympathize wholeheartedly with the crying, disillusioned son. Only as the scene progresses does Willy try to fill Biff's empty space by moving a suitcase to sit next to him. Although we now can see Willy in close-up, it is always with Biff's out-of-focus profile in the foreground, until the son finally accuses, "You gave her Mama's stockings!" and the scene erupts into physical violence.

This emphasis on Biff continues into the final confrontation in the kitchen. During the scene, John Malkovich, the actor who plays Biff, has more close-ups than any other performer. Schlöndorff also composes long-shot compositions to center on him, as in the shot of the family around the table when Biff slams down the rubber tube and confronts his father with the latter's plans for suicide. In the son's final embrace of his father, Schlöndorff holds on the shot of Malkovich over Hoffman's shoulder so that we experience a close-up of Biff rather than one of his father. We see Biff's lips kiss his father's neck, and it is only after Biff leaves that we know Willy's reaction. The kiss is not in Miller's text (although it may have been in the Broadway production). When Biff says the line, "Will you take that phoney dream and burn it before something happens?" Miller simply indicates, *"Struggling to contain himself, he pulls away and moves to the stairs"* (133). Both kiss and Schlöndorff's close-up of it are additions, and they create the most affectively potent moment in the whole film.

Although Schlöndorff would not be responsible for the casting of John Malkovich as Biff, he can surely take credit for the subtle visual highlighting of the actor. One is also struck by the particular quality of Malkovich's voice. If anything, it has a certain shallowness whereby it takes on a certain hoarseness whenever he raises volume. It is a voice well suited to Biff, for the actor sounds soft-spoken even when he is shouting. Surrounded as he is by performers who let loose in orally virtuoso fashion, Malkovich's softness becomes markedly and effectively contrasting.

For Biff's voice is the voice of reason and the voice of Miller's political conscience. And it is here that we can see at least a partial reconciliation between *Death of a Salesman*'s unanalytical, emotional side and its committed, reformist

31. *Death of a Salesman.* The tableau of Willy Loman's funeral. Photo: Deutsches Filmmuseum Fotoarchiv.

(although hardly revolutionary) side. Willy's death is not simply a pathetic shame; it takes Biff's anger and lucidity to give it meaning, and if Miller stops short of posing a political solution to the problem of capitalist alienation, he at least suggests the futility of buying into the American Dream.

Indeed, the speeches at Willy's funeral become remarkably close to being Brechtian social gests. Biff's praise of his father's natural love for working with his hands, Charley's humanistic defense of Willy, Happy's use of Willy's death to justify his own venality, Linda's concentration on personal freedom, all relate to the characters' economic conditions and rank in the class structure, as does the conspicuous lack of other mourners. Schlöndorff stages this scene in unnatural, symmetrically formal style—as a final tableau. Far from being a departure from Schlöndorff's earlier Brechtian interests, *Death of a Salesman* shares a number of Schlöndorff's continuing concerns with similar issues: with the use of socially typed characters, with affect and its purposeful manipulation, with the effects of economic forces on personal freedom and happiness. (See illustration 31.)

As one critic commented, the only lapse in the television film "was the increase in commercial breaks as the tragedy accelerated toward its climax—the commercials ironically underscoring the play's criticisms of an image-obsessed mercantile society" (Humm). *Death of a Salesman* is a clear attempt to use the mass media for the political and aesthetic education of a large population. One may quibble with *Death of a Salesman* as inadequate political drama; on its own terms, however, as a faithful adaptation of a major postwar dramatic text, the movie seems a hardly mitigated artistic triumph.

Schlöndorff had successfully negotiated a production mine field: he had managed as a foreigner to bring a noted Broadway production to the screen intact, in a version satisfactory to the playwright, without sacrifice of cinematographic qualities, in a manner attractive to an American network television audience. As Jonathan Hart has argued at length, Schlöndorff successfully balanced, in functional cinematic terms, the play's realist and expressionist elements. One may miss the intellectual daring of some of Schlöndorff's earlier works; one may be aware of a certain modesty of ambition about the whole enterprise; one may even accuse Schlöndorff of surrender to a Hollywood aesthetic of mere political liberalism. But as a preservation of Arthur Miller's play, as a vehicle to make *Death of a Salesman* both physically and psychologically accessible to a mass audience, and as an intelligent example of stage-to-screen adaptation, the Schlöndorff film is to be counted as a major success.

21

A Gathering of Old Men

To some extent, Volker Schlöndorff's well-received *Death of a Salesman* may have been something of a "calling card" picture, a work designed to prove to American producers that Schlöndorff could work in English and make a film acceptable to a mass American market. For much of the late 1980s, Schlöndorff worked from a New York base, and his next project, an adaptation of black American novelist Ernest Gaines's *A Gathering of Old Men*, was a fully American-made work.

A Gathering of Old Men (1987) was realized for CBS television and shown in the United States as a Sunday night movie before a subsequent video release as *Murder on the Bayou*. Coproduced with Hessischer Rundfunk, the film was shown at the 1987 Cannes film festival, had a theatrical release in Europe, and was therefore more characteristically "amphibious" on the other side of the ocean. The result is filled with tantalizing contradictions, as the work simultaneously meets requirements of cinematic genre, of the made-for-TV movie, of serious literary adaptation, and of calculated political statement. Let us consider it from two general perspectives—first, as genre film, specifically a variant on the Western; and second, as literary adaptation of a major work of African American literature, one that examines significant issues of race, culture, and civil rights in the United States and experiments with the use of multiple points of view.

German-American Precedents

In *A Gathering of Old Men*, Schlöndorff returns to the theme of collective rebellion that he explored in *Michael Kohlhaas* and *The Sudden Wealth of the Poor People of Kombach*. The film is set in rural Louisiana in 1972 and shows how a group of African American men successfully avoid a lynching after the shooting in self-defense of a white man by a black. The story harks back to *Kohlhaas* and

Kombach in its portrayal of the sudden self-assertion of an exploited class and the reactions against such rebellion by the dominant class. Like *Kohlhaas* and *Kombach*, it is a quasi Western, a work that takes elements from the Western genre and applies them to a different historical and geographic setting.

A Gathering of Old Men differs from earlier works in one major way: in this case, the rebellion is successful. Where *Kohlhaas* and *Kombach* are pessimistic works that portray the crushing of rebellion as a near inevitability, *Gathering* shows the willful blacks as victorious in changing an oppressive social system. In this respect, as Schlöndorff's second American film, *A Gathering of Old Men* stands in marked contrast to *Death of a Salesman*. Where the latter work portrays U.S. society as one in which economic ambition has destroyed family and social values, *A Gathering of Old Men* suggests just the opposite, a vigorous society with a capacity to correct its faults, with the potential to become more open to all classes of people.

Schlöndorff is of course not the only representative of the New German Cinema to work in the United States and explore aspects of the country's life and culture. Perhaps the most obvious examples of this are Werner Herzog's *Stroszek* (1977) and Wim Wenders's *Paris, Texas* (1984), not to mention Percy Adlon's *Bagdad Cafe* (1988), all works set at least in part in the American West. Yet Schlöndorff's approach to looking at the United States is almost antithetical to that of Herzog, Wenders, or Adlon. The other filmmakers put an emphasis on landscape and environment, on the beauty and grandeur of nature and the simultaneous encroachment of commercialism and urbanization. Both natural landscape (bleak and desolate) and urban cityscape (forbidding and alien) become metaphors for characters' internal states. Schlöndorff's emphasis, by contrast, is on the social situation of the American South: places are specific rather than metaphoric; people are representatives of real social classes rather than demonstrators of any existential human condition; and the narrative becomes a specific demonstration of social change rather than a device for musing on philosophical questions of language, identity, and communication.

Both Schlöndorff and Wenders have in their American films looked back to the American work of Fritz Lang, perhaps the major father figure of the New German Cinema. The major elements of *A Gathering of Old Men*'s story line— the lynch mob, the fugitive seeking freedom and vindication, the manipulation of evidence and testimony to call into question judgments of truth—all hark back to Lang's American movies, from his first efforts in *Fury* (1936) and *You Only Live Once* (1937) to *Beyond a Reasonable Doubt* (1956). Above all, *A Gathering of Old Men* takes part in what critics have customarily seen as the overreaching Langian theme, that of justice and equality in society. It is as if Schlöndorff, in developing his second American project, looked directly to the model of Lang for both subject matter and style.

Given his interest in American institutions, it makes full sense that Lang would have shot several Westerns, namely *The Return of Frank James* (1940), *Western Union* (1941), and *Rancho Notorious* (1952). For the Western has traditionally been a genre in which filmmakers explored the fundamental contradictions of American society. Although it is set in the South rather than the West, *A Gathering of Old Men* bears a number of structural and thematic similarities to the traditional Western, most of which are already present in Ernest Gaines's novel. Any discussion of *A Gathering of Old Men* should consider how its treatment of themes and motifs of the good-bad hero, personal freedom, gender roles, and violence are in ways similar to and different from treatments of these same issues in the American Western.

Relation to the Western

A Gathering of Old Men's resetting of the Western's narrative configurations in the deep South of the 1970s realigns a number of traditional structures. Like many Westerns, *A Gathering of Old Men* centers thematically on an issue of vengeance; the story begins when Beau Bouton, a Cajun farmer, is shot in the front yard of an old black man, Mathu (Lou Gossett Jr.), after having beaten and chased a younger black man, Charlie. Aware of the almost certain reprisals to come from the Bouton family, eighteen old black men, all of them armed with comparable shotguns, assemble on Mathu's porch, all claiming responsibility for the killing. They are organized by Candy Marshall (Holly Hunter), daughter of the main white landholders in the area, who, like everyone else, wrongly thinks Mathu is the killer rather than Charlie, who has fled. Caught in the middle is the sheriff of the town, Mapes (Richard Widmark), whose main responsibility is to keep order and to establish the truth. (See illustration 32.)

The assembly of black men resembles the preparations of Western homesteaders against an impending Indian attack, ranchers against rustlers, or in more modern Westerns, Indians against white attackers. The threat of impending violence hangs over the entire movie. The motives are the same: the protection of one's own safety, family, and property. In Schlöndorff's case, white rednecks are the potential savages who threaten civilization and peace.

The casting of Richard Widmark as Mapes, and of Woody Strode as Clatoo, one of the more outspoken old men, is a direct invocation of the universe of John Ford. Strode, who was John Ford's favorite black actor, appeared in Ford's *Sergeant Rutledge* (1960), *The Man Who Shot Liberty Valance* (1962), and *Seven*

32. *A Gathering of Old Men*. Louis Gossett Jr. as Mathu *(left)*, Holly Hunter as Candy, and Richard Widmark as the sheriff. Photo: Museum of Modern Art/Film Stills Archive.

Women (1966). Widmark not only appeared in Ford's *Cheyenne Autumn* (1964) but acted with Strode in the director's *Two Rode Together* (1961). Thematically, *A Gathering of Old Men* echoes John Ford in its emphasis on the development and preservation of a community. The film's conclusion, in which the fiddler plays and victorious people begin to dance, serves the same function as Ford's famous square dance scenes, in which peace and community are overtly cele-brated. The preservation of community serves as the justification for violence in Ford's films; so it is also, implicitly, in Schlöndorff's.

The figure of Mapes extends and challenges two stereotypes: that of the Western sheriff and that of the redneck Southern sheriff. In contrast to the cliché Southern sheriff, Mapes recognizes that times have changed, that both blacks and whites deserve protection under the law, that violence is an inappropriate solution to social conflict. Indeed, Widmark's appearance and performance as Mapes gives the character remarkable dignity. Widmark's Mapes is far trimmer and neater than the character described in Gaines's novel, in which the sheriff is characterized as overweight and sloppy. Widmark creates a figure far closer to the character of the Western sheriff. He is a lawkeeper, a representative of civilization, an antidote to savagery. And if Mapes takes the place of the Western sheriff, the character of Lou Dimes (Will Patton) evokes the archetypal Western newspaperman, the bearer of civilization who will use the publication of truth to mold public opinion in the cause of justice.

The mythology of the Western is often, in effect, a mythology of masculinity. Proof of manhood, for the Western hero, comes through lack of cowardice and successful self-defense. Both Gaines's novel and Schlöndorff's film measure manhood through this successful self-defense, most pointedly through the character of Charlie. At the beginning of the film, we see Charlie running from Beau Bouton and we hear his voice-over on the sound track, quoting, with some modifications, a passage from later in the book: "All my life, that's all I ever done, was run from people" (Gaines 188). Yet when Charlie goes off with Mapes at the end, he says, "A man come back to pay up, sheriff, stops running." Both book and movie clearly connect the blacks' assertiveness and self-defense with a necessary passage toward manhood.

The role of women in the Western is always in comparison with and contrast to this masculinity. Women, with the exception of Candy, play a secondary role in *A Gathering of Old Men.* At first they assume the role, typical for many women in the Western, of antiviolence supporters of peace and domesticity, even at the expense of some freedom. The black women oppose their husbands' involvement in the defense of Mathu. One of them stays home to clean the catfish her husband has caught and is told by her husband, in a line paraphrased from the book, "If them fish ain't ready for me to eat when I get back, I'm go'n do myself some shooting right here" (Gaines 33). As the film progresses, however, the black women, although they remain secondary figures, become supportive and speak out.

Candy is a different figure from the other women in the film. She is somewhat mannish, a leader, and the instigator of the organized resistance to the expected lynching. In the context of the Western genre, she becomes like the woman in the Western who achieves power and prominence by behaving like a man, like Calamity Jane, Annie Oakley, or the heroines of numerous Howard Hawks films. As an assertive woman in a world dominated by men, she is also an American cousin to Sophie in *Coup de Grâce*, a movie not without, as we have mentioned, its own bows to the Western. Where Gaines describes Candy as wearing khaki pants, Schlöndorff dresses her in blue jeans, clothing that only reinforces this analogy to the Western. One of the key scenes in the film, however, involves the point at which, when they have heard that Fix will not come to lynch Mathu, the old men decide to meet as a group to decide what to do next. They exclude Candy, which brings out in her a patronizing, plantation owner quality that "deheroicizes" her. Just as Mapes is in some moments the Southern sheriff, in others the Western sheriff, so, too, Candy flip-flops from a Western role to a less attractive, more rigid Southern one. At this point, Lou Dimes acts like a Western hero: he carts Candy off physically to remove her from the action. It is a gesture of male assertion, a taming-of-the-shrew image, and one appropriate in its evocation of the traditional Western, even while its sexual politics may be questioned.

Central to any Western is the question of violence, and this threat drives *A Gathering of Old Men*'s suspense mechanisms. The initial shooting begins the movie, and the attempted vengeance for Beau's death by Fix Bouton seems inevitable as the film builds up to an expected final showdown between blacks and whites. Here the contrasts to *Kohlhaas* and *Kombach* are most noteworthy. Where the earlier two films are significantly lacking in suspense—any lasting success by the two sets of rebels is always clearly impossible—*A Gathering of Old Men* avoids the same sense of futility and the outcome is always uncertain. Whether the blacks will triumph or be repressed is never taken for granted. On the one hand, this suspense allows *A Gathering of Old Men* to function as a mass audience genre film for which the good guys will triumph. On the other hand, the movie's approach to violence is always ambiguous, and while much violence is threatened in *A Gathering of Old Men,* very little is seen. The movie is something of a Western without action.

Consider, for example, the scene in which Mapes, in questioning the black men, strikes those who are lying to him. One notices, especially on repeated viewings, that these are clearly rather undisguised stage slaps that are deemphasized through Schlöndorff's discreet use of cutaways and a lack of strong aural reinforcement on the sound track. The effect is that the slap comes off more as an insult to dignity than as physically violent abuse. This is in marked contrast to Gaines's novel, in which Mapes's actions seem far more ugly, brutal, and uncalled for, due no doubt to the written description and psychological development that accompanies them on the printed page. In this way Schlöndorff is able to keep Mapes a largely sympathetic character. Candy's slapping of Lou later on in the film is similarly tame and almost ritualistic.

The film continually sees violence as inappropriate and dysfunctional: Mapes's slaps do nothing to get him the information he wants. After Charlie confesses, the black men who want to follow him with their guns to Bayonne are talked out of it by the more reasonable ones who prefer to trust the law. And Luke Wills's vigilante attack on the black men becomes simply ludicrous.

In this respect, Schlöndorff's message is more optimistic than Gaines's. Where Gaines ends his novel with a shoot-out in which both Luke and Charlie are killed, Schlöndorff presents the success of all involved as lying in their ability to sidestep violence. Although the Western may traditionally present violence as an inevitability, as does Gaines's novel, Schlöndorff seems to be saying that it is not and that the strength of U.S. culture may be in its ability to achieve social change with a minimum of violence. When Gil Bouton, Fix's son and Beau's brother, throws a gun to the ground and says "When will this all stop?", he seems to be speaking for the filmmaker.

Although it follows many of the conventions and narrative configurations of the Western, *A Gathering of Old Men,* as a made-for-television movie in the United States, also participates in what may be considered another genre, the social problem television film. Although it has a number of admirable and distinctive qualities, *A Gathering of Old Men* may have been a network attempt to reduplicate the success of an earlier Gaines adaptation, John Korty's *The Autobiography of Miss Jane Pittman,* which in 1976 received both high ratings and several awards. *Gathering*'s very existence as a film in the United States might not have been possible outside the context of the made-for-television movie. Its optimism, its safely moderate liberal politics, and its reliance on genre elements fit the requirements of that mode of production.

As a social problem film, *A Gathering of Old Men* can be read as a commentary about the American civil rights movement, a reading reinforced by the shot of Lou Dimes in his office as he looks at a bunch of civil rights news photos tacked to his wall. At the beginning, Candy organizes the blacks' resistance, giving them leadership, credibility, and necessary support. If read in this metaphoric way, the film suggests how necessary the white liberal's support was in the early stages of the civil rights movement. Schlöndorff has even said, "Candy is me. I am the liberal who wants to do a favor for the blacks. She believes that they need her, just as I believe that they need for me to make a film about them and for them. At some point I must efface myself. Just as Candy must" (Siclier 10).

Coming in the late 1980s, *A Gathering of Old Men* can only be seen as a statement against Reagan-era complacency and an attempt to revive the civil rights question. To what extent did the subject appeal to Schlöndorff because *A Gathering of Old Men* presents a model of social action and resistance opposite in strategy and effect to the suicidal, self-defeating terrorist actions of the Germany of the 1970s? In this regard, *A Gathering of Old Men* becomes a liberal fantasy of success, a flirtation with violence that results in nonviolence, an act of resistance that results in social change rather than repression, an encouragement to continue with political struggle through the apathetic 1980s. It is ironic that *Michael Kohlhaas,* shot in the optimistic and militant 1960s, should portray its revolution as failure, while *Gathering*, shot in the reactionary 1980s, shows its rebellion as a success.

A Theater-Oriented Adaptation

In *A Gathering of Old Men* Schlöndorff collaborated with two of the United States' foremost black literary figures, Ernest J. Gaines, the author of the novel, and Charles Fuller, who wrote the screenplay. Fuller was the playwright who won the Pulitzer Prize in 1982 for *A Soldier's Play*, which was since turned into the film *A Soldier's Story* (1984). He represents a major voice in the black American theater. This literary pedigree may have allowed for the marketing of the project to European public television.

As a novel, *A Gathering of Old Men*'s most formally experimental aspect is its use of multiple narrators. Each chapter is written from a different point of view. One might argue that this experiment with point of view is Gaines's least successful achievement in the book: on occasion the different voices in the storytelling seem too similar, indistinguishable. The political implications of the technique are nonetheless clear: it presents the old men's actions as collective action, emphasizing the community rather than the individual.

Both the book and the movie continually emphasize, although in different ways, this tension between the individual and the community. As we look at Fuller and Schlöndorff's adaptation strategies, we see how all of them emphasize this sense of the individual within the community, creating a text that works on two overlapping levels—one political, the other psychological. We consider first the structural changes made at the beginning of the narrative; second, Fuller's creation of a series of monologues that give voice to different sides of the black experience; third, the creation of extended single-set scenes, in which groups of characters, individually and collectively, face off in arenalike confrontation; and finally, Fuller and Schlöndorff's use of multiple voice-over narrators. The result is a precise political analysis of collective action, even while it raises some unsettling questions on the psychological level.

Although *A Gathering of Old Men* is a generally faithful adaptation, Fuller's screenplay makes two structural changes to the narrative, one at the beginning, one at the end. We have already mentioned the ending, which softens the fatalism of Gaines's novel and provides for uplift and optimism. The difference in beginnings is more complex. Gaines does not reveal until the end that it was Charlie who killed Beau. Rather, the reader discovers along with many of the characters the specific nature of the violence. Fuller's screenplay begins with the killing, so we are constantly aware of what has happened, even while many of the story's participants are not. Whereas Gaines's work takes on the tone of a mystery novel in places, Schlöndorff, much in the manner of Lang, is more concerned with the game of concealing and revealing a truth that the audience already knows. The screenplay removes the story from mysterylike questions of individual responsibility and personal motive to focus on people's responses, individual and collective, to the violence. Although the opening killing may also have been required to fulfill the usual commercial television requirement of strong action within the first few minutes to hook the audience, Charlie's flight and return give the film a symmetry and dramatic coherence.

Our knowledge that Charlie is the killer particularly enriches the scene in which the group of black men assemble before marching to Mathu's house. We see Charlie, unseen by the others, crouched in the grass. Although we learn later that he is some distance away, Schlöndorff's editing patterns suggest that he is spying on the men, watching them prepare to take action. This motivates all the more clearly his return and provides a focus and point to the scene: the collective's strength gives, in effect, Charlie the strength to do the right thing. Whereas Charlie's return in the novel seems a bit of a contrivance, it becomes logical and consistent in the film, and Charlie's speech when he does return refers back to the scene:

> Then I ran. I ran. I ran. And everywhere I turned I was still on the Marshall place. Like a wall everywhere. I fell down and screamed, ate dirt. Then I heard a voice coming across the swamp, coming from the graveyard. I thought it was the demons awakened when you fired them shots over the graves. I listened and I listened. I heard that voice say, "Come back."

Fuller emphasizes this thematic concern with both collective action and individual experience when he makes occasional digressions into theatrical speeches, with a style of writing that shows clear affinities to the playwright's stage experience. Schlöndorff apparently encouraged him in this approach and wished the monologues to structure the film something like an opera, with each character having his own aria, and giving the whole a ballad- or fablelike quality (Siclier 10). As critic Thulani Davis has written about the old men: "At times they appear to be a ring of singers, taking solos in turn" (55).

For example, we hear Coot's speech about how he served in World War I, and although it occurs somewhat earlier on film than in the book, it is lifted almost verbatim from it (Gaines 103–5). It is an unusually wordy, if effective, digression for a commercial motion picture, and one perhaps more suited to the small television screen, with television's emphasis on dialogue, close-ups, and personal psychology. Similarly, Clatoo gives a speech later in the film about how his brother Silas successfully plowed a field more quickly than Fix Bouton's tractor, only to be beaten by whites for winning the race. Although in the book the description is given by a character named Tucker, who is not present in the film, Fuller's text is an effective paraphrase of Gaines's (96–98). Schlöndorff shoots it in a single take lasting almost a full minute, with framing that carefully puts Mathu slightly out of focus in the background behind Clatoo. Near the end of the take, the camera follows Clatoo as he paces, then continues on to rest on Mapes at the end, as Clatoo confronts him by asking where the law was at the time. It is a theatrical text, rendered subtly cinematic.

A similarly theatrical approach occurs in sections of *A Gathering of Old Men* that bring together a collection of characters in a single location for an extended period, presenting dramatic action in a unified space and continuous time. Central to *A Gathering of Old Men* are two continuous scenes, both of which take place in front of Mathu's house, interrupted only by a twenty-five-second segment in which we see Fix being told of his son's death. The first scene lasts a full fifteen minutes, the second twelve, so that together they constitute almost a third of the running time of the movie. We see the old men arrive at Mathu's, then Lou Dimes, then Mapes, then the undertaker, and witness Mapes's questioning and striking of the old men. They are scenes that could be performed on a full-sized stage, but given the large number of characters involved in the single setting, Schlöndorff's camera provides for the centering of attention and emphasis. Similarly, in the shorter but central scene in which Gil and Fix confront one another about changing times and attitudes, Schlöndorff assembles a large number of people in a single room, even while portraying the core conflict between father and son. In both cases, a single setting becomes an arena, a place for the display and resolution of conflict, in a way comparable much more to dramatic literature than to narrative literature. Fuller and Schlöndorff apply in these relatively long scenes a theatrical unity of time and place exploited successfully in *Death of a Salesman* but not that evident in Schlöndorff's work up to this point.

Schlöndorff's mise-en-scène in these sequences is rich because it plays with constantly shifting points of view and the constant graphic reformulation of the basic situation. Consider, for example, the sequence of shots in which Mapes, sitting in front of his car, calls Mathu up to him and implores him to send everyone home. Through both editing and camera movement that reframes the action, the image alternates between frontal compositions of Mathu or Mapes individually and lateral ones of the two together, squared off against one another. In the frontal shots of Mathu, some of which are from

Mapes's point of view, the composition invariably displays the lined-up black men behind him, showing his collective support. The contrasting lateral shots emphasize visually the psychological push and pull between the two characters. In one of the climactic shots in the encounter, we see Mathu with Candy and Lou together behind him at his left, the assembled men behind him at his right: the shot summarizes all the pressures coming to bear on Mathu at that moment, from whites on one side, blacks on the other, and his unity with all. Schlöndorff's mise-en-scène is classic and unobtrusive, but it exploits the film medium's ability to represent a political conflict through a graphic assembly of visual elements, even while providing through close shots for psychological individuation of its participants.

Ambiguities of Point of View

The question of point of view is perhaps the most central one to any discussion of *A Gathering of Old Men* as a literary adaptation. Gaines's device of switching narrators with each chapter is central to the book's implicit premise that no one person is responsible for the social advances that are taking place in Mathu's yard. As both a book and a movie, *A Gathering of Old Men* avoids creating a single heroic figure. Indeed, the narrative teases us, setting up Candy as the film's heroine, only to undercut her authority and moral position when it reveals her own underlying racism, and it is only on reflection that we can fully appreciate Gil's harsh accusation to Candy, "You're pathetic!"

The film attempts to preserve the book's shifting points of view through a series of changing voice-overs, which fill in occasional background information. Yet, as Thulani Davis has observed, the device seems to add little (55). The voice-overs often feel unnecessary, and because they are often spoken by minor characters, that character's voice cannot always meaningfully color the viewer's perception of the material. It may well be that in the traditional coding of voice-overs, we expect a single, more unified point of view, and Schlöndorff and Fuller's innovation may for many audience members seem more disorienting than enlightening.

What is more, it brings up an issue of psychological imbalance that may go back to the book itself. Within Gaines's novel, although the number of pages narrated by white characters is almost exactly even to those narrated by blacks, the white characters are far more likely to narrate more than one chapter and thus gain individual importance. Lou Dimes, for example, is the narrating voice for a total of four chapters; Gil's friend Sully, a much less significant character in the film, narrates two. The boy Snookums is the only black character to return as a narrator, and both of his chapters are minor. The result may be in part to blur together and deindividualize the black characters, at least in contrast to the white.

In his review of *A Gathering of Old Men* in the French journal *Positif*, Eric Derobert argues that the film itself is characterized by an implicit racism. The collection of black characters contrasts to only a few white ones, all of whom are more developed and show more psychological subtlety (73). Derobert may have a point. Surely Candy and Mapes represent far more ambiguous characterizations than those of Mathu or Charlie. And why is it that Candy and Lou Dimes are entitled to romantic lives in the film, but the black characters are not? This is, in effect, the same argument that has been used against other works about white-black relations, like Richard Attenborough's *Cry Freedom* (1987) and Alan Parker's *Mississippi Burning* (1988), both films in which the white characters, by getting more attention and psychological development, are implicitly presented as more important than the blacks. We can remember it as an argument that had been used, in somewhat different form, against Schlöndorff's own *Circle of Deceit*.

To defend Schlöndorff, however, one can point out that any highly developed individuation of the African Americans in *A Gathering of Old Men* would run the risk of undermining the film's theme of collective rather than individual action. To have overemphasized a single protagonist would be to fall into the trap of suggesting that it is individual heroism, rather than group effort, that causes social change. What we get in *A Gathering of Old Men* is not individual rebellion, like Kohlhaas's or Elisabeth's in *A Free Woman*, both doomed to failure, but the unified rebellion of a whole repressed class of people who must act together, first along with allies from within the oppressing classes, then without them. And, as the "arias" make clear, each of the African Americans has a story. Schlöndorff has perhaps created a film in which we identify with the whites as individuals, with the blacks as a race and class of people. (See illustration 33.)

In summary, then, *A Gathering of Old Men* allowed Schlöndorff to find in the United States a set of sentiments and experiences that have not been present in his German works—a sense of powerful and successful political action, a sense of admiration for a society relatively united in seeking to preserve its positive aspects and correct its negative ones. *A Gathering of Old Men* presents an all but idealized United States, particularly in comparison to the Europe Schlöndorff has previously shown. Some might argue that the film may be the product of a certain naïveté.

Schlöndorff, in his collaboration with politically committed American writ-

33. *A Gathering of Old Men.* The group of black rebels at Mathu's place. Photo: Museum of Modern Art/Film Stills Archive.

ers working within a largely commercial format, produced a calculated recipe, a mixture of political commitment with Hollywood genre. The film contains a number of Schlöndorff's previous preoccupations, that is, with the adaptation of a significant literary source in a straightforward but faithful manner; with exploring the nature of political rebellion and commitment and the reactionary repression that can potentially result; with bringing important and provocative ideas to a mass audience. *A Gathering of Old Men* has its contradictory aspects, in the form of a sexual politics that seems not fully worked out, in what may be an imbalance of psychological development between white and black characters, in what may be the optimism of a fantasist rather than an objective onlooker. Although its happy ending and dramatic directness make it somewhat different from the rest of Schlöndorff's oeuvre, *A Gathering of Old Men* develops and varies the filmmaker's established concerns.

22

The Handmaid's Tale

*T**he** Handmaid's Tale* represents Schlöndorff's first feature-length contribution to the science fiction genre, but it also continues some of his earlier thematic and structural preoccupations. It is one of a number of works exploring,
both in print and in screen adaptations that usually followed the novels, the
science fiction subgenre that portrays dystopian societies in the future. Among
the most famous literary works of this genre are George Orwell's *1984,* Aldous
Huxley's *Brave New World,* and Anthony Burgess's *A Clockwork Orange.* In writing the novel on which the film was based, Margaret Atwood saw herself as
extending this literary genre. Beginning with Fritz Lang's *Metropolis* (1926) and
William Cameron Menzies's *Things to Come* (1936), up to more recent works
such as François Truffaut's *Fahrenheit 451* (1966), Ridley Scott's *Blade Runner*
(1982), and Terry Gilliam's *Brazil* (1985), filmmakers have used this same genre
to provide both entertainment and commentary on their present-day societies.
Schlöndorff himself toyed with this approach in his contribution to the
omnibus film *War and Peace* (1983). Within the dystopian genre, however,
Schlöndorff in *The Handmaid's Tale* manages to pick up and rework a number
of ideas, ideological concerns, and rhetorical and poetic strategies that have
characterized much of his earlier work. In many ways, *The Handmaid's Tale* represents a return to the Schlöndorff of the 1970s in its focus on a woman's right
to personal and sexual fulfillment.

Writers and filmmakers have long used science fiction as a way to present
relatively abstract ideas about society. Many critics have also argued that science fiction works, although set in the future, are always about the society in
which they are produced. Margaret Atwood's *The Handmaid's Tale* is part of this
tradition. Atwood's view of the future involves a feminist concern with the role
of women and with issues of sexual equality and reproductive rights. She presents a world in which the radical religious right has transformed North
American society. She creates for liberal readers an embodiment of their worst

nightmares of conservative backlash against civil rights, feminism, sexual rev-olution, and the ideal of personal freedom. Atwood's approach to depicting an oppressive, totalitarian state is a familiar one. Her originality lies in her apply-ing this familiar vision of the future to the concerns of women and feminists.

In terms of themes, *The Handmaid's Tale* confronts issues of fascism, patri-archy, conformity, individualism, and rebellion already explored in Schlöndorff's German-made films. The film continues the director's struggle to come to terms with the political past of Germany at the same time as it pres-ents a skeptical view of a potential neofascist societal evolution in America. In terms of form, it extends Schlöndorff's involvement with episodic story struc-tures, with questions of point of view and subjectivity, and with the look as a mechanism of power. As a work based on a novel by one of North America's most prestigious woman writers, *The Handmaid's Tale* also continues Schlöndorff's involvement in literary adaptation.

The story is set at around the turn of the twenty-first century. Kate (Natasha Richardson), her husband, and her small daughter are attempting to flee their North American homeland after a right-wing fundamentalist coup. But border guards intercept them, kill the husband, and cart off Kate and her daughter sep-arately. Along with a mass of other women and minority prisoners, Kate is sub-jected to a selection process. Pollution has rendered the majority of Gilead's women sterile. Having passed a fertility test, Kate is interned along with other handmaids who are to assure the continuation of the Gilead elite. After extended indoctrination, drills, and brainwashing, the handmaids are placed with individual families.

Commander Fred (Robert Duvall) and his wife Serena Joy (Faye Dunaway) "adopt" Kate, who henceforth will be addressed as Offred. The Commander directs the ongoing war against the rebels in the mountains. The ultraconser-vative Christian Gileadites have legitimized by Biblical rituals the triangular relationship of husband, wife, and biological handmaid-mother. The veiled wife is supposed to be present whenever the male attempts to impregnate the surrogate mother. When repeated intercourse fails to produce pregnancy, Serena suspects the Commander's sterility and arranges a liaison between Kate and Nick (Aidan Quinn), the Commander's chauffeur. The Commander also infringes on the rules by secretly taking Kate out to a nightclub off-limits to any-one but the male hierarchy, diplomats, and foreign trade commissions. There she finds one of her former cohandmaids, Moira, who fled but was appre-hended and condemned—like prostitutes, former career women, and other would-be refugees—to serve the men's whims at the club.

Kate learns she is pregnant and wishes to save her child. She wants Nick to escape with her. Ofglen, a neighboring handmaid and a secret underground member as well, passes a knife to Kate for her to kill the Commander. The same day, Serena discovers the dress Kate wore to the nightclub, and the Commander refuses any help to the handmaid. He insists, however, on a sentimental parting embrace, which Kate utilizes to slash his aorta. Soldiers appear to arrest her. Not until later does it dawn on the handmaid that this force, including Nick, is in reality part of the underground. An epilogue shows Kate living in a mountain refuge, awaiting childbirth and Nick's return.

References to the Third Reich

To turn to issues of content first, both the conception and the reception of *The Handmaid's Tale* have special relevance to the German experience. The *Neue Zürcher Zeitung* reports that the film's literary model was conceived "in the shadow of the Berlin Wall" (Frosch, 56). In the novel's inside cover, the author specifically acknowledges her Berlin fellowship made possible by the DAAD German Academic Exchange Service. As to the reception of *The Handmaid's Tale,* Germans responded favorably to the film, indicating a cultural and political preparedness to enter into dialogue with the ideas expounded in this work (Karasek, "Blick").

The *Handmaid's Tale* is filled with allusions and references to the specifically German experience of totalitarian regimes, although many of these historical references may have been lost on the American and other Western viewers. These are most conspicuous in the early parts of the film, but they underlie its social order throughout. There are contemporary allusions to the former GDR's restricting travel for its citizenry, especially outgoing travel—note the failed border crossing at the outset of the film. Schlöndorff reportedly had a replica of the Berlin Wall erected on the North Carolina set, but a blizzard on the day of shooting almost obscured it (Johnson 44). There are the historical references to the Holocaust—observe the processing of women and minority prisoners, especially their selection in huge halls resembling railroad station platforms, their being marched off in columns and being deported in cattle cars. There are uniformed guards everywhere overseeing troops of drably dressed, stooped workers who mechanically perform menial tasks in the background. This imagery evokes the concentration camps and is extended in later settings in the film. The searchlight that constantly circles about the Commander's house at night suggests a prison camp. Scenes of the handmaids in group formation in a setting of monumental architecture call to mind the Nuremberg spectacles. Military uniforms and insignias are ubiquitous. The implication is clearly to relate the past to the present. A German commentary on *The Handmaid's Tale* could well conceive of its images as "description of conditions of our time" *(Gegenwartsbeschreibung)* ("Kühle Bilder" 21).

This imagery is reflective of the neofascist social system portrayed in the film. Ideals of order, racial purity, biological determinism, and authoritarian religion create a mythology that dictates a forced return to an ultratraditional, sex role–divided family. This "cultification" of the traditional family implies a repression of nonconformity and sexual desire even while the widespread sterility in Gilead has clearly destroyed the biological base of the family unit. The breeding program presented in *The Handmaid's Tale* has parallels with the Nazi *Lebensborn* project. In that policy, the regime recruited unwed young women and SS elite studs to breed successive "pure" Nazi generations. Also, "Aryan"-looking foreign children were taken from their families to be raised as Germans, thus, in fact, historically dismantling existing families much as Kate's daughter Jill is placed with a "fit family" in the film. Gilead's ideology cultifies the family at least to the extent that it serves to preserve a white middle-class ideal. Feminism, sexual freedom, birth control, abortion, religious celibacy, and lesbianism are all seen as undermining this idealized family structure needed to preserve an orderly and (re)productive society. According to Aunt Lydia, at once boot camp sergeant and concentration camp guard to the handmaid recruits: "Before we had freedom to, now we have freedom from."

The reengineering of society into a neofascist hierarchy is implemented through a strong program of propaganda and indoctrination similar to that of the Third Reich, which reacted to women's liberation and reduced the place and status women had historically achieved in the post–World War I Weimar society. In the words of Alfred Rosenberg, chief ideologue of the Nazi movement, "Emancipation of woman from the women's emancipation movement is the first demand of a generation of women which would like to save the *Volk* and the race" (512). The restoration of women to *"Kinder, Küche, Kirche"* (children, kitchen, church) in the Third Reich finds its parallel in the world of Gilead.

Gilead, not unlike fascist Germany, presents a militaristic society where men spend considerable time in soldierly and policing pursuits. Both the fictional and the historical fascist regimes are radical patriarchies. It is true for both regimes what a Nazi propagandist included in a 1933 definition of National Socialism: "The German resurrection is a male event" (Huber 121–22). This denigration of women is cloaked in an ideology that pretends to idealize them. Just as the National Socialists awarded prolific mothers medals at ritualistic assemblies (Medals Day, Mother's Day) and made them the object of routine honors and deference, so too does Gilead. Gilead is worse in that it often does not even reward its biological mothers with the opportunity to rear their own children.

Almost all the major characters in *The Handmaid's Tale* are women, a characteristic that puts the film apart from the usual science fiction works in which women are secondary figures. The two exceptions are Nick, the chauffeur, and the Commander, who most represents the patriarchy. The Commander is the film's villain who, as played by Robert Duvall as a smiling good ol' boy, nonetheless makes understandable how the society might buy into the repressive ideology he represents. The Commander embodies the naive petit-bourgeois idealism that hid the inhumanity of an Adolf Eichmann under a surface of patriotism, efficient management, politeness, and good family values. At one point the Commander patronizingly explains to Kate that the overthrow of democracy has been a necessary response to those pressure groups, "the blacks, homos, all those persons on welfare." "And women, " Kate replies. To which he reacts, agreeing, "And women," with his usual boyish smile that is at once ingenuous and horrifying.

This is not the first time that Schlöndorff has dealt with the superficial appeals of fascism. Both *The Tin Drum*'s family fathers—petit bourgeois like the Commander—and Reiting and Beineberg, the friends of the title figure in *Törless*, impress those around them as good-natured, decent people. In reality, they are, as revealed by Schlöndorff's films, radical in their fascist pursuits and hence dangerous to others. Schlöndorff's concept of fascism, then, includes this superficial appeal. This concept further has the elements, strongest in *The Tin Drum,* of the petit bourgeois wanting "to clean up" all that is perceived as "foreign" and to counteract a sense of powerlessness with a feeling of omnipotence (here, in *The Handmaid's Tale,* the Commander). It also includes the psychosocial feature, as visible in *Törless,* whereby the fascist manipulates victims and groups (here, the group therapy exercise persuading Jeanine that she should feel guilty about having been raped and aborting the baby). It finally is connected with the mythical power of visual display familiar from Leni Riefenstahl's *Triumph of the Will* and parodied in the Nazi rally sequence of *The Tin Drum* (here, the ritualistic public execution of a handmaid). *The Handmaid's Tale* employs all these elements, reiterating for the 1990s what Schlöndorff expressed for the previous decades and would express again in 1996's *The Ogre.*

If one is looking for the Schlöndorff film most comparable to *The Handmaid's Tale,* however, it is probably *The Lost Honor of Katharina Blum.* In both, violence leads to violence in a patriarchal society with neofascist components. Both works involve a female victim who begins by being passively involved in an oppressive situation but who is finally driven to murder of a man who has been exploiting her. In both films, the woman's assertion of her sexuality is either forbidden or punished. In both, the woman is the object of constant abuse and degradation.

Yet the works have important differences. Most important would be that where *Katharina Blum* portrays an individual woman fighting almost alone against the male-dominated institutions of court system, police, and press, in *The Handmaid's Tale* Kate has both women allies and women opponents. The latter have been incorporated into the system and have internalized its values. *The Handmaid's Tale* is thus a problematic film from a feminist perspective and might even be termed a postfeminist film. On the positive side, its emphasis on female characters in itself asserts the importance of women. On the other hand, Kate is hardly the feminist role model of the independent, strong woman interacting mainly with other "sisters." She is passive: she is literally swept off her feet by Nick and, at the end of the film, instead of actively participating in the struggle against the neofascist Gilead regime, simply awaits his return from the conflict.

In a feminist discussion of Schlöndorff's film, Marianne Barnett argues that the movie's Kate is basically a weak, nonthinking protagonist who is preoccupied with sexual happiness (9–12). We would respond that it is not so much that Kate is necessarily weak (she does kill the Commander and she does help Moira tie up Aunt Lydia) or nonthinking (when she tells the Commander "I don't think," it seems clear that this thought-through response is the only one acceptable under the circumstances).

Rather, the problem with Kate as a character may have more to do with the qualities of the cinematic medium and certain decisions made in the adaptation process. In reading the book, which tells the story from Kate's point of view, the reader admires Kate for her intelligence and ability to analyze her own situation. The movie, by contrast, presents Kate from a far more detached perspective. We are deprived of her reasoning and motivations and see her actions only from the outside. Important in this context is the omission from the film of Kate's reflections on her relationship with her own mother, a 1960s feminist. Kate is thereby positioned in the book as a specifically postfeminist woman, and the growing political awareness that she experiences becomes tied to her personal reconciliation with her mother's values. In the screen medium's rendering from the outside, Kate becomes a less interesting character than Moira or Serena Joy, and this lack of a highly defined protagonist may be one of the reasons why so many reviewers have reacted coolly to the film. What is more, Kate's striving for sexual happiness through Nick must be understood in the context of the movie's subtextual "family romance," which we examine shortly.

Pinter, Adaptation, and Structure

One might blame the relative one-dimensionality of Kate's character on Harold Pinter, who wrote the film's screenplay. A critic looking for the same complexity as in Atwood's book could fault Pinter on other grounds as well. Any viewer who has read the book is struck by the way in which Pinter leaves out much of the background and explanation of Kate's situation. Part of this would be due to a decision to tell chronologically a narrative that in book form jumps around in time and makes associations between Kate's past and her present. Pinter completely eliminates all of the flashbacks apart from the movie's repeated inserts portraying Kate's memories of her husband's death and her nightmares about her separation from her daughter. There is certainly evidence that Schlöndorff supported and encouraged Pinter's adaptation strategies. The director has commented that he did not want to make the character of Kate too sympathetic: "If you were to identify more with the main figure of Kate . . . that would in my view become unbearable for the audience and border on kitsch. . . . Crying is cheap. Understanding is more difficult, yet also more important" (Schlöndorff, "Weinen" 78). And elsewhere Schlöndorff has commented on his long-standing dislike of flashbacks ("Coming" 22).

At first glance, the screenplay throws away some of the novel's greatest riches. In the print version, we learn, for example, of Kate's affair with her husband when he was still married to his first wife. This mirrors provocatively Kate's situation with the Commander and his wife Serena Joy. In the novel, Moira is Kate's best friend from college rather than someone she has just met. And we have already discussed the importance Atwood puts on Kate's relation to her mother.

Equally frustrating may be Pinter's deletion of basic pieces of exposition. Only a reader of the book will recognize, for example, that when Nick whispers the word "Mayday" to her as he pushes her out of the house near the film's end that he has said to her the password of the resistance group (although one can surmise this when one hears, on a later news broadcast, the group referred to as the Mayday terrorists). Similarly, the uninitiated viewer is left to figure out for himself that Gilead has banned reading for its ordinary citizens.

Such indirection might be characterized as sloppy screenwriting, but one should bear in mind that Pinter's other work as a playwright and scriptwriter has often been characterized by incomplete exposition and ambiguities of context. Pinter's refusal to explain everything is perhaps maddening to a literalist of adaptation theory, but it raises provocative questions. Is the film *The Handmaid's Tale* really less rich because it does not spell everything out? Is it necessarily an inferior film because the details become more meaningful to the spectator who has read the book? Or are not Pinter and Schlöndorff respecting the audience's intelligence by assuming that its members can fill in ellipses and understand connections that are only implied?

As with his adaptation of Proust's *Remembrance of Things Past*, Schlöndorff works in *Handmaid* from a script that opts for simplicity rather than complexity of structure, and the response among critics has in many cases been the same: the accusation that the result is schematic and one-dimensional. Structurally, *The Handmaid's Tale* consists of a highly episodic series of short scenes. This "string of pearls" narrative design is a throwback to Schlöndorff's storytelling patterns in films from the 1970s, such as *Katharina Blum* or *Coup de Grâce*. Yet it is a format much like that of Atwood, who also tells her story in brief scenes that link together both everyday and significant actions to combine an abstract, hypothetical portrait of a dystopic community with more conventional narrative elements. If Schlöndorff's film lacks Atwood's multiple time layers and background information, it nonetheless remains close to its source work in mood and ultimate effect. Unlike Atwood, whose concluding chapter unexpectedly recasts her tale in the context of an historical document being examined by stuffy scholars years later, Pinter and Schlöndorff give the story a cyclical pattern. At the film's end, we return to the snowy mountains where it began, with Kate once again in flight.

Where the novel plays with different time levels, the film plays with juxtapositions of different settings. At the center of the film are the domestic spaces of the Commander and Serena's household. Related to this center are the large public spaces of group regimentation or public rituals; contrasting to these two are the taboo spheres of the Commander's study, Nick's apartment, and the Jezebel nightclub. The domestic space around which much of the movie is structured is set in a small guarded estate in an upscale suburban location. Serena Joy frequently is shown here in the midst of plants and flowers; outside and interior gardens and their growth contrast with her inability to bear children. We associate the domestic space with the bright light of day and with clean, white surroundings and see it at night only during the sex ritual and when rules are being broken (as when Kate goes to steal the scissors or visits the Commander in his study or Nick in his apartment) These bright, well-lit scenes and settings correspond to the idealized order and conformity of Gilead. Nighttime, by contrast, is the time of rule violation, forbidden activity, and sex.

Those settings associated with unsanctioned activities are invariably dark, as seen in the brown wood and leather of the Commander's study, the low-key lighting used in Nick's apartment, and the black walls of the nightclub hotel room. *The Handmaid's Tale* uses setting and lighting to delineate character and situation and to this extent comes out of the expressionist tradition.

Closely related to such patterning is the film's color system. Blacks and browns, as worn by the Commander, the guardians, and the military as well as the "Aunts," the female commissars, denote force and masculinity. Whites, grays, and primary colors, by contrast, signify the various roles, places, and status positions of women in the society. For instance, a gray habit characterizes either a servant or—indicated by an additional wimple and a surgical mask—a member of the slave-labor decontamination force. The handmaids wear white during their indoctrination period, as do little girls and the young brides of guardians (identifiable as such only to readers of Atwood's novel). As the handmaids are placed in households, they gradually change to red costumes. The elite wives wear royal blue. This creates a patriotic red-white-and-blue configuration, evocative of the American flag, when the three groups of wives, brides, and handmaids are assembled together. Taken as a whole, this rigid color system reflects the strict, simplistic order of the Gilead society. It also echoes the Nazi creation of analogues to female religious orders, such as the "Brown Sisters" who worked in Himmler's *Lebensborn* maternity hospitals (Grunberger 246).

This color coding exemplifies Gilead's need for social conformity: it visually expresses the regime's urge to crush any surviving sense of individuality and personal integrity in favor of depersonalization. The central sociological issue of *The Handmaid's Tale* is the individual's need for personhood in the face of oppression. The visual articulation of this issue of individuality versus conformity is one of *The Handmaid's Tale*'s biggest successes. There is a constant play in the film, in a way reminiscent of Fritz Lang's *Metropolis,* between geometric groupings of people and the position of the individual within such groupings.

Consider, for example, the early scene in which the handmaids-to-be have gone to bed in the gymnasium dormitory. Their equally spaced cots, set out in a perfect grid, and all bathed in an eerie blue light, suggest uniformity and conformity. Yet, as the camera passes over them, we hear each girl whisper her name to the others, claiming her individuality. Schlöndorff carries through this motif of repetitive similarity in a later overhead shot of cups containing pills, presumably tranquilizers, that will be administered to the girls. Gilead is a society in which uniform submission is the ideal.

This issue of naming is central to the film. Each handmaid is given a name beginning with the letters "of" as in Offred, Ofglen, Ofwarren. The name does not belong to the person, we find out, but rather to the position in the house-hold. Her name indicates that her master, be it Fred, Glen, or Warren, owns her. Kate discovers that she is not the first Offred. Similarly, the Ofglen she befriends, and who urges her to join the resistance, is without warning replaced by another. In this context, Kate's statement to Nick, after they have made love, "My name is Kate," becomes an act of rebellion. When the Commander takes Kate to the nightclub, he introduces her as "Mary Lou," which suggests both his throwing away the rule book for a night and the transformation of Offred-Kate into someone following yet another social role, that of "evening rental." Might this also imply that he has never bothered to learn her real name? It is true that the Commander, having asked Kate to his study for her first evening visit, suggests: "I thought I'd like to get to know you a little." But he hardly intends to break the depersonalization. His suggestion rather is an outgrowth of the curiosity of the cat for its prey, of the sentimentality of the petit bourgeois for conquest, of the thrill of the forbidden, and of the lust that goes through the motions of intimate contact. His suggestion is not unlike his attempt, which provokes Serena Joy's hasty intervention, to touch Kate's breast during the sex ritual. "I find it impersonal," he justifies his gesture later—he craves the curves, the appeal of the surface; he is not, however, prepared to acknowl-edge Kate's personality.

As with these naming patterns, sexuality in Gilead is either done by the rules or becomes an expression of rebellion and personal identity. The formal insem-ination ceremony is between impersonal robed role players. By contrast, Kate allows herself to be seen nude by Nick at the window. In their sexual encoun-ters the two join their undressed bodies. Correspondingly, Nick privileges Kate as a person, repeatedly addresses her by name, and both his "Hallo lolo" greet-ing and the occasional crudeness of his language (comparable to Moira's) demonstrate that he takes exception to the proper conformity of Gilead. Kate and Nick's sexual encounter develops into a healthy, loving relationship in con-trast with the sanctioned but sick triangle consisting of Commander, Serena, and Offred-Kate.

Power, Punishment, and Family Structures

Schlöndorff portrays the officially sanctioned relationship as following arche-typal dominance-submission patterns along the lines of a subtextual family romance. According to the Gilead concept, the three form a family for the purpose of procreation. In a Freudian conceptualization, this triangle can assume features of an incestuous constellation: the "father" Commander cohabits with the "daughter" while "mother" Serena Joy is at hand sanctioning the relations. Interactions between the Commander and Serena, on the one hand, and Offred-Kate, on the other, are couched in characteristically parent-child terms. For instance, the Commander repeatedly invites Offred-Kate to join him in board games like Scrabble and checkers. He launches into a patronizing presentation of his *Weltanschauung* after an even more patronizing use of the phrase, "Let me explain something to you." He lays out the fancy boa and evening dress for the secret night out at the Jezebel club with the typical fatherly "I have a surprise for you." He stipulates at the club, "You can have one drink"—the father lays down the strict rules of conduct for the younger set. Finally, both he and Serena lower the parental boom on the disobedient child, once the visit to the nightclub is discovered, by the "mother's" "Go to your room" and, respectively, the "father's" "You better go to your room now." Kate's situation as child or "adopted" child is only reinforced by the parallel to her own daughter Jill, who also was adopted by a Gilead family.

Daughter Offred-Kate thus in the sex ritual participates in her "parents'" lovemaking. Are we, in similar oedipal terms, to read the "rape" of Aunt Lydia by Moira as a farce that metaphorically spoofs and condemns the Gilead sex ritual? A third party is involved as in the ritual above; Moira sexually taunts the woman-"commissar" in Kate's presence. This violent incident in the gymnasium restroom contrasts starkly with Moira's and Kate's cordial reunion in the nightclub's washroom. Kate genuinely respects and appreciates this strong, independent young woman; Gilead, in its intolerance toward lesbianism, perceives in her solely the embodiment of "gender treachery."

This social order brutally enforces conformity, especially in regard to sexual life. In addition to Moira, two handmaids are singled out for exemplary punishment. One has her feet broken for alleged masturbation. This is the very handmaid who is later executed because of the sin of sexual intercourse with a person other than her officially chosen provider-"father." The other handmaid, Jeanine, as a teenager under parental pressure allowed her fetus to be aborted. Now she is put to the pillory. The instrument of flogging in Gilead is no longer, however, the whip; in its stead, we observe a psychological "whipping"— Jeanine is publicly denounced by all other present handmaids. She is punished to the point of insanity. Gilead employs brainwashing methods to crush individuality, as well as to induce a conformity of attitudes among the handmaids.

A number of sequential punishment episodes—starting with the concentration camp–like selection process extending to the public hanging and thence to the Jezebel club—helps to lend shape to the film. Moreover, such structured punishment is frequently associated with two extremely significant formal features in *The Handmaid's Tale:* the circle and the look. Both merit closer analysis.

When punishment is meted out in Gilead terms, it frequently is administered in situations arranged in circular order. For instance, as Jeanine stands accused of abortion, she is ringed by the other handmaids. Similarly, the execution of the "adulterous" handmaid is associated with the figure of the circle. An early shot in the execution sequence focuses on the hangman's rope, now laid out on the grass in a loop. In the presence of the other handmaids, the noose, by its nature round, is slipped over the sinner's head. Subsequently, the handmaids collectively pull the rope that hangs her. Immediately afterward, during a second ritual punishment in which the handmaids again are made to function as the execution squad, they encircle the victim, a physician alleged to have seduced a handmaid, and lynch him. In both cases, encirclement attests to powerlessness. Yet the terrible lethal power wielded by these handmaids is at once testament to their own utter powerlessness: they themselves are victimized by being forced, brainwashed into their destructive actions against one of their own and against the doctor who, according to Ofglen, is in reality a member of the underground. (See illustration 34.)

In punishment episodes such as the one involving Jeanine, exposure to the gaze of others becomes a powerful instrument of penal judgment. Seeing, in fact, generally equates with power in *The Handmaid's Tale.* This relates to the destructive, negative power of Gilead as well as to the opposing, positive power of its oppressed subjects. An eye adorns the icon of Gilead's supremacy, the pyramid. It casts about the traveling cone of light and, in a wider sense, equates with the omnipresent searchlight beams that control life at Gilead during the nocturnal hours. The system's video monitors are also ubiquitous.

But the might of Gilead's eyes can be broken. During the "rape" episode in the gymnasium restroom, Moira and Kate take away Aunt Lydia's power to see by blindfolding her. In a related sequence, Serena Joy's seeing, that is, power, is shown to exert no grip over Nick and Kate. The two sleep with one another after the sexual rituals with the Commander have repeatedly failed to impregnate Kate. Serena has taken the liberty to "correct her fortune" by adding a surrogate father, too, and has persuaded Kate to engage secretly in this union with the chauffeur. This sequence then continues with a cut from the lovers in Nick's apartment to a shot of Serena observing herself, in her erstwhile Tammy Faye Bakker role, as a hymn singer on television. As her version of "Amazing Grace" rings out on the sound track, the film shifts from the close shot of Serena on the television screen to a frontal, semiclose frame of her as the observer. Subsequently,

34. *The Handmaid's Tale.* A circle of handmaids surrounding a condemned man. Photo: Deutsches Filmmuseum Fotoarchiv.

the camera zooms closer as Serena's gaze shifts from the contact with her own television image and turns inward. The camera tracks to a more lateral semi-close up of her face as she breaks into a smile and turns her head sideways as she is about to stand up. During this process the lovers' moans have become audible under the hymn.

In the next shot, with the camera positioned outside Nick's bedroom window looking in, the view is blocked by the blue tint in the lower glass panels. As the camera moves upward and tilts downward, it presents almost an overhead side view of the lovers. Toward the end of the scene Kate says her name and Nick, in whispers, repeats it before they part. The basic meaning conveyed suggests that Serena, the woman of the Gilead elite, enjoys the prospect of the intrigue's intended consequence: Kate's baby, which she eventually expects to become hers. The visual shift from her observation of the television image to the outside window of the lovers' room implies her power over the two. The blue window film blocks Serena's view inside, however, suggesting that she does not have the complete control over the lovers that she had manipulating her own image. This blockage harks back to an earlier, related shot in which Kate was able to peek out through a bus's glass window only because someone had scratched a tiny opening into its similar blue tinting.

Looks and exchanges of looks establish and charge the meaning of seeing in *The Handmaid's Tale*. Kate and Nick are repeatedly seen looking at each other, thus relating to each other, and this is often associated with looking at one another through a window. Even more important have been the couple's exchanges of eye contact in the car's rearview mirror. Serena's control fails, and the two have increased both their familiarity with and power over each other.

The interpersonal exchange of looks, in fact, signifies a liberation from the regime's power of seeing in *The Handmaid's Tale*. Kate's friend Moira, the most rebellious spirit among the handmaids, attests to this. After the reunion of the two friends at the Jezebel club and their private talk, a shot presents Moira on a balcony, dressed resplendently in the red of the handmaids, but in a miniskirt version that mocks the original. The frame positions her in front of a circle lit in blue—shape and color both signify the power of Gilead. She is looking out over the nightclub, exchanging glances with Kate. Repressed, abused, injured, even physically harmed by the regime and its conformity, she has maintained human dignity and independence. Kate's reunion with Moira and the women's rebellious gazes prepare the spectator for Kate's ultimate rebellion—the slaying of the Commander—and her liberation by the Mayday underground. Gilead's insistent repression of women's rights sparks a degree of rebellion. This rebellion keeps alive a modicum of hope in the face of the dominant patriarchal, even neofascist rule portrayed in Schlöndorff's dystopia.

Thus, although *The Handmaid's Tale*'s screenplay falls short in providing satisfying context and back story for the action and hence lacks a dynamic protagonist, the resultant film is by no means cinematically unsophisticated. The movie's designation of meaning through environment, visual patterning, color coding, and gaze structures is always interesting and often compelling. All of these visual aspects are never just decorative. Rather, they are linked to a discourse about power, gender, family structures, and sexual freedom that go beyond the immediate text.

In view of this analysis, our response to critics of *The Handmaid's Tale* in general and feminist critics in particular would be to refer them to important larger cultural contexts they fail to address. These contexts involve, first, the film's attack on fascism in its Third Reich manifestation. Criticizing the reactionary historical movement that squashed Germany's women's liberation of the 1920s and early 1930s can be read here as profeminist discourse. (Scenes in the handmaids' dormitory clearly allude to the fascism addressed in *Girls in Uniform*

[Mädchen in Uniform], the 1931 movie about a girls' boarding school that expresses feminist attitudes in the Weimar Republic.) Such specific historical references to Nazi actions against women are easily lost on the film's American critics and viewers, which may account for the work's being more warmly received in Germany than in the United States.

Second, the Atwood novel and the screen adaptation are best appreciated as reflections on feminism from a postfeminist sensibility. Both speak directly to the circumstances of the 1980s and 1990s whereby young women growing up have taken for granted the victories won by their mothers and grandmothers and women in their thirties and forties who had previously chosen career over motherhood have begun to have children. By deleting the relationship between Kate and her mother, an ardent 1960s feminist, Schlöndorff and Pinter can express only obliquely what Atwood says more directly, namely, that the liberation of women must come from women's own choices. It is not that Moira or Kate or Ofglen chooses the politically perfect path, but rather that each has coped with oppression in a way that has maintained personal dignity.

Part Five

THE POST-WALL
SCHLÖNDORFF

23

A Filmmaker for the European Community

Schlöndorff's next period, which we call his "Post-Wall" period, is not marked by a completely clear transition but essentially comprises the director's work from 1990 until the present. One might see the period beginning with the fall of the Berlin Wall on November 9, 1989. With the subsequent reunification of Germany, Schlöndorff reorients his attention toward creating a European cinema, first with the production of *Voyager* and later with his taking over the Babelsberg film studios in Berlin. *The Ogre*, released in October 1996, is also decisively European in its orientation. This is also a period during which Schlöndorff completed a short television concert documentary, *The Michael Nyman Song Book* (1992). In a six-part television documentary about Hollywood filmmaker Billy Wilder and in *Palmetto* (1998), Schlöndorff acknowledges the strong ties Wilder had to Central European traditions and the inverse debt that the younger filmmaker owes to Wilder. He returns to specifically German subject matter in a short film about personnel land mines along the Wall and in *The Legend of Rita* (2000).

Although *Voyager* was released in Germany in late 1991, this film, an adaptation of Max Frisch's novel *Homo Faber,* was one that Schlöndorff had thought about for a long time and had planned to begin even prior to *The Handmaid's Tale.* Schlöndorff has described what happened in an interview given just before starting *Voyager:* "I thought it had been waiting 30 years so it could wait a little longer, while *The Handmaid's Tale* had to be done right away. So I had it postponed. I'm glad I did. I have at last one truly American film behind me, and I can again do this truly European piece" (Van Gelder).

Although it was shot in English with an American star, Sam Shepard, *Voyager* nonetheless marks a turn away from the American subjects of his preceding three films. Schlöndorff in the same interview described the project as a "strictly European production" and "a trans-Atlantic enterprise." And at the time of its release, Schlöndorff told the French film magazine *Cahiers du cinéma* that *Voyager* was "my first German film in ten years" ("Rencontre" 53). We shall see in our discussion of *Voyager* how some of these characterizations may be a bit simplistic, but there is no question of the European nature of the film's cultural sources.

Changes in the Director's Personal Life

Schlöndorff has described how the period around which he decided to shoot a film from *Homo Faber* was a time of personal uncertainty for him:

> A few years ago, after my move to New York, I doubted almost everything in general and my career in particular. I toyed with the idea that it was time after thirty years of making films to learn something decent and to study, for instance, architecture or medicine. For many reasons, I wasn't doing very well. ("Wem wird man" 236)

This apparent midlife crisis may have to do with the way his American stay had disrupted his marriage to Margarethe von Trotta. (See illustration 35.) Von Trotta has described something of how the marriage fell apart:

> Just as I had this unconscious knowledge when I got to know him, so I did this time. I had the premonition that the geographic separation was the prologue to the real separation. At first he frequently came flying over, then he noticed that he could not stand the permanent jet lag, and the trips became more and more rare. (Freyermuth 97)

Schlöndorff has acknowledged that the content of *Voyager*, whose main character travels from New York to remote sites in Latin America and from one end of Europe to the other, in many ways reflected his own personal situation (Strauss 50). The director said in 1990, "Somehow, I sort of have a suitcase existence. With the eternal dream to settle down with a home" (Zehle).

Not long after this statement, Schlöndorff may have made an attempt to realize this dream. After renewing an acquaintance with Angelika Gruber, who had worked as an editor on *Circle of Deceit*, he began an affair with her that resulted in a pregnancy and a subsequent marriage. From all indications, Schlöndorff had by 1992 settled into a more stable domestic situation with his wife and daughter Elena. It is striking how Schlöndorff's making of a seemingly traditional home parallels his homecoming to Germany and his ending of an itinerant period in his life.

35. Margarethe von Trotta and Schlöndorff at the Montreal film festival in the early 1980s. Photo: Bernard H. Bergman and Sally Schoen Bergman.

In the years that followed, up to the shooting of *The Ogre,* Schlöndorff was to preoccupy himself more with managerial duties at the Babelsberg studio than with creative production. In some ways, rather than become an architect or physician, Schlöndorff became a businessman. The nature of the Babelsberg enterprise, however, made it no ordinary business, and we see in Schlöndorff's involvement in it an extension of many of the ambitions he has had throughout his career. On the surface, this is a period of artistic void. Schlöndorff goes for a five-year stretch without a theatrical feature to his credit. Prior to signing on with Babelsberg, Schlöndorff had agreed to direct a screen adaptation of Dashiell Hammett's *Red Harvest* for Italian producer Alberto Grimaldi, who had been trying for seventeen years to produce the film ("Harvest Time?"). The project, like several to follow, went unrealized.

The Michael Nyman Songbook

Schlöndorff's last completed movie before taking on the Babelsberg project was *The Michael Nyman Songbook* (1992), essentially a music documentary of a concert given by actress and chanteuse Ute Lemper, along with the Michael Nyman band, at the Hamburg Musikhalle on February 4, 1992. The program was of music by Michael Nyman, the British composer who had begun to achieve a cult following, especially in connection with his work with filmmaker Peter Greenaway (*Drowning by Numbers*, 1988; *The Cook, the Thief, His Wife and Her Lover*, 1989).

Although the film begins with an instrumental rendition of the "Miranda" theme from Greenaway's *Prospero's Books* (1991), its main interest is in three vocal pieces, in which Nyman sets to music texts by Wolfgang Amadeus Mozart ("A Letter and a Riddle"), Arthur Rimbaud ("L'Orgie parisienne"), and Paul Celan ("Six Celan Songs"). A common preoccupation with themes of love and death links the texts, all set to music in Nyman's distinctive postmodern, postminimalist style. Lemper sings the first in English, the second in French, and the third in German, perhaps as a way to give the film appeal to public television stations throughout Europe.

One is struck by how the concert itself, pitched somewhere between the classical and popular music traditions, attempts a bridge between high art and popular art that is comparable to what Schlöndorff has attempted in film. It has the seriousness of the concert hall and the literary salon. At the same time, Lemper cultivates a persona of movie-star glamour: she has the self-consciously arched eyebrows and sleek hair of Greta Garbo at her peak and a bit of the timbre and swagger of Marlene Dietrich. And the music, with its emphasis on pounding rhythms, has one foot in the baroque and another in rock, even while it evokes the romanticist song cycle tradition.

The song setting of the Paul Celan poems is the longest work on the program and the one that most dominates the fifty-five-minute document. Celan, an ethnic Austro-German from the Bukovina, a Romanian German-language enclave, survived Russian occupation and escaped German deportation, even as his kin disappeared in the Nazi gas chambers. His verse articulates the suffering of Jews in Eastern Europe and presents some of the most hermetic and yet most eloquent German-language testimony to the Holocaust. This confrontation of issues and feelings connected to the Holocaust links *The Michael Nyman Songbook* to a 1990s sensibility that has sought to come to terms with this aspect of German history, one that Schlöndorff was to explore in much more depth in his subsequent production of *The Ogre*.

For the most part, Schlöndorff maintains a low profile as a director here, allowing the words and music to speak for themselves. The sole exception is his periodic use of interpolated images from other sources—a silhouette and etchings from Mozart's times for the first song, images from the paintings of

James Ensor for the Rimbaud work, and most strikingly, footage from Alain Resnais's *Night and Fog* (*Nuit et brouillard,* 1955) and Alexander Dovzhenko's *Earth* (*Zemlya,* 1930), as well as photographs of Celan himself—for the last cycle of songs. Schlöndorff's cannibalization of the footage from Resnais's landmark documentary on the concentration camps is particularly striking, especially for the viewer aware of the carefully contrapuntal image-narration interplay in the original. The rhythms of Nyman's music form a different but fully appropriate dialectic with the images. One might complain that the end result is not quite pure concert film, not quite music video, but it at least has a dignity worthy of its subject matter.

Babelsberg

Schlöndorff became officially associated with the Babelsberg Studios in August 1992. After the fall of the Berlin Wall, there was considerable uncertainty about what would happen to the old East German DEFA studios located in Potsdam, on the outskirts of Berlin. The studio complex, as a government-owned entity under the post–World War II GDR, first fell to the Treuhand (a German equivalent to the Resolution Trust Company, which resolved the 1980s savings and loan crisis in the United States), which would then oversee the privatization process. Although any number of proposals were made, three major interests finally competed to take over the studio. One set of potential investors centered around several modest-sized Berlin media operations in general and that of producer Regina Ziegler in particular. The second embodied the Munich filmmaking establishment, represented by the Werbe-Filmhaus Berndt, a company concentrating on industrial moviemaking and commercials. The third was the French corporate mammoth Compagnie Générale des Eaux (CGE), represented by its branch Compagnie Immobilière Phénix (CIP). Among its subsidiaries, CGE counted the French Billancourt and Boulogne studios. Schlöndorff associated with this French third group (now a part of the corporate conglomerate Vivendi), and it was the one that won out.

All three accused one another of being more interested in real-estate investment than in film production. Given the speculative real-estate market of the time, with Berlin scheduled to once again become Germany's capital, such accusations had credibility in a city that was popularly being referred to with the words, "All of Berlin is an *Immobilie,* a real-estate parcel." There were also suspicions raised by Schlöndorff and others that the Werbe-Filmhaus Berndt was primarily a front for interests dedicated to keeping Munich as the center for German filmmaking and that the Berlin-based group ultimately was manipulated by or allied with Munich counterparts seeking to serve the same purpose (Schlöndorff and Fleischmann). In addition, in promoting their point of view, Schlöndorff and Peter Fleischmann argued that their competitors were too unambitious and provincial to be committed to running a studio that would have international commercial and cultural impact. Although it may never be clear how much the different competing parties were motivated by the real-estate value of the property rather than by cultural interests, Schlöndorff was obviously convinced enough of CGE's intent to make a go of the movie studio operation that he accepted the job of becoming the studio's manager, with Fleischmann as his assistant.

Post-Wall Context: Rescuing Tradition or Colonizing?

To understand the importance of this opportunity and the significance that it clearly had for Schlöndorff, one must remember the history of the Babelsberg Studios. We have already discussed the role that the Babelsberg Studios played in the creation of the Weimar cinema to which Schlöndorff feels such an affinity. In addition to this, the East German cinema that came out of Babelsberg represented a substantial tradition that Schlöndorff may have wanted to extend. Schlöndorff has expressed admiration for the training of the filmmakers who emerged from the Konrad Wolf Film and Television Academy and in 1990, at least, saw these filmmakers as essential to any artistic flowering of the post-Wall German cinema (Müry 17). The DEFA Holocaust films or works by Wolfgang Staudte (*Rotation,* 1948) and Konrad Wolf (*Stars [Sterne],* 1959) share with Schlöndorff's films political commitment, sobriety of style, and literary sophistication.

Schlöndorff clearly took on his new job as manager of the studio with the somewhat grandiose aim of making the new Babelsberg a cultural force worthy of its former glories. He projected intense optimism during the initial months of this operation. Many of the tasks to be accomplished had to do with updating a somewhat archaic facility and streamlining a cumbersome infrastructure. As time went on, however, different problems set in. The most serious problem seems to have been a lack of business. Schlöndorff complained about the dearth of support from the film industry in Berlin, which sought its film production services elsewhere ("Ich dachte" 13). At the same time, Schlöndorff's hope to provide a film facility for all of Europe also met with resistance. In France, film industry unions opposed the making of French productions on foreign soil, and according to one report, French film industry personnel were afraid to be seen talking to Schlöndorff at the Cannes film festival for fear of being considered traitors (Freyermuth 81). Although two major French productions, *La machine* (1994) and *Une femme française* (1995), came to Babelsberg in the early 1990s, neither was a particular critical or box office success. Moreover, there were repeated reports of productions that considered using the Babelsberg facility but which producers took elsewhere. Among these are *City of Lost Children* (*La cité des enfants perdus*, 1995), *Johnny Mnemonic* (1995), *The House of Spirits* (1993), and Doris Dörrie's *Nobody Loves Me* (*Keiner liebt mich*, 1994) (Williams; Molner 54; Schlöndorff, "Ich dachte" 14).

There are several reasons for these difficulties. A first major factor would be competition from other studios, in particular the domestic German Munich Bavaria unit; Berlin's own Tempelhof, Spandau, and Wedding complexes; and facilities in North Rhine Westphalia. The Berlin-Wedding and the North Rhine Westphalia operations both are newly expanded studio plants furbished respectively by the Berlin Senate and the Ruhr state. In addition, the latter's facilities have been generously financed by the aggressive North Rhine Westphalia film bureau, source of what has been the continent's second-richest film fund (Dalichow 440; Lieb, "Will New German" 31). By contrast, Babelsberg has suffered, much to Schlöndorff's chagrin, from lack of underwriting by the local film subsidy boards of both the state of Brandenburg and the city-state of Berlin (Schlöndorff, "Ich dachte" 14; Lieb, "Will New German" 90).

These troubles are wrapped up with the general economic problems that have followed German reunification in general and the reunification of Berlin in particular. Economic unification was to prove difficult and costly, coming at the outset of infrastructural changes demanded by the industrial globalization of the 1990s, a deep economic downturn in the West, and a complete collapse of East European trade relations. To modernize the communications, transportation, general commercial, and industrial systems of the territories of the former GDR has taken untold billions of deutschmarks. High unemployment was to drive up the social welfare expenditures, especially in the new federal states in the East, where the loss of East European customers and antiquated plant equipment were to force the majority of employers into bankruptcy. Domestic and international investment has been lacking. Deficit spending has become the norm. Public funding has been curtailed everywhere. The governmental entities that Babelsberg would ordinarily depend on, Brandenburg and Berlin, have acutely felt these effects of reunification. At the same time, despite a critical shortage of capital, speculation has driven up prices, thus making filming in the larger Berlin area an expensive proposition.

In more recent reflections on his experience as a studio head, Schlöndorff has not avoided acknowledging his failures and the possible need for a change of direction in the project. He has seemed particularly frustrated that not one of the first seventeen theatrical features shot at Babelsberg has been an unqualified success ("Ich dachte" 13). He has said: "If in 10 years Babelsberg does not make money, that will mean there is no European cinema anymore" (Boulet-Gercourt). At the same time, by the end of 1996, Babelsberg's three profitable enterprises were the studio tour, German television series production, and sound mixing ("Erstens" 238), not feature film production. Nonetheless, between 1996 and 1997, studio losses fell from $5.9 million to $1.7 million. With the expiration of his contract, Schlöndorff in September 1997 announced his intention to leave his position but would continue to serve as "Chairman of the Supervisory Board of the Medienstadt Holding Babelsberg" (Hils 18).

By the end of the 1990s, the entire German film industry was restructuring through mergers and buyouts. Schlöndorff's own production company, Bioskop, was acquired by Kinowelt ("Kinowelt" 34). In the course of these fusions, the new larger units, including Wenders's Road Movies, began issuing shares and capitalizing on the stock market ("Goldrausch").

Throughout this period, Schlöndorff repeatedly considered taking the reigns of a succession of projects. Among those announced but either unrealized or directed by others were "The Siege of Leningrad" and "A Season in Hell" ("Eine Zeit in der Hölle"), from a play by Christopher Hampton about Arthur Rimbaud and Paul Verlaine (Lieb, "Film Centers" 34, 36). It was eventually filmed by Agnieszka Holland at Babelsberg under the title *Total Eclipse* (1995). Although neither of these projects reached fruition under Schlöndorff, this period did contain small-scale creative activity in a variety of areas. We have already discussed Schlöndorff's work for the opera during the 1990s in a previous section. He also served as a performer in Bernhard Sinkel's *The Movie Narrator* (*Der Kinoerzähler*, 1993).

Parallel to this, Schlöndorff continued to play the role of advocate for a film industry policy that would promote a creative and vital German cinema within the context of a healthy European film culture. He became a particularly strong spokesman for defending the European film against the threat of obliteration that arose when some promoters of the GATT trade agreements envisioned them as applying also to motion pictures. Many observers, particularly those in the French film industry, rose up in defense of preserving some degree of trade restriction designed to protect European national cinemas. In a piece in *Die Zeit* from October 1993, Schlöndorff argued both for quotas and subsidies to promote Europe's individual film industries, particularly given that the United States already controlled 90 percent of the market. In arguing for specific national cinemas, Schlöndorff stated:

Jean-Claude Carrière has summarized the GATT philosophy in the following manner: "As the Irish listen mainly to German music (Bach, Beethoven, Brahms) and the rest of the world couldn't give a hoot for Irish music, as the Portuguese read much French literature, and the rest of the world, however, hardly buys Portuguese books, one therefore ought to stipulate that in the world order the Irish should no longer compose, the Portuguese no longer write—in the future music will come from Germany, literature from France . . . and film, of course, from Hollywood." ("Deutscher Masochismus" 62)

To some extent, Schlöndorff and his allies were successful in their struggle, and the GATT treaty was accepted without the feared inclusion of the motion picture industry. Indeed, after this international trade scuffle, Jack Valenti, the primary American lobbyist for Hollywood's interests during the ratification process, made significant gestures toward peacemaking when he visited the 1994 Berlin film festival and described himself as being "almost in love with the Babelsberg studio head" ("Brief aus").

Throughout this discourse, and indeed, throughout much of the discourse surrounding the Babelsberg project, Schlöndorff articulated a kind of European Community approach to developing both a film industry and a market for its products. There has been an engaging tension between what one might call Schlöndorff's nationalist orientations and his more internationalist sentiments, both of which make an enemy of the industrialized Hollywood product. At the same time, there is an irony in this configuration. To the extent that the reunification process can be seen as a colonization of the former East Germany by the West Germans, one could argue that Schlöndorff's position toward the former East German film studio was analogous to Hollywood's stance toward Europe. Schlöndorff's industrial model left little real room for the film culture of the former GDR.

For it would be simplistic to characterize this Schlöndorff as merely anti-Hollywood and simplistic, too, to label him merely a West German opportunist. In proposing to make of Babelsberg a Hollywood-in-Europe, he was reacting against a low-budget European cinema that has been so marginalized that it becomes insignificant, as much as he was reacting against Hollywood commercialism. At the same time, implicit in Schlöndorff's actions was the conviction that even large-scale European filmmaking should be different from large-scale Hollywood filmmaking. The specific traditions of individual countries and cultures should not be lost. Schlöndorff would return to this theme in a February 1999 *Der Spiegel* article in which he wrote, "But the soul still needs the familiar, the indigenous" ("Der Verlust" 196).

With *The Ogre,* Schlöndorff may have been suggesting the kind of product he would like to see more of. It was a large-scale production, with an international cast, aimed at a mass audience but ambitious in its artistic aspirations. We see once again Schlöndorff's attempt to resolve the contradictions of commercial filmmaking. With the commercial and critical failure of *The Ogre,* however, Schlöndorff achieved no such resolution. In his next two projects, Schlöndorff explores diametrically opposed alternatives. On the surface, *Palmetto* would seem like a retreat into blatant commercialism. In the project that follows, *The Legend of Rita,* he moves in the other direction, toward a low-budget, culturally specific German product. Although the former would appear to be a mainstream Hollywood film, it was produced by a German with significant technical and artistic roles assumed by Central Europeans. And the latter, although localized in its orientation, contains a significant dose of Wilder-like satire and has appealed to international critics and audiences. With these films and the Billy Wilder documentary, Schlöndorff suggests that a creative dialogue between Europe and Hollywood has been a major heritage and may point to the future.

24

Voyager

> I wanted to focus on my Teutonic inheritance, the 1950s, Existentialism, the question of guilt.
>
> —Schlöndorff, "The Last Days of Max Frisch"

Almost immediately after the American release of *The Handmaid's Tale*, Schlöndorff began production of "Last Call for Passenger Faber," an adaptation of Max Frisch's 1957 novel *Homo Faber*. The project, which was finally released under the title *Voyager* in the United States and *Homo Faber* in Germany, was one that Schlöndorff thought about for a long time. Indeed Paramount offered him an opportunity to adapt the novel in 1978, but he turned down the project. On the one hand, he thought incest such a taboo that he doubted it could be presented on screen (Schlöndorff, "Wem wird man" 236; Traub 198; Wetzel). On the other hand, as a member of the German protest generation, the filmmaker had turned to political issues and solutions rather than to the existential questions of guilt and angst (Tobis, Press notes for *Homo Faber* [13]). Schlöndorff returned to the project after the film rights to the novel again became available in January 1988 (Schlöndorff, "Last Days" 1). The final film was not completed until the Spring of 1991.

Frisch's *Homo Faber* as Source Material

Voyager is thus another adaptation of a renowned literary classic, in this case one of the major German-language novels of the 1950s. Its title, *Homo Faber*, means "man, the maker," and it touched the existentialist nerve of that Central Europe of the post–World War II economic miracle in which the "doers" dominated. It linked itself to the romantic element in German cultural tradition that criticized, even despised technocracy as a social norm. At the same time, *Homo*

Faber was only indirectly a political novel. It was far more concerned with metaphysical and personal questions.

The personal angle, in fact, relates to novelist Frisch's life and, perhaps in an extension, to that of filmmaker Schlöndorff, as well. Not only had Frisch, an architect and technology-oriented person, turned toward the arts. Frisch, who was in his midforties when he wrote the book, also underwent experiences analogous to protagonist Faber's life: near-marriage in the 1930s to a Jewish student from Berlin (Frisch, *Tagebuch* 173; Frisch, "Montauk" 727–29; Bircher 710–75), travels in South America, separation from his first wife, conflicts with her about visitation of their daughter (Tobis, Press notes for *Homo Faber* [26]). Schlöndorff has claimed Frisch to have modeled the character Sabeth on a woman with whom he maintained a relationship until his death and has described conversations with Frisch in which the author told him specifics about their shipboard romance ("Last Days" 22–23; "Wem wird man" 241).[1]

Schlöndorff himself has cautiously but repeatedly alluded to connections between the *Homo Faber* story line and his own private life. The filmmaker writes about how, in 1987,

> when I was living in New York, separated from my wife, incapable of experiencing another love, hence depressed, nearly 50 years old—then, somewhere on 55th Street, it flashed through my head: *Homo Faber*! I wrote a letter to Max Frisch, and that's how it all started. (Tobis, Press notes for *Homo Faber* [9–10])

The filmmaker has acknowledged the desire to restart life at fifty with another, much younger woman, and he has suggested he realized this during the filming (Interview with Terry Gross). At the same time, Schlöndorff repeats with *Voyager* a pattern, established with *The Tin Drum, Swann in Love*, and *Death of a Salesman*, of choosing a literary source that had impressed him as a youth. "When Frisch's novel came out in 1957 I was in a Paris café drinking my first espresso, wearing jeans and a black turtleneck sweater—one full generation younger than the author" ("Last Days" 1).

Frisch's novel is composed of a number of disparate elements, which at first glance seem unrelated. The first quarter of the book deals with the main character, Walter Faber, a Swiss engineer of about fifty, employed by UNESCO, who is in a commercial airplane that goes down over the Mexican desert. On the plane with him is Herbert Hencke, the brother of Joachim Hencke, a friend from Faber's university days. Having survived the plane crash and delayed rescue in the desert, Faber impulsively decides to join Herbert to visit Joachim in the Guatemalan jungle, where the latter has embarked on a questionable tobacco-growing project. After much struggle, the men arrive at Joachim's, only to find the man has committed suicide.

The middle half of the novel goes off in a different direction. On returning home to New York, Faber chooses to take a ship rather than a plane to an important meeting in Paris and on board meets a young woman, Sabeth, with whom he falls in love—not knowing, in fact, that Sabeth is his own daughter. He had fathered her with Hanna, whom he has not seen in twenty years, and who had later married Joachim. Again acting impulsively, Faber joins Sabeth in a trip by car across Europe to Athens, where she will join her mother. On reaching Greece and shortly after Faber has figured out that Sabeth is his daughter, Sabeth dies after an accident, and Faber must acknowledge to Hanna his unwitting incest.

The last fourth of the book forms a coda to the main action in which Faber is hospitalized with presumably terminal stomach cancer, the description of which is interrupted by Faber's reflections on further events: a return visit to Guatemala to see Herbert, who had remained behind; a stopover in pre-Castro Cuba, during which Faber's anti-American feelings spill forth; the description of a disastrous and awkward screening of 8-mm films Faber had taken during his travels.

One of the book's most interesting qualities is the way in which the South American story and the European story complement one another and are ultimately united. These two relatively separate narratives allow Frisch to set up a system of contrasts that can be seen as a series of binary opposites. Although Faber is a scientist, a man of impersonal detachment, he must confront experiences more easily explained by art or mythology. Although he is a man who tries dispassionately to control the world, he must confront a series of improbable coincidences that can only suggest something akin to fate or predestination. Where Faber is a man of reason, he must experience an awakening of passion that he has presumably never felt before. Where Faber is a man of the machine age, he must see in Central America a death and decay that only animal flesh can undergo. The narrative presents a series of contrasts: primitive jungle to comfortable New York apartment; New World of science, technology, and industrial development to Old World of museums, the opera, and antiquity; nightmarish travel by plane to idealized travel by ship; role of father to role of lover; jaded experience of the middle-aged male to spontaneous enthusiasm of the 20-year-old female. Frisch's narrative is a rich one precisely because out of the central contrast of Faber to the strange, unreliable world around him comes a set of variations of these polar opposites: reason/passion, technology/art, machine/flesh, experience/youth, chance/fate, North/South, America/Europe.

Schlöndorff streamlines and reduces the literary narrative without sacrificing the model's thematic richness. The Latin American episodes are presented swiftly and efficiently without Frisch's sense of lingering, of wasted time, and of boredom, and they account for only about twenty-three of the film's 113 minutes. In addition, Schlöndorff omits the entire coda from the film. Schlöndorff's story concentrates on the central romance, the autobiographical part of the book that most interested him ("Wem wird man" 238). Schlöndorff's greatest change is in making Faber an American. Although this change was in part motivated by economic constraints that required such a medium-budget movie with international locations to be shot in English, it nonetheless produces a reconfiguration of the story's fundamental oppositions (Schlöndorff, "Wem wird man" 245). Faber (Sam Shepard) becomes a direct representative of American technical expertise and cultural semiliteracy as opposed to both Third World primitiveness and European aesthetic and philosophical tradition. What in the novel is a contrast between Northern and Southern European sensibilities is simplified into a European-American dichotomy. Schlöndorff himself has said,

> It appeared more plausible and exciting that it be an American who for the first time sees the Louvre, the cathedral of Orvieto, the Ludovician Altar, rather than that some European who is 50 years old claims that he never traveled to Italy or Greece. The entire trip becomes more interesting, it turns into an initiation. The technological man, the American, returns to the origins of our culture. ("Wem wird man" 245)

The structure of *Voyager* thus involves two roughly parallel journeys, each of which bridges a number of the binary oppositions: Faber's trip to see Joachim Hencke (August Zirner) and his trip with Sabeth (Julie Delpy) to Athens. Both connect North and South, present and past, the controlled and the unpredictable. Both end in death, and both represent a movement from an impersonal technological world to one suggestive of primal origins. By implication, Faber's confrontation with Joachim's death becomes a confrontation with his own death, producing an awareness of mortality that would be a central part of any midlife crisis. The structure of the journey makes movement in space and time a metaphor for the life cycle. Schlöndorff thereby uses in *Voyager* a structure comparable to that of *Swann in Love* in which a progression from rising to going to bed becomes a metaphor for birth and death. Faber's affair with Sabeth becomes a kind of second life, a rebirth, a starting over. It is a structure that is actually clearer in Frisch's novel, which ends with Faber's implied death.

In the system that Frisch and Schlöndorff set up, love is the opposite of death, and *Voyager* becomes fundamentally a love story (Schlöndorff, "Wem wird man" 238). As such, it extends the pattern developed throughout Schlöndorff's work of presenting love relationships that cannot survive because of society's disapproval or their own self-destructive unconventionality. Schlöndorff in *Voyager* raises the question of what is a "natural" or "normal" love relationship. In contrast to Sabeth, who seems normal, unspoiled, and authentic, Schlöndorff presents the characters of both Ivy and the airline stewardess. As critic Charles Helmetag has observed, these two, together with the female Americans surrounding Faber and Sabeth on their transatlantic cruise, are thickly made up and thus contrast dramatically with Sabeth and her mother (7–8). Schlöndorff adds to the binary oppositions found in Frisch a new one of "artificial" American women as opposed to the "natural" European woman. He presents the former as flirt and the latter as serious. If the airline stewardess who calls Faber to his plane is, as Helmetag noted, a kind of siren, leading Faber to near death, Sabeth, by contrast, brings him to life. It is he who becomes a kind of Hades character pulling a Sabeth-Persephone into the underworld. *Voyager* presents a fundamental paradox: Faber's most perfect love is the most unacceptable to human society. The film pushes to an extreme one of the fundamental principles of the classic love story—that the strength of the love must be in direct proportion to its impossibility .

Looking, Seeing, and Eroticism

In presenting a radical situation of forbidden love, *Voyager* is reaching for something far beyond a realistic portrayal of accidental incest, and the movie, with its ultimate setting in Athens, deliberately invites comparison to Greek myth. Yet *Voyager* is not a simplistic retelling of classic myth in modern dress. Rather, it explores in concrete dramatic terms philosophical questions related to chance and destiny. Although imagery suggestive of antiquity and mythology surrounds Sabeth and Faber, the movie leaves inconclusive whether old classic ideas or modern scientific ones could better explain a situation like Faber's, whether an empiricist can see a situation more clearly than a believer. Is the story tragedy, or simply one of, as the song over the concluding credits of the German prints says, "Careless Love"?

Schlöndorff alludes to Oedipus in both visual and verbal references to blindness. There is a scene in which Sabeth, having spotted Faber at the Louvre, where he has been looking for her, approaches quietly from behind the park bench on which he is sitting and playfully covers his eyes with her hands. This gesture lends an ominous note to a scene of joyous reunion. As the two are driving through Europe at night, Sabeth at one point must steer the car because Faber's eyesight is inadequate in the darkness. In the scene at the Athens airport that, at the beginning and end of *Voyager,* frames the story, we see repeated a close shot of Faber sitting, expressionless, having not boarded the plane that has just been announced. He is wearing dark glasses, and his near catatonic manner calls to mind the image of the blinded Oedipus. Schlöndorff reinforces this with Faber's voice-over in which he says: "I have nothing to see any longer, her hands, which do not exist any more, her movements when she tossed her hair back, her teeth, her lips, her eyes which no longer see anything." Like the ancient tragic hero, Faber finds the premises of his world questioned.

Looking and seeing therefore become central motifs in *Voyager* just as they had been in Schlöndorff's previous *The Handmaid's Tale.* In both, looking becomes a source of pleasure and power. And Schlöndorff's treatment of the look becomes one of the ways in which *Voyager* succeeds at being cinematically expressive. The development of Faber and Sabeth's love is specifically embodied in their mutual exchange of looks. At first it is Faber who looks at Sabeth, but in a key scene, during a group discussion of art versus science in the ship's lounge, we see Faber become very deliberately the object of Sabeth's gaze. The succession of shots in this scene provides for the film's first shifting of point of view from Faber to Sabeth, and this point of view periodically transfers from one to the other as the film progresses. To the audience, this shifting provides for the intensifying emotional force of the love story as each member of the couple becomes both subject and object of the gaze. Faber's falling in love involves a surrender of power as he becomes both looker and looked-at in an equal and symmetrical relationship. To become a lover, he must give up the power of being a father.

At key moments, Schlöndorff shifts the point of view to Sabeth. The director makes a major departure from Frisch's description of the scene in the Louvre. In both book and film, Faber, who has never before been a museum goer, visits the Louvre in the hope that he will see Sabeth there. Where the novel describes him as eventually finding her there on a repeat visit, the movie handles the situation differently. Schlöndorff shows Faber looking at the Venus de Milo and other female nudes, and thereby expresses, through editing, a sexual desire only implied previously. Just near closing time, Sabeth spots Faber, watches him leave and then follows him to the park bench as we described earlier. Schlöndorff places Sabeth among ancient statuary, thereby connecting the episode to the film's conclusion in Athens. By making Sabeth the looker, Schlöndorff expresses visually Faber's increasing emotional vulnerability. Schlöndorff connects both art and love to the pleasure of looking.

Schlöndorff reinforces these connections in a later scene in which Faber and Sabeth visit an Italian cloister and see a sculpted female head of a sleeping Erinys. They discover that the statue looks more impressive when one of them stands in a certain spot, creating a particular lighting. In a subsequent shot Schlöndorff creates a visual echo by having Faber in bed lying on his back with his profile comparable to that of the Erinys. Sabeth is hovering over him and he becomes again the object of her loving look. Matthias Rüb has argued that Schlöndorff ignores how the Erinys is a figure of revenge who punishes guilt, and hence the director misses the way in which the Erinys scene in Frisch may foreshadow Faber's coming sorrow. Although Schlöndorff's Erinys may be seen as either placid or threatening, the director's intelligent mise-en-scène ties the image into *Voyager*'s developed pattern of the gaze.

Given this system of looking, it is interesting that Schlöndorff does not pick up on one of the key scenes in Frisch in which Sabeth looking at Faber is emphasized. In the novel, Frisch describes Sabeth as being bitten by the snake while Faber is swimming nude. As Faber approaches to help the victim, she backs away slowly at the sight of his nakedness, which causes her to fall from the embankment. In Schlöndorff's version, not only does Faber swim with his clothing on but there is no indication that Sabeth even sees him coming toward her. As Daniela Berghahn points out, in Frisch's version, Sabeth's accident immediately follows her recoiling from her father's sexuality (85). This metonymic equating of the father with the snake becomes in the film merely an accident seen largely in the long shot from Faber's point of view. Frisch's version more pointedly suggests a disrupted Eden in which Sabeth may be responding to her father's unacknowledged sexual aggression against her.

Throughout the story, Faber continually takes 8-mm movies of what he sees, and Schlöndorff incorporates these movies into *Voyager,* where they come to embody a number of the movie's formal and thematic concerns. The home movie sequences are another link in the film's system of looks. Significantly, even before first standing in line with the young woman for the cruise's table assignments, Faber records her on film as she steps into his field of vision. Likewise, the very last images of Sabeth in the film resemble home movie footage and are intercut with the final image of Faber in the airport; they are indicated to be his memory of Sabeth. The home movie sequences thus in general equate with Faber's memory, allowing the film to be told alternately in both the present and past tense. This 8-mm cinema also becomes a self-reflexive metaphor both for Schlöndorff's own craft and, perhaps, also for his memories of the book and the period in which it was written.

That Faber should take home movies is fully in character, for as a technology-oriented person he should enjoy experimentation with this sort of device. Yet it is through these movies that Faber begins to become an artist; he begins to make images of his surroundings and of Sabeth; he begins to unite his mechanical instincts with aesthetic ones. He begins to unite, as Schlöndorff also does as a filmmaker, art and technology. What is more, as *Voyager* progresses, we see a similar change of point of view to Sabeth, as she begins to take movies of Faber. He becomes as much the object of her camera as she is of his, something he seems to find disconcerting in the scene on the Greek boat where his sour expression and his withdrawn posture tell her, in effect, to turn off the camera. He has alternated between father and lover role, and since learning of Hanna (Barbara Sukowa) and Joachim Hencke as her presumed parents, is in transition between the two roles, sensing the need to emphasize the pole of father.

Fathers and Lovers

Two scenes in particular both reinforce this father-lover bivalence and complement one another with a certain visual symmetry. In the first, Sabeth and Faber have left the shipboard party, and Faber asks her to marry him. As the scene progresses, he is clearly both serious and fanciful, with the fatherly, rationalist side at war with the impulsive lover. Schlöndorff adds irony to this scene by having the band in the adjacent room play a wailing version of "Careless Love." The couple is interrupted by Kurt (Thomas Heinze), Sabeth's younger boyfriend, the presence of whom clearly makes Faber seem all the more father-like. Sabeth walks off screen with Kurt, only to return presently. The pattern of absence and return beautifully complements the entire sense of hesitation about the scene.

This pattern is repeated in the episode that follows the couple's reunion at the Louvre in which they sit together in a café. The episode starts with Faber being the dutiful father in extracting from her two promises: not to hitchhike to Rome and not to become an airline stewardess. He insists that he needs to get back to his conference and asks her to send him an occasional card or letter so he knows that she has reached her destination. In a movement that becomes a mirror image of Sabeth's in the previous shipboard scene, Faber says good-bye and leaves the frame. After a pair of reverse-angle shots through the café window, Faber surprises Sabeth who is so wrapped in thought that she does not see him return. In both scenes Schlöndorff skillfully uses the absence of a character from the frame to suggest the momentary loss sensed by the one who remains. Space and framing become a metaphor for feeling. Being a father implies eventual separation from one's child; being a lover involves joining and union.

Schlöndorff summarizes this conflict between father and lover roles near the end of the film when Faber sees Sabeth in the hospital garden. This is the device Schlöndorff employs to resolve the narrative and do so in a manner different from Frisch: in a dramatic rather than novelistic manner. This resolution presents a unified scene rather than Frisch's mosaic of episodes. As Hanna is accompanying Sabeth back to her room, Faber calls to her, and the two exchange looks. No doubt because he is inhibited by Hanna's presence, Faber does no more and begins to cry as they leave. He can be neither father nor lover to the woman he loves most. It is a classic double bind.

In the way that these scenes vary the father-lover poles, they develop the leitmotif technique prevalent throughout Schlöndorff's work and thus extend the continuities in his oeuvre. One can find in *Voyager* both traditional, symbolically loaded leitmotifs and more casual, less thematically weighted, almost playful "echo structures." Both lend the film structural coherence. The relationship between Sabeth and the stewardess from the plane crash can serve to illustrate the more traditional leitmotif. In one sense, the stewardess functions as an alter ego to Sabeth; she varies, in a somewhat negative way, the relationship between the older man, Faber, and a youthful woman. The stewardess represents the female adapted to the machine age. Schlöndorff keeps the connection between these two characters alive by reminding the spectator of the stewardess in the dialogue. At one point, Sabeth tells Faber of her job goal to become a stewardess; at another, as mentioned, Faber extracts from her the promise not to pursue this career objective.

The "threshold motif" exemplifies a more loosely connected echo structure. Repeatedly in *Voyager,* characters come to another's door and meet with varying degrees of acceptance. Faber returns to his New York apartment and is greeted through the chain bolt by Ivy, his girl friend, who then lets him in. The protagonist brings medicine to a seasick Sabeth, who accepts it through the only narrowly opened door. In a French hotel, Sabeth goes to Faber's room where they make love for the first time, an episode that is repeated as a flashback from Faber's point of view right after he admits to Hanna that he has had sex with Sabeth. (See illustration 36.) In a final variation that immediately follows, Faber goes to the door of Hanna who is sobbing in her room. He tries the locked door, and the film cuts to the next scene. These echo structures unify the film visually rather than thematically. One can see this visual unity in the

36. *Voyager.* Faber (Sam Shepard) and Sabeth (Julie Delpy) at a threshold. Photo: Deutsches Fimmuseum Fotoarchiv.

way in which Kurt and Sabeth, running through the rain with a canvas over their heads, reflect Faber and Ivy's earlier lovemaking in the shower during which he pulls her gown over their heads. Similarly, the proliferation of statues throughout the European sections constantly brings to mind the film's central dichotomy between the material and the spiritual.

This use of leitmotifs and echo patterns is not the only quality *Voyager* has in common with Schlöndorff's earlier work. Schlöndorff's reflective male hero in *Voyager* is in many respects similar to Benyon of *Georgina's Reasons*, Laschen of *Circle of Deceit*, and the title figure of *Swann in Love.* All are suffering heroes characterized by a cool stoicism, and indeed at one point Schlöndorff had planned to cast Bruno Ganz, his star of *Circle of Deceit*, in the role of Faber. Instead, Sam Shepard joins the ranks of leading men in Schlöndorff films criticized for being too inexpressive and aloof. A *Washington Post* critic commented of the actor: "Shepard seems to wander about in a fog of navel-gazing self-absorption. As Faber, he gives so little away that, aside from an air of weary glamour and his reliance on rationality and fact, the man seems virtually without personality" (Hinson). A similar opinion was expressed by German critic Günther Bastian of *film-dienst* who quipped, "This film's [positive] impression is impaired only in places by the actor portraying Faber who evokes the image of Arthur Miller, looking like he was entertaining doubts about whether or not it was right to marry Marilyn Monroe." Yet Shepard has not been without his staunch defenders. Calling the casting of Shepard as Faber "inspired," Caryn James of *The New York Times* wrote:

> With his 1950s fedora and impassive face, he looks and sounds like the old-fashioned, terse masculine ideal. Still, his intense eyes and his very presence . . . suggest more depth than Gary Cooper ever did. Sam Shepard is an intelligent icon who depicts the complex currents beneath the still surface of *Voyager.*

In its treatment of women, *Voyager* goes back to the prefeminist Schlöndorff, the filmmaker of *Young Törless* and *Michael Kohlhaas.* In each of these earlier films, a central male protagonist encounters different women in the course of the narrative. The women represent a range of types and contrasts. Törless's mother, for example, exists in opposition to Bozena, the prostitute, just as Kohlhaas's wife forms a contrast to the nuns who are raped, the ladies at court, and Katrina, the camp follower. In both cases, women are defined by the males' perception. There is a similar pattern in *Voyager.* The film defines women from a masculine viewpoint as mother, daughter, flirt, or mistress.

This is not to say that Schlöndorff's treatment of women in *Voyager* is completely retrograde. The character of Hanna, as played by Barbara Sukowa, is an independent woman with a successful career who has perhaps been more skilled than Faber at uniting intellect and feeling. Although Julie Delpy's Sabeth is frequently childlike, the character shares much of her mother's independence. Both women are assertive and, in the context of the film's setting in the late 1930s and 1950s, even liberated. Schlöndorff's Sabeth is far more active than Frisch's in pursuing Faber and in asking for what she wants. And as we have suggested above, Faber's ability to find love arises in direct proportion to the equality he and Sabeth have in the relationship.

The similarity between mother and daughter and their mutual strength supports a second mythological reading that has been advanced by Schlöndorff himself ("Das ist der Sinn" 12, 16). The film evokes not only Oedipus but the myth of Demeter and Persephone, the latter also known as Kore. According to the legends, Demeter lost her daughter Kore after the latter had been abducted by Hades. Out of Demeter's efforts to retrieve her daughter from the underworld comes a mythological explanation for the change of seasons whereby Kore, now called Persephone, returns to Hades with each winter. Like the manipulative Demeter, Hanna has engineered the situation to suit herself. She refuses both an abortion and marriage to Faber, even though she is pregnant, yet maneuvers into subsequent marriages as they become convenient. She controls what her daughter knows about her past and thereby unwittingly contributes to Sabeth's involvement with Faber. Indeed Schlöndorff himself has described Hanna as the only guilty party, a statement that surprised his interviewer, who was expecting a more profeminist position (Müry 15). Hanna and Faber's conflict near the end of *Voyager* comes to suggest a clash among imperfect gods in which the female god is an equal match to the male. The analogy between Hanna-Sabeth and Demeter-Kore is, of course, a loose one and more of an allusion than an exact parallel. But it adds one more layer to Schlöndorff's film.

An Existentialist Art Film

Throughout *Voyager* Schlöndorff equates myth and art. In *Voyager* Schlöndorff picks up a line of discourse that had been particularly heavy in his films of the 1970s. He presents a consideration of the role of art and the artist in human experience. One recalls the visits to museums featured in both *The Morals of Ruth Halbfass* and *A Free Woman* and the different, even contradictory attitudes these earlier works expressed about art. *Voyager* is closer to a *Free Woman* in that it sees art as liberating, as expressing a person's passionate, and, indeed, feminine side, and as an antidote to the impersonality of the modern world. Where works like *The Morals of Ruth Halbfass* and *Swann in Love* emphasize the decadent, petit-bourgeois aspects of culture, *A Free Woman* and *Voyager* are far more optimistic about the value of aesthetics. Sabeth's naïveté, like her namesake Elisabeth's, is still unspoiled in its belief that art can transform human experience.

The tension between the roles of art and technology in the changing human condition is a theme relating contemporary films as different as *Voyager* and Wim Wenders's *Until the End of the World,* films that have some remarkable parallels. As the two major international productions directed by German filmmakers released in 1991, *Voyager* and *Until the End of the World* share similarities of structure, style, and even narrative. Both are episodic works that resemble road movies, although both use multiple means of transportation to move their characters across continents, oceans, and national borders. In both, an oddly matched mixed-gender couple (rather than buddies) travel together to rejoin parents who had been uprooted by the Third Reich. Both contrast primitive surroundings with high technology. In both, characters take moving pictures of what they experience. Both may reflect the condition of a German filmmaker who, facing an inhospitable domestic cinema economy, has been forced into the rootlessness of large-scale international coproduction.

Both the Wenders and Schlöndorff films met with mixed critical reception and box office results. On both counts, *Voyager* was more successful in Germany than in the rest of the world. German critical reaction was warmer, and the film stayed for a number of weeks among the ten top-grossing films in the country, earning almost $5 million within sixteen weeks (Groves). In addition, the film was nominated for three Felix Awards, considered to be the united Europe's answer to the Oscar: for European film of the year, European actress, and European supporting actress. Although *Voyager* received an excellent number of positive reviews from the New York critics—one count put it at eighteen positive out of twenty-four write-ups (*"Shining"* 18), the movie did only modest business there and in other major American cities.

Voyager's positive and negative reviewers for the most part repeat the usual divisions in reception for Schlöndorff's work, with one side praising the film's intelligence and craftsmanship, the other side finding in it a vapid academicism and a simplistic and unfocused illustration of a work of literature. Although we would tend to hold the former opinion, we find a major puzzlement in Schlöndorff's attempt to treat existential issues on screen. Given the classicism and simplicity of style with which *Homo Faber* has been adapted, the film all but ignores the developments in cinema that grew out of existentialist thought itself. Consider, for example, the way in which Michelangelo Antonioni in *L'avventura* (1960) or Ingmar Bergman in *The Silence* (1963)—to give just two examples—apply existentialist thought to the formal structures of their films. These movies play with time and duration, suggest that the possible meaninglessness of human existence might be expressed through the boredom of their antinarratives and treat their characters' confusion of sex and love as parallel to the audience's simultaneous experience of titillation and thoughtfulness. The result is a coherent merger of existentialist content with particular existentialist forms. It is a coherence characteristic of many of the great art films of the 1960s.

Much of Frisch's book—and especially the Latin American section—reads, in effect, like a description of an Antonioni film in which characters are bored, directionless, and vaguely anguished. It is quite the opposite of Schlöndorff's terse, matter-of-fact summary of the search for Joachim. Although Schlöndorff keeps many of Frisch's existential themes, he loses much of the author's existential rhythm whereby details often unimportant to the narrative receive special emphasis. *Voyager* takes a more traditional approach, one more comparable, let us say, to David Lean's *Brief Encounter* than to Antonioni's *Red Desert*. The film has one foot in direct narrative, the other in more philosophical discourse. The result is less radical than it might have been but is nonetheless distinctive.

This direct narrative quality has greatly bothered Matthias Hurst, a critic who has written extensively about *Voyager*. Hurst's argument is that Schlöndorff loses much of the subjectivity inherent in Frisch's telling the story so intensely from Faber's point of view. Although Hurst is pleased with the director's use of voice-over narration to retain what he calls Frisch's "I narrator," he claims that Schlöndorff undercuts this effective tool of first-person cinema narration with a visual style that is too detached and omniscient (230, 243). Hurst is accurate in much of his description of the adaptation, but one might argue that only through a disjunction between image and sound could Schlöndorff get a sense of Faber's tale not as lived by the character but as remembered. That *Voyager* is not completely Frisch need not, as Hurst maintains, make it a failure as a movie.

Voyager breaks a certain amount of new ground for Schlöndorff. He himself sees it as a response to the new world situation of the 1990s in which the fall of Communism has created an intellectual climate comparable to that in Europe after World War II. He proposes that artists and writers are again ready to confront questions of guilt and fate (Tagliabue 22). Although those same questions have always been present in Schlöndorff's work, they have frequently remained secondary to his political and social interests. One could argue that Schlöndorff is in *Voyager* retreating into the kind of politically quietist bourgeois material that the left of the late 1960s would have found culturally offensive. In the case of Max Frisch, however, the book is an anomalously apolitical work from an author who maintained his political commitments. Although it was not a bestseller when first published, *Homo Faber* has since become one of the author's most popular works. One wonders whether Schlöndorff's adaptation may have comparable long-term appeal. Only time will tell whether *Voyager*'s new emphasis on the personal and metaphysical is a digression in Schlöndorff's career or a new direction. On the other hand, one can also see *Voyager* as extending the line in Schlöndorff's work last established by *Swann in Love*, foregrounding a preoccupation with love, eroticism, memory, guilt, and loss.

25

The Ogre

A superficial viewing of Volker Schlöndorff's *The Ogre* (1996) cannot fail to produce in the mind of the spectator familiar with Schlöndorff's earlier work a whole network of references and parallels to the director's other films. The opening scenes in a boys' boarding school rework elements of *Young Törless*. A naive hero who has a boy's psyche in a mature man's body can be seen as an inverse of *The Tin Drum*'s Oskar, who had a mature psyche in a boy's body. *The Ogre*'s spectacle of collective Nazi rituals recalls comparable assemblies in *The Handmaid's Tale*. And the director's fascination with the war-torn areas of the Baltic region and East Prussia, established in *Coup de Grâce* and *The Tin Drum*, returns here in yet another inverted variant on the *Heimatfilm*.

At the same time, *The Ogre* explores new ground for Schlöndorff. In it, the filmmaker treats the themes of innocence and guilt, suggesting that guilt about the Third Reich should include guilt not just about the Holocaust but also about the lives of thousands of young German men who were sacrificed. Schlöndorff's treatment of this era differs from that of others in his use of a central character who is a kind of mythic, ahistoric archetype, resulting in a collision between specific historical details and a poetic figure whose narrative function is to provide a point of view about these details. In addition, *The Ogre* employs an overarching metaphor that disturbingly compares the seductive qualities of fascism to pedophilia. The result is a narrative that encourages and then discourages—in repeated alternation—identification with the hero, that piles on ideological contradictions, and that ultimately confused and offended critics and audiences.

Schlöndorff's source material is the novel by Michel Tournier called *Le roi des aulnes* (1970) and retitled *The Ogre* in its English translation (1972). The original title is a direct reference to Goethe's poem "Der Erlkönig," a romantic ballad celebrating childhood, imagination, and the magic of nature. *Erlkönig* is also the title of Tournier's book in German, although Schlöndorff deliberately used the more generic title *Der Unhold*, to avoid an excessively charged reference to

Goethe (Schlöndorff, "Nachwort" 188). Tournier has been a controversial figure in European letters, in part because some critics saw *Le roi des aulnes* as a
novel as much entranced by the mystique of fascism as it was critical of it
(Douin). In preunification West Germany, Jean Améry, formerly exiled during
the Third Reich, attacked "Tournier's Aestheticism of Barbarism" (73). For
this reason, Schlöndorff himself described the project as risky (Jenny 199) and
has admitted that his interest in it emerged from his own naive, juvenile fascination with the glamour of Nazi artifacts and ideology ("Nachwort" 175–77).
Although it incorporated extensive factual research, Tournier's novel is an elaborately written, fanciful work that combines fictional diaries with third-person
narrative—the kind of nonrealistic book that would traditionally be thought
impossible to render on the screen.

The book is divided into six main sections. Part 1 focuses on the main character, Abel Tiffauges, owner of a middle-class Parisian car repair shop in the
late 1930s, as he remembers his youth in a boarding school and as he pursues
a hobby of photographing school children. Tiffauges befriends a schoolgirl who
later falsely accuses him of raping her. Because France is preparing to enter
World War II at the beginning of September 1939, the judge allows Tiffauges,
in lieu of standing trial, to enlist in the army.

Part 2 describes Tiffauges's work with homing pigeons that he collects and
trains to deliver messages for the French army.

In part 3, Tiffauges, captured by the Germans, works in an East Prussian
prison camp, where he enjoys closeness to nature. He finds he can even slip off
to a deserted woodland cabin where he feeds a blind elk, whose lack of connection to the herd clearly parallels Tiffauges's own loner status. He also meets
the head forester, who recommends him for a position at the hunting lodge of
Field Marshall Hermann Göring, Hitler's second in command.

In part 4, Tiffauges works as a factotum at the lodge and observes Göring in
hunting, partying, and boasting, until the fall of Stalingrad disperses the hunters.

In part 5, Tiffauges is sent to a "Napola," an elite residential school for the
indoctrination and military training of teenage boys. He begins as custodian
but rises to become chief recruiter for the school, and finally, as the crisis war
situation pulls the school's leaders to the front, becomes the authority figure in
charge.

In the final section, Tiffauges learns of Germany's impending defeat and res-
cues from death a boy who has escaped from Auschwitz. After hiding the boy
in the school's attic and nurturing him back to health, Tiffauges, amid the chaos
and slaughter by the invading Russian army of the teenage boys around him,
carries the Jewish boy Ephraim on his shoulders into an icy swamp.

Given the story's requirements for elaborate period re-creation, its several major changes of international locations, and its elements of spectacle, *The Ogre* needed to be an expensive, large-scale production. Indeed, the project originated with a former East German director, Rainer Simon, and Schlöndorff took it over in part because financiers were more comfortable with Schlöndorff as a proven talent (Wahl). The film was budgeted at 26 million marks, or almost $17 million. Given this kind of budget, the film took on an international quality, with shooting in English and a mixture of American, French, and German performers. At one point, Gérard Depardieu was envisioned for the lead role of Abel Tiffauges; with his passing on the project, Schlöndorff went next to the American actor John Malkovich. Others involved in the production were Jean-Claude Carrière, who had previously helped script both *The Tin Drum* and *Swann in Love;* the Belgian Bruno de Keyzer, most famous for his cinematography of several major films by Bertrand Tavernier; and British composer Michael Nyman, with whom Schlöndorff had previously collaborated on *The Michael Nyman Songbook. The Ogre* was clearly a prestige production, and Schlöndorff, aware of the risks involved, commented, "If we fail, the German and European film will once again be buried" (Wahl 25).

Schlöndorff's adaptation stays faithful to the book's basic structure, although he speeds through the first third of the narrative in about twenty minutes of screen time and emphasizes the last third so that it comprises almost half of the final film. However, a simple outline of the story's somewhat picaresque structure fails to convey the elements that make the narrative rich. Schlöndorff claims he was trying for a mixture of styles in *The Ogre,* something that would have the raucous effect of a balladeer's broadside, with a vibrant mixture of short scenes and elaborate tableaus, a contrasting of mythic, utopian pastoral elements with folksy, operetta-like comedy ("Nachwort" 178, 182–84). Two major aspects of Tournier's novel are carried into the film and make it unusual: the mythic quality of Abel Tiffauges's character and an allusive web of metaphors and leitmotifs. Both elements give the story, in print and on the screen, a poetry and lyricism that take it beyond being merely a realistic portrayal of an historical period.

A Mythological Hero

Surrounding Abel Tiffauges is an array of biblical, Christian, historic, and fairy-tale references that merge and overlap. The character's very name is a mixture of the sacred and the profane. His first name clearly refers to the biblical son of Adam and Eve—the wandering shepherd who is slain by his brother

Cain. (Indeed, just before he is wrongly arrested for the rape of Martine, the cinematic Tiffauges bumps his head on a beam, producing a bloody, erroneous "mark of Cain.") The surname is identical to the name of the castle of the legendary Gilles de Rais, slaughterer of women and children and source of the storybook figure of Bluebeard. Throughout the film, Tiffauges is associated with the figure of St. Christopher, carrier of the Christ child through threatening waters. We see the allusion to this Biblical image from the first image of the film—of students at St. Christopher's boarding school perched on one another's shoulders in a school yard fight—to the very last image, of Tiffauges and Ephraim in the swamp. (See illustration 37.) Alternating with this image of a saintly rescuer, however, is that of Tiffauges as a grim reaper, seen most vividly in the sequences in which the character, dressed in a black cape and riding a black horse, picks up and carries off young boys who will later die in battle. (See illustration 38.) In a variation of this last figure, when Tiffauges first recruits a group of young men, he plays a handmade recorder, taking on the persona of the pied piper.

Through most of the film, Tiffauges is convinced that he is not an ordinary man and that, although he does not know what it is, he has a special mission and unique destiny. Twice in the early part of the narrative he escapes punishment for something of which he is falsely accused. When St. Christopher's school catches on fire and his friend Nestor is killed, the school officials forget or ignore an appointment at which the boy Abel was supposed to be disciplined. That escape, which in voice-over Tiffauges tells us was his fate, prefigures his avoidance of jail for a rape charge. Given these seemingly contradictory references, part of the challenge to the audience is to figure out what Tiffauges's fate might be and what his destiny might mean.

Abel Tiffauges appears as a fully ordinary, though not very well adjusted man. At the same time, both Tournier and Schlöndorff present him as an almost spiritual figure. The ambiguity in Tiffauges's character is embodied most uncomfortably in the sexual aspects of the narrative. Early in the film we see Tiffauges in his apartment with his mistress Rachel. He takes pictures of her clothed only in lingerie. The resulting association of his camera with sexuality makes his having taken pictures of Martine and other children seem somewhat less than innocent. Later on in the film, when we see his delight in being among the boys in the Napola, we feel the same distrust. We are never quite sure whether the filmmaker is simply being discreet about Tiffauges's sex life or whether the protagonist is a metaphysical character who transcends ordinary sexuality. Writing in his "Nachwort" afterword about the character of Tiffauges, who he argues "cannot be explained by psychology," and who "remains for-

37. *The Ogre.* John Malkovich as Abel Tiffauges, who becomes a St. Christopher figure when he attempts to carry a Jewish boy from the battle site. Photo: Courtesy of Kino International.

ever a child and will never be older than twelve years" (182), Schlöndorff has commented, "his sexuality is not exactly genital" (180).

Disturbing Metaphors

The suggestion of pedophilia then becomes a major metaphor in the film, one that is problematic, ambiguous, and highly discomforting. The boys are

38. *The Ogre.* A pied piper Abel stealing children on behalf of the Nazi recruitment. Photo: Courtesy of Kino International.

seduced by Nazism in much the same way they would be sexually seduced—in a way that initially seems exciting, adventurous, and loving. This metaphor proposes that just as the universally admired value of the love of children is perverted by inappropriate sexuality, so also were positive values of self-sacrifice, self-discipline, and love of country perverted by National Socialism. In a self-reflexive way, the audience may also feel itself to be a target for seduction, in that the movie's narrative mechanisms make us want to like a character whom we see behaving like a pedophile. It is not consoling to the spectator that we see no evidence of Tiffauges using children sexually. On the contrary, our projection of feelings of lust onto Tiffauges extends the metaphor of innocence and guilt. Becoming emotionally excited by images of Nazi spectacle violates a taboo comparable to that of feeling sexual excitement at the images of children. Schlöndorff is asking us to confront and compare these two kinds of ecstasy. One may be offended by the facile quality of the comparison, but one cannot deny that it is a potent one.

One result of this metaphor is that it is almost impossible for the viewer to identify fully with Tiffauges. Although the movie offers little in the way of a Brechtian separation of elements, as a central character, Tiffauges is as Brechtian a hero as any in Schlöndorff's work. Rather than feel what the protagonist feels, we more often than not feel emotions that differ. When he picks up Martine after her accident, we feel uncertainty as opposed to his euphoria. When Tiffauges becomes successful at working for the Nazis, we feel concern as opposed to his pride. As he recruits the boys, we feel horror at their exploitation, as opposed to his elation or tenderness. He is an unreflective protagonist who acts on instinct but who causes the audience to be thoughtful and to reflect on the implications of his actions. One is reminded of Godard's observation that the only really effective, nonmelodramatic way to present the Holocaust would be to show it from the Nazi point of view and let the audience be shocked: Schlöndorff takes something of the same approach here (Godard 54). Only at the end of the movie, when Tiffauges realizes the danger to the boys and attempts to rescue Ephraim, do the emotions and desires of the audience coincide with those of the hero. Schlöndorff himself has said that Tiffauges's change of heart comes not from political awareness but from his love of children: "As a fool, he is not receptive to ideas; hence he cannot be corrupted, but he can be seduced" ("Nachwort" 187). Even though there is not much visually or stylistically in *The Ogre* that would link it to the *Verfremdungseffekt*, *The Ogre* uses Brechtian dramaturgy in its naive hero, whose sexual and other motivations are never fully specified and whom the audience sees almost exclusively from the outside.

At the same time, Tiffauges becomes an appropriate stand-in for the audience. As a Frenchman, he is an outsider and an observer, in much the same way that a large number of viewers of *The Ogre* would not have experienced the Third Reich firsthand. An audience member can identify with the character's love of animals and of nature and can easily root for his success in negotiating the difficulties of serving in the army, surviving prison camp life, working for a crazed, psychotic Göring, and finally being responsible for several hundred teenage boys. Schlöndorff alternately creates identification with Tiffauges, only to block it through sexual ambiguity and the protagonist's political naïveté.

The appeal of Abel Tiffauges as a nature-loving loner links this character to the universe of the Western, and *The Ogre* shares with both *Coup de Grâce* and the filmmaker's other anti-*Heimatfilme* Schlöndorff's affinity for this enclosed world. Even the Cain and Abel motif reflects the central opposition in the Western between the settled farmer and the wanderer and the violence that comes between them. As in the Western, *The Ogre* presents an almost entirely masculine world, and all of its female characters, such as Rachel, Martine, and

Frau Netta (Marianne Sägebrecht), the housekeeper for the Napola, are either only fleetingly present or marginal to the story. The director clearly sees in the movie's eastern Prussia landscape a parallel to the Western: "Each nation likes to have a far away landscape, that can serve as safe site for its dreams and into which it can send its saints and its rogues" ("Nachwort" 189).

As the last half of *The Ogre* develops, Schlöndorff digresses from the letter of the book by emphasizing and directly contrasting the characters of Göring (Volker Spengler), the field marshall and Hitler's second in command, and Count Kaltenborn (Armin Mueller-Stahl), the aristocratic heir to the castle that houses the Napola. Here the movie shifts to a more abstract and theoretical plane, and the scenarists seem more interested in opposing ideas and attitudes than in moving a story forward. Göring comes to represent the vulgarity, violence, greed, and excess of the new regime—comparable to the Western's get-rich-quick miner, gambler, or bank robber who threatens social stability. Kaltenborn becomes comparable to the homesteader who represents values of tradition and family-oriented community. Throughout the scenes at the hunting lodge and the military school, Kaltenborn hovers quietly like a silent but disapproving grandparent.

Perhaps the most representative episode that includes the rivals occurs in the hunting scene in which dozens of hare, deer, and other wildlife are shot and then piled up at the entrance of the hunting lodge. The scene shows us that what had once been skillful sport has become sadistic slaughter and also works as a disturbing prefiguring of the roundup and killing of the boys later in the film. Kaltenborn is present at the hunt but is unenthusiastic and hardly participates in this conspicuous consumption of wildlife. The analogy is clear: Kaltenborn represents those Germans in positions of power who tolerated a government they knew was destructive.

In a related scene, the chief forester persuades Göring not to shoot a gigantic stag so that it can breed for one more season. Soon after, the field marshall throws a tantrum when he learns that Kaltenborn has shot the same stag. With one shot, Kaltenborn asserts his aristocratic privilege and expresses without words his disdain for the new order. The moment is not without irony, for Kaltenborn has had to destroy one more animal to make his point.

Schlöndorff and Jean-Claude Carrière further try to visualize this Göring-Kaltenborn opposition through the use of a monologue that Armin Mueller-Stahl gives as Kaltenborn is being arrested for his alleged link to the July 20, 1944, assassination attempt on Hitler's life. In the speech, the character rails against the destruction of the noble German nation by National Socialism: "It's a whole beautiful country, to which we have given our souls. It is utterly doomed. It's going to be wiped out of human memory, our entire heritage, even our name, even our ancestors' names, wiped out, all wiped out." Although this and other scenes with Kaltenborn and Göring certainly have an intellectual appeal, they contain very little emotionally involving dramatic action. Kaltenborn's cool haughtiness makes him appealing only in relation to the vulgar Göring; at one point Göring rather nastily puts down SS officer Raufeisen, head of the Napola, for being the son of a grocer. The reduction of Tiffauges to a marginal observer slows the dramatic momentum of the movie even more.

An emotionally somewhat more involving character, although he is horrible in his own way, is that of the pseudoscientist Professor Blaettchen (Dieter Laser), who tries to determine the viability of each recruited boy on the basis of superficial genetic traits. In a series of intercut scenes, Schlöndorff juxtaposes Tiffauges's hunt through the countryside for boys with Blaettchen's explanations of his judgments about such things as body type and measurements, eye and hair coloring, and even smell. In this extended sequence, Schlöndorff finds a cinematically effective way to present certain abstract ideas from Tournier's novel. He does this by using powerful images, structuring them rhythmically into short scenes, and anchoring the audience's emotions to Tiffauges's increasingly sinister character. An alert viewer will pick up on the underlying contradiction: that if heredity is of utmost importance, then the snobbish Kaltenborn, not Göring, should be the leader. Just as Göring's excesses have perverted the hunt, Blaettchen's pseudoscience perverts biology.

Unifying Leitmotifs

Two things unify this fragmentary and diverse narrative: Tiffauges's naive point of view and Tournier's elaborate system of leitmotifs for which Schlöndorff provides cinematic equivalents. We have already suggested how the image of St. Christopher opens and closes the film, and to those examples we add the image of Tiffauges carrying Martine after her accident and, later, the injured body of a young boy who has been fatally burned by the backfiring of a *Panzerfaust* antitank rocket. Although there are other motifs, the most prominent additional ones in the film are that of the ogre, the Canadian wilderness, and a flaming holocaust.

Considering first the image of the ogre, one might suggest that Abel Tiffauges is not the only ogre in the story. Our first introduction to a creature of gigantic body and ravenous appetite is through Abel's boarding school friend Nestor, who is the overweight son of the school caretaker. Nestor's position at the school allows him to enjoy late-night gluttonous raids on the school's kitchen, which Abel watches. In a subsequent scene, we see Nestor on a throne-like toilet, and Abel dutifully obeys a command to wipe the boy's backside. Later in the film, Göring provides a visual echo of Nestor. Volker Spengler, who plays the field marshall, has the same pudgy baby face and massively round body as the boy Nestor. In addition, we see elaborate banquets at the hunting lodge. Göring shows a comparable fascination with feces when, out in the woods, he explains to Tiffauges the subtle differences between different animal droppings and even pops a turd into his factotum's mouth, a gross touch that doesn't appear in the original novel.

Tiffauges himself is also identified as an ogre, and early in the film he comments that "somehow I always inspire fear in people." We hear Rachel call him a monster in response to his rough lovemaking. Later in the film, after the head forester has described to him how the blind elk is feared by the locals as an agent of evil, we connect Tiffauges as an ogre even further to the elk ogre when the human's eyeglasses are crushed and he must carry Ephraim while effectively blinded. We most clearly see Tiffauges as an ogre when he collects the children in his grim reaper costume, although he himself becomes aware that he is seen this way only when he and Frau Netta read a circular distributed among the peasants that warns them not to surrender their children to the traveling ogre.

A third major motif is the one related to Canada. We first see the boy Abel Tiffauges reading an adventure book about the Canadian wilderness to his friend as Nestor eats. Tiffauges later tries unsuccessfully to interest Martine in the same book, and he himself becomes lost in rereading the book just before Martine's cries call him to her incriminating side. When Tiffauges arrives at the Prussian prison camp, he sits and turns himself around ecstatically on the ice, and his later discovery of the cabin and the elk confirms for him that his so-called imprisonment is actually the realization of a childhood dream. The story's conclusion in the icy swamp brings the character back to a Canada-like environment.

In contrast to this motif related to cold, ice, and snow is the leitmotif of flaming destruction. We see it first when the boys spill lighter fluid on the floor of the school chapel and then accidentally ignite it, causing the fire in which Nestor is killed. The fire is a clear foreshadowing of the destruction of the Kaltenborn castle by the Russian troops, an event that itself was preceded by the fiery *Panzerfaust* accident. As Tiffauges reads in Kaltenborn's diary late in the film: "These people started a fire, and now the house is going to be burned down." Although leitmotif structures are present in almost all of Schlöndorff's films, perhaps no other work of his so directly invites the viewer to interpret

the filmic narrative through these leitmotifs and so directly depends on them
for structural unity.

When they function most effectively, the leitmotifs give *The Ogre* much of its
visual interest. Schlöndorff's challenge in making *The Ogre* was to find a fresh
way to represent the Nazi era, whose visual icons have through overuse
become cinematic clichés. The piling up of the wildlife carcasses in front of
the lodge still has the capacity to shock, while the parties within the lodge or
the torch-lit rituals of the military students seem overfamiliar. Göring's appearance with a live lion by his side allows the animal to embody visually the
power, anger, impulsiveness, and potential for violence in the character. In fact,
this visual metaphor is more effective than the caricatural performance that
Schlöndorff gets from Spengler as Göring and its counterpart from Heino Ferch
as Raufeisen.

On occasion, Schlöndorff can take a cliché image and turn it into a commentary on itself. A soft-focus shot of a group of shirtless boys crossing through
water on horseback is at once a *Heimatfilm* commonplace, and a reference to
nineteenth-century romanticist painting. Schlöndorff establishes the link
between a certain cultural ideology and a political system that both grew out
of it and perverted it. Similarly, the images of Tiffauges among the boys as they
exercise, practice tumbling, or stand in elaborate formations manage to modify and spoil what would otherwise be the perfection of their physical achievements. Neither completely a participant nor completely an observer in their
training, Tiffauges becomes an almost comic visual intrusion. His presence
pulls the viewer's attention away from a Riefenstahl-like idealization of the
body to develop the narrative point that Tiffauges is becoming accepted by the
boys and feels happy and fulfilled in his role at the school. In a similar subversion of cliché Nazi imagery, Schlöndorff shows Tiffauges crouched at the
feet of Lothar, the awkward boy who is later killed by the *Panzerfaust*, adjust-
ing the child's socks at a supremely solemn ceremony in which the boy is given
his sword.

Equally successful but in a contrasting mood, Schlöndorff invests the comparatively ordinary image of Tiffauges escaping, Ephraim on his shoulders,
with the gravity of myth. Using a simple voice-over on the sound track, in
which John Malkovich refers back to St. Christopher, Schlöndorff creates a coupling of image and sound that together provide a coherence to the preceding
hour and fifty minutes. Tiffauges, the image and sound imply, has met the destiny toward which he has been moving all his life. As Tiffauges and Ephraim
enter the icy swamp, the director cuts to a shot of the blind elk, expressionistically lit by the flashing lights of the warfare going on at the castle. The animal's

calmness becomes a counterpoint of stillness to the chaos the pair has left. It suggests a spiritual strength analogous to the way that Tiffauges's dogged persistence allows him to endure the heaviness of the child in the deepest part of the water. This switch from confusion to focus and from disorder to calm is skillfully marked by a transition in Michael Nyman's music from a manic, turbulent theme to one that is soothing. As the pair begin to pull out of the low point, Malkovich reads the final words of the film, words from Abel's boarding school youth:

> Remember that you are under the sign of St. Christopher. You are a child-bearer. Remember that when you carry a child, you will be able to avoid harm by taking shelter under the mantle of innocence. And you will go through rivers. And you will go through tempests. And you will go through the flame of sin. And then—

The final image of the film is an extreme long shot in which the tiny figures of the survivors are dwarfed by an icy wilderness. It is an image that glitters and offers, in the sun we see rising, the promise of freedom but that also expressionistically presents a cold, cosmic space suggestive of eternity.

Germans as Victims

What exactly is Schlöndorff saying with this ending and the narrative that precedes it? The ending differs from Tournier's, in which Tiffauges and Ephraim drown. Schlöndorff reportedly shot more than one version and experimented with both upbeat and downbeat conclusions (Kinzer). For Tournier, the figure of Tiffauges surely represents French collaboration with the Germans during World War II. Schlöndorff has gone on to suggest that one can also see Tiffauges as exemplifying the kind of German who became naively involved with the Third Reich (Frank 137). The ending implies that redemption may be possible even for a human being—and by extension for a nation—who has been through the fires of even so clearly mortal a sin as the Holocaust. But it also suggests that such redemption may require discomfort, risk, self-sacrifice, and awareness of previous guilt—the substantive guilt of doing, the passive guilt of tolerating the wrongs of others, and the more ephemeral guilt of imagining and admiring evil.

In the context of the German cinema of the 1990s, *The Ogre* can be seen as part of a trend toward presenting World War II from the German point of view. One can see precedent for this as early as 1980 with Wolfgang Petersen's *The Boat (Das Boot)*, which depicted wartime submarine life as experienced by

German sailors. This tendency develops further in the 1990s with work like Joseph Vilsmaier's *Stalingrad* (1993), which portrayed the defeat from the point of view of the vanquished German foot soldier. One can also cite a documentary like *My Private War* (*Mein Krieg*, 1990) by Harriet Eder and Thomas Kufus, which was assembled from home movie footage shot by German soldiers at the front, or Helke Sander's *Liberators Take Liberties* (*Befreier und Befreite*, 1992), drawn from interviews with German mothers who conceived illegitimate children when they were raped by soldiers occupying Germany in 1945.

All of these films have produced uncomfortable reactions in those who fear that the showing of Germans victimized by the war experience will somehow take away from the nation's guilt about the war or diminish outrage at the atrocities committed against Jews, other German minorities, and non-Germans. Yet one can also see in this development a move away from a Manichaean, melodramatic mode of portraying the war and toward a more ambiguous and multidimensional one. Taken as a whole, these films, like *The Ogre,* display an inclination to find nuances apart from the conventional perpetrator-victim formula. They are films that attempt to engage the German audience in a discourse of national mourning. They extend and develop from earlier works of the New German Cinema, such as those by Syberberg, Fassbinder, Reitz, and Schlöndorff, which had begun a process of examining the World War II experience in an attempt to come to terms with it (Elsaesser, *New;* Santner). *The Ogre* completes a kind of trilogy, which began with *Young Törless*'s examination of the roots of fascism and continued with *The Tin Drum,* that saw Hitler's strength as lying in the false sense of empowerment that he gave the petite bourgeoisie.

The Ogre premiered at the 1996 Venice Film Festival where, according to one report, it provided the first moment of controversy in a festival that had been uneventful up to that point (Seidel). Although, according to reports, the local Italian critics were relatively positive, the film was much more negatively received elsewhere (Schulz-Ojala). Its German premiere followed only a week or so later. Reviews were highly mixed as was the evaluation of John Malkovich in the lead. Opening week box office receipts were a disappointment, and the number of tickets sold formed only about 5 percent of those sold for *Twister,* which was the number one ranking film at the German box office in early September 1996 ("Schwacher Start"). The film's French premiere about a month later was equally unimpressive, with the same combination of unenthusiastic reviews and disappointing sales. Although the film was among the top ten grossing movies for the week, it ranked only number ten and was on the list for one week only, this ranking representing a gross of only $332,146 ("*Variety*

International Box Office"). The film was not released in the United States until December 1998. It went largely unnoticed.

One imagines that *The Ogre* had too many things going against it to gain either widespread critical acceptance or to find a mass audience. Given the already suspect nature of Tournier's novel, one critic referred to a situation in which German reviewers came into the film ready "to reach for their antifascist fire extinguishers" (Kilb). It would be hard to expect uniform critical praise for a work that, on the one hand, treats the Nazi era with such a high degree of allusion and ambiguity and, on the other, seems to resort to familiar caricature and cliché in its portrayal of Nazi characters. In addition, *The Ogre* asks its audience to identify with a central character who behaves like a child molester and who enthusiastically recruits adolescent cannon fodder. A lack of physical dramatic action and of any feminine love interest would further discourage a traditional audience.

At the same time, one cannot but admire Schlöndorff's audacity and risk taking in pursuing the project. *The Ogre* contains moments of lyricism and poetic ambiguity that are powerful both artistically and as political discourse. Perhaps the filmmaker was right in his ambition when he says, about his flirtation with Nazi imagery, "It is more dangerous to abandon the potential of these myths and images to the skinheads" ("Nachwort" 194). Unlike Schlöndorff's other big-budget international literary adaptations such as *Michael Kohlhaas* or *Swann in Love*, which are commonly considered overly conventional failures, *The Ogre* could almost be considered too ambitious, too formally radical, and too demanding of its audience. In this sense, the film is far more a failure of the producer and entrepreneur in Schlöndorff than it is a failure of the artist.

26

Billy, How Did You Do It? and *Palmetto*

During this period, Schlöndorff's model became Billy Wilder, whose negotiation of the commerce-art high wire was the subject of *Billy, How Did You Do It?* (1992). Schlöndorff's relation to Wilder had gone back to the 1970s when Wilder, having seen *The Lost Honor of Katharina Blum,* sent the younger director a note, calling it the best German film since Fritz Lang's *M.* Later, the two met in Hollywood when Schlöndorff screened *Coup de Grâce* for Wilder (Schlöndorff, "Nobody" 12). As head of Babelsberg, Schlöndorff honored Wilder at the studio several times, most notably in connection with Wilder's receiving the 1992 Felix, the European film prize, for lifetime achievement (Schäfer and Schobert 393; Jurczyk). This moment publicly proposed a symbolic family line between the seasoned Central European, who embodied Hollywood professionalism, and the new enterprise, which would connect the cinema of a newly reunited Berlin with that of its pre–World War II predecessors.

Wilder as a Model: *Billy, How Did You Do It?*

In the context of the 1990s, *Billy, How Did You Do It?* may well provide a key to understanding Schlöndorff's evolving attitudes toward the profession of film-making. Let us look at this work in some detail. Schlöndorff began the documentary in 1988 as an oral history drawn from interviews with the Hollywood filmmaker. It was not completed until 1992, when it took the form of a six-part television presentation broadcast over several weeks in August and September of that year. *Billy, How Did You Do It?* is a career survey of the director's major works, and one gets the sense that Schlöndorff wanted to capture, as he had done about a decade earlier with Valeska Gert, the personality of an artist advanced in years, before death would make such a venture impossible. In this effort, as well as in Schlöndorff's subsequent work to revitalize Berlin's

Babelsberg Studios, we see the filmmaker trying to connect to a whole set of German filmmaking traditions, including those that arose in Hollywood after the exile there of much of the Weimar Republic's top filmmaking talent.

Billy, How Did You Do It? consists of a collage of materials including interview footage with Wilder himself, direct-address commentary by Schlöndorff, clips from Wilder's films and other related works, and newsreel footage and stills from the periods treated. Technically, the work mixes both film footage and materials shot on video, which gives it a somewhat patchy appearance. The credits indicate Gisela Grischow as codirector and Hellmuth Karasek as cointerviewer. Karasek, longtime editor of the movie and theater pages of the prominent *Der Spiegel* magazine, was working with Wilder on their book *Billy Wilder: Eine Nahaufnahme* (1992) during this period.

The documentary is oriented toward the television medium, and most of it consists either of the talking head of Billy Wilder answering questions from off-screen interviewers or Volker Schlöndorff addressing the audience with observations about Wilder's work. In these latter segments, the only visual variation comes from occasional changes of clothing and the change of still images, mainly of Wilder's face, that appear on video monitors positioned behind Schlöndorff. Interspersed among the talking heads are the clips and stills, making for a somewhat minimalist document drawn from deliberately restricted materials. There are, for example, no interviews with anyone other than Wilder—no collaborators or critics.

Just as the documentary switches between film- and video-generated materials, it also constantly shifts between German and English. The effect of this constant alternation reminds the viewer of Wilder's central European roots and repositions Wilder as part of a German filmmaking tradition. Schlöndorff's entire career as a filmmaker has contained homages to his predecessors in both the German film and in Hollywood. *A Degree of Murder* cites the film noir at a time when the very term *film noir* was in general use nowhere outside France; one can see the hallway murder of Tötges in *Katharina Blum* as an homage to the scene in *Double Indemnity* in which Phyllis Dietrichson shoots an incredulous Walter Neff; the Wilder documentary then is only an extension of this historically conscious, cinephilic temperament. Of all his affinities, Schlöndorff's attachment to the tradition of Weimar film and its surrounding culture may be his most central.

Schlöndorff's Wilder television project can be seen as part of a larger movement in German film culture to acknowledge and incorporate into itself the exile tradition, one in which anti-Nazi European filmmakers worked in the Hollywood studios. A leader in this acknowledgment was, of course, Rainer

Werner Fassbinder, whose stylistic bowing to the Hollywood efforts of Douglas Sirk–Detlef Sierck calls into question the assumptions of the narrative. We have discussed how *A Gathering of Old Men* forms a link to the Westerns of Fritz Lang. Retrospectives of the work of exile filmmakers such as Douglas Sirk; Curtis Bernhardt, honored at the Deutsche Kinemathek in 1981 (Belach, Gandert, and Prinzler 7); and Billy Wilder, honored in 1980, were held under the auspices of the "Forum des Jungen Deutschen Films" at the Berlinale. All of this suggests the claiming by German cinéastes of an exile heritage previously unrecognized.

One of the results of this reclamation has been a turning away in the 1980s and 1990s from the assumption that a German film must necessarily be dour and humorless. For example, the comedies of Doris Dörrie, particularly *Men* (*Männer*, 1985), have been compared to those of Ernst Lubitsch. Schlöndorff's inclusion of Wilder and, by extension, Wilder's mentor Lubitsch in his list of filmmakers worthy of major consideration forms part of an aesthetic reorientation within German film culture of the 1980s and 1990s that has led to production both lighter in tone and more popular with domestic audiences. Cases in point are Helmut Dietl's *Schtonk* (1991), *Rossini* (1997), and *Late Show* (1998); Sönke Wortmann's *Maybe . . . Maybe Not* (*Der bewegte Mann*, 1994); actor-producer Til Schweiger's *Knockin' on Heaven's Door* (1997); and Detlev Buck's *Jailbird* (*Männerpension*, 1995). This is not at the risk of a certain contradiction. When in the Wilder documentary the older filmmaker advises "Don't let them realize 'Look, this is only a movie,'" we are obviously faced with an aesthetic at odds with Schlöndorff's previous orientation toward Brecht.

At the same time, some of the most interesting moments of *Billy, How Did You Do It?* deal with Wilder's more serious and political side. Particularly striking is the treatment of *Mills of Death (Todesmühlen)*, a re-editing by Wilder of a documentary that Hanus Burger had made for the U.S. government right after World War II (Karasek, *Billy Wilder* 309–10; Jaeger and Regel 42). *Mills of Death* shows the horrors of the concentration camps and the devastation of the war. Wilder describes a German preview of the film at which audience members, asked to evaluate it, left the forms blank and instead stole the pencils provided—an anecdote that adds a touch of black comedy to the report. As Schlöndorff describes how Wilder lost most of his family in the death camps, one becomes particularly aware of a kind of dark underside to the filmmaker. Schlöndorff's documentary momentarily becomes another way to confront the Holocaust and suggests different modes of resistance to this negative legacy.

Most of *Billy, How Did You Do It?* looks at how Wilder was able to produce good work within a commercial Hollywood system. Schlöndorff's approach is to pick the brain of a professional whom he clearly admires. The documentary provides extended discussions of stars with whom Wilder worked, including the director's observations about the unique qualities of Marlene Dietrich, William Holden, and Marilyn Monroe. His most renowned cowriters, Walter Brackett and I. A. L. Diamond, receive similar treatment, with the latter being granted a particularly moving eulogy by Wilder.

Of perhaps greatest interest, however, is Wilder's discussion of particular techniques and commercial strategies. Extended question-and-answer sessions treat issues such as using voice-over narration, constructing the opening of a film, and devising comic scenes with the right balance between straight lines and punch lines and the right timing between them. Wilder also describes his preference for the adaptation of stage plays rather than novels and discusses methods of reaching a wide audience. This concern for commercial viability eventually extends to Wilder's telling of anecdotes about disastrous previews, quarrels with studio heads about film titles and about the tag line of *Some Like It Hot*, "Nobody's perfect," which proved far more popular with audiences than the writers ever expected. In a particularly telling exchange, Schlöndorff asks Wilder whether he would still want to make films even if nobody paid him to do so. Wilder scoffs at the idea, indicating his comfort with a commercial system. If there is one theme that strikes us about *Billy*, it is that of the coexistence of art and commerce. Indeed, at one point Wilder boasts that he never made a film lacking in integrity. He may have made artistic mistakes, but he never sold out. One senses Schlöndorff's agreement and admiration.

Palmetto

Palmetto is to date Schlöndorff's most Wilder-like movie. One of a string of neonoir films that emerged in the late 1990s, its narrative contains the full range of archetypal elements characteristic of the genre: a tough hero who becomes vulnerable to a glamorous, dishonest, and manipulative woman; a city victimized by corrupt policemen and government officials; a rich, powerful patriarch surrounded by insincere schemers; and the standard noir settings of seedy bars, cheap hotel rooms, opulent mansions, dark and rainy streets, and forbidding police headquarters. The film conjures up numerous noir icons: fedora hats, martinis, cigarettes, high-heeled shoes, and whirring fans. It strives for an atmosphere of lust and greed comparable to Wilder's classic *Double Indemnity*.

After the extraordinary ambition and failure of *The Ogre*, Schlöndorff claims to have seen in *Palmetto* a chance to take a reprieve from seriousness (Tobis, Press notes for *Palmetto* 2801, 8 of 11). The film was in many ways comparable to

Schlöndorff's *A Degree of Murder,* itself made right after the grim austerity of *Törless.* In both cases, Schlöndorff was defying an accepted image of himself as a humorless anticommercial aesthete. Perhaps coincidentally, perhaps not, both works milk black humor and suspense from scenes of corpses locked in car trunks and cranes lifting, in one case, a cadaver over a junk yard and, in *Palmetto,* the hero over a vat of acid. In both instances, critical reaction was negative.

Palmetto is difficult to defend critically. One may admittedly have to grant that it probably achieves what it set out to do. Schlöndorff has spoken of the delight he took in working with deliberate clichés and in having fun creating garish images ("Palmetto" 2803 4–6 of 7). It is easy to see what attracted Schlöndorff to the source novel by James Hadley Chase, *Just Another Sucker* (1961). The book is a tightly plotted, slickly written page-turner. It has few original ideas but is admirably executed. As a film, however, it is handicapped by unmotivated elements in the overly complicated narrative, a decidedly unsympathetic hero, and a lack of any ideological center. Because the book is narrated in the first person, the reader has an easier time buying into the narrative's less credible elements: when we see things solely from the point of view of the hero, Harry Barber, they make more sense. Furthermore, the print Barber elicits more sympathy from the reader, doubtless because his is the only point of view. Schlöndorff and his screenwriter, E. Max Frye, have also added plot twists not in the original and thereby multiplied occasions for the viewer to quit suspending disbelief. Individual scenes may be skillful but are never really innovative: Schlöndorff has nothing new here to add to the film genre.

Perhaps the problem is that Schlöndorff has imitated Wilder without updating him. Although Wilder is now considered a classicist filmmaker, he did not always seem that way in his heyday. Often Wilder pushed the limits of cynicism and vulgarity beyond what was acceptable in his time. One has only to recall how *Double Indemnity* was seen by many in the 1940s not as fun but as morally specious sensationalism. In the world of the 1990s, of course, cynicism and vulgarity have become the norm rather than the exception. In spite of its hot and heavy sex scenes, *Palmetto* appears routine by today's standards. Lacking a standardized morality against which to play, the movie's portrayal of moral transgressions generates little excitement. We feel almost more concern for Harry Barber when he wants to light a cigarette in the smoke-free police building than when the seventeen-year-old jailbait Odette comes on to him.

Palmetto's most interesting aspect is the way in which its main characters mislead one another, creating a parallel to the way in which the film deliberately misleads its spectators. Elizabeth Shue's femme fatale lures Woody Harrelson's Harry Barber into a phony kidnapping scheme through a mise-en-scène of appearances comparable to Schlöndorff's manipulation of his audience. The Shue character lies and withholds information from Barber. Barber himself, hired by the police as press agent, gives journalists misinformation about the crime in which he has participated and deceives his audience in a comparable way. Despite the story's being told firmly from Barber's point of view, Schlöndorff elides key material, only to reveal it later. For example, he waits to make clear whether the "kidnapped" Odette actually had sex with Barber. Similarly, the director withholds the details of how the police and Barber planned to entrap the villains until after we have witnessed the capture. Schlöndorff compromises the movie's first-person point of view. The audience becomes one more in a succession of "victims."

Although American in subject matter, *Palmetto* was financed by Rialto Films, a company associated with the commercial German cinema since the 1950s. Its technical credits list the Austrian cinematographer Thomas Kloss, Wim Wenders's longtime editor Peter Przygodda, and music by Klaus Doldinger, who had collaborated with Schlöndorff on *Baal* and *The Sudden Wealth of the Poor People of Kombach*. An American-European hybrid, *Palmetto* was also Schlöndorff's first film in Cinemascope. Its creators, however, clearly took pains to make it "television safe," for many of its compositions work on the small screen as well as or better than they do in the theatrical version. It is a new variation in Schlöndorff's relation to television.

Palmetto may qualify as Schlöndorff's least politically committed film. Like others of the director's less political works, for example, *Swann in Love* or *Voyager*, it has a quality of nostalgia for an aestheticized past. One can acknowledge its craftsmanship and even moments of visual and poetic distinction, but its lack of any rhetorical edge renders it insignificant. Its stylistic conviction may allow it to escape, if we recall Billy Wilder's self-satisfaction at his own integrity, the category of "selling out," but it does not so easily avoid the label of "mistake."

27

The Legend of Rita and "The Perfect Soldier"

Schlöndorff's next film, *The Legend of Rita* (*Die Stille nach dem Schuss*, 2000), took an approach almost totally antithetical to that in his preceding feature, *Palmetto*. *The Legend of Rita* was a low-budget film, made without stars, in a deliberately drab, realistic manner. It also marked a return by Schlöndorff to German-language production and a specifically German subject. In *Rita*, Schlöndorff comes back to his familiar subject of terrorism and tells the story of Rita Vogt, a fictionalized character modeled on members of the anarchist Red Army Faction of the 1970s. Although the beginning of the movie portrays Rita in her lawless activities of robbing a bank, springing her terrorist boyfriend from jail, and shooting a French police officer, most of the story has to do with her seeking asylum in the former German Democratic Republic and the bleakness and frustration of daily life there. Critics heralded *The Legend of Rita* as a marked "return to form" (Elley 42; Hoberman 117; Scott E5).

Our discussion of *The Legend of Rita* examines how it intertwines concerns with women's issues with specifically German political questions. Rita herself becomes a metaphoric figure for the May 1968 generation coming to terms with the legacy of a previously divided Germany. Although narratively coherent, the movie's formal structure involves an assembling of small details and comparisons that accumulatively embody the contradictions within a reunited Germany.

"The Perfect Soldier"

Schlöndorff had already shown an interest in a specifically German problem of unification in a short film he made for a collection entitled *Spotlights on a Massacre*. A brief digression to examine this four-minute work is appropriate here. This 1997 project was organized by Handicap International, a nonprofit

309

agency devoted to the elimination of land mines worldwide. *Spotlights on a Massacre* consisted of ten short films, each about four minutes long and directed by a group of renowned filmmakers, including Youssef Chahine, Mathieu Kassovitz, Coline Serreau, and Fernando Trueba. The project was supervised and produced by Schlöndorff's old friend Bertrand Tavernier, who also contributed a segment.

Unlike some of his colleagues, Schlöndorff took a documentary approach in which he zeroed in on the particularly German aspect of the problem, the remaining land mines on the old East-West border. Schlöndorff opens and closes his segment with the image of a man walking near a guard tower inside the "death strip" that rimmed the Berlin Wall, triggering an explosion. In between, the filmmaker presents the audience with a Brechtian montage of sounds and images from three points of view. We hear Schlöndorff's own voice in French, articulating his dismay at the problem. A mine victim, a middle-aged man who shows us his prosthesis, describes the experience of losing a foot. A military expert discusses the extraordinary efficiency of mine use—the episode's informal title is "The Perfect Soldier"—and the extent to which these weapons were employed. On screen, we see images of the latter two speakers, texts of documents (sometimes superimposed, with the texts crawling up or across the screen, over each other or over photographic images), and shots of the green countryside and ruins of the Wall. Some of the documents are lists of medical injuries; others are diagrams of mine-related military structures. We hear statistics of the costs of planting mines, implicitly compared with the human costs of being unable to remove them. Schlöndorff contrasts the cold detachment of the military expert with the physical effects on individuals. The result is visually sophisticated and compresses much material, articulated by the three voices, into its very short running time. It works as persuasive rhetoric on both the mind and the heart. It shows the same dialectical combination of detachment and sympathy that Schlöndorff was also to use in *The Legend of Rita*.

A Film for Both Germanies

In terms of content, *The Legend of Rita* was a unique postunification attempt to portray life in the former East German state. Schlöndorff wrote the screenplay with Wolfgang Kohlhaase, one of the most renowned screenwriters of the GDR. Kohlhaase was most famous for his collaborations with directors Gerhard Klein (e.g., *Berlin—Schönhauser Corner* [*Berlin—Schönhauser Ecke*, 1957] and *The Gleiwitz Case* [*Der Fall Gleiwitz*, 1961]) and Konrad Wolf (especially *I Was 19* [*Ich war neunzehn*, 1967], *Mama, I Am Alive* [*Mama, ich lebe*, 1976], and *Solo Sunny* [1979]). Kohlhaase's 1965 project *Berlin Around the Corner (Berlin um die Ecke)* was filmed by Gerhard Klein but banned by the Socialist Unity Party's Eleventh Plenum, which suppressed until post-Wall times some of the strongest products of GDR cinema culture.

Schlöndorff and Kohlhaase wrote a first screenplay for *Rita* in the early 1990s but were unsuccessful in financing it. The initial version of the screenplay was written with consultation from Inge Viett, who was largely the model for the character of Rita. Schlöndorff even had an associate attend Viett's trial to provide information with which to develop the narrative. Viett later accused the filmmakers of using material from her autobiography without permission, but the case was settled out of court. The filmmakers, in creating the character of Rita, also drew on the real-life models of Silke Maier-Witt and Susanne Albrecht. After *Palmetto*, Schlöndorff and Kohlhaase rewrote the script, fictionalizing the new version more than the older one (Weingarten 222; Schlöndorff, "Coming" 20; Schlöndorff, "Ohne Glanz" 14–15).

Schlöndorff's collaboration with Kohlhaase is particularly important because *The Legend of Rita*, although originally conceived in the early 1990s, was to be Schlöndorff's first nonadaptation fiction feature in almost thirty years. Schlöndorff shares screenwriting credit with Kohlhaase but in an interview gave the screenwriter credit for all dialogue and small details ("Coming" 21). For convenience sake, the discussion that follows attributes to Schlöndorff the movie's range of narrative tactics. The authors acknowledge this approach must surely result in some simplification.

Schlöndorff chose as his director of photography Andreas Höfer, who was also a product of East German training and experience. The movie represents a Babelsberg project, coproduced with branches of German television in the formerly communist areas and subsidized by boards in those regions. In both subject matter and production procedures, *Rita* is a kind of cross-cultural enterprise, bridging the two Germanys.

Politics Without Propaganda

The Legend of Rita is a political film but one that examines political ambiguities and contradictions rather than one that has a propagandistic agenda. Indeed, one of its most provocative aspects is its rendering as sympathetic both a terrorist heroine and members of the Stasi state security police who watch and control her even as they give her refuge. The traditional image of the Stasi official has been that of a ruthless thug who suppresses all personal and civil liberties for the sake of the state. But Schlöndorff refuses to give *Rita* a villain. He has commented,

> The behavior of the old Stasi was surprising—they came out of the Spanish Civil War, out of the resistance against Hitler, out of the partisan fighters. . . . Weren't they romantics themselves—idealists, who still believed that through certain means a better world could be fashioned? (Schlöndorff and Kohlhaase [9])

Still, all of *Rita*'s characters must surrender to practicality and in one way or another compromise their ideals.

The Legend of Rita is built on a central irony: the so-called revolutionary and liberating communist state pushes Rita Vogt (Bibiana Beglau) into an increasingly conformist and confining lifestyle. At first, Rita assumes the fictitious identity of Susanne Schmidt and goes to work in a textiles factory. She strikes up a friendship with Tatjana (Nadja Uhl), a rebellious young divorcée who drinks too much and mistrusts authority. (See illustration 39.) The relationship develops into a sexual one, only to be cut short when Tatjana figures out aspects of Rita's past and the Stasi agents must move Rita and assign her a new "legend." (Originally, the film's English title was to use the plural form "legends," in line with Rita's three lives.) In her new identity, as Sabine Walter, Rita falls in love again, this time with a male colleague, but she is forbidden to marry Jochen (Alexander Beyer) and follow him to a position near Moscow. In each step of the process, Rita comes closer to living a staid, conventional life.

In terms of narrative structure, *Rita* has major similarities to both *The Lost Honor of Katharina Blum* and *The Handmaid's Tale*. In all three, a rebellious young woman is coerced into conformity. In all three, the woman must relate to a paternalistic authority figure. Unlike the villainous Beizmenne and Robert Duvall's commander, however, the character of Erwin Hull (Martin Wuttke) is much more sympathetic. He admires Rita's ideals and shows some concern about her welfare. He and Rita share both positive motives and the decisiveness to use physical or emotional violence to achieve goals. In a scene immediately after Rita chooses to stay in the GDR rather than join her anarchist friends on a trip to Beirut, Rita asks Hull whether he ever thinks in terms of the individual people he controls. "It's about making people happy," he replies. But his later actions toward Rita contradict this assertion. In its portrayal of social structures that render love relationships impossible, *The Legend of Rita* joins the list of other Schlöndorff movies that articulate the same theme.

Central to *The Legend of Rita* are issues of gender. Schlöndorff himself has

39. *The Legend of Rita.* Bibiana Beglau as Rita, former terrorist, and her rebellious GDR coworker Tatjana (Nadja Uhl). Photo: Courtesy of Kino International.

commented that the story would be unthinkable with a male terrorist as its central character ("Coming" 19). The story's fascination lies in its presentation of a transgressive female figure. *Rita* is as much about the roles of women in German society as it is about terrorism. In her progression from outlaw to factory worker to her final job with a children's camp, Rita moves gradually toward the traditional feminine role of caretaker of children. Each of these roles carries with it a different kind of love relationship. Her "crush," as she herself describes it, on the group's leader, Andi (Harald Schrott), ties her to her revolutionary persona. When she loses his affections, she splits from the group. Her lesbian attachment to Tatjana is to a woman who still embodies a spunky antiauthoritarian attitude. As Rita becomes compliant in the world of work, she becomes adventurous in the world of love. By contrast, her later love, Jochen, is a propary conformist who asks her to give up a career to follow him to Russia.

Each role that she plays represents a different role for women in general, a different model. One of the most telling scenes in the film occurs after Rita by chance encounters Friederike (Jenny Schily), a member of the gang who is now herself leading a conventional life as a wife and mother in the GDR. When Rita tells Friederike that she is so pleased to see her happy, Friederike replies, with her child by her side: "Where did you get that idea?" One can compare this scene to the one in which Hull comes on to Rita and she rebuffs him by indicating that she thought he was married. "It's expected," is his laconic response. Traditional gender roles are no guarantee of happiness.

Rita's identity seems defined by those around her. When Tatjana learns of Rita's criminal past, she nonetheless accepts her. Jochen, on the other hand, seems to push Rita toward a more passive role. One of the first things he says to her when they meet on the beach and she confirms that she is watching the children, is "then I'll be watching you." In this scene, Schlöndorff plays with the convention, in the love story, of the rescuing white knight, creating audience expectations of a savior who will sweep Rita away and give her lasting happiness. In scenes that follow, however, Schlöndorff skillfully undercuts these expectations. Key to this is a scene in which Rita and Jochen have been watching slides from the previous summer, most of which are of Rita in a skimpy bathing suit. In this scene, Schlöndorff sets Rita up as the traditional object of the male gaze, but he also has Jochen discover that Rita's hideous eyeglasses are of window glass and she unconvincingly says that she wears them "for fun."

In a subsequent scene, Jochen is taking a bath with Rita in the room. As he emerges from the tub, Rita tells him of her violent past. Unlike Tatjana, he is unaccepting and comments that she should not be telling him this. Schlöndorff's canny staging of this scene, one involving male nudity, reverses the usual gender roles and makes the male vulnerable and threatened. Revealed as a terrorist, Rita undermines a patriarchal order, and Jochen clearly cannot accept it. In the scenes that follow, Rita, now unable to be protected in a reunified Germany, resumes her role as a fugitive from justice.

In his examination of social roles within the GDR, Schlöndorff periodically moves into the lighter realm of satire. In their attempt to size up the refugee revolutionaries, the Stasi agents throw a bratwurst barbecue for them. The long-haired radicals become incongruous participants in a banal middle-class social ritual. In a later scene, the Stasi bureaucrats play at being gentlemen hunters but prove to be inept sportsmen who cannot shoot a single wild boar herded in front of them or who get a finger stuck in the barrel of the rifle. As the men talk shop, the older general comments on the revolutionaries' proposal to be sent to Africa: "But Angolans are black." A seemingly irrelevant comic interlude occurs when Rita tries to teach Tatjana to drive the former's new baby-blue Trabi, the cheaply made two-cycle East German people's vehicle, the

GDR's answer to the West German Volkswagen. As Tatjana gently backs the car into a tree, a rear fender separates from the body. But the scene makes several points. When a policeman drives by, Rita protects Tatjana by saying she herself was driving her car and the cop pulls the fender off to free the car from the tree. The joke about the junkiness of the car is obvious, but the scene also shows Rita being pulled into a middle-class ideal—out for a Sunday drive, wearing a pretty Sunday-best dress. The most comic figure is that of Hull's young assistant, Gerngross (a play on the German word for "upstart"). Gerngross (Thomas Arnold) appears as a kind of feminized bureaucrat. He wears an apron at the barbecue, pours coffee for his boss, brings in flowers, and loses to Rita at Ping-Pong. He becomes a direct inverse of the activist Rita.

Music and Motifs

Part of the movie's satire occurs in its use of music. In the opening bank robbery, we hear what sounds like a music box playing the "Internationale" workers' anthem. In contrast, the final scenes of the movie feature a gentle harpsichord-like playing of the German national anthem, suggesting a triumph of nationalism. At different points in the motion picture, different styles of music create a kind of cross-section of the East German culture. While socializing at the hunting lodge, the Stasi agents and their revolutionary guests sing familiar communist party propaganda songs. At a later motivational party for the factory workers, a pop band plays diluted Western-style rock music to which Rita dances with abandon. At a birthday party for Tatjana's father, we hear an old-fashioned accordionist. And when Rita runs into Friederike, her ex-extremist friend is singing on a town square of a seaside resort in a traditional German folk song chorus. *The Legend of Rita* assembles a range of popular music forms to weave together the different strands that make up a culture. The impact of this is all the stronger because the motion picture had no music written for it. Schlöndorff in effect expresses a kind of cultural neutrality in giving the movie no musical voice of its own; it simply presents the voices of others.

These periodic parties, each with its own type of music, provide a structuring device for the film. Schlöndorff employs a another set of motifs to further unify his narrative. Most prominent among these is the use of the gun. Rita's attempt to bring a revolver into East Berlin is the incident that establishes her relation to Hull: that he lets her pass creates the bond between them. Later, Rita shows a kind of aggressive playfulness in handling the gun among the other gang members. She sticks it in the top of her jeans in a way that claims phallic power, and she will shortly discharge it when she shoots the policeman. In a later comic scene with Gerngross, she teaches the young wimp how to carry a gun and accidentally fires it, breaking a window and upsetting her guardian. Near the end of the movie, as Germany reunifies, we see the Stasi agents surrendering their firearms to yet other bureaucrats in a scene that echoes the gun confiscation that begins the GDR narrative.

Related to the motif of the gun is that of the motorcycle. Motorcycles have long carried connotations of personal freedom, individualism, and antiauthoritarian defiance. Rita rides around Paris on her red Honda, a luxury that some of her comrades chide her for indulging in. Later, when she is stopped by a cop for not wearing a helmet, she attempts an escape, and a chase ensues. It ends with her shooting him. Rita's shift to driving a Trabi indicates her change of attitude and position. At the end of the story, we see Rita accompanying a West German on a motorcycle headed for the border with the West. He comments that they may have trouble with the law because she is not wearing a helmet. As he stops to urinate by the side of the autobahn, Rita steals the bike. As she reaches the border and sees guards, she tries to run through the border without stopping. (See illustration 40.) She is shot down by a guard in a way that uncomfortably mirrors the way in which she herself killed the Paris cop. Freedom has led to danger.

In contrast to her negative motorcycle encounters with the police, her meeting with the policeman after the Trabi fender bender has a benign quality. Although he speaks to her and Tatjana patronizingly, he is unthreatening and projects an ethos of solidarity with a fellow citizen. Social constriction has led to security.

This imagery gives the story an almost circular structure whereby it begins and ends with violence. Imposed on this visual structure, however, is a set of repeated voice-overs whereby Rita, after the fall of the Wall, is writing her story for Tatjana. This device allows for a shifting of points of view within the story. In some places, we experience things through Rita's eyes, coming to experience along with her life in the GDR. At other points, however, the movie portrays her as naive. Two parallel scenes show her inability to fully grasp the situation around her. Both occur in workers' cafeterias. In the first, in the textile factory, Rita is the only worker at her table to give money in support of the Nicaraguan Sandinistas, and her coworkers glare disapprovingly at her generous gift. In the second, at the movie's end, she appeals to her coworkers not to give up the dream of a socialist utopia. Her sentiments may be valid, but she seems clueless about the negative response they were bound to engender. The scene creates in the viewer an unusual split. On the one hand, we admire and are moved by her idealism. On the other, we see how little she understands.

40. *The Legend of Rita*. Rita's final escape upon the unification of the two Germanies. Photo: Courtesy of Kino International.

In this sense, *The Legend of Rita* embodies a successful dialectic between the appealing romanticism of the entire May 1968 generation and the realistic awareness of the failure of communism.

The Legend of Rita was warmly received in its premiere at the 2000 Berlin Film Festival where its two lead actresses, Bibiana Beglau, who played Rita, and Nadja Uhl, who played Tatjana, shared the best actress award. Although it was a critical success in Germany, it was a part of what *Der Spiegel* described as a particularly unsuccessful box office year for motion pictures or "an audience-deficient autumn" (Weingarten and Wolf 188). The reception was also good abroad but given the movie's specifically German subject matter, there was little hope of wide-audience mainstream popularity. Almost all critics had high praise for Bibiana Beglau, who, according to one,

> has a challenging stare and a ferocious will that seems to originate somewhere in her lower back and goes straight up her spine into her neck and head, which is held proud and high, like a ballerina's. Beglau throws her sinewy body into whatever she does, whether it's work, sex, or stickups. She is a great camera

subject: urgent yet pliant and yielding; not beautiful, exactly, but radiant and sympathetic. (Denby 93)

At the end of the film, Rita joins the ranks of Schlöndorff's failed revolutionaries. What is different here is little sense of a revolutionary fervor to be passed on to future generations. *The Legend of Rita* looks back to the past. Schlöndorff described the film as "closing a chapter on terrorism rather than reopening it" ("Coming" 19). Schlöndorff seems in this work to be wanting to heal the wounds of a Germany divided into East and West after World War II and along generational lines in the 1960s. The filmmaker's ambitious program is to reflect on several recent decades of German political history and encapsulate that history into a set of characters who are imperfect and contradictory but ultimately sympathetic.

28

Conclusion

In writing this book, we intended to be neither uncritical champions of Volker Schlöndorff nor completely detached reporters. Rather, the book's goal has been to assess a film career whose significance has come largely from works categorized either as qualified successes or interesting failures. Schlöndorff is important not because he has directed an astonishing string of indisputable masterpieces but because he has pursued strategies of film production that defy easy categorization. Any conclusions drawn about this body of work must consider Schlöndorff's penchant for jumping into waters whose currents pull in two directions. To sum up this study's concerns, let us propose five axioms for the appreciation of Schlöndorff's movies.

1. Schlöndorff's films are not for those who would create a false dichotomy between film and literature. Critics who decry the disfiguring of literature by cinematic adaptation usually believe that something has been lost of the complexity, the vividness, or the resonance of the original. We have instead seen how Schlöndorff's works, when successful, have a cinema-specific complexity, vividness, and resonance. This applies to both successful adaptations and works written directly for the screen.

Too often, those who complain about the oversimplifications of popular movies locate their lack of complexity in the medium itself, as though literary expression by definition is more complicated than cinematic expression. These critics automatically oppose literature to film and refuse to value the cinematic pleasures of direct sensory involvement. Schlöndorff's films make the compelling argument that screen adaptations need not be simple-minded nor mere illustrations of an author's story. Rather, they may combine the immediacy of a visual medium with at least some of the reflectiveness of the written word.

In response to cinema purists who argue that the director's repeated reliance on literary sources merely indicates a lack of a fully developed cinematic imagination, we counter that Schlöndorff in no way proposes his style of literary adaptation as the only mode of filmmaking. Indeed, in an interview from the

319

mid-1990s, Schlöndorff advocated that a revived German cinema needed to
come from projects that would not be literary adaptations, would be set in the
present, would use popular genres, and would speak to mass audiences about
current issues in society ("Ich dachte" 14). He acknowledged immediately that
on at least three of these points his own work was different. Schlöndorff's
movies call not for a move to an institutionalized cinema of literary adaptation
but rather to a pluralism whereby the use of prior works of literature is one of
many resources at the filmmaker's disposal.

2. Schlöndorff's films are not for those who would create a false dichotomy
between art and commerce. Critics have sometimes reproached Schlöndorff
for striving for popular success, as with *A Degree of Murder, Michael Kohlhaas,*
and *Palmetto*. At other times they have simply seen him as part of a dour,
unappealing New German Cinema popular only with non-German intellectuals.

It is perhaps more accurate to conceive of Schlöndorff's cinema as one calculated to achieve popular success as part of its artistic success; that is, the project of bringing important images, thoughts, and ideas to a mass audience
involves, for Schlöndorff, an aesthetic strategy as much as a commercial one.
His colleague Alexander Kluge, for example, has written of *The Tin Drum,*

> I don't consider it right to say that *The Tin Drum* is a commercial film; because a
> part of the success of this film could not be explained in this way. The concep-
> tion of the *one* public sphere (contrast: ghetto formation), which Schlöndorff advo-
> cates; the self-confidence, which is the quality of an *auteur,* and which grows out
> of the manner in which he proceeds with the history of 1945. . . . Things, which
> would not stir in the case of a literal adaptation, are in motion in this film. . . .
> That's something I could not reduce to the simple formula of a commercial film;
> there is within it a piece of realism. ("Künftige Filmpolitik" 111–12)

Schlöndorff's use of conventional film genres is as much an artistic choice as
a commercial one. His exploitation of conventions from the Western, the
Heimatfilm, the thriller, the love story, and the war film has allowed for accessible storytelling. At the same time, many of his works contain elements of
irony, reversal of expectations, caricature, and metaphor that transform them
into anti-Westerns, anti-*Heimatfilme,* antithrillers, anti–love stories, and
anti–war films. As critical viewers we enjoy them, even when we are being
pulled into awareness of the conventions being used.

3. Schlöndorff's films are not for those who would create a false dichotomy
between political activism and tradition. Politically, Schlöndorff has been crit-

icized by the right wing as a leftist, proterrorist, profeminist propagandist.
Leftist critics, by contrast, have characterized him as a would-be sympathizer
whose ties to commercial filmmaking and artistic tradition neutralize what
would be positive political messages. These critics follow the now all but
clichéd dictum that a radically political work must be stylistically radical.

We concur that Schlöndorff's style is less consistently radical than those of
Rainer Werner Fassbinder, Jean-Marie Straub and Danièle Huillet, and Jean-
Luc Godard. At the same time, we assert that the search for purely radical stylistics can only result in a political dead-end whereby the work produced loses
all potential to reach the very masses it would rouse to action. The mistake
comes in assuming that extreme stylistic radicalism is better than moderate stylistic exploration, much like the naive medical patient who assumes that five
pills will be more effective than one.

We have demonstrated how aspects of Bertolt Brecht's political theories of
drama have infused Schlöndorff's work not only during the 1970s but at other
points as well. That Schlöndorff is not always an extreme Brechtian does not
make him an irrelevant one. To those who argue that Schlöndorff's love of literature and other artistic traditions is retrograde, we suggest that Brecht, too,
performed literary adaptation of a different sort when he used sources like John
Gay's *Beggar's Opera* or Sophocles' *Antigone,* updating them for a different time
and place.

This is not to say that Schlöndorff's work is lacking in political contradictions and ideological problems. Some feminists might complain, for example, that an excess of male protagonists in his stories is fundamentally
patriarchal. The same commentators might also argue that the conventional
structure of *The Lost Honor of Katharina Blum* may invite spectators to take
pleasure in the abuse of the film's heroine. Is it enough that Schlöndorff subverts conventional cinematic illusionism through a carefully developed pattern of gaze structures and self-reflexive devices? We have seen how, in a
similar manner, some critics have regarded *Circle of Deceit* and *A Gathering of
Old Men* as implicitly racist because they develop white characters more fully
than their Arab or African American ones.

All of this criticism points not to a lack of political commitment but rather to
a lack of ideological perfection. It might be useful to examine how Schlöndorff's
attachment to commercial narrative structures and to artistic tradition may
sometimes subvert his political messages. But in many cases, those political
messages are pointed, intelligent, and well articulated. In particular, the discourses about fascism contained in *Young Törless, The Tin Drum,* and *The
Handmaid's Tale* show both political commitment and formal invention. That

some of Schlöndorff's films, like *A Degree of Murder* or *Swann in Love* or *Voyager*, are relatively apolitical in orientation in no way detracts from those that do contain successful political discourse.

4. Schlöndorff's films are not for those who would create a false dichotomy between narrative film and cinematic formal invention. Because Schlöndorff works within traditional narrative forms, it may actually become easier to overlook the structural complexities of his movies. We have identified in our study three major areas that show particular formal sophistication: the use of voice-over narration, the positioning of the spectator in ways that creatively manipulate point of view, and the use of leitmotifs and visual associations.

Schlöndorff's use of voice-overs in some instances becomes a deft Brechtian device to provide for careful interplay between what we see on the screen and distancing, contrapuntal verbal commentary. In other cases, it grows out of the image-sound experiments of the French New Wave that sought to give subjective resonance to objective images. The filmmaker's constant preoccupation with issues of point of view throughout his career shows a similar variety of intents and purposes, from the way in which the observer in *Young Törless* flip-flops between being a detached onlooker and a guilty participant, to the complex patterns of visual desire in *Voyager*.

Most important, however, is Schlöndorff's use of leitmotifs, which at their best overlay a musical structure of repetition and variation onto more conventional narratives. The circular structures of *Törless, Georgina's Reasons, The Tin Drum, Circle of Deceit* and *Voyager* establish themes in the opening scenes, return to them periodically, and conclude with them in a way that is formally satisfying beyond any kind of narrative closure. In each case, the device gives the film a quality of reflection, of wistfulness, of remembered past. Far more than from their choice of literary source materials, Schlöndorff's movies are literary in the positive sense through this sophisticated use of structure.

5. Schlöndorff's films are not for those who create a false dichotomy between the German cinema and international film. In the period immediately following *The Tin Drum*, it was a commonplace to consider Schlöndorff the most German of directors due to the particularly German subject matter of so many of his works from the 1970s. As Schlöndorff became more of an international figure, his critical reputation declined somewhat, as though it were this specific "Germanness" that had given the earlier work its quality. By Germanness we are referring here—along with Mary Fulbrook—to "a self-identifying community of common memory and common destiny" (21), an involvement with issues of national identity. This involvement with a national memory, language, and culture during the period from the midsixties to mideighties specifically frequents the Third Reich past. The German protest generation of the 1960s saw itself as speaking out against injustice in ways that its parents had failed to do: radicalism was an attempted atonement for the sins of the fathers, finding in the Vietnam War another Holocaust. This specifically German sensibility also attempts to share with the pre–Third Reich tradition or, to be more precise, traditions, for as we have shown, Schlöndorff leans on both the classical model of Fritz Lang and the oppositional one of Bert Brecht.

Part of the post–World War II German sensibility has been an attempt to reconcile shame of the recent German past with pride about a wide range of achievements of German culture. Heide Fehrenbach has argued that cinema culture in postwar Germany was marked by a profound ambivalence toward both Hollywood and the Hollywood-like production system that the Third Reich had encouraged. If the redeveloping country were to reassemble its recent production system, how would it distinguish itself from an industry that was complicit with Nazi war crimes? Next to this rock, however, was the hard place of merely surrendering a cultural identity to American consumerism, hedonism, and superficiality. This ambivalence was felt on the political right by church groups concerned about immoral entertainment. Its presence on the left can be seen in a figure like Schlöndorff.

We have striven to demonstrate how much of the filmmaker's later work maintains distinctively German attributes. The connection of *Death of a Salesman* to German expressionism, the homage to the American work of Fritz Lang contained in *A Gathering of Old Men*, the references to the Third Reich that appear throughout both *The Handmaid's Tale* and *The Ogre*, all point to an extension of Schlöndorff's German heritage. *The Legend of Rita* is the key German film to date for examining in retrospect the culture of East Germany.

One must also point out that one characteristic of Germanic people has traditionally been their eagerness to travel and to learn new languages. In some respects, the voyager of Max Frisch's *Homo Faber* is representative of a particular national type, of which Schlöndorff himself would be one example. From his early experiences in France, Schlöndorff has always had one metaphoric foot in Germany and one outside it. One can view much of his career as an attempt to bring into the German film world the best aspects of French film culture and the best qualities of American movie professionalism. Schlöndorff's internationalism is a part of his "Germanness." As one who has constantly moved between insider and outsider status, it is hardly surprising that in recent years Schlöndorff has tried to promote both a vital German cinema and a lively cross-national European one, with the former uniting the film centers of both Munich and Berlin. Schlöndorff may have failed to overcome the harsh eco-

41. German chancellor Gerhard Schröder *(center)* with a group of filmmakers in 2001 *(from left):* Hark Bohm, Volker Schlöndorff, Katja von Garnier, Caroline Link. Photo: Michael Jung/dpa (Deutsche Presse Agentur).

nomic realities of the 1990s, but one can only admire his dream of a cultural post-Wall Weimar in Berlin.

In this study, we traced Volker Schlöndorff's career from its tentative beginnings and early success, through its sophomore commercial failures and a subsequent regrouping within the subsidy-rich television culture of the 1970s. We looked at Schlöndorff's triumphs from the end of that decade and his experimentation with different production situations throughout the 1980s. And we saw his return to Germany and Europe in the 1990s in the executive role of studio manager. There can be no doubt that Schlöndorff has evolved in the process. Gundolf S. Freyermuth, in his 1993 reportage on the Babelsberg Schlöndorff, *Der Übernehmer,* views the director-manager as metamorphosing from the longtime "artistic only child" to the increasingly worldly "paterfamilias." "In the past months," Freyermuth continues, "he has thus traveled the path from the son who was partly lost, partly recalcitrant, to the responsible father, from outsider to professional leader, from rebel to representative" (120). (See illustration 41.)

We have not argued in the above pages that Volker Schlöndorff is a great film director; only that he is a significant one who is inadequately appreciated. There can be no argument, however, that in the budding and flowering of the New German Cinema, in the development of survival strategies following the drying up of the New German Cinema in the 1980s, and in the articulation of a vision for a post-Wall European Community film industry, Schlöndorff has been a major player.

Filmography

Appendix

Notes

Works Cited and Consulted

Index

Filmography

The following abbreviations are used in this filmography:

C   camera
D   direction
L   length
P   production company or producer
Sc   screenplay

Who Cares? (*Wen kümmert's?*, 1960. Also called *Watch on the Rhine*)
    Short. Sc: Volker Schlöndorff; C: Herbert Rimbach; L: 11 min.

Young Törless (*Der junge Törless*, 1966)
    P: Filmproduktion Franz Seitz/Nouvelles Editions de Films (Franz Seitz, Louis Malle); Sc: Volker Schlöndorff, Herbert Asmodi (based on the novella *Die Verwirrungen des Zöglings Törless* by Robert Musil); C: Franz Rath; Cast: Matthieu Carrière, Bernd Tischer, Marian Seidowsky, Alfred Dietz; L: 87 min.; Awards: West German Bundesfilmpreis 1966 for screenplay and direction; International film critics award (FIPRESCI), Cannes; Max Ophüls-Preis 1966.

A Degree of Murder (*Mord und Totschlag*, 1967)
    P: Rob Houwer Film; Sc: Volker Schlöndorff, Gregor von Rezzori, Arne Boyer, Niklas Frank; C: Franz Rath; Cast: Anita Pallenberg, Hans Peter Hallwachs, Werner Enke, Manfred Fischbeck; L: 87 min.; Awards: Bundesfilmpreis 1967 in Silber, Goldenes Band für Kamera.

"An Uneasy Moment" ("Ein unheimlicher Moment," 1967)
    P: Franz Seitz Filmproduktion; D: Volker Schlöndorff, Herbert Rimbach; Sc: Volker Schlöndorff, Herbert Rimbach; C: Werner Kurz; L: 13 min. Part of the episode film *Der Paukenspieler (The Kettledrummer)*, a Franz Seitz production that was not released until 1981. Shown theatrically as a short in 1970.

Michael Kohlhaas (*Michael Kohlhaas—Der Rebell*, 1969)
    P: Oceanic Film/Rob Houwer Film for Columbia Pictures (Elliot Kastner, Jerry Gershwin); Sc: Volker Schlöndorff, Edward Bond, Clement Biddle-Wood (based on the novella of the same title by Heinrich von Kleist); C: Willi Kurant, Herwig Zürkendörfer; Cast: David Warner, Anna Karina; L: 100 min.; Awards: Drehbuchprämie, Ehrenurkunde "Dama del Paragua," Human Rights Award (Preis der Menschenrechte), Strasbourg.

Baal (1969)

P: hr (Hessischer Rundfunk)/BR (Bayrischer Rundfunk)/Hallelujah Film; Sc: Volker
Schlöndorff (based on the play of the same title by Bertolt Brecht); C: Dietrich Lohmann;
Cast: Rainer Werner Fassbinder, Margarethe von Trotta, Siegfried Graue, Günter Neutze,
Hanna Schygulla; L: 87 min.; Broadcast premiere: January 7, 1970, hr 3.

The Sudden Wealth of the Poor People of Kombach (*Der plötzliche Reichtum der armen Leute
von Kombach*, 1970)

P: hr/Hallelujah Film; Sc: Volker Schlöndorff, Margarethe von Trotta; C: Franz Rath;
Cast: Reinhard Hauff, Georg Lehn, Margarethe von Trotta; L: 102 min.; Awards:
Bundesfilmpreis for direction, 1971; first prize, Agrarfilmfestival, Portugal.

The Morals of Ruth Halbfass (*Die Moral der Ruth Halbfass*, 1971)

P: hr/Hallelujah Film (Eberhard Junkersdorf); Sc: Volker Schlöndorff, Peter Hamm;
C: Klaus Müller-Laue, Konrad Kotowsky; Cast: Senta Berger, Helmut Griem, Peter
Ehrlich, Margarethe von Trotta, Walter Sedlmayer; L: 94 min.

A Free Woman (*Strohfeuer*, 1972)

P: hr/Hallelujah Film (Eberhard Junkersdorf); Sc: Volker Schlöndorff, Margarethe
von Trotta; C: Sven Nykvist; Cast: Margarethe von Trotta, Friedhelm Ptok, Martin
Lüttge, Walter Sedlmayer; L: 101 min.; Awards: International Film Festival, Chicago,
1973—Golden Hugo for von Trotta; Brussels, 1973—Prix Femina for von Trotta;
Deutscher Kritikerpreis 1972 for von Trotta.

Overnight Stay in Tyrol (*Übernachtung in Tirol*, 1973)

P: hr/Hallelujah Film (Eberhard Junkersdorf); Sc: Volker Schlöndorff, Peter Hamm;
C: Franz Rath; Cast: Margarethe von Trotta, Reinhard Hauff, Herbert Achternbusch; L:
78 min. Broadcast premiere: October 8, 1974, ARD television.

Georgina's Reasons (*Georginas Gründe*, 1974)

P: Bavaria on behalf of WDR/ORTF (Werner Kliess); Sc: Peter Adler (based on the story
of the same title by Henry James); C: Sven Nykvist; Cast: Edith Clever, Joachim Bissmeyer,
Margarethe von Trotta; L: 63 min.; Broadcast premiere: April 27, 1975, ARD television.

The Lost Honor of Katharina Blum (*Die verlorene Ehre der Katharina Blum*, 1975)

P: Paramount/Orion/Bioskop Film/WDR (Eberhard Junkersdorf); D: Volker
Schlöndorff, Margarethe von Trotta; Sc: Volker Schlöndorff, Margarethe von Trotta
(based on the novel of the same title by Heinrich Böll); C: Jost Vacano; Cast: Angela
Winkler, Mario Adorf, Dieter Laser; L: 106 min.; Awards: International Film Festival, San
Sebastian, 1975—Bundesfilmpreis for Camera and Best Actress (Angela Winkler).

Coup de Grâce (*Der Fangschuss*, 1976)

P: Bioskop Film/Argos, Paris/hr (Eberhard Junkersdorf); Sc: Margarethe von Trotta,
Geneviève Dormann, Jutta Brückner (based on the novel by Marguerite Yourcenar); C:
Igor Luther; Cast: Margarethe von Trotta, Matthias Habich, Rüdiger Kirchstein; L: 95
min.; Awards: Premio Vittorio de Sica, Naples, 1976; Bundesfilmpreis for Direction, 1977.

Just for Fun, Just for Play—Kaleidoscope Valeska Gert (Nur zum Spaß, Nur zum Spiel—Kaleidoskop Valeska Gert, 1977)
Documentary. P: Bioskop for ZDF (Eberhard Junkersdorf); C: Michael Ballhaus; Cast: Valeska Gert, Pola Kinski; L: 60 min.

Germany in Autumn (Deutschland im Herbst, 1978)
Omnibus film. P: Project Filmproduktion/Filmverlag der Autoren/Hallelujah Film/Kairos Film (Theo Hinz, Eberhard Junkersdorf); D and Sc: Alf Brustellin, Rainer Werner Fassbinder, Alexander Kluge, Maximiliane Mainka, Peter Schubert, Edgar Reitz, Katja Rupé, Hans Peter Cloos, Volker Schlöndorff ("Antigone" episode, Sc with Heinrich Böll), Bernhard Sinkel; Cast: Angela Winkler, Francisca Walser, Helmut Griem, Wolfgang Bächler, Heinz Bennent, Mario Adorf; L: 124 min.

Der zoologische Palast (1978)
P: hr (Wolfgang Völker); Sc: Thomas Jahn, on the basis of texts by English students; D: Volker Schlöndorff, Matthieu Carrière; C: Werner Rosemann, Helmut Kühn, et al.; Cast: John Venning, Claus-Peter Corzilius, Thomas Schulze, Walter Groh, Paul Danaher, Brenda Jackson. L: 81 min. Broadcast: December 27, 1978, ARD television.

The Tin Drum (Die Blechtrommel, 1979)
P: Franz Seitz/Bioskop Film/Artemis Film/Hallelujah Film/Argos Film/hr, in cooperation with Jadran Film Zagreb and Film Polski Warsaw (Franz Seitz, Eberhard Junkersdorf); Sc: Jean-Claude Carrière, Franz Seitz, Volker Schlöndorff, Günter Grass (based on the novel of the same title by Günter Grass); C: Igor Luther; Cast: David Bennent, Mario Adorf, Angela Winkler, Katharina Thalbach, Daniel Olbrychski, Charles Aznavour, Tilo Prückner, Heinz Bennent; L: 145 min.; Awards: Goldene Schale des Bundesfilmpreises, 1979; Golden Palm, Cannes, 1979; Oscar, Best Foreign Film, 1980.

The Candidate (Der Kandidat, 1980)
Omnibus film. P: Project Film im Filmverlag der Autoren Film/Bioskop Film/Kairos Film (Theo Hinz, Eberhard Junkersdorf); Sc: Stefan Aust, Alexander von Eschwege, Alexander Kluge, Volker Schlöndorff; C: Igor Luther, Werner Lühring, Jörg Schmidt-Reitwein, Thomas Mauch, Bodo Kessler; L: 129 min.

Circle of Deceit (Die Fälschung, 1981)
P: Bioskop Film/Artemis/Argos, Paris/hr; Sc: Volker Schlöndorff, Jean-Claude Carrière, Kai Hermann, Margarethe von Trotta (based on the novel by Nicolas Born); C: Igor Luther; Cast: Bruno Ganz, Hanna Schygulla, Gila von Weitershausen, Jerzy Skolimowski; L: 110 min.; Awards: International Film Festival, Strasbourg, 1982—Best Camera for Igor Luther; Deutscher Filmpreis, Best Supporting Actor for Jerzy Skolimowski.

War and Peace (Krieg und Frieden, 1983)
Omnibus film. P: Project Film im Filmverlag der Autoren Film/Bioskop Film/Kairos Film (Gerd von Halem, Daniel Zuta); D and Sc: Alexander Kluge, Volker Schlöndorff (Sc with Heinrich Böll), Stefan Aust, Axel Engstfeld; L: 120 min.

Swann in Love (*Un amour de Swann, Eine Liebe von Swann,* 1984)
   P: Les Films du Losange/Gaumont Paris/FR3. S/F.P.C. Paris/Nicole Stéphane/Bioskop Film/WDR (Margaret Menegoz, Emmanuel Schlumberger, Nicole Stéphane); Sc: Peter Brook, Jean-Claude Carrière, Volker Schlöndorff (based on "Swann's Way" from *Remembrance of Things Past* by Marcel Proust); C: Sven Nykvist; Cast: Jeremy Irons, Ornella Muti, Alain Delon, Marie-Christine Barrault, Fanny Ardant; L: 110 min.

Death of a Salesman (*Tod eines Handlungsreisenden,* 1985)
   P: Punch/Roxbury Productions New York/Bioskop (Robert F. Colesberry); Sc: Volker Schlöndorff, based on the stage play of the same title by Arthur Miller; C: Michael Ballhaus; Cast: Dustin Hoffman, Kate Reid, John Malkovich, Stephen Lang; L: 136 min. Awards: Golden Globe for Dustin Hoffman.

"Helmut Schmidt in the German Democratic Republic" ("Helmut Schmidt in der DDR," 1986). Contribution to *Odds and Ends/Miscellaneous News (Vermischte Nachrichten),* a film by Alexander Kluge.
   P: Kairos Film, ZDF (Alexander Kluge); Sc: Volker Schlöndorff; C: Franz Rath; L: 10 min. (of 103 min. total).

A Gathering of Old Men (*Ein Aufstand alter Männer,* 1987)
   P: Consolidated Productions Los Angeles/Jennie & Co. Film Productions New York/Zenith Productions London/CBS/hr/Bioskop (Gower Frost, Michael Deely, Eberhard Junkersdorf); Sc: Charles Fuller (based on the novel by Ernest J. Gaines); C: Edward Lachman; Cast: Louis Gossett, Jr., Richard Widmark, Holly Hunter, Joe Seneca; L: 91 min.

The Handmaid's Tale (*Die Geschichte der Dienerin,* 1990)
   P: Bioskop film/Cinetudes Film/Odyssey Distributors/Cinecom International (Daniel Wilson); Sc: Harold Pinter (based on the novel of the same title by Margaret Atwood); C: lgor Luther; Cast: Natasha Richardson, Faye Dunaway, Robert Duvall, Aidan Quinn; L: 108 min.

Wilder-Auktion (1989)
   P: ZDF (Johannes Willms, for the ZDF TV magazine "Aspekte.") Sc.: Volker Schlöndorff, Marianne Trench; C: George Paris, Yahir Tropen; C: Billy Wilder, Claudette Colbert, Volker Schlöndorff; L: 8 min. Broadcast: November 17, 1989, ZDF.

Voyager (*Homo Faber,* 1991)
   P: Bioskop Film/Action Films Paris/Stefi 2 Home Video Hellas Athens (Eberhard Junkersdorf); Sc: Volker Schlöndorff, Rudi Wurlitzer (based on the novel by Max Frisch); C: Yorgos Arvanitis, Pierre L'homme; Cast: Sam Shepard, Julie Delpy, Barbara Sukowa, Dieter Kirchlechner; L: 117 min. Awards: Deutscher Filmpreis, 1991—Filmband in Silber (production); Bavarian Film Prize, 1992.

The Michael Nyman Songbook (1992)
   Documentary for television. P: Bioskop Film/Decca Record Co./hr/Arte, Strasbourg

(Eberhard Junkersdorf); Sc: Volker Schlöndorff; Music: Michael Nyman; with Ute Lemper, the Michael Nyman Band; L: 53 min. Broadcast premiere: May 30, 1992, Arte.

Billy, How Did You Do It? (1987, 1992)

Documentary (Billy Wilder in conversation with Volker Schlöndorff and Hellmuth Karasek). P: Bioskop Film/hr/WDR/BR (Eberhard Junkersdorf); D: Volker Schlöndorff, Gisela Grischow; C: Bodo Kessler; L: six episodes, 45 min. each; Broadcast premiere: August 16, 18, 22, 27, 29, and September 3, 1992, WDR West 3.

The Ogre (Der Unhold, 1996)

P: Studio Babelsberg/Renn Prods. Paris/Recorded Pictures London/WDR, France 2 Cinema (Ingrid Windisch); Sc: Jean-Claude Carrière and Volker Schlöndorff (based on the novel *Le roi des aulnes [The Ogre]* by Michel Tournier); C: Bruno de Keyzer; Cast: John Malkovich, Armin Mueller-Stahl, Marianne Sägebrecht, Gottfried John, Volker Spengler; L: 117 min.

"The Perfect Soldier," episode for *Spotlights on a Massacre* (1997)

P: Babelsberg, Handicap International and Little Bear. (Bertrand Tavernier); C: Ingo Baar. L: 4:10 min.

Palmetto (1998)

P: Rialto Film Berlin/Neverland Films Los Angeles/Castle Rock (Matthias Wendlandt); Sc: E. Max Frye (based on the novel *Just Another Sucker* by James Hadley Chase); C: Thomas Kloss; Cast: Woody Harrelson, Elisabeth Shue, Gina Gershon, Rolf Hoppe, Tom Wright; L: 114 min.

The Legend of Rita (Die Stille nach dem Schuss, 2000)

P: Babelsberg Film, Mitteldeutsches Filmkontor, and MDR (Arthur Hofer, Emmo Lempert); Sc: Wolfgang Kohlhaase and Volker Schlöndorff. C: Andreas Höfer; Cast: Bibiana Beglau, Martin Wuttke, Nadja Uhl, Harald Schrott, Alexander Beyer, Jenny Schily, Thomas Arnold; L: 101 min.; Awards: Silberner Bär, best actress for both Bibiana Beglau and Nadja Uhl and Blue Angel (Best European Film) at the Berlin Film Festival.

Appendix:
U.S. Film, DVD, and Video Sources

Facets Video
1517 W. Fullerton Ave.
Chicago, IL. 60614
(800) 331-6197
Website: www.facets.org

Video: *Young Törless, The Lost Honor of Katharina Blum, Le Coup de Grâce*, "*Antigone*" of *Germany in Autumn, The Tin Drum, Death of a Salesman, The Handmaid's Tale, Michael Nyman Songbook, Voyager, The Ogre, Palmetto, The Legend of Rita.* DVD: *The Tin Drum, The Legend of Rita.*

Films Incorporated
5547 N. Ravenswood Ave.
Chicago, IL 60640-1199
(800) 323-4222
FAX (773) 878-8648

Goethe-Institut, German Cultural Centers
Website: goethe.de

Contact your regional Center in Atlanta, Chicago, New York, San Francisco, et cetera. Video: *Young Törless*, "*Antigone*" of *Germany in Autumn, The Tin Drum.* Holdings may vary.

Goethe-Institut, Inter Nationes New York
   (former West Glen collection)
(212) 439-8690
e-mail: filmdepot@goethe-newyork.org
Website: www.goethe.de/wk/ney/filmkat/film.htm

Video: *Young Törless, The Lost Honor of Katharina Blum, Coup de Grâce*, "*Antigone*" in *Germany in Autumn, The Tin Drum, Swann in Love, Death of Salesman, The Handmaid's Tale, Voyager, The Ogre.*

Home Film Festival
P.O. Box 2032
Scranton, PA 18501
(800) 258-3456
Website: homefilmfestival.com

Video: *Young Törless, The Lost Honor of Katharina Blum, Coup de Grâce,* "Antigone" in *Germany in Autumn, The Tin Drum, Swann in Love, Death of Salesman, The Handmaid's Tale, Voyager, The Ogre, The Legend of Rita.*

Kit Parker Films
1245 10th St.
Monterey, CA 93940
(408) 649-5573

35-mm: *Swann in Love.*

Kino International
333 W. 39th St.
New York, NY 10018
(212) 629-6880
FAX (212) 714-0871
e-mail: kinoint@infohouse.com
Website: www.kino.com

Video: *The Tin Drum, The Ogre.* DVD: *The Tin Drum.* 35-mm: *The Tin Drum, The Ogre, The Legend of Rita, The Legend of Rita.*

New Yorker Films
16 W. 61st. St.
New York, NY 10023
(212) 247-6110
FAX (212) 307-7855
e-mail: info@newyorkerfilms.com
Website: www.newyorkerfilms.com

Video, DVD, 16-mm, and 35-mm: *The Sudden Wealth of the Poor People of Kombach, A Free Woman.* 16-mm and 35-mm: *Young Törless.*

Swank Motion Pictures
201 S. Jefferson Ave.
St. Louis, MO 63103-2579
(800) 876-5577
Website: www.swank.com

16-mm: *Circle of Deceit.* Video: *The Handmaid's Tale.* Video, DVD, 16-mm, and 35-mm: *Palmetto.*

West Glen Communications

German feature film collection now distributed by Goethe-Institut Inter Nationes New York (seeentry on p. 334).

Mail Order Kaiser
D-80791 Munich/Germany
E-mail: kaiser@mokm.de
Website: www.mokm.de

An overseas source for nonsubtitled German-language videocassettes in PAL format of recent features, e.g., *Die Stille nach dem Schuss (The Legend of Rita).*

Notes

6. "Amphibious" Movies and Formal Experiments

1. Note the credits in Volker Schlöndorff and Günter Grass, *Die Blechtrommel als Film* (1979; Frankfurt/M.: Verlag, 2001) N. pag. (penultimate page), "sowie dem Hessischen Rundfunk," and, for *Circle of Deceit*, respectively, Hans-Michael Bock, ed., *CineGraph* (Munich: edition text + kritik, 1984 ff), "Volker Schlöndorff," Lg. 2, F 11, although the actual prints fail to list these contributions. For *Gathering of Old Men, CineGraph,* Lg. 23, F 14.

2. On the other hand, we should not fail to recognize that von Trotta drew significant impulses from Schlöndorff and other male New German Cinema filmmakers, not to mention a gain in experience from Schlöndorff and profit from his film production company, Bioskop, on which she could rely. In many ways, von Trotta's *The Second Awakening of Christa Klages* is a reworking of themes, ideas, and motifs found earlier in *The Lost Honor of Katharina Blum,* not surprising in that both employed elements of the Margit Czenki case. Bonds also clearly exist between *Marianne and Juliane* and Schlöndorff's "Antigone" episode from *Germany in Autumn.* Both deal with clashes between the state and female characters. In each case, one sister is rebellious, the other—Juliane-Ismene—nonrevolutionary. Besides such affinities in content and motifs, parallels in cinematic style are clear as well. From another male filmmaker, Fassbinder, von Trotta took on the *Rosa Luxemburg* project after his death.

13. *Coup de Grâce*

1. The script of *Coup de Grâce* is printed in French in *L'avant-scène du cinéma* 181 (Feb. 1, 1977), 3–22, 43–59; excerpted in German in Rainer Lewandowski, *Die Filme von Volker Schlöndorff* (Hildesheim: Olms, 1981), 229–35. From the unprinted script, it is apparent that Margarethe von Trotta and Jutta Brückner were responsible for the scenario and Geneviève Dormann only for the French edition.

15. *The Tin Drum*

1. Any filmmaker faced with the task of adapting a novel of the length and breadth of Grass's *Tin Drum* would have to make economies. Even after cutting the last third of the novel, Schlöndorff was forced to make more cuts. The different birthday parties in the Matzerath house, for instance, had to be collapsed into one scenic block. Oskar's unique educational experience, a blending of Goethe and Rasputin, was deleted. Also dropped was the chapter "Shopwindows" in which Oskar tries to tempt passersby with thievery by shattering jewelers' display windows with his vitricidal voice. Nearly the entire block of three chapters dealing with Maria's brother ("Herbert Truczinski's Back," "Niobe," and "Faith, Hope, Love") was sacrificed—a fortunate choice for deletion, since this Gothic tale is the most autonomous part of the first half of the Grass novel. Also omitted is the "Duster" section (the chapter of the same name and "The Christmas Play" as well as much of "The Ant Trail"). The spheres of adolescence and Catholicism, both among the chief targets of Grass's satirical pen, had to be reduced. Some characters are also modified. Jan Bronski appears single rather than married as in the novel. And the toy merchant Markus, in an addition to the text, returns by night to the cemetery and recites the *Kaddish* at Agnes Matzerath's grave, thus allowing the filmmaker to collapse multiple references in the text to Markus's Jewishness into one succinct scene.

16. *Just for Fun, Just for Play—Kaleidoscope Valeska Gert, The Candidate,* and *War and Peace*

1. Missing from the American version of *War and Peace* are an interview with Heinrich Böll, a lengthy section of the Bonn antinuclear protest of October 1981, and a documentation of the celebration and demonstration that accompanied the twenty-fifth anniversary of the Bundeswehr. The interview with Sam Cohen was moved from near the end of the film and put in the middle, and the Versailles sequence was trimmed from eight minutes to four. (Linda Duchin, Teleculture, Inc., letter to the authors, January 12, 1984.)

2. The first two playlets, "Gespräche im Weltraum" (or "Conversations in Space") and "Atombunker," are roughly continuous with one another.

3. Although J. Hoberman has asserted that the scene with Sam Cohen was played by an actor-surrogate (*Village Voice*, December 6, 1983, 62), other reports indicate that this is not the case and that Cohen himself does appear in the film. See endnote 13 in Patricia Thomson, "Atomic Reactions," *Afterimage* 11.9 (April 1984): 10.

18. *Swann in Love*

1. Frank Kermode has argued that all beginnings and endings in literature suggest birth and death, respectively. See *The Sense of an Ending: Studies in the Theory of Fiction* (New York: Oxford UP, 1967). *Swann in Love* would simply make more obvious this quality common to all fictional narratives.

2. Henze, one may recall, used a female vocalist to similar effect as part of his score for Alain Resnais's *Muriel* (1964). In this earlier film, the voice also suggests an absent figure, that of the title figure Muriel, a victim of torture during the Algerian war.

19. A German Filmmaker in the United States

1. In his notes accompanying the German re-edition of Miller's play, which uses the filmmaker's own translation, Schlöndorff writes of how the playwright borrowed Willy Loman's name from words used in one of Lang's *Dr. Mabuse* movies. Volker Schlöndorff, "Anmerkungen." *Tod eines Handlungs-reisenden,* by Arthur Miller. Deutsch von Volker Schlöndorff mit Florian Hopf (Frankfurt/M.: Fischer Taschenbuch Verlag, 1987) 118.

24. *Voyager*

1. Cf. the novelist's relationships to Madeleine Seigner and, much later, her daughter as described by his biographer Urs Bircher: "Ihre Tochter Karin Pilliod war, rund 50 Jahre nach der Mutter, Frischs letzte Lebensgefährtin" (248).

Works Cited and Consulted

Researchers may wish to consult, at the Deutsches Filmmuseum Frankfurt/M., the "Sammlung Volker Schlöndorff," a collection of materials from both the filmmaker's private archives and Bioskop Film. A "Findbuch" inventory has been established, and the museum is entertaining plans to post it to the museum's website, www.deutsches-filmmuseum.de.

Améry, Jean. "Gespräch über Leben und Endes des Herbert Törless." *Leporello fällt aus der Rolle.* Ed. Peter Härtling. Frankfurt: S. Fischer, 1971. 185–97.

———. "Michel Tourniers Ästhetizismus der Barbarei." *Merkur* 27 (Jan. 1973): 73–79.

Amiel, Mireille. "*La soudaine richesse des pauvres gens de Kombach.*" *Cinéma* Jan. 1972: 136–37.

Andrew, Dudley. *Concepts in Film Theory.* New York: Oxford UP, 1984.

Appel, Paul H., Bavaria Atelier GmbH, Munich. Letter to the authors. May 24, 1984.

Aust, Stefan. *The Baader-Meinhof Group: The Insider Story of a Phenomenon.* Trans. Anthea Bell. London: The Bodley Head, 1985.

Baer, Harry. *Das atemlose Leben des R. W. Fassbinder.* Cologne: Kiepenheuer and Witsch, 1982.

Barnett, Marianne. "Atwood's Seduction: *The Handmaid's Tale.*" Rocky Mountain Modern Language Association Convention. University of Utah, Salt Lake City. Oct. 12, 1990. We are indebted to the author for a copy of the manuscript.

Baroncelli, Jean de. "Le jour où Oskar cessa de grandir." *Le monde* Sept. 22, 1979: 1+.

———. "Sous les yeux d'un enfant." *Le monde* May 20, 1979: 1+.

Barthes, Roland. *Image-Music-Text.* New York: Hill and Wang, 1977.

Bastian, Günther. "*Homo Faber.*" *Film-Dienst* 44. Jahrgang. Mar. 5, 1991: 33.

Bazin, André. *What Is Cinema?* Trans. Hugh Gray. 2 vols. Berkeley: U of California P, 1967.

Belach, Helga, Gero Gandert, and Hans Helmut Prinzler, eds. *Aufruhr der Gefühle: Die Kinowelt des Curtis Bernhardt.* Munich: Bucher, 1982.

Bellour, Raymond. "Alienation, Segmentation, Hypnosis." Interview with Janet Bergstrom. *Camera Obscura* 3–4 (1979): 71–103.

Bergala, Alain. "Rivette, Baptiste et Marie." *Cahiers du cinéma* Mar. 1982: 5–7.

———. "Le vrai, le faux, le factice." *Cahiers du cinéma* 351 (1983): 4–9.

Berghahn, Daniela. "Fiction into Film and the Fidelity Discourse: A Case Study of Volker Schlöndorff's Re-interpretation of *Homo Faber.*" *German Life and Letters* 49 (1996): 72–87.

Berghahn, Wilfried. *Robert Musil in Selbstzeugnissen und Bilddokumenten.* Series: rowohlts monographien. Reinbek: Rowohlt, 1963. 28–29.

Bernhard, Thomas. *Frost.* Frankfurt: Insel, 1963.

Beuth, Reinhard. "Sisyphos im sibirischen Straflager." *Die Welt* Mar. 18, 1988.

Bircher, Urs. *Vom langsamen Wachsen eines Zorns: Max Frisch 1911–1955*. Zürich: Limmat Verlag, 1997.

Blot, Jean. *Marguerite Yourcenar*. Ecrivains d'hier et d'aujourd'hui 39. Paris: Editions Seghers, 1971.

Blume, Mary. "Schlöndorff Dares to Tread in Proust's Way." *International Herald Tribune* Jan. 20, 1984: 5.

Blumenberg, Hans C. "Deutsche Ängste, deutsche Bilder." *Die Zeit* Apr. 25, 1980.

———. "Das war der Wilde Osten." *Kinozeit*. Frankfurt: Fischer Taschenbuchverlag, 1980. 204–8.

Böll, Heinrich. *Die verlorene Ehre der Katharina Blum. Mit Materialien und einem Nachwort des Autors*. Cologne: Kiepenheuer and Witsch, 1984.

———. "Die verschobene Antigone. Drehbuchentwurf für Volker Schlöndorffs Beitrag zu dem Film *Deutschland im Herbst*." *Heinrich Böll Werke: Hörspiele, Theaterstücke, Drehbücher, Gedichte 1952–1978*. Ed. Bernd Balzer. Cologne: Kiepenheuer and Witsch, 1978. 609–15.

———. "Will Ulrike Gnade oder freies Geleit?" Letter. *Der Spiegel* 31 (Jan. 20, 1972). Rpt. in Böll, *Die verlorene Ehre* 193–208.

———. *Women in a River Landscape*. Trans. David McLintock. New York: Knopf, 1988.

———. "Zehn Jahre später. Ein Nachwort von Heinrich Böll." Böll, *Die verlorene Ehre* 259–69.

Born, Nicolas. *Die Fälschung*. Reinbek: Rowohlt, 1979. Pub. in English as *The Deception*. Trans. Leila Vennewitz. Boston: Little, Brown, 1983.

Boulet-Gercourt, Philippe. "Berlin's Hollywood." *World Press Review* Dec. 1992: 52.

Brecht, Bertolt. "Anmerkungen zum Volksstück." *Gesammelte Werke*. Werkausgabe. Frankfurt: Suhrkamp, 17 (1967): 1163–69, 1172.

———. *Baal, A Man's a Man and The Elephant Calf*. Ed. and with an introduction by Eric Bentley. New York: Grove, 1964.

———. *Brecht on Theatre: The Development of an Aesthetic*. Ed. and trans. John Willett. New York: Hill and Wang, 1964.

———. "Ist ein Stück wie *Herr Puntila und sein Knecht Matti* . . . noch aktuell?" Schriften zum Theater 3, *Gesammelte Werke*. Werkausgabe. Frankfurt: Suhrkamp, 17 (1967): 1174–75.

———. *Poems*. Ed. John Willet and Ralph Manheim with cooperation of Erich Fried. London: Eyre Methuen, 1976.

"Brief aus Berlin Zeitmosaik." *Die Zeit* Feb. 25, 1994: 14.

Brode, Hanspeter. *Günter Grass*. Munich: Beck, 1979.

Bronnen, Barbara, and Corinna Brocher. *Die Filmemacher*. Munich: Bertelsmann, 1973.

Brückner, Jutta, and Margarethe von Trotta. "Der Fangschuss." Unpublished screenplay. N.d., 138 pp.

Brückner, Jutta, Margarethe von Trotta, and Geneviève Dormann. *"Le coup de grâce."* *L'avant-scène du cinéma* 181 (Feb. 1, 1977): 3–23, 43–59.

Buck, Joan Juliet. "On the Set with Marcel Proust." *Vogue* Dec. 1983: 392.

Buckley, Tom. "Character Disorders." *New York Times* Dec. 19, 1980: C12. Rpt. in *New York Times Film Reviews, 1979–1980.* New York: *New York Times* and Arno Press, 1981. 308.

Callenbach, Ernest. "*Young Törless.*" *Film Quarterly* Winter 1966–67: 42–44.

Canaris, Volker. "Theaterinszenierungen im Fernsehen." *Sachwörterbuch des Fernsehens.* Ed. Helmut Kreuzer. Series: UTB 1185. Göttingen: Vandenhoeck and Ruprecht, 1982. 184–87.

Canby, Vincent. "*Coup de Grâce,* a Film Parable." *New York Times* Feb. 6, 1978: C15.

———. "Mankind's Folly: The Dark Side of Three Movies." *New York Times* Mar. 7, 1982, sec. 2: 15+.

———. "A 16th-Century Tale." *New York Times* June 20, 1980: C12. Rpt. in *New York Times Film Reviews, 1979–1980.* New York: *New York Times* and Arno Press, 1981. 226.

Cattini, Alberto. *Volker Schlöndorff.* ii castoro cinema 78. Florence: La Nuova Italia, 1980.

Chabrol, Claude. "Little Themes." *The New Wave: Critical Landmarks.* Ed. Peter Graham. Garden City, NY: Doubleday, 1968. 73–77. Rpt. from *Cahiers du cinéma* 100 (1959).

Chase, James Hadley. *Just Another Sucker.* London: Robert Hale, 1961.

Collins, Richard, and Vincent Porter. *WDR and the Arbeiterfilm.* London: British Film Institute, 1981.

Comolli, Jean-Louis. "Cléopatre, le jeu, l'échec." *Cahiers du cinéma* Mar. 1964: 32–40.

Constantin-Film. Press notes for *Mord und Totschlag.* Mar. 1967. 17 pp.

Corino, Karl. "Törless Ignotus." Spec. issue of *Text + Kritik, Robert Musil* 21/22.2 (1972): 61–72.

Corrigan, Timothy. "Types of History: Schlöndorff's *Coup de Grâce.*" *New German Film: The Displaced Image.* Rev. ed. Bloomington: Indiana UP, 1994. 54–73.

Coursodon, Jean-Pierre. "Lettre de New York." *Cinéma* Feb. 1985: 22+.

Cowie, Peter, ed. *International Film Guide 1967.* London: Tantivy, 1967.

———, ed. *International Film Guide 1988.* New York: Zoetrope, 1987.

Crary, Jonathan. "War Games: Of Arms and Men." *Arts* 56.8 (Apr. 1982): 77–79.

Dalichow, Bärbel. "Von den Mühen der Großartigkeit. Das Babelsberger Filmstudio nach der Wende." *Fischer Film Almanach 1994.* Ed. Horst Schäfer and Walter Schobert. Frankfurt: Fischer Taschenbuch Verlag, 1994: 436–42.

Davis, Thulani. "*A Gathering of Old Men:* Volker on the Bayou." *Village Voice* May 12, 1987: 55–56.

"'Death of a Salesman' Doubles 1966 Audience." *New York Times* Sept. 17, 1985: C17.

Denby, David. "Society Dictates." *The New Yorker* Feb. 5, 2000: 92–93.

Derobert, Eric. "*Colère en Louisiane (A Gathering of Old Men).*" *Positif* Jan. 1988: 73.

Derrida, Jacques. *The Ear of the Other: Otobiography, Transference, Translation: Text and Discussions.* Ed. Christie McDonald. Trans. Peggy Kamuf. Lincoln: U of Nebraska P, 1988.

Deschner, Günter. "Das Baltikum im groben Raster. Schlöndorff's neuer Film *Der Fangschuss.*" *Die Welt* Nov. 4, 1976.

Deutsches Institut für Wirtschaftsforschung. "Zur Entwicklung der Filmwirtschaft in der BRD." *Wochenbericht* 7 (Feb. 13, 1986): 90–96.

"Les 10 films des redacteurs." *Positif* May 1992: 25–30.

Dommermuth, Marianne. *"Mord und Totschlag."* *Express International* May 17, 1967, "Film-TV-Buch" sec.

Donner, Wolf. "Himbeerwasser mit Schuss." *Die Zeit* Apr. 21, 1972.

———. "Der lüsterne Meinungsterror." *Die Zeit* no. 42 (Oct. 10, 1975): 44.

Douin, Jean-Luc. "Volker Schlöndorff prend les risques de porter à l'écran *Le roi des aulnes,* roman de Michel Tournier." *Le monde* Oct. 3, 1996: 28.

Ducouré, Alexis. "*The Legends of Rita.* Sombres destins." *Séquences* no. 213 (May–June 2001): 49.

Durgnat, Raymond. *Nouvelle Vague: The First Decade.* London: Motion, 1963.

Duve, Freimut. "Moral des Friedens." *Die Zeit* (U.S. ed.), no. 3 (Jan. 22, 1982): 5.

Eco, Umberto. "Die Krise der Vernunft." *Merkur* 436 (1985): 531.

Eder, Klaus. "Ein Starfighter, der fliegt." *Deutsche Volkszeitung* no. 18 (Jan. 5, 1980).

———. "Vom Umgang mit Leichen." *Film* 5 (1967), cited in Constantin-Film [16–17].

Elley, Derek. "*The Legends of Rita.*" *Variety* Feb. 28–Mar. 5, 2000: 42.

Elsaesser, Thomas. *New German Cinema. A History.* New Brunswick, NJ: Rutgers UP, 1989.

———. "Tales of Sound and Fury: Observations on the Family Melodrama." *Film Theory and Criticism: Introductory Readings.* 4th ed. Ed. Gerald Mast, Marshall Cohen, and Leo Braudy. New York: Oxford UP, 1992: 512–35. Rpt. from *Monogram* 4 (1972).

Engelhard, Günter. "Bohème schwarzweiss." *Weltwoche* July 5, 1984.

"Erstens kommt es anders . . ." *Der Spiegel* Nov. 18, 1996: 236–38.

"Erwacht der deutsche Film?" Press Materials for *Der junge Törless.* Munich: Nora Verleih, 1966. N. pag.

Étudiants des 27ᵉ et 28ᵉ Promotions de l'IDHEC. "L'IDHEC en 1973." *Positif* 54 (Sept. 1973): 56–60.

Even, Martin. "Un film émancipé sur l'émancipation de la femme." *Le monde* Jan. 19, 1973: 13.

Fassbinder, Rainer Werner. "Insects in a Glass Case: Random Thoughts on Claude Chabrol." *Sight and Sound* Autumn 1976: 205+.

Fehrenbach, Heide. *Cinema in Democratizing Germany: Reconstructing National Identity after Hitler.* Chapel Hill, NC: U of North Carolina P, 1995.

Fink, Adolf. "Eine ganz gewöhnliche Geschichte." *Frankfurter Allgemeine Zeitung* July 27, 1981.

Fischer, Robert, and Joe Hembus. *Der Neue deutsche Film 1960–1980.* Munich: Goldmann, 1981.

Fleischmann, Peter. Telephone interview. Aug. 17, 1994.

Frank, Niklas. "Requiem für deutsche Pimpfe." *Der Stern* Aug. 29, 1996: 134+.

Franklin, James. *New German Cinema: From Oberhausen to Hamburg.* Twayne's Filmmaker Series. Boston: Twayne, 1983.

Franz, Carl, ed. "Der Postraub in der Subach." Giessen: H. Hase, 1825. Rpt. in *Vereinsblatt des Geschichtsvereins für den Kreis Biedenkopf* Jg. 3 no. 9. Nov. 6, 1909. N. pag.

Frayling, Christopher. *Spaghetti Westerns: Cowboys and Europeans from Karl May to Sergio Leone.* London: Routledge, 1981.

Freyermuth, Gundolf S. *Der Übernehmer. Volker Schlöndorff in Babelsberg.* Berlin: Ch. Links Verlag, 1993.

Friedman, Lester. "Cinematic Techniques in *The Lost Honor of Katharina Blum.*" *Literature/Film Quarterly* 7.3 (1979): 244–52.

Frisch, Max. "Montauk." *Gesammelte Werke in zeitlicher Folge.* Ed. Hans Mayer. Vol. 6. Frankfurt: Suhrkamp, 1976. 617–754.

———. *Tagebuch 1966–1971.* Frankfurt: Suhrkamp Verlag, 1971.

Frosch. "Gruselmärchen aus dem Patriarchat." *Neue Zürcher Zeitung* Mar. 3, 1990: 56.

Fulbrook, Mary. *German National Identity after the Holocaust.* Cambridge: Polity Press, 1999.

Funk-Uhr no. 20 (1969). Cf. "Große Schweinerei." *Bild und Funk* no. 20 (1969).

Gaines, Ernest J. *A Gathering of Old Men.* New York: Vintage, 1984.

Gambrell, J. "Disarming Metaphors." *Art in America* 72 (Jan. 1984): 83–87.

Garsault, Alain. "Le temps d'aimer et le temps de mourir: *Le coup de grâce.*" *Positif* 189 (Jan. 1977): 63.

Gellert, Christian Fürchtegott. *Werke.* Ed. Gottfried Honnefelder. Vol. 1. Frankfurt: Insel, 1979.

"German Film Production." *Variety* Feb. 19, 1986: 230.

"Gespräch zwischen Margarethe von Trotta und Christel Buschmann." *frauen und film* 8 (1976): 29–33.

Gill. "*Vermischte Nachrichten (Odds and Ends).*" *Variety* Mar. 11, 1987: 124.

Godard, Jean-Luc. "Des traces du cinéma." Interview with Michel Ciment and Stéphane Goudet. *Positif* 456 (1999): 50–57.

"Goldrausch in der Kinowelt." *Der Spiegel* Oct. 4, 1999: 284–87.

Gotthelf, Jeremias. "The Broommaker of Rychiswyl." *Tales of Courtship.* Trans. Robert Godwin Jones. New York: Peter Lang, 1984. 217–35.

Grass, Günter. *Kopfgeburten oder Die Deutschen sterben aus.* Darmstadt: Luchterhand, 1980. Pub. in English as *Headbirth, or The Germans Are Dying Out.* New York: Harcourt Brace Jovanovich, 1982.

———. *The Tin Drum.* Trans. Ralph Manheim. New York: Vintage Books, 1964.

———. *Über das Selbstverständliche. Reden.* Neuwied: Luchterhand, 1968.

———. "Wie Literatur in Bildern laufen lernt." Forum series, Berlin Akademie der Künste. Panel discussion on *Die Blechtrommel.* June 14, 1979.

Grass, Günter, and Volker Schlöndorff. "Infantilismus einer ganzen Epoche." Interview. *Der Spiegel* Apr. 30, 1979: 186.

Grélier, Robert. "*Le coup de grâce.*" *L'image et son* 320–21 (Oct. 1977): 70–71.

Griffith, James. *Adaptations as Imitations: Films from Novels.* Cranbury: U of Delaware P, 1997.

Grosser, Alfred. *Das Deutschland im Westen.* Munich: Hanser, 1988.

Groves, Don. "Scandi B.O. Picks Up." *Variety* July 22, 1991: 80+.

Grunberger, Richard. *The 12-Year Reich.* A Social History of Nazi Germany 1933–1945. New York: Holt, Rhinehart, and Winston, 1971.

Habe, Hans. "Jagd frei auf Journalisten." *Die Welt* Oct. 1975. Photocopy on file.

Handy, Ellen. "Chris Burden." *Arts* 58.4 (Dec. 1983): 39.

Hans. *"Der Junge Törless."* *Variety* Apr. 27, 1966: 19.

Harcourt, Peter. *"The Sudden Wealth of the Poor People of Kombach."* *Film Quarterly* 34.1 (1980): 60–63.

Hart, Jonathan. "The Promised End: The Conclusion of Hoffman's *Death of a Salesman.*" *Literature/Film Quarterly* 19.1 (1991): 60–65.

"Harvest Time?" *Variety* Mar. 2, 1992: 79.

Haustrate, Gaston. *"Le faussaire."* *Cinéma* Nov. 1982: 104–5.

Head, David. "'Der Autor muß respektiert werden'—Schlöndorff-Trotta's *Die verlorene Ehre der Katharina Blum."* *German Life and Letters* 32.3 (Apr. 1979): 248–64.

———. "West German Television and the Work of Volker Schlöndorff." Address. University Film and Video Association Conference. Southern Illinois University at Carbondale. Aug. 1982.

Hebecker, Klaus. "Junger deutscher Film mit neuem Treffer." *Westfälische Rundschau.* Dortmund Apr. 21, 1967.

Held, Jean-Francis. "Sodome et Gaumont." *Les nouvelles litteraires* Feb. 23–29, 1984: 19.

Helmetag, Charles. "Volker Schlöndorff's 'American' Adaptation of Max Frisch's *Homo Faber."* Annual AATG Meeting. Baden-Baden, Germany. July 19–23, 1992. We are indebted to the scholar for perusal of his manuscript.

Hensel, Georg. "Lebenslauf eines dicken Mannes, Baal genannt." *Fernsehen + Film* Jan. 1970: 40–41.

Henze, Hans Werner. *Katharina Blum.* Concert Suite for Orchestra in Six Movements. Side 2 of *Swann in Love.* Perf. Basel Radio Symphonie Orchestra. Varese Sarabande Records, 1984.

Hickethier, Knut. "Der Film nach der Literatur ist Film. VS's *Die Blechtrommel* (1979) nach dem Roman von Günter Grass (1959)." *Literaturverfilmungen.* Ed. Franz-Josef Albermeier and Volker Roloff. Frankfurt: suhrkampTb Vlg., 1989. 183–98.

———. *"Der plötzliche Reichtum der armen Leute von Kombach."* *Filmklassiker.* Ed. Thomas Koebner. Vol. 3. Stuttgart: Reclam, 1995. 224–26.

Hils, Miriam. "Schlöndorff Ankles Babelsberg Post." *Variety* Sept. 8–14, 1997: 18.

Hinson, Hal. "*Voyager:* Passport to Angst." *Washington Post* May 27, 1992: C4.

"Hit der Woche." *Gong* 20 (1970).

hmb [Helmut M. Braem]. *"Georginas Gründe."* *Stuttgarter Zeitung* Apr. 29, 1975.

Hoberman, J. "Fables of Reconstruction." *Village Voice* Jan. 30, 2001: 117.

Holetz, Lotte. "Zwischendurch Obst verkauft. Bölls *Katharina Blum*-Verfilmung. Gespräch mit Angela Winkler." *AZ* Oct. 10, 1975.

Holl. [Holloway, Ronald.] *"The Candidate."* *Variety* May 21, 1980: 24.

Hopf, Florian. "Fragen an junge deutsche Regisseure. Gespräch mit Volker Schlöndorff über *Mord und Totschlag."* *Die Welt* Dec. 17, 1966, Feuilleton.

———. "Ein Individuum kämpft gegen ein System. Gespräch mit Volker Schlöndorff." *Die Welt* Feb. 15, 1969.

Horak, Jan-Christopher. "West German Film Politics: From A to Zimmermann." *Afterimage* Apr. 1984: 2.

Howe, Desson. "Educating 'Rita.'" *Washington Post* June 15, 2001, weekend sec.: 42–43.

Huber, Engelbert. *Das ist Nationalsozialismus.* Stuttgart: Union Deutsche Verlagsgesellschaft, 1933.

Hughes, Robert, ed. *Film: Book II—Films in Peace and War.* New York: Grove Press, 1962.

Humm. "Death of a Salesman." *Variety* Sept. 18, 1985: 54.

Hunter, Stephen. "*Legend of Rita:* Lives of a Terrorist." *Washington Post* June 15, 2001: C5.

Hurst, Matthias. *Erzählsituationen in Literatur und Film.* Reihe Medien in Forschung und Unterricht 40. Tübingen: Niemeyer Verlag, 1996.

hy. "Nicht zu aktualisieren. *Baal.*" *epd/Kirche und Fernsehen* 16 (Apr. 25, 1970): 12–14.

Infratam Rating Report. Oct. 8, 1974.

"Infratest." Rating report documents at Hessischer Rundfunk, Abteilung Fernsehspiel, Frankfurt/M.

Jacobson, Egon. "Die 100 wichtigsten deutschen Filme." *SKD Newsletter* (Deutsche Kinemathek) Nov. 6, 1995: 61–63.

Jaeger, Klaus, and Helmut Regel, eds. *Deutschland in Trümmern. Filmdokumente der Jahre 1945–1949.* Oberhausen: Laufen, 1976.

Jaeggi, Bruno. "Appell an die Mündigkeit." *Baseler Nachrichten* Aug. 18, 1976.

James, Caryn. "*Voyager:* Good Crew, Slow Trip." *New York Times* Feb. 23, 1992, sec. 2: 13.

James, Henry. "Georgina's Reasons." *The Complete Tales of Henry James.* Ed. Leon Edel. Philadelphia: Lippincott, 1963: 13–86.

Jansen, Peter W. "Klassenliebe und Klassenhass." *Vorwärts* Nov. 4, 1976.

Jenny, Urs. "Ich rieche Menschenfleisch." *Der Spiegel* Sept. 18, 1995: 198+.

Jeremias, Brigitte. "Das Abenteuerliche an Männerbündnissen." *Frankfurter Allgemeine Zeitung* Oct. 22, 1976.

"Jetzt hilft nur noch die Flucht nach vorn." *Der Spiegel* no. 16 (Apr. 14, 1986): 233–42.

Johnson, Brian. "Returning to a New Berlin." *MacLean's* Feb. 26, 1990: 44–45.

Jurczyk, Guenter. "Billy, How Did You Do It?" *Tagesspiegel* Dec. 6, 1992.

Kaes, Anton. *From Hitler to Heimat: The Return of History as Film.* Cambridge, Mass.: Harvard UP, 1989. Pub. in German as *Deutschlandbilder.* Munich: text + kritik, 1987.

Kanzog, Klaus. "Wege zu einer Theorie der Literaturverfilmung am Beispiel von Volker Schlöndorffs Film *Michael Kohlhaas—Der Rebell.*" *Methodenprobleme der Analyse verfilmter Literatur.* Ed. Joachim Paech. Münster: MAkS, 1984. 23–52.

Karasek, Hellmuth. *Billy Wilder.* 3rd ed. Munich: Heyne, 1995.

———. "Ein Blick ins künftige Glück." *Der Spiegel* Feb. 12, 1990: 230–31.

Kayser, Wolfgang. *Das sprachliche Kunstwerk.* 15th ed. Bern: Francke, 1971.

Kellermann, Volkmar. *Brücken nach Polen.* Stuttgart: Verlag Bonn aktuell, 1973.

Kifner, John. "Fact vs. Fiction in Beirut: A Reporter Views *Circle of Deceit.*" *New York Times* Mar. 2, 1982, sec. 2: 15+.

Kilb, Andreas. "Das Gespenst von Kaltenborn." *Die Zeit* no. 36 (Aug. 30, 1996): 49.

Kilborn, R. W. "Whose Lost Honor?" *Scottish Papers in Germanic Studies* 4 (1984): 21.

"Kinowelt Boosts Production Ties." *Variety* Jan. 17–23, 2000: 34.

Kinzer, Stephen. "Rampant Signs of Life at a Legendary Studio." *New York Times* Dec. 31, 1995, sec. 2: 22.

Kitses, Jim. *Horizons West.* London: Secker and Warburg/BFI, 1969.

Kleist, Heinrich von. *Michael Kohlhaas.* Trans. James Kirkup. London: Blackie, 1969.

Kluge, Alexander. "Künftige Filmpolitik." *Ulmer Dramaturgien.* Ed. A. Kluge and Klaus Eder. Munich: Hanser, 1980. 108–15.

———. "Über Gefühl." Program for *La Bohème,* Oper Frankfurt. Frankfurt: Stadt Frankfurt am Main, June 16, 1984. 5.

Kluge, Alexander, and Volker Schlöndorff. Interview, with a statement by Stefan Aust. *Filmfaust* 32 (Feb.–Mar. 1983): 3–24.

Knilli, Friedrich, Knut Hickethier, and Wolf Dieter Lützen, eds. *Literatur in den Massenmedien.* Reihe Hanser Medien RH 221. Munich: Hanser, 1976.

Korn, Karl. "Mord und Totschlag." *Frankfurter Allgemeine Zeitung* Apr. 22, 1967.

Kreimeier, Klaus. *Die Ufa-Story. Geschichte eines Filmkonzerns.* Munich: Hanser, 1992.

Krekeler, Elmar. "Der Mensch quält ewig sich im Kampf von Trieb und Sehnsucht." *Die Welt* July 3–4, 1993, Feuilleton.

Kreuzer, Helmut. "Zu Aufgaben und Problemen einer philologischen Medienwissenschaft am Beispiel des Fernsehens." *Film- & Fernsehwissenschaftliche Mitteilungen* 3.4 (1990): 7–15.

Ein Krieg wird vermarktet. Die Rolle der Medien im Libanon-Konflikt. A TV discussion with Volker Schlöndorff, Kai Hermann, Gerhard Konzelmann, and Erika Görke. Moderator: Manfred Buchwald. Dir. by Heinz Camus. Hessischer Rundfunk, 1984.

"Kühle Bilder und schroffe Striche: 40. internationale Filmfestspiele Berlin." *Die Welt* Feb. 12, 1990: 21.

Kurowski, Ulrich. "Junger deutscher Film." *Lexikon Film.* 2nd ed. Goldmann Sachbücher Nr. 11136. Munich: Goldmann, 1976. 71–77.

———. "Rückblende." *Lexikon Film.* 2nd ed. Goldmann Sachbücher Nr. 11136. Munich: Goldmann, 1976. 139.

Lardeau, Yann. "Le décor et le masque." *Cahiers du cinéma* 351 (1983): 4–9.

Lellis, George. *Bertolt Brecht, Cahiers du Cinéma and Contemporary Film Theory.* Ann Arbor, MI: UMI Research Press, 1982.

Lenz, Siegfried. Interview on NDR Radio. Mar. 6, 1976. Pub. in Knilli 171–74.

Le Pavec, Jean Pierre. "*Apocalypse Now* de Francis Ford Coppola." *Cinéma* Oct. 1979: 68–71.

Lewandowski, Rainer. *Die Filme von Volker Schlöndorff.* Hildesheim: Olms, 1981.

Lieb, Rebecca. "Film Centers Thinking in Two Lingos." *Variety* Sept. 20, 1993: 34+.

———. "Will New German Studio Fly with Euros?" *Variety* Apr. 26, 1993: 31+.

Limmer, Wolfgang. *Rainer Werner Fassbinder, Filmemacher.* Spiegel-Buch. Reinbek: Rowohlt, 1981.

Lotz, Sebastian."Trivialität des Luxus: Interview mit Volker Schlöndorff über seinen neuen Film." *Stuttgarter Zeitung* Mar. 24, 1972.

Lukasz-Aden, Gudrun, and Christel Strobel. *Der Frauenfilm.* Munich: Heyne, 1985.

Magretta, William R., and Joan Magretta. "Story and Discourse. Schlöndorff and von Trotta's *The Lost Honor of Katharina Blum.*" *Modern European Filmmakers and the Art of Adaptation.* Ed. Andrew S. Horton and Joan Magretta. New York: Ungar, 1981. 278–94.

Marcus, Millicent. *Filmmaking by the Book.* Baltimore: Johns Hopkins UP, 1993.

Markham, James L. "Beirut Ex-Premier Balks at Return Without Truce." *New York Times* Jan. 20, 1976: A1+.

———. "Lebanese Planes Attack Leftists and Palestinians." *New York Times* Jan. 17, 1976: A1+.

———. "Strife in Lebanon Falls as Town Falls to Moslems." *New York Times* Jan. 21, 1976: A1+.

Martin, Marcel. *"Le faussaire."* *La révue du cinéma* Nov. 1981: 23–25.

———. *"Feu de Paille."* *Écran* Feb. 1973: 68.

———. *France.* London: A. Zwemmer, 1971.

Mathers, Pete. "Brecht in Britain: From Theatre to Television (on *The Gangster Show*)." *Screen* 16.4 (1975–76): 81–93. With subsequent discussion, 93–100.

McCormick, Richard W. *Politics of the Self.* Princeton: Princeton UP, 1991.

McFarlane, Brian. *Novel to Film: An Introduction to the Theory of Adaptation.* New York: Clarendon Press, 1996.

Meitzel, Matten. "A propos du nouveau Heimatfilm allemand: *La soudaine richesse des pauvres gens de Kombach.* " *Les cahiers de la cinémathèque* 32 (1981): 133–37.

Methner, Caroline. "Volker Schlöndorff macht seine erste Oper für die Berliner." *Berliner Zeitung* June 30, 1976.

Metz, Christian. *The Imaginary Signifier: Psychoanalysis and Cinema.* Bloomington: Indiana UP, 1982.

Miller, Arthur. *Death of a Salesman.* New York: Penguin, 1976.

Milne, Tom. *"Circle of Deceit."* *Monthly Film Bulletin* May 1982: 85.

Moeller, Hans-Bernhard. "Productive Filmmaking and Personal Partnership." *Schatzkammer* 14.2 (Fall 1988): 2–11.

Molner, David. "Babelsberg Boost." *Variety* Sept. 19–25, 1994: 53–54.

Monaco, James. *How to Read a Film.* Rev. ed. New York: Oxford UP, 1981.

Montaigne, Pierre. "Schlöndorff: le cinéma à l'heure allemande." *Le figaro* Jan. 18, 1973: 24.

Munziger-Archiv./Internat. Biograph. Archiv. "Volker Schlöndorff." Lieferung 39/80. Sept. 27, 1980. K: 13049.

Müry, Andres. "Vorleser der Filmnation: Volker Schlöndorff." *Frankfurter Allgemeine Zeitung Magazin* Feb. 16, 1990: 14–17.

Musil, Robert. "Über Robert Musils Bücher." *Tagebücher, Aphorismen, Essays und Reden.* Ed. Adolf Frisé. Hamburg: Rowohlt, 1955. 775–80.

———. *Young Törless.* New York: Pocket, 1978. Trans. of *Die Verwirrungen des Zöglings Törless.* Series rororo Taschenbuch Ausgabe. Reinbek: Rowohlt, 1959 and 1962.

Nagel, Ivan. "Triumph der Angst." *Der Spiegel* 34 Jg. no. 17. Apr. 21, 1980: 245–52.

Nasri, Samir. *"Le faussaire en questions."* *Cinéma* Feb. 1982: 47–52.

Nemeczek, Alfred. "Die Blonde mit dem festen Blick." *Der Stern* Oct. 28, 1976.

Netenjakob, Egon. "Volker Schlöndorff." *TV-Film Lexikon 1952–1992.* Frankfurt: Fischer-Bücherei, 1994. 343–46.

Nettelbeck, Uwe. "Die Beseitigung einer Leiche." *Die Zeit* Apr. 21, 1967.

Noelle-Neumann, Elisabeth, and Winfried Schulz, eds. *Publizistik. Fischer Lexikon.* Frankfurt: Fischer Taschenbuchverlag, 9 (1971): 220–41.

Nogueira, Rui., ed. *Melville on Melville.* New York: Viking, 1971.

"Oklahoma Judge Says German Film Not Porn." *Daily Texan* Oct. 21, 1998: 3.

"Oklahoma Police Seize Foreign Movies Deemed Obscene by County Court." ACLU Press Release. June 27, 1997. <http://www.aclu.org/news/no6797c.html>.

"Opera *Katherina Blum.*" *German Quarterly* 60.3 (1987): 519.

Orr, Christopher. "The Discourse on Adaptation." *Wide Angle* 6.2 (1984): 72–76.

Patalas, Enno. "Die zerrissene Leinwand." *Die Zeit* no. 44 (Oct. 28, 1999): 61–65.

Peter, Frank-Manuel. *Valeska Gert.* Berlin: Edition Hentrich, 1987.

Peters, Karsten. "Weder Schuld noch Sühne." *AZ* Apr. 19, 1967.

Pflaum, Hans Günther. "Adler/Schlöndorff, *Georginas Gründe.* " *Fernsehdienst* 14 (1975).

———. "Jagdfest bis zum Ende." Volker Schlöndorffs neuer Film *Der Fangschuss.*" *Süddeutsche Zeitung* Nov. 20, 1976.

———. "Konzertierte Aktionen: Materialien zu einem Fall." *Jahrbuch Film 83/84.* 21–29.

———. "Ein vergebliches Suchen." *Süddeutsche Zeitung* Feb. 12, 1983.

———. Pflaum, Hans Günther, and Hans Helmut Prinzler. *Cinema in the Federal Republic of Germany.* Bonn: InterNationes, 1993.

Pflaum, Hans Günther, and Hans Helmut Prinzler. *Film in der Bundesrepublik Deutschland.* Rev. ed. Bonn: InterNationes, 1992.

Phillips, Klaus, ed. *New German Filmmakers. From Oberhausen Through the 1970s.* New York: Ungar, 1984.

Piccadilly. "Filmisches Geschick im Umgang mit Günter Grass." *Neue Zuercher Zeitung* May 31, 1979.

Pietropaolo, Laura, and Ada Testaferri. *Feminisms in the Cinema.* Bloomington: Indiana UP, 1995.

Piontek, Heinz. "Der unheilige Christophorus." *Rheinischer Merkur* Nov. 24, 1972.

Plard, Henri. "Sur le film *Die Blechtrommel:* de Grass à Schlöndorff." *Etudes germaniques* 35 (Jan.–Mar. 1980): 69–84.

Pollet, Jean-Daniel. "Profiter de tout pour faire des films." Interview with Antoine de Baecque. *Libération* Oct. 8, 2001 <www.liberation.com/cinema/archives/retro/20011008pollet.html>.

Powers, John. "Saints and Savages." *American Film* Jan.–Feb. 1982: 38–43.

Powrie, Phil. "Marketing History: *Swann in Love.*" *Film Criticism* 12 (1988): 33–44.

Prinzler, Hans Helmut. "Die Bewerbung." *R. W. Fassbinder Werkschau.* Ausstellungskatalog. Ed. Marion Schmidt and Herbert Gehr. Berlin: Argon, 1992. 56–76.

Private Conversations . . . On the Set of "Death of a Salesman." Dir. Christian Blackwood. A Castle Hill release. New York: Punch Productions, 1985.

Prokop, Dieter. "*Michael Kohlhaas* und sein Management." *Massenkultur und Spontaneität.* Zur veränderten Warenform der Massenkommunikation im Spätkapitalismus. Edition suhrkamp. Frankfurt: Suhrkamp, 1974. 36–41.

Ray, Robert B. *A Certain Tendency of the Hollywood Cinema, 1930–1980.* Princeton: Princeton UP, 1985.

"Register." *Der Spiegel* Dec. 21, 1981: 176.

Reimer, Robert C. "Applause and V. Schlöndorff and M. von Trotta's *Die verlorene Ehre der Katharina Blum.*" *Proceedings of the Fourth Annual International Conference on Film.* Ed. Douglas Radcliff-Umstead. Kent, OH: Kent State U., 1988. 63–67.

Reimer, Robert C., and Carol J. Reimer. *Nazi-retro Film. How German Narrative Cinema Remembers the Past.* Twayne's Filmmaker Series. New York: Twayne, 1992.

Rentschler, Eric. "Deutschland im Vorherbst: Literature Adaptation in West German Film." *Kino: German Film* 3 (1980): 11–19.

———. "Deutschland im Vorherbst: The Literature Adaptation in West German Film 1976–1977." Special Session 190. MLA Convention. San Francisco. Dec. 28, 1979.

———. "Specularity and Spectacle in Schlöndorff's *Young Törless.*" *German Film and Literature: Adaptations and Transformations.* Ed. E. Rentschler. New York: Methuen, 1986. 176–92.

———. *West German Film in the Course of Time: Reflections on the Twenty Years Since Oberhausen.* Bedford Hills, NY: Redgrave, 1984.

Rivette, Jacques. "Entretien avec Jacques Rivette." *Cahiers du cinéma* Sept. 1981: 9–21.

Rosen, Marjorie. "Is *A Free Woman* the Woman We've Been Waiting For?" *The New York Times* July 7, 1974, sec. 2: 11.

Rosenbaum, Jonathan. Review of *Michael Kohlhaas. Chicago Reader* June 8, 1990, sec. 2: 40.

Rosenberg, Alfred. *Der Mythus des XX. Jahrhunderts.* Munich: Hoheneichen-Verlag, 1930.

Rotermund, Uta. "Weiß, männlich. Normal? Schlöndorff-Film *Die Geschichte der Dienerin.*" *Marabo* no. 3 (Mar. 1990): 32–34.

Roud, Richard. "Anguish: *Alphaville.*" *Sight and Sound* 34 (Autumn 1965): 164–66.

Rouse, John. *Brecht and the West German Theatre.* Ann Arbor: UMI Research Press, 1989.

Rüb, Matthias. "Ödipus hat heute frei." *Frankfurter Allgemeine Zeitung* Mar. 21, 1991.

Rühle, Günther. "Die vier schrecklichen Tage der Katharina Blum." *Frankfurter Allgemeine Zeitung* Sept. 26, 1975.

Ruther, Rainer. "Le Heimatfilm un genre typiquement teutonique." *Les cahiers de la cinémathèque* 32 (1981): 130–32.

Sandford, John. *The New German Cinema.* Totowa, NJ: Barnes and Noble, 1980.

Santner, Eric. *Stranded Objects.* Ithaca, NY: Cornell UP, 1990.

Sarris, Andrew. "The Father, the Son, and the Holy Revolution (II). *Village Voice* Mar. 2, 1982: 45.

sb. "*Mord und Totschlag.*" *Neue Zürcher Zeitung.* Fernausgabe. Feb. 8, 1968: 32.

Schäfer, Horst, and Walter Schobert, eds. *Fischer Film Almach 1993.* Frankfurt: Fischer, 1993.

"Schlöndorff, Herzog and the Others." *Scala* no. 5 (1985): 26–27.

Schlöndorff, Volker. Acceptance speech. Text of Academy Award address contained in a letter to the authors. Aug. 10, 1993, from the Academy of Motion Picture Arts and Sciences. Copyright © Academy of Motion Picture Arts and Sciences, 1980.

———. *Un amour de Swann.* Spec. issue of *L'avant-scène du cinéma* 321–22 (1984): 118 pp.

———. "Anmerkungen von Volker Schlöndorff." Arthur Miller. *Tod eines Handlungsreisenden.* Neu übersetzt von Volker Schlöndorff mit Florian Hopf. Frankfurt: Fischer Taschenbuch Verlag, 1987. 117–19.

———. "Avec l'opéra, je recharge mes batteries." *L'avant-scène opéra* 107 (Mar. 1988): 86–87.

———. *Baal* press materials. Hessischer Rundfunk, Bayrischer Rundfunk, Hallelujah Film, [1970].

———. *Die Blechtrommel: Tagebuch einer Verfilmung.* 2nd ed. Neuwied: Luchterhand, 1979.

———. "Coming to Terms with the German Past. An Interview with Volker Schlöndorff." Conducted by Gary Crowdus and Richard Porton. *Cineaste* 26.2 (2001): 18–23.

———. "Das ist der Sinn der Elegie. Aus Volker Schlöndorffs Arbeitsjournal." *Jahrbuch Theater 1991.* Zürich: Orell Fuessli and Friedrich Verlag, 1991. 10–23.

———. "Demnächst im Programm." Interview. *Deutsches Fernsehen* 47.1 (1972): 7–8.

———. "Deutscher Masochismus." *Die Zeit* Oct. 11, 1993: 62.

———. "Entretien avec Schlöndorff." With Jean-Loup Passek. *Cinéma* Jan. 1972: 138–41.

———. "Entretien avec Volker Schlöndorff." *Écran* Feb. 1973: 68–69.

———. "Entsetzliches ist selbstverständlich." Interview with Kai Niemeyer. *AZ* Apr. 19, 1967, Feuilleton.

———. "*Le faussaire* en questions." *Cinéma* Feb. 1982: 40–46.

———. "Der Filmregisseur geht zur Oper." Interview with Uta Gote. *Die Welt* Jan. 30, 1974, "Kultur" sec.: 23.

———. "Ich dachte, das mache ich im Schlaf." Interview with Andreas Kilb and Christiane Peitz. *Die Zeit* Sept. 8, 1995: 13–14.

———. "Inside Europe." Interview conducted by Hans Juergen Neumann. Deutsche Welle European Report. KUT-FM, Austin, TX. Nov. 23, 1992.

———. "An Interview." Conducted by Barry and Greg Thomson. *Film Criticism* 1.3 (Winter 1976–77): 26–37.

———. Interview with Terry Gross. National Public Radio. KSTX, San Antonio. Nov. 18, 1991.

———. "Ist Michael Kohlhaas eine politische Leitfigur? Gespräch mit Volker Schlöndorff." Interview with Heiko R. Blum. *Frankfurter Rundschau* Mar. 29, 1967.

———. "*Der junge Törless.*" *Film* (Velber) 4.6 (1966): 45–56.

———. "The Last Days of Max Frisch." *New York Times Book Review* Apr. 5, 1992: 1+. Cf. the longer version of the same material in the German original ("Das ist der Sinn der Elegie").

———. "The Limits of Journalism: An Interview with Volker Schlöndorff." With Al Auster and Leonard Quart. *Cineaste* 12 (1982): 47.

————. "Michael Kohlhaas. Drehbuch." Unpublished manuscript. Houwer-Film Munich. N.d.: 117 pp.

————. "Mit Oskar zum Oscar. Der Regisseur Volker Schlöndorff." Interview. Ein Film von Ilona Kalmbach und Jürgen Bischoff. 24 min. Coproduction of Deutsche Welle TV and hr. 1999.

————. "Nachwort." *Der Unhold* nach dem Roman *Der Erlkönig* von Michel Tournier mit Auszügen aus dem Drehbuch von Volker Schlöndorff und Jean-Claude Carrière. By Volker Schlöndorff. Göttingen: Steidl, 1996. 175–202.

————. "Nett sein bringt nichts." *Rainer Werner Fassbinder. Werkschau.* Exhibition catalogue. RWF Foundation. Ed. Marion Schmid and Herbert Gehr. Berlin: Argon, 1992. 99–103.

————. "Nobody Is Perfect." *Süddeutsche Zeitung* June 20, 1991: 12.

————. "Notes on Making *Swann in Love.*" Press notes for *Swann in Love.* New York: Orion Classics, 1984. N. pag.

————. "Ohne Glanz, Glamour und Glätte. Gespräch mit Volker Schlöndorff." Interview with Margret Köhler. *Film-Dienst* 53 Jg. Sept. 12, 2000: 14–15.

————. "Oskar Matzerath im Dritten Weltkrieg." Interview mit Bion Steinborn und Reiner Frey. *Filmfaust* 24 (Oct.–Nov. 1981): 3–19.

————. "A Parisian-American in Paris." *Village Voice* July 6, 1982: 44–45.

————. *Der plötzliche Reichtum der armen Leute von Kombach.* Ed. Hilmar Hoffmann and Walter Schobert. Reihe Filmtexte. Frankfurt: Kommunales Kino, 1970.

————. Preface. *Histoire du cinéma allemand.* By Roland Schneider. Paris: Éditions du Cerf, 1990. 13–14.

————. Press notes for *Der plötzliche Reichtum der armen Leute von Kombach.* [Munich:] Verleih Neue Filmkunst Walter Kirchner, Hessischer Rundfunk, Hallelujah Film, [1966]. 9 pp.

————. "Die Prinzessin aus dem Tiergarten." *Der Spiegel* Dec. 17, 1984: 164, 168–169.

————. "Rencontre avec Volker Schlöndorff." Interview. *Cahiers du cinéma* Sept. 1991: 53.

————. "La résurgence nécessaire des utopies." Interview with Élie Castiel. *Séquences* no. 123 (May–June 2001): 23.

————. "Schlöndorffs Traum/Schlöndorff's Erwachen." Joe Hembus. *Der deutsche Film kann gar nicht besser sein.* Munich: Rogner and Bernhard, 1981. vi–viii.

————. "Souvenirs de Louis Malle." *Positif* 471 (May 2000): 66–69. A revised, enlarged version of the director's "Nachwort" epilogue in the German translation of *Malle über Malle.* Ed. Philipp French. Berlin: Alexander, 1998.

————. "Sur le tambour." Interview. *Jeune cinéma* 121 (Sept.–Oct. 1979): 18–20.

————. "*The Tin Drum:* Volker Schlöndorff's 'Dream of Childhood'." Interview with John Hughes. *Film Quarterly* 35 (Spring 1981): 2–10.

————. "Der Verlust der Liebe." *Der Spiegel* Feb. 15, 1999: 196–97.

————. "Volker Schlöndorff bleibt ein Außenseiter." Interview with Wilhelm Ringelband. *Die Tat.* [1967]. Photocopy on file.

————. "Volker Schlöndorff: un Proust sensuel." Interview. *Les nouvelles littéraires* Feb. 23–29, 1984: 20–22.

———. "Von den 'Alten' war sie uns die Nächste." *Süddeutsche Zeitung* Apr. 15–16, 1978: 115. This is an edited, abbreviated version of Schlöndorff's eulogy given on Apr. 5, 1978, at the Berlin Ruhleben cemetery on the occasion of Valeska Gert's funeral.

———. "Warum *Frauen vor Flusslandschaft?*" Spielzeit 77. Heft 4. Munich: Schauspielhaus Münchener Kammerspiele, 1988. No pag.

———. "Weinen ist so billig! Interview mit Volker Schlöndorff." Conducted by Jochen Schütze. *Prinz* Feb. 1990: 78–79.

———. "Wem wird man schon fehlen?" Interview. *Der Spiegel* no. 12 (Mar. 18, 1991): 236–51.

———. "Der Wille zur Unterwerfung." *Augenzeugen.* Ed. Hans Helmut Prinzler and Eric Rentschler. Frankfurt: Verlag der Autoren, 1988. 248–55. Originally published in *Frankfurter Rundschau* Feb. 16, 1980.

———. "Zimmermanns Hinrichtungslinien." *Augenzeugen.* Frankfurt: Verlag der Autoren, 1988. 91–95. Rpt. from *Die Zeit* Dec. 16, 1983.

———. "Zu meinem Film über Valeska Gert." Eulogy delivered at Ruhleben cemetery, Berlin, on Apr. 4, 1978. Press Materials for *Just for Fun, Just for Play.* 1–7. Rpt. in different form as "Von den 'Alten' war sie uns die Nächste."

Schlöndorff, Volker, and Günter Grass. *Die Blechtrommel als Film.* 1979. Frankfurt: Verlag, 2001.

Schlöndorff, Volker, and Margarethe von Trotta. Interview. 1979. G. S. Tel Aviv. Video Archive. Goethe Institute Munich.

———. Schlöndorff, Volker, and Margarethe von Trotta. "Melville und der Befreiungskampf im Baltikum." Interview with Horst Wiedemann regarding *Der Fangschuss.* *Film und Ton* 12 (1976): 56–59.

Schlöndorff, Volker, and Peter Fleischmann. "Selbstverständlich ein Immobiliengeschäft." Interview with Guenther Jurczyk. *Der Tagesspiegel* May 9, 1992, Feuilleton.

Schlöndorff, Volker, and Wolfgang Kohlhaase. "A Discussion with Screenwriter Wolfgang Kohlhaase and Volker Schlöndorff." Pressbook for *The Legend of Rita.* New York: Kino International, n.d., [8–11].

Schlöndorff, Volker, et al. "*La Bohème.*" *Musiktheater Hinweise.* Oper Frankfurt. June–July 1984: 2–5.

Schlöndorff, Volker, Nicolas Born, and Bernd Lepel. *Die Fälschung als Film und der Krieg im Libanon.* Frankfurt: Zweitausendeins, 1981.

"Schlöndorffs Requiem für Böll." *Der Spiegel* Mar. 3, 1986: 223.

Schmidt, Eckhart. "Oskar trommelt nur Effekte." *Christ und Welt* May 4, 1979: n. pag. Photocopy on file.

Schostakowitsch, Dimitri. "Meine Auffassung der *Lady Macbeth.*" 1935. *Programmheft zur Münchner Erstaufführung der Urfassung von "Lady Macbeth von Mzensk."* Munich: Bayrische Staatsoper, 1993. 37–39.

Schubert-Scheinmann, Petra. "Literaturverfilmung als Interpretation. Vergleichende Analyse von Erzählung und Film *Die verlorene Ehre der Katharina Blum.*" Magisterarbeit, Technische Universität Berlin, 1983.

Schulz-Ojala, Jan. "Der Rattenfänger von Kaltenborn." *Tagespiegel* Sept. 2, 1996.

Schütte, Wolfram. "Der Durchbruch." *Frankfurter Rundschau* Sept. 13, 1975.

"Schwacher Start für Schlöndorff's *Unhold*." *Tagespiegel* Sept. 19, 1996.

Scott, A. O. "In 1970s Germany, a Young Terrorist Keeps Changing Her Identity, Not Her Ideals." *New York Times* Jan. 24, 2001: E5.

"Seidel, Hans-Dieter. "Und bist du nicht willig." *Frankfurter Allgemeine Zeitung* Sept. 2, 1996, Feuilleton.

Shattuck, Roger. *Proust's Way: A Field Guide to* In Search of Lost Time. New York: W. W. Norton, 2000.

Shewey, Don. "TV's Custom-Tailored Salesman." *New York Times* Sept. 15, 1985, sec. 2: 1+.

"*Shining* espying some glowing notices." *Variety* Feb. 3, 1992: 18.

Shipman, David. "Cinema: A Quarterly Review." *Contemporary Review* 248 (1985): 155–59.

———. "*Circle of Deceit*." *Films and Filming* June 1982: 32.

Siclier, Jacques. "*Colère en Louisiane* de Volker Schlöndorff." *Le monde* Nov. 22–23, 1987: 10.

Sontag, Susan. *Against Interpretation and Other Essays.* New York: Farrar, Straus, and Giroux, 1966.

Stam, Robert. "Television News and Its Spectator." *Regarding Television: Critical Approaches.* Ed. E. Ann Kaplan. American Film Institute Ser. 2. Frederick, MD: University Publications of America, 1983. 23–43.

Stoll, Dieter. "Ich will nicht den Zeigefinger schwingen." *AZ* Oct. 2, 1975: 17.

Storznowski, Julius. *Polen und Deutsche.* Stuttgart: Seewald, 1973.

"Straub-Huillet." *CineGraph.* Lexikon zum deutschsprachigen Film. Ed. Hans-Michael Bock. F 1. Munich: edition text + kritik, 1984– .

Strauss, Frédéric. "Paysage après la bataille." *Cahiers du cinéma* Sept. 1991: 47–59.

Strick, Philip. "*Death of a Salesman*." *Monthly Film Bulletin* 55 (Aug. 1988): 655.

———. "*The Handmaid's Tale*." *Monthly Film Bulletin* 57 (Nov. 1990): 682.

Studlar, Gaylyn. "Visual Pleasure and the Masochistic Aesthetic." *Journal of Film and Video* 37.2 (1985): 5–26.

Tagliabue, John. "A Director Who Pursues the Inner Demons." *New York Times* Jan. 26, 1992, sec. 2: 22.

Tarqui, Anne. "Un amour de Swann." *Cinéma* Mar. 1984: 53.

Thomas, Kevin. "*Tin Drum* Marches to a German Beat." *Los Angeles Times* Mar. 4, 1980, sec. 6: 1+.

Thomson, Patricia. "Atomic Reactions." *Afterimage* 11.9 (Apr. 1984): 5–10.

Tichy, Wolfram, ed. *rororo Film Lexikon. Filme.* 3 vols. Reinbek: Rowohlt, 1978.

Tieck, Ludwig. "Vorrede" zu Heinrich von Kleist. *Hinterlassene Schriften.* 1821. Cited in Heinrich von Kleist. *Michael Kohlhaas. Erläuterungen und Dokumente.* Ed. Günter Hagedorn. Stuttgart: Reclam, 1970. 87–88.

Tobis. Press notes for *Homo Faber.* 1991. N. pag.

Tobis. Press notes for *Palmetto.* 1998. http://www.tobis.de//palmetto/2801-2803.

Tournier, Michel. *The Ogre.* Trans. Barbara Bray. Garden City, NY: Doubleday, 1972. Trans. from the French *Le roi des aulnes.* Paris: Gallimard, 1970.

Traub, Rainer. "Bauchlandung eines Machers." *Der Spiegel* no. 24 (1990): 195–201.

"Tribüne des Jungen Deutschen Films: Volker Schlöndorff." *Filmkritik* 10 (June 1966): 307–09.

Truffaut, François. "A Certain Tendency of the French Cinema." *Movies and Methods.* Ed. Bill Nichols. Vol. 1. Berkeley: U of California P, 1976. 224–36.

Van Gelder, Lawrence. "At the Movies." *New York Times* Mar. 16, 1990: C12.

"*Variety* International Box Office." *Variety* Oct. 14–20, 1996: 18.

Verleih Neue Filmkunst Walter Kirchner et al. Press notes for *Der plötzliche Reichtum der armen Leute von Kombach.* [Munich, 1970–71].

Vielain, Heinz. "Ein SPD-Mann fördert Film und Verteidiger der RAF." *Die Welt* Sept. 27, 1976. Rpt. in Schlöndorff, *Die Blechtrommel. Tagebuch* 42.

Vinocur, John. "Schlöndorff's Latest Movie Looks at the Lebanese War." *New York Times* Feb. 7, 1982, sec. 2: 1+.

"Volker Schlöndorff." *CineGraph.* Lexikon zum deutschsprachigen Film. Ed. Hans-Michael Bock. Munich: edition text + kritik, 1984– .

Vom Erlkönig zum Unhold. Volker Schlöndorffs Tournier Verfilmung. A film by Ralph Eue, Sibille Gerhards, and Thorsten Johanningmeier. Studio Babelsberg/WDR, 1996.

von Mengershausen, Joachim. "Beine breit. Zu Volker Schlöndorffs *Michael Kohlhaas, der Rebell.* Anstelle einer Kritik." *Film* (Velber) 7 (May 1969): 30–32.

von Trotta, Margarethe. "Husbands, Wives, Men, Women . . ." Interview with Marjorie Rosen. *Millimeter* 4.3 (Mar. 1976): 36–38.

———. *Die verlorene Ehre der Katharina Blum.* Bühnenstück. Berlin: Kiepenheuer und Witsch Bühnenverlag. N.d.

Wahl, Torsten. "Görings Schloss in Marlenes Halle." *Berliner Zeitung* no. 282 (Dec. 13, 1995): 25.

"*War and Peace.*" *Variety* Mar. 9, 1983: 322.

Weigend, Friedrich. "Kritisch gesehen. *Baal.*" *Stuttgarter Zeitung* Apr. 23, 1970.

Weingarten, Susanne. "Grillparty mit der Stasi." *Der Spiegel* Feb. 14, 2000: 222–23.

Weingarten, Susanne, and Martin Wolf. "Wir haben uns verrechnet." *Der Spiegel* Dec. 18, 2000: 188–90.

Wenders, Wim. "Der Filmverlag gegen die Autoren." *Augenzeugen. 100 Texte deutscher Filmemacher.* Ed. Hans Helmut Prinzler and Eric Rentschler. Frankfurt: Verlag der Autoren, 1988. 100–101.

Wendt, Ernst. "Ein Jugendbildnis." *Film* (Velber) 5 (1966): 16–19.

Westlake, Donald. "Du *Point de non-retour* aux *Arnaquers.*" *Positif* no. 359 (Jan. 1991): 10–15.

Wetzel, Kraft. "Volker Faber Vater." *die tageszeitung* Mar. 21, 1991.

Wiegand, Wilfried. "Interview." *Rainer Werner Fassbinder.* Hanser Reihe Film 2. 3rd ed. Munich: Hanser, 1979. 63–90.

———. "Nationalhymne einer Leidenschaft." *Frankfurter Allgemeine Zeitung* Feb. 22, 1984.

Wilder, Billy, and Hellmuth Karasek. *Billy Wilder. Eine Nahaufnahme.* Hamburg: Hoffmann und Campe, 1992.

Williams, Michael. "*Lost Children* Pair Find Homes in French Studio." *Variety* Jan. 10–16, 1994: 14.

Wink, Andrea, and Thilo Wydra. *Katalog Filmreihe Volker Schlöndorff.* Wiesbaden: Verein Wiesbadner Kinofestival e.V., 1996.

Wirsing, Sibylle. "Baal heute." *Tagesspiegel* Apr. 23, 1970.

WMH. "Die Premiere." *Hamburger Abendblatt* Apr. 22, 1967.

Wydra, Thilo. *Volker Schlöndorff und seine Filme.* Heyne Filmbibliothek Nr. 32/256. Munich: Heyne, 1998.

Yourcenar, Marguerite. *Der Fangschuss.* Trans. Richard Moering. Cologne: Kiepenheuer und Witsch, 1968. Pub. in English as *Coup de Grâce.* Trans. Grace Frick. New York: Farrar, Straus and Giroux, 1957.

Zehle, Sibylle. "Er ist ein Läufer." *Die Zeit* July 16, 1990.

Zeutzschel, Günter. "*Der plötzliche Reichtum der armen Leute von Kombach.*" *Das Fernsehspiel—Archiv* 4.71: P18.

Zipes, Jack. "The Political Dimensions of *The Lost Honor of Katharina Blum.*" *New German Critique* 10–12 (1977): 75–84.

Index

357

Hans-Bernhard Moeller is the author of "Literatur zur Zeit des Faschismus," in *Geschichte der deutschen Literatur,* edited by Ehrhard Bahr, and editor of *European Exiles and Latin America.* He has contributed critical film studies to many omnibus volumes and to journals such as *Quarterly Review of Film Studies, Film Criticism, Jump Cut, Journal of Film and Video, Wide Angle,* and *Monatshefte.* In conjunction with the Stiftung Deutsche Kinemathek, he has conducted the biannual survey on "Der deutsche Film in amerikanischer Forschung und Lehre." His Ph.D. is from the University of Southern California. He teaches German cinema and twentieth-century German literature at the University of Texas at Austin.

George Lellis is the author of the book *Bertolt Brecht, Cahiers du Cinéma and Contemporary Film Theory* and the coauthor, with George Wead, of *Film: Form and Function* and *The Film Career of Buster Keaton.* His Ph.D. is from the Department of Radio, Television, and Film at the University of Texas at Austin. He has contributed reviews and articles to *Film Quarterly, Sight and Sound, Screen,* and *Take One.* A professor of communication at Coker College, he is a member of the Society for Cinema Studies, the University Film and Video Association, and the Carolinas Communication Association, for which he has served as president.